Data Analytics and Artificial Intelligence for Predictive Maintenance in Industry 4.0

Edited by

Tanu Singh & Vinod Patidar
School of Computer Science
University of Petroleum and Energy Studies
Dehradun, Uttarakhand, India

Arvind Panwar
School of Computing Science and Engineering
Galgotias University
Gr. Noida, Uttar Pradesh, India

&

Urvashi Sugandh
School of Computer Science and Engineering
Bennett University
Greater Noida, India

Data Analytics and Artificial Intelligence for Predictive Maintenance in Industry 4.0

Editors: Tanu Singh, Vinod Patidar, Arvind Panwar and Urvashi Sugandh

ISBN (Online): 979-8-89881-087-0

ISBN (Print): 979-8-89881-088-7

ISBN (Paperback): 979-8-89881-089-4

First published in 2025.

need for a court order if at any point you breach any terms of this License Agreement. In no event will any delay or failure by Bentham Science Publishers in enforcing your compliance with this License Agreement constitute a waiver of any of its rights.

3. You acknowledge that you have read this License Agreement, and agree to be bound by its terms and conditions. To the extent that any other terms and conditions presented on any website of Bentham Science Publishers conflict with, or are inconsistent with, the terms and conditions set out in this License Agreement, you acknowledge that the terms and conditions set out in this License Agreement shall prevail.

Bentham Science Publishers Pte. Ltd.
No. 9 Raffles Place
Office No. 26-01
Singapore 048619
Singapore
Email: subscriptions@benthamscience.net

CONTENTS

FOREWORD

The convergence of Data Analytics and Artificial Intelligence (AI) has unlocked transformative possibilities across industries, and their application in predictive maintenance within the Industry 4.0 framework stands as a testament to this progress. The chapters in the book *Data Analytics and Artificial Intelligence for Predictive Maintenance in Industry 4.0* comprehensively explore the intersection between cutting-edge technology and maintenance practices, offering invaluable insights for researchers, practitioners, and industry leaders.

This anthology begins by establishing a foundational understanding of predictive maintenance, detailing how Industry 4.0's enabling technologies—such as the Internet of Things (IoT), cloud computing, and big data analytics—pave the way for smarter, data-driven decisions. Subsequent chapters delve into innovative methodologies, showcasing machine learning, deep learning, and generative AI implementation in predictive maintenance systems. These techniques address challenges such as real-time monitoring, fault detection, and optimization of resources, significantly reducing downtime and improving operational efficiency.

The book emphasizes technical advancements and contextualizes them within diverse applications, ranging from agriculture and manufacturing to disaster resilience and healthcare. Unique perspectives on federated learning, bibliometric analyses of AI innovation, EEG-based IoT for human-machine interaction, and optimization strategies further broaden the scope of discussion. Integrating novel approaches like homomorphic encryption in healthcare predictive analytics highlights the commitment to balancing technological progress with ethical considerations like privacy and security.

Readers will also find forward-looking perspectives in chapters discussing quantum computing, augmented and virtual reality, and blockchain as potential disruptors in predictive maintenance. This book equips readers to navigate the complexities of implementing predictive maintenance systems in dynamic industrial environments by addressing challenges such as interoperability, workforce upskilling, and data governance.

This book represents the collective expertise and forward-thinking vision of its esteemed editors—Dr. Tanu Singh, Dr. Vinod Patidar, Dr. Arvind Panwar, and Dr. Urvashi Sugandh—and its contributors. Together, they provide a robust academic and practical framework to harness the potential of predictive maintenance in shaping the future of Industry 4.0.

With the advent of Industry 4.0, the industrial landscape is undergoing a significant transformation, driven by the integration of data analytics and artificial intelligence into predictive maintenance. *Data Analytics and Artificial Intelligence for Predictive Maintenance in Industry 4.0* captures this dynamic shift, offering a balanced mix of foundational knowledge, pioneering advancements, and innovative perspectives. This book is a vital resource for academics, industry professionals, and policymakers aiming to navigate and shape this evolving field.

Manju Khari
School of Computer and Systems Sciences
Jawaharlal Nehru University
New Delhi India

PREFACE

The rapid technological advancement in the era of Industry 4.0, led by the integration of cutting-edge technologies such as data-driven systems, smart factories, the Internet of Things (IoT), big data analytics, artificial intelligence, and machine learning, is revolutionizing manufacturing and industrial processes. The adoption of such technologies has innovated a diverse range of solutions, such as predictive maintenance, directing a shift from a reactive and preventive maintenance approach to a highly proactive maintenance approach. The predictive maintenance approach is a key enabler of efficiency in Industry 4.0 due to its ability to anticipate equipment failures, optimize maintenance schedules, and reduce downtime, leading to cost savings and overall increased productivity along with the improvement in safety measures. Artificial Intelligence and data analytics have emerged as crucial technologies in predictive maintenance due to their capabilities of processing vast amounts of data, identifying patterns, and providing actionable insights that improve overall maintenance processes.

The book *Data Analytics and AI for Predictive Maintenance in Industry 4.0* offers a thorough overview of how data analytics and artificial intelligence are applied to predictive maintenance across various industries. The chapters in this edited book offer in-depth analyses of the fundamental principles, practical resources, optimization methods, and smart uses of AI and machine learning algorithms, advanced sensor technologies, and resilience against natural disasters for predictive maintenance. These contributions also include real-world case studies on predictive maintenance ensuring that readers gain theoretical as well as practical insights into the application of these technologies.

The book is divided into 13 chapters. Each chapter highlights a key aspect of predictive maintenance and has been carefully selected and peer-reviewed, ensuring that the book offers both theoretical insights and practical applications. The first few chapters offer core principles and knowledge on data analytics, machine learning, and IoT technologies, preparing readers for in-depth exploration of the challenges and opportunities in predictive maintenance. The later chapters provide a thorough overview of big data analytics integration, federated learning techniques for the advancement of agriculture, healthcare predictive analysis, and advanced optimization methods, demonstrating their potential to revolutionize maintenance strategies and improve decision-making. Overall, the book provides a comprehensive summary for a broad audience that includes academics, professionals, and researchers keen to apply data analytics and artificial intelligence for predictive maintenance in a wide spectrum of industries, from agriculture and healthcare to disaster management and manufacturing.

We are grateful to all the authors who have shared their expertise in the form of contributed chapters in this edited volume. Their expertise, diverse experiences, and practical insights offer readers a comprehensive view of the emerging landscape of predictive maintenance.

As editors of this book, our role has been to oversee the organization and compilation of the chapters and to ensure coherence across the content. The responsibility for the integrity, accuracy, and reliability of the scientific material rests with the respective authors. The views and findings expressed in the chapters are those of the authors and do not necessarily reflect those of the editors.

We would like to extend our gratitude to our institutions for their support, resources, and encouragement, without which this book would not have been possible. Special thanks go to our editorial team for their meticulous work in ensuring the quality of this publication.

As the industry undergoes digital transformation, we are sure that this book will inspire innovative ideas and applications in predictive maintenance, leading to more intelligent and resilient industrial operations in the future.

Tanu Singh & Vinod Patidar
School of Computer Science
University of Petroleum and Energy Studies
Dehradun, Uttarakhand, India

Arvind Panwar
School of Computing Science and Engineering
Galgotias University
Gr. Noida, Uttar Pradesh, India

&

Urvashi Sugandh
School of Computer Science and Engineering
Bennett University
Greater Noida, India

List of Contributors

Aditya Kejrewal	UBS, Pune, India
Ashif Ali	Noida Institute of Engineering and Technology, Greater Noida, Uttar Pradesh, India
Ankush Kumar Gaur	UPES, Dehradun, Uttarakhand 248007, India
Arvind Panwar	School of Computing Science and Engineering, Galgotias University, Greater Noida, Uttar Pradesh, India
Achin Jain	Department of Information Technology, Bharati Vidyapeeth's College of Engineering, New Delhi, India
Arul A. Prakash	Department of Computer Science and Engineering, Sathyabama Institute of Science and Technology, Chennai, India
D. Saravanan	Department of Computer Science and Engineering, Sathyabama Institute of Science and Technology, Chennai, India
Harsh Taneja	Department of CSE, Graphic Era Deemed to be University, Dehradun, Uttarakhand, India
Jessica Singh Syal	Bharati Vidyapeeth's College of Engineering, New Delhi, India
Joseph Arul Valan	National Institute of Technology Nagaland, Chumukedima, Dimapur, Nagaland, India
Kiran Deep Singh	Chitkara University Institute of Engineering and Technology, Chitkara University, Rajpura, Punjab, India
Kim Ho Yeap	Department of Electronic Engineering, Universiti Tunku Abdul Rahman, 31900 Kampar, Malaysia
Kuldeep Singh Kaswan	School of Computing Science and Engineering, Galgotias University, Gr. Noida, Uttar Pradesh, India
Kareena Tuli	School of Computer Science Engineering & Technology, Bennett University, Greater Noida, India
Manu Singh	School of Computing Science and Engineering, Galgotias University, Gr. Noida, Uttar Pradesh, India
Mukesh Kumar	Department of Computer Science & Engineering, National Institute of Technology Patna, Patna, Bihar, India
Manish Kumar	School of Computing Science & Engineering, Galgotias University, Greater Noida, India
Neha Sharma	Department of Information Technology, Bharati Vidyapeeth's College of Engineering, New Delhi, India
Prabh Deep Singh	Department of Computer Science and Engineering, Graphic Era Deemed to be University, Dehradun, India
Phey Phey Lim	Intel Corporation, Penang, Malaysia
Prokash Gogoi	National Institute of Technology Nagaland, Chumukedima, Dimapur, Nagaland, India

Pranav Shrivastava   Department of Computer Sciences, Galgotias College of Engineering and Technology, Greater Noida, India

Prerna Agarwal   School of Computer Science Engineering & Technology, Bennett University, Greater Noida, India

Rahin R. Batcha   Department of Computer Science and Engineering, Sathyabama Institute of Science and Technology, Chennai, India

Rakesh Sharma   McDermott International, Pune, Maharashtra, India

Sunakshi Mehra   Galgotias College of Engineering and Technology, Greater Noida, Uttar Pradesh, India

Sonu Kumar Jha   Department of Computer Science & Engineering, National Institute of Technology Patna, Patna, Bihar, India

Somaraju Suvvari   Department of Computer Science & Engineering, National Institute of Technology Patna, Patna, Bihar, India

S. Vignesh   Department of Computer Science and Engineering, Sathyabama Institute of Science and Technology, Chennai, India

Saquib Hussain   School of Computer Science Engineering & Technology, Bennett University, Greater Noida, India

Tanu Singh   School of Computer Science, University of Petroleum and Energy Studies, Dehradun, Uttarakhand, India

Urvashi Sugandh   School of Computer Science and Engineering, Bennett University, Greater Noida, India

Varun Kumar Singh   Galgotias College of Engineering and Technology, Greater Noida, Uttar Pradesh, India

Veerendra Dakulagi   Department of CSE (Data Science), Guru Nanak Dev Engineering College, Bidar, Karnataka, India

Vaswati Gogoi   School of Computer Science, University of Petroleum and Energy Studies, Dehradun, Uttarakhand, India

Vinod Patidar   School of Computer Science, University of Petroleum and Energy Studies, Dehradun, Uttarakhand, India

Vijay Ramalingam   Department of Computer Science and Engineering, Sathyabama Institute of Science and Technology, Chennai, India

Yu Jen Lee   Department of Electronic Engineering, Universiti Tunku Abdul Rahman, 31900 Kampar, Malaysia

Understanding the Basics of Data Analytics and AI for Predictive Maintenance in Industry 4.0

Arvind Panwar[1,*], **Urvashi Sugandh**[2], **Neha Sharma**[3], **Manish Kumar**[1] and **Kuldeep Singh Kaswan**[1]

[1] *School of Computing Science and Engineering, Galgotias University, Greater Noida, Uttar Pradesh, India*

[2] *School of Computer Science and Engineering, Bennett University, Greater Noida, India*

[3] *Department of Information Technology, Bharati Vidyapeeth's College of Engineering, New Delhi, India*

Abstract: Industry 4.0 marks a transformational era in industrial practices, defined by the merging of cutting-edge technologies such as the Internet of Things, cyber-physical systems, extensive data examination, cloud computing, artificial intelligence, and machine learning. This chapter, entitled "Understanding the Basics of Data Analytics and AI for Predictive Maintenance in Industry 4.0," offers an inclusive exploration of how data examination and AI are revolutionizing predictive servicing strategies to improve functional efficacy, decrease expenses, and enhance safety. To commence with an outline of Industry 4.0 and the evolution of servicing strategies—from reactive and preventative to predictive—the chapter underscores the pivotal role of data-driven decision-making in modern industrial operations. It delves into the basics of data examination, analyzing the kinds of industrial data, methods of obtaining information, and preprocessing techniques. Core analytical techniques, like descriptive, diagnostic, predictive, and, briefly, prescriptive analytics, are inspected to demonstrate their applications in servicing contexts. The chapter further examines the joining of AI in predictive servicing, detailing machine learning algorithms. It also highlights the instruments and platforms usually used in data examination and AI, together with programming languages like Python and R, specialized software, and data visualization instruments. The advantages, like reduced downtime, servicing cost savings, extended equipment lifespan, and enhanced decision-making capabilities, are balanced against challenges, for example, data quality management, scalability, cybersecurity concerns, skills gaps, cultural resistance to change, and investment considerations. The chapter also explores emerging developments and future directions, like edge computing, digital twins, comprehensible AI, merging with other Industry 4.0 technologies, and the concept of Predictive Servicing as a Service (PMaaS), analyzing their possible influence to further transform servicing practices and contribute to sustainability. By providing foundational knowledge and practical insights and highlighting both oppor-

---

* **Corresponding author Arvind Panwar:** School of Computing Science and Engineering, Galgotias University, Gr. Noida, Uttar Pradesh, India; E-mail: arvind.nice3@gmail.com

Tanu Singh, Vinod Patidar, Arvind Panwar & Urvashi Sugandh (Eds.)

tunities and challenges, this chapter aims to provide readers with the understanding necessary to leverage data examination and AI for innovative and efficient predictive servicing in the evolving landscape of Industry 4.0.

Keywords: Artificial intelligence (AI), Data analytics, Industry 4.0, Internet of things (IoT), Machine learning (ML), Predictive maintenance.

INTRODUCTION

The dawn of Industry 4.0 has transformed how industries function, communicate, and conceive [1]. This section intends to offer a thorough comprehension of the fundamental principles of data examination and synthetic consciousness for anticipatory servicing in Industry 4.0. In this section, we will plunge into the overview of Industry 4.0, its progression, and the importance of predictive servicing at this time. Additionally, industries must leverage novel technologies to optimize operations whilst ensuring worker safety through automation. While change can inspire apprehension, an open mind to emerging tools may reveal opportunities to enhance productivity, quality, and outcomes [2].

OVERVIEW OF INDUSTRY 4.0

Industry 4.0 and the fusion of cyber systems will revolutionize manufacturing like never before. While companies scramble to integrate networks of intelligent devices and technologies capable of autonomous action, profound transformation lies ahead. Already, robots work alongside workers on factory floors, communicating in real time through IoT platforms to autonomously complete tasks. Machines learn from vast torrents of big data, enabling precision and customization at scale. Human and artificial intelligence will cooperate as never before to realize smart factories envisioned since the dawn of computational might, though challenges remain to full realization [3]. Optimists point to skyrocketing productivity and emancipation from dreary tasks, while others fear widespread economic upheaval and profound social changes as old jobs become obsolete. One thing is clear - a new industrial age defined by sentient systems and omnipresent information looms on the horizon, for good and for bad [4].

The Evolution of Industrial Revolutions

The novelty concept of Industry 4.0 does not exist alone and is deeply rooted in the flow of industrial revolutions that took place in a certain chronological order. The first industrial revolution took place in the late 18th century and tended to associate with the transition from manual labor to the operation of machines [5]. The second revolution unfolded in the late 19th and early 20th century and involved the further development of machinery, as well as the new concept of mass production, which was represented by conveyor belts. The third industrial revolution started in the mid-20th century and was based on the vastly spread computer, automation, and mechanization of production. The fourth industrial revolution, which is sometimes called Industry 4.0, is fuelled by the integration of digital, physical, and biological systems, which provides for the creation of levels of automation, service, and innovation that were not experienced before by the manufacturing industry. The fundamental transformation of Industry 4.0 is not only in industrial facilities' widespread adoption of modern and highly efficient technologies but also in the development of an entirely new ecosystem where machines, humans, and data interact with each other harmoniously and effectively [6]. Industry 4.0 ecosystem is built on interconnectivity, automation, and the ability to exchange data for the foundation of smart factories, which create smart products and carry out smart services.

In the next sections, the basics of data analytics and AI in predictive maintenance will be discussed. These will include types of data and data analytics techniques, AI algorithms, integration of these technologies in Industry 4.0, benefits, and challenges of the implementation.

Key Technologies Driving Industry 4.0

The hallmarks of Industry 4.0 are the convergence of a number of essential technologies that revolutionize manufacturing. The technologies are the foundation on which smart factories, smart products, and smart services are built. It can be said that the key technologies of Industry 4.0 are:

- **Internet of Things:** The term Internet of Things refers to the interconnection of devices and machines using sensors to collect data and exchange it. In other words, IoT refers to the connection of anything from house appliances and motor vehicles to the entire factory and networks, enabling their communication. For example, in the case of predictive maintenance, IoT sensors can be used to monitor equipment and detect and possibly predict undesired anomalies and failures. Other uses for IoT devices are keeping track of inventory levels, monitoring the supply chain, and optimizing logistics [7].
- **Cyber-Physical Systems (CPS):** Cyber-physical systems amalgamate computational and physical mechanisms to generate ingenious infrastructures. CPS combines the tangible with the digital, permitting live observation, administration, and optimization of corporeal processes. In prescient servicing, CPS can monitor hardware performance, distinguish anomalies, and foresee failures. CPS can furthermore optimize fabrication techniques, diminish energy usage, and improve merchandise quality [8].
- **Big Data and Analytics:** Vast data alludes to the expansive and intricate

information assemblages that are created by different sources like gadgets, machines, and sensors. Big data investigation includes breaking down these information accumulations to acquire experiences and settle on educated choices [9]. In prescient support, enormous information examination can dissect hardware execution information, identify examples, and foresee disappointments. Big data investigation can likewise be utilized to streamline upkeep timetables, diminish downtime, and improve general hardware viability.

- **Cloud Computing:** Cloud computing alludes to the utilization of a distributed computing framework for information stockpiling, handling, and investigation. Distributed computing empowers the adaptability, scalability, and monetary knowledge required for the examination of enormous information accumulations. In prescient upkeep, distributed computing can utilize and handle significant measures of hardware execution information, enabling live checking and prescient investigation [10].

- **Artificial Intelligence (AI) and Machine Learning (ML):** AI and Machine Learning (ML) are key advancements driving Industry 4.0. AI alludes to the advancement of keen frameworks that can perform obligations ordinarily requiring human insight. ML is a subset of AI, including the utilization of calculations to dissect information and make expectations. In prescient upkeep, AI and ML can break down hardware execution information, recognize anomalies, and anticipate disappointments [11]. AI and ML can likewise streamline support timetables, diminish downtime, and improve general hardware viability.

The Impact of Industry 4.0 on Manufacturing and Maintenance

Industry 4.0 is radically transforming how goods are crafted through introducing novel technologies, processes, and commercial models. The impact of Industry 4.0 on manufacturing and upkeep is multi-faceted and far-reaching, with sizeable implications for productivity, efficiency, and competitiveness. Employing Industry 4.0 technologies like IoT, AI, and robotics permits the automation of fabrication workflows, resulting in boosted efficiency and productivity. Predictive servicing, empowered by these technologies, curtails downtime and heightens overall equipment performance. Breaking down enormous datasets provides insights into equipment functioning, manufacturing procedures, and supply chain administration, improving operational efficiency, decreasing costs, and boosting competitiveness. Novel commercial models and opportunities are emerging, such as predictive servicing as a service, data examination as a service, and equipment tracking as a service, cultivating new income streams and prospects for manufacturers and service providers [12, 13]. However, adopting Industry 4.0 technologies also spawns a skills void in the labor force, necessitating investment in workforce progression to ensure the necessary abilities to back these technologies. Additionally, the increased utilization of IoT devices and cloud computing raises cybersecurity concerns, obligating manufacturers to invest in cybersecurity steps to shield their operations. Overall, Industry 4.0 is revolutionizing manufacturing and upkeep, presenting both opportunities and obstacles that must be addressed [14].

Maintenance Strategies in Industrial Settings

It is vital for industrial settings to employ effective maintenance strategies to preserve equipment and machinery's reliability, cogency, and longevity. The common maintenance approaches utilized include reactive maintenance on the one hand and preventative maintenance and predictive maintenance on the other [15]. Each of them varies significantly in terms of applied methodology and implication for the type of operational performance.

Reactive Maintenance

Reactive maintenance is often referred to as "run-to-failure" maintenance as it presumes that the equipment should only be serviced after it has already broken down or failed. This method makes virtually no demands on planning and investment in advance, as off-cycle servicing is avoided, and at the same time, it is available for utilization at no additional cost, given that the action is taken as a result of a prevailing breakdown. Although it may entail reduced maintenance costs, given the associated delays and investments, in the long run, the reactive approach is linked to high economic costs of spontaneous downtimes, premature equipment wear, and malfunctioning. I agree that unplanned maintenance can result in unsafe conditions and should be avoided because of costs at this site as well. Besides the associated financial expenses, this type of maintenance is linked to unpredictability and requires constant revision of production schedules, which is inherently disruptive of overall efficiency.

Preventative Maintenance

Preventative maintenance requires regularly scheduled servicing of equipment, irrespective of its current state of operation, *via* either time or usage-oriented intervals. The notion ordains that wearing and malfunction can be observed and corrected in a timely manner, before the equipment breaks down altogether. The approach allows for systemizing equipment monitoring and focuses on the detection and replacement of specific components, which can preserve equipment reliability and longevity while keeping unexpected breakdowns at bay [16]. At the same time, preventative maintenance may introduce significant operational costs since potentially optimal equipment has to be extensively and, therefore, overly serviced.

Predictive Maintenance

Predictive maintenance utilizes modern technologies, such as big data and artificial intelligence, to continuously monitor integrated sensors and thus track equipment conditions. Based on such data, patterns and changes can be recognized and responded to in case the equipment is on the verge of malfunctioning. The quickest and cheapest possible means can then be employed to service the equipment, and the action can be taken exactly when it is needed rather than in advance and in cases when it may not be necessary. According to the corresponding research regarding vibration prediction of turbine generator units in eastern China, the introduction of predictive maintenance is associated with significantly improved efficiency and reduced costs [17, 18].

The Synergy of Data Analytics and AI in Predictive Maintenance

Transition from Data to Insights

The information sources available in industrial environments are formed by a huge amount of data generated by various machines, sensors, and systems and transmitted over the network. Such data can be characterized as parameters of operation, environmental conditions, and metrics of equipment performance. However, the accumulation of these sources does not in itself bring any new value. The main problem in the context of Industry 4.0 is the transformation of the information into valuable insights that can be used for better decisions and improvements in maintenance practices [19]. The purpose is achieved through various data analytical techniques and artificial intelligence algorithms.

The transformation starts at the initial data stage when patterns and trends can be extracted on the basis of past operations and historical information. Machine learning and other artificial intelligence approaches are used in order to predict potential problems in the future. Because machines, systems, and sensors collect data at a rapid rate, people cannot interpret these datasets manually [20]. At the same time, the analytical process might be beneficial for identifying anomalies, coincidence, and other signals that are not visible before the analytical treatment. Therefore, the vendors spend significant investments for the remediation of such data.

In the case of predictive maintenance, the role of AI and data analysis is critical because it helps to replace traditional tools such as reliably scheduled overhauls and repair requests that are activated by operators when the machine breaks down. With the help of data over numerous parameters, it is possible to apply a vibration analysis of the historical cases of bearing breakages for the prediction of new malfunctions [21]. By integrating data over an appropriate time period and using modern ML approaches, the bearing failure can be predicted with a probability of 95%. Costly data and system damages can be eliminated due to the timely reaction. Overall, it is possible to say that the use of AI and data analysis for proactive maintenance is extremely important for modern organizations that want to optimize their operations and costs and reduce the risk of unpredictable failures.

Importance of Data-Driven Decision Making

The predictive maintenance method is often applied to modern industrial management, where data-driven decision-making is important. By using empirical data and analytical models, organizations can arrive at decisions that are evidence-based, independent, clear, and repeatable. Doing this offers better insights, efficiency, risk management, improvement, and strategic capabilities. In the era of Industry 4.0, the ability to react and adjust quickly on a platform that takes into account incoming data is critical for companies wanting to stay competitive in their respective markets. Maintenance is evolving from a cost center to a strategic asset that contributes to overall business objectives through data-driven decision-making [22].

Objectives of the Chapter

Predictive Maintenance in Industry 4.0 Using Data Analytics and Artificial Intelligence: The overarching goal is to outline the basic understanding of theoretical terms and concepts, establish the traditional *vs.* predictive maintenance transition synergized with data analytics and AI, put weight on a need for data-driven decision-making processes in this field, and share more practical insights on real-world problems as well as some challenges and future trends that this industry is facing. The chapter accomplishes these objectives by providing readers with a guided walk-through on how to use data analytics and AI to improve predictive maintenance, making the connection between theoretical concepts and real-world technology.

FUNDAMENTALS OF DATA ANALYTICS IN PREDICTIVE MAINTENANCE

Understanding Industrial Data

In the instance of Industry 4.0, predictive maintenance is more dependent on industrial data analysis, and so far, deployment of maintenance resources to expected failures can be scheduled. Data analytics plays an important role in this, helping businesses identify legible facts from their big data sources and make informed decisions based on that [23].

Understanding Industrial Data

Industrial data ultimately originates from all over the place, like sensors, machines, operational systems, *etc*. This data may also be heterogeneous because of its origin. It may be complicated by complexity and often appears not to have a fixed structure, which all require expert tools and algorithms for treatment [24].

Types of Data Sources

Industrial data comes from many origins and has many facets that describe its content. There are basically four types of data sources:

- **Sensor Data:** Sensor data includes temperature, vibration, pressure, and other parameters —anything that comes from your sensors or IoT devices that can help you understand the performance and condition of equipment [25].
- **Machine Logs:** This includes data on how the machines are being utilized, what work orders have been reallocated to them, their performance, and the upkeep narrative. This kind of data is frequently used to recognize examples and patterns in the conduct of hardware [26].
- **Operational:** This data is produced by operational systems such as manufacturing processes, inventory levels, and supply chain information [27].
- **Environment Data:** In this, environment data is related to the external factors that can affect equipment functionality, *i.e.*, temperature, humidity, and weather conditions.

Data Characteristics

Industrial data has the 4 Vs of big data: volume, velocity, variety, and veracity. These attributes are essential for realizing the nature of industrial data and the complexities involved in analysis.

- **Volume:** Industrial data is generated in vast quantities, often in real-time, from various sources such as sensors, machines, and operational systems.
- **Velocity:** Industrial data is rapid — it requires real-time analytics to keep up with the speed at which the industrial use case generates and processes this data.
- **Variety:** Industrial data comes in various formats, including structured, semi-structured, and unstructured data, such as text, images, and videos.
- **Veracity**: Minimizing the error in data to newer dimensions of making an accurate data source available is crucial; inaccurate, incomplete information results in incorrect insights and wrong decision-making.

Additionally, industrial data can be classified into structured and unstructured data:

- **Structured Data:** This kind of data is in a certain organized fashion that can be easily queried by humans and machines. For instance, relational databases and spreadsheets.
- **Unstructured Data:** The data is not formatted, and hence, it is less easy to analyze. Examples are text files, images, and videos.

To implement an effective predictive maintenance strategy, we need to understand what industrial data looks like. This presents the organization with more options for data management systems and analytics tools to process data relevant to their type of industry by understanding how much it is available and at what speed it becomes available.

In the next sections, we will deal with the data analytics process of predictive maintenance, such as data preprocessing, feature engineering, and modeling techniques. We will also talk about machine learning, artificial intelligence in predictive maintenance, and the difficulties and advantages of implementing that in industries.

Data Acquisition and Preprocessing

For predictive maintenance, data acquisition and preprocessing are two necessary steps in the chain of any data analytics solution. The worse the data collected and its preprocessing, the more inaccurate the insights obtained.

Data Collection Methods

There are multiple ways to collect industrial data, such as:

- **Data Collection *via* IoT Devices and Sensors:** Industrial sensors and IoT devices are used to collect real-time diagnostic data on equipment performance and environmental conditions (only some examples). The devices can connect over the web, providing remote control, monitoring, and data retention [28].
- **Data Logging Systems:** Data logging systems collect data from multiple sources such as sensors, machines, and operational systems and store it. These systems can capture data in a range of frequencies, be it on a periodic basis or every second [29].

The choice of data collection method depends on the specific requirements of the predictive maintenance application, the type of data needed, and the infrastructure available.

Data Preprocessing Techniques

Data preprocessing is an important step in preprocessing industrial data before analysis. Data preprocessing generally includes solving data quality problems, dealing with missing values, and transforming data into some other format suitable for the downstream tasks.

- **Data Cleaning and Handling Missing Values:** Data cleaning is all about dealing with errors and generalization of data. Dealing with missing values is essential because any data that is incomplete can lead to a biased, incorrect conclusion [30].
- **Data Transformation or Normalization:** Data is convertedfrom one format to another suitable for analysis. Complex models require all variables to be on the same scale, so different normalization techniques are applied to make fair comparisons and predictions [31].
- **Feature Extraction and Selection:** Feature extraction is to identify features or variables that can represent the equipment behaviour or failure better than raw data. Feature selection is the process of reducing the number of input variables when developing a predictive model; often, it will help to reduce overfitting and more robust unseen data by removing some features [32].

Data preprocessing is a laborious and time-consuming but essential step to ensure that the insights produced are accurate and reliable. These methods, when applied, can help organizations ensure that their data quality is up to the mark, which not only reduces the chances of errors but also improves the efficiency of their predictive maintenance activities.

Core Data Analytics Techniques

In the case of Industry 4.0, data analytics plays a crucial role in enabling organizations to use predictive maintenance by allowing them to extract insights from massive amounts of data and make more informed decisions [33]. The primary methods of core data analytics at the heart of predictive maintenance can be grouped into four main categories – Descriptive Analytics, Diagnostic Analytics, Predictive Analytics, and Prescriptive Analytics.

Descriptive Analytics

Descriptive analytics is the analysis of historical data to understand and explain what has happened in the past (in terms of patterns). Descriptive analytics is mainly used to summarize and describe the data, which helps in understanding what has happened.

- **Statistical Summaries:** In this step, we do the calculation of statistics like mean, median, mode, and standard deviation to find out the central tendency and variability of data [34].
- **Visualization Techniques:** It consists of histograms, box plots, series, and scatter and graphically displays data, facilitating its interpretation and allowing the identification of patterns.

Descriptive analytics allows you to spot trends, outliers, and correlations in your data.

Diagnostic Analytics

Analyzing data to discover why some action happened is known as diagnostic analytics (because you are diagnosing the root cause of an event). Diagnostic analytics have the main goal of delving into why equipment fails and what different types of relationships exist among different types of variables.

- **Root Cause Analysis:** This allows companies to identify the root causes of equipment failures in real time so they can address underlying issues instead of just treating the symptoms [35].
- **Correlation *vs.* Causation:** Correlation analysis identifiesthe kind of relationship each variable has, and causation analysis figures out if such relationships are causal.

This is where diagnostic analytics comes into play with predictive maintenance and offers the ability to diagnose why the equipment is failing and take preventative measures.

Predictive Analytics

Predictive analytics predict the future using statistical models and machine learning algorithms. The two main goals of predictive analytics include predicting the failure of equipment and predicting how much life (*i.e.*, RUL — Remaining Useful Life) is left in the asset.

- **Time Series Analysis:** Time series analysis is the process of analyzing time series data to extract meaningful statistics, *etc.* One considers ARIMA, exponential smoothing, or seasonal decomposition techniques to forecast future values [36].
- **Regression Models**: Regression models, such as linear regression and logistic regression, are used to predict continuous and binary outcomes, respectively. Regression models are used to predict the output value of a dependent variable

based on an independent variable. For example, the number of sales a company makes in a month is dependent upon its spending on advertising in that month.

At the heart of predictive maintenance is predictive analytics, which helps users predict when an in-service machine will start to have issues so that maintenance can be planned in advance.

Prescriptive Analytics in a Nutshell

Prescriptive analytics is about running optimization and simulation techniques to suggest what should be done. Prescriptive analytics is mainly focused on maintenance strategies as well as the capability and spare part management. One of the most rapidly developing areas in predictive maintenance, prescriptive analytics has the capability to greatly improve existing maintenance strategies. But it does require advanced data analytics and modeling.

In the next section, we will then dive into artificial intelligence and machine learning-based predictive maintenance, as well as supervised, unsupervised, and reinforcement learning used in it.

ARTIFICIAL INTELLIGENCE IN PREDICTIVE MAINTENANCE

Artificial Intelligence (AI) and Machine Learning (ML) have been introduced to predictive maintenance in Industry 4. By taking advantage of these technologies, organizations are able to sift through vast piles of data and gain insights into relationships and future equipment failure events. This section will begin by introducing AI and ML, discussing important concepts related to both, followed by how theywork in predictive maintenance [37].

Introduction to Artificial Intelligence and Machine Learning

AI and ML are disruptive technologies in the field of predictive maintenance, as they enable users to sift manually through mountains of available data points and make highly reliable predictions on when a machine or asset might break down. AI revolves around creating smart systems liable for performing tasks that require human intelligence, whereas ML denotes the ability of machines to learn from data without being programmed explicitly. The advent of AI and ML in predictive maintenance has an even more significant chance to change the tide on how maintenance is scheduled and prevents downtime while also enhancing overall equipment effectiveness.

Definitions and Key Concepts

As we already discussed previously about the basics of machine learning, deep learning, and AI, let's go through how all these fit into the paradigms of predictive maintenance using AI.

- **AI (Artificial Intelligence):** AI refers to developing intelligent systems that are capable of performing tasks that would require human intelligence, such as learning, problem-solving, and decision-making. In terms of their various capabilities, AI systems are generally thought to fall into two groups: (i) narrow/weak AI, which is designed to perform a particular task, and (ii) general /strong AI, which operates at the same intellectual level as a human being across the full range of cognitive functions [38].
- **Machine Learning (ML):** It refers to the predictive analysis of data and is often considered a subset of AI. It is a way of making a computer learn from data in such a way that the systems will be able to do some tasks without being programmed explicitly. It is classified as supervised, unsupervised, and reinforcement learning algorithms [39].
- **Deep Learning (DL):** A subset of ML, DL uses neural networks to analyze data. DL is especially valuable in image recognition, speech recognition, natural language processing, and sophisticated pattern recognition. DL models are stacked with artificial neurons, which makes DL able to learn and represent intricate patterns in data.

The Predictive Maintenance AI Workflow

The AI workflow in predictive maintenance is multi-stage; it includes data collection, model training, and deployment.

- **Data Collection:** Data is collected from multiple sources like sensors, machines, and operational systems. This can involve everything from sensor readings and machine logs to operational data.
- **Data Preprocessing:** We clean the data and transform it to prepare the data for analysis by normalizing it. This remains an important step in ensuring data/module quality and building insights.
- **Developing the Model:** Using this pre-processed data, ML algorithms are trained and developed. The specific algorithm you choose is dependent on the problem and the data available.
- **Model Evaluation:** The performance of the ML model is evaluated using metrics like accuracy, precision, and recall. This is a very crucial step to make the model robust and reliable.

- **Model Deployment:** The model trained is deployed in a production environment to predict in advance if any equipment will fail. This can mean you want to interface the model with other systems, such as Computerized Maintenance Management Systems (CMMS) or Enterprise Resource Planning (ERP) systems.
- **Refine Model:** The model is continuously updated through new data and feedback. This makes sure that the model is still relevant and performs well over a certain period of time.

AI workflow combines the power of AI and ML to predict when equipment fails, minimize downtime, and optimize maintenance schedules. Next up, we will discuss the different types of ML algorithms used for predictive maintenance, such as supervised, unsupervised, and reinforcement learning algorithms.

AI Benefits in Predictive Maintenance

Advantages of AI in predictive maintenance:

- **Increased Accuracy:** AI models are able to process more data and recognize patterns that might not be noticed by humans, resulting in a greater likelihood of predicting failures.
- **Improved Efficiency:** AI models can predict when equipment is going to fail automatically; this eliminates the need for manual analysis, and hence maintenance teams can be used elsewhere.
- **Predict Failures to Schedule Maintenance during Downtime:** You can actually predict equipment failures and then schedule the maintenance activities during planned downtime, minimizing the impact on production.
- **Cost Savings**: AI-powered predictive maintenance reduces the need for unplanned repairs and decreases the spare parts process.

The remainder of this section explains the 3 types of ML algorithms applied to predictive maintenance (supervised, reinforcement, and unsupervised). We will also cover the challenges and pitfalls of leveraging AI in predictive maintenance.

Machine Learning Algorithms for Predictive Maintenance

Predictive maintenance in Industry 4.0 makes extensive use of machine learning algorithms, allowing companies to process vast amounts of data and accurately predict failures in equipment. Supervised, unsupervised, and reinforcement are the most popular families of machine learning algorithms utilized in predictive maintenance.

Supervised Learning

In supervised learning, models are trained on labeled data where the target output is given. Supervised learning is primarily used to build models that are able to classify equipment states or predict a continuous outcome, such as Remaining Useful Life (RUL) [40].

Classification Algorithms

- **Decision Trees:** These are simple models that you can understand due to the format of how the predictions are made based on a series of decisions that classify machine conditions. They are used for categorical data and for interpreting which features are most important.
- **Support Vector Machines:** Support Vector Machines (SVM) are high-performance models that can work exceptionally with high data and data containing outliers. They are typically used in binary classification problems. Like SVM (Support Vector Machines), we can have SVR (Support Vector Regression). They are good at capturing non-linear relationships they can handle outliers [41].
- **Random Forests:** Random forests work by aggregating the predictions of multiple decision trees to increase their accuracy and reduce overfitting. They are good for large datasets and feature selection.

Regression Algorithms

- **Linear Regression:** This algorithm measures the linear relationship between the input features and the target variable, RUL, and other continuous output predictions.
- **Polynomial Regression:** Polynomial regression models play an important role in non-linear and linear regression. They are really good at modeling non-linear relationships between the input features and the target variable [42].

Unsupervised Learning

In unsupervised learning, models are trained on unlabelled data where the output is unknown. Here, the main goals are to find patterns, anomalies, and clusters in the data.

Clustering Algorithms

- **K-Means Clustering:** K-means clustering is an algorithm that attempts to divide the dataset into K clusters based on similarities. It is great at recognizing patterns and anomalies in data.

- **Hierarchical Clustering:** Agglomerative hierarchical clustering is a type of hierarchical clustering that builds a hierarchy based on distance similarity. It serves to detect nested patterns and outliers within data.
- **Anomaly Detection Techniques:** Anomaly detection goes the extra mile **through** which prominently disparate data points are recognized. Popular techniques for anomaly detection include Density-Based Spatial Clustering of Applications with Noise (DBSCAN) and isolation forests [43].

Reinforcement Learning

With reinforcement learning, models are trained to respond based on rewards or penalties. The reinforcement learning problem that we want to solve is to determine this policy so that the sum of rewards over a sequence of decision-making would be the largest. While reinforcement learning does hold the possibility to greatly improve predictive maintenance, it is a nascent field and is currently still under research.

INTEGRATION OF DATA ANALYTICS AND AI IN INDUSTRY 4.0

The integration of data analytics and AI is critical for the success of predictive maintenance in Industry 4.0. This integration enables organizations to leverage the power of data analytics and AI to predict equipment failures, reduce downtime, and optimize maintenance schedules.

Building a Predictive Maintenance System

The constituents required to build a predictive maintenance system include architecture, workflow, and interoperability with current industrial systems.

System Architecture

The three main layers of system architecture for predictive maintenance are as follows:

- **The Data Layer:** This is where data is collected and stored from many sources—sensors, machines, and operational systems. This layer is responsible for some of the most important things, such as making sure that data quality is acceptable and so on. Data Storage Layer — Relational Databases, NoSQL databases, and Data Warehouses [44].
- **Analytics Layer:** Analytics has become an essential part of companies trying to extract information from the data using different methods, such as ML and DL. This layer is extremely important in mining useful information from the data. It houses the data analytics tools (Python, R, SQL, *etc.*) and machine learning

libraries (TensorFlow, Pytorch).

- **Visualization Layer:** This layer is concerned with the showcasing of insights in a simple and understandable way. This is important in letting decision-makers make sense of the data-driven insights and take proper action. This layer is the visualization layer, which contains data visualization tools like Tableau, Power BI, D3, *etc.*

Workflow from Data Collection to Decision Making

The process from data capture to decision-making entails several steps, including:

- **Data Collection:** Data is collected from various sources, including sensors, machines, and operational systems. This data can include sensor readings, machine logs, and operational data.
- **Data Preprocessing:** The necessary data cleaning, transforming, and normalization are done to prepare the data for analysis. You must pay close attention to details at this step so you can minimize low-quality data while getting accurate insights.
- **Model Development:** Models in machine learning are built and trained with the help of pre-processed data. The selection of the model is based on the nature of the problem and also on the kind of data we have available in the dataset.
- **Model Evaluation:** Performance metrics like accuracy, precision, and recall are calculated to evaluate the performance of the machine learning model. This step is very important as it will help ascertain that the model has the right prediction [45].
- **Model Deployment:** A trained model is deployed in production to predict equipment failure. This entails integrating the model with other systems (such as CMMS or ERP systems)
- **Decision Making:** The predictions can be leveraged to make smarter decisions about when and how to carry out maintenance, such as when work orders will be due on assets and which resources need staffing. This might include determining the most important pieces of equipment, streamlining maintenance, and focusing on resource allocation [46].

Interrelated with Current Systems of Industries

Seamless operation and benefits realization are only possible when predictive maintenance systems are integrated with the existing industrial system. Here are the basic components these predictive maintenance principles touch on for most general systems.

- **Computerized Maintenance Management Systems (CMMS):** They are used for automating maintenance operations, which includes scheduling and assigning resources. APIs to CMMS allow your organization to benefit from automatic maintenance scheduling, accurate resource allocation, and full data integration [47].
- **Enterprise Resource Planning (ERP) Systems:** ERP systems are highly integrated computer-based systems used for managing business operations, such as accounting, management of inventory and materials, and supply chain. They are more easily integrated with ERP systems to maximize inventory levels and supply chain operations throughout the organization [48].
- **Industrial Automation Systems:** Industrial automation systems are used to control and monitor industrial processes, such as production and manufacturing. Through the integration with industrial automation systems, businesses can further streamline their production processes and minimize downtime.

Predictive maintenance systems integrated with these also provide companies the ability to tap into data analytics and AI capabilities for their maintenance practices, hence helping them achieve high equipment effectiveness.

CHALLENGES AND FUTURE DIRECTIONS

Predictive maintenance in Industry 4.0 has benefits as well as challenges and areas for future development. This section will elaborate on the technical challenges, organizational and operational challenges, and the future direction of predictive maintenance.

Technical Challenges

Manufacturing industries that are looking to adopt Industry 4.0 for the implementation of predictive maintenance should recognize that they face ecosystems of some technical challenges that need to be dealtwith adequately in order to implement these technologies successfully.

Data Quality and Management

There is a significant difficulty in predictive maintenance related to data quality and management. As always, the quality of data collected and analyzed has a significant impact on the accuracy of valuable insights. If predictions are based on poor-quality data, these will likely be inaccurate and may lead to maintenance alerts that are not required, or the early signs of an equipment failure would have gone undetected.

Quality of Data

It is important to have proper data management strategies in place while adopting any ML/AI model, like data cleaning, preprocessing, scaling, normalization, *etc*. There are several reasons that can lead to data quality issues, such as sensor failures, data transmission errors, or inconsistent formats of the same. Identifying and cleaning these issues requires a rock-solid Data Quality Control framework and the deployment of modern AI/ML techniques to find and fix bugs in our data [49].

Scalability and Processing Speed

One of the most significant technical difficulties in predictive maintenance is scalability and processing speed. Industrial equipment generates mountains of data, which is computationally expensive to analyze [50]. Scalable architectures and services like high-performance computing are needed to enable the data to be processed as fast as possible. This involves everything from leveraging distributed computing, cloud computing, and high-performance databases to meeting the massive volume and velocity of industrial data.

Data Privacy and Cyber Security

Cybersecurity and data privacy are common nightmares of anybody working with predictive maintenance. IoT devices and cloud computing are more likely to be susceptible to cyber-attacks or data leaks. In addition, ensuring the security and privacy of the data revealed in this context of use is crucial to ensure trust in it and prevent unauthorized access. This involves adding strong securityand data encryption measures and making sure it complies with Data Protection Regulations.

Business and Operational Challenges

Of course, as with any initiative in the space of Industry 4.0, predictive maintenance also faces a set of organizational and operational challenges that must be dealt with if it is to be successful in the long run [51].

Skills Gap and Workforce Training

Predictive maintenance technologies that can be adversely affected need specialized skills like data analytics, machine learning, and AI adoption. The companies deploying the technologies have to lean more heavily on workforce investments, making sure their people can support them. It consists of training programs to re-skill and upskill the workforce for using Industry 4.0 technologies [52].

Cultural Resistance to Change

Predictive maintenance is ultimately a cultural shift from traditional preventative engine maintenance to more predictive, data-driven predictive maintenance alternatives. Organizations must work on addressing cultural resistance to change and ensuring that all stakeholders have been brought in line with the new maintenance strategy. This involves initiatives around change management, communication strategy, and training programs to make the stakeholders understand the benefits and implications of predictive maintenance well enough [53].

Investment and Cost Considerations

Predictive maintenance technology is both hardware and software and requires thousands of dollars in investment. Each initiative requires significant investments, and thus, organizations need to rethink these approaches strategically based on overall business objectives. This requires conducting cost-benefit analysis, quantifying potential ROI, and providing business cases for predictive maintenance projects.

Emerging Trends and Technologies

The future of predictive maintenance in Industry 4.0 is being shaped by a few big trends and technologies.

Edge Computing in Predictive Maintenance

Edge computing is where you move data processing closer to the source of data, at the edge of your network. This approach minimizes latency and enables better real-time processing, making it more secure.

Real-time machine learning data analysis on IoT: Machine Learning requires a lot of processing power, and doing the process on edge devices, such as Raspberry Pi or other smart cameras from OpenCV, can help in making the decision based on many sensors around a conveyor belt, which then sends inference alerts to inform maintenance team about equipment failures [54].

Digital Twins

In essence, digital twins offer virtual copies of real-world machinery. These digital twins can be leveraged to model the behavior of equipment, forecast failures, and optimize maintenance operations. They can also test and validate predictive maintenance models, helping to minimize the necessity of physical prototypes and improve prediction accuracy.

Explainable AI (XAI)

Explainable AI (XAI) refers to the development of AI models that are transparent and can be interpreted. This is something that is super important in the realm of predictive maintenance, where overall adaptability and dependability can be heavily dependent on understanding what causes our AI-driven predictions. Explainable AI can be used to provide insights into the decision-making process of AI models, enabling maintenance teams to understand why certain predictions were made and how they can be improved [55, 56].

Predictive maintenance for Industry 4.0 can deliver substantial advantages in terms of increased efficiency, reduced downtime, and superior competitiveness. Yet it also poses a number of challenges, along with future growth opportunities. Overcoming these challenges and adopting new trends and technologies will help organizations implement predictive maintenance successfully and enjoy its rewards.

The Future Landscape of Predictive Maintenance

Luckily, we see a bright future for predictive maintenance in Industry 4.0, with some upcoming trends and technologies galvanizing its destiny. In this regard, this section looks into how predictive maintenance is cooperating with other Industry 4.0 technologies and the feasibility of introducing predictive maintenance as a service, as well as discusses sustainability issues and economic aspects of these technologies.

Integration with Other Industry 4.0 Technologies

It is expected that in the future, predictive maintenance will merge with other Industry 4.0 technologies such as augmented reality, blockchain, and 5G networks. These integrations will strengthen predictive maintenance capabilities and open the door to a range of potentially transformative new business models.

- **Augmented Reality (AR):** Service workers can be guided while performing maintenance-related activities by a custom AR application to make the maintenance task easier by providing real-time information on how to perform clips and connections between machines. The AR can simulate maintenance scenarios in which the technician may carry out accurate practices and training in the AR world [57, 58].
- **Blockchain:** Blockchain can enhance the integrity and security of the maintenance data, providing a secure and transparent approach to tracking ghosted activities. This allows for an auditable record of repairs on blockchain

by demonstrating ownership, accountability, and traceability.

• **5G Networks:** Essential for ultra-fast data transmission in real time, which is necessary to perform faster and more reliable equipment failure predictions. Likewise, 5G networks will make IoT more popular, and predictive maintenance will become even more sophisticated [59, 60].

Predictive Maintenance as a Service (PMaaS)

PMaaS (Predictive Maintenance as a Service) will become the most significant trend in predictive maintenance. Predictive Maintenance as a Service is delivering predictive maintenance capabilities as cloud-based services, so companies can have access to top-notch predictive maintenance services without making huge investments upfront.

• **Advantages of PMaaS:** There are many benefits that come with using PMaaS, for example, decreased costs, improved scalability and more flexibility. It allows organizations to enjoy extensive predictive maintenance by opting for this technology without making any significant initial investment in hardware, software, and training. This flexibility helps organizations to scale their predictive maintenance capabilities up or down quickly, enhancing agility and responsiveness [61, 62].
• **Challenges of PMaaS:** The adoption of PMaaS also presents several challenges, including data security and privacy concerns, integration with existing systems, and ensuring the reliability and accuracy of the service. Organizations must carefully evaluate these challenges and develop strategies to address them [63, 64].

Sustainability and Environmental Impact

One of the most promising areas is predictive maintenance and it has the ability to contribute to the achievement of sustainability [65]. Less downtime and more efficient maintenance processes help lower energy usage, waste generation, and consumption output for businesses.

• **Energy Efficiency:** Properly maintaining equipment will result in better energy efficiency by ensuring that equipment operates at optimal performance levels and decreasing the occurrence of maintenance tasks that are not needed. Ultimately, this can result in deep cost savings and lower CO_2 emissions [66, 67].
• **Less Wastage:** Predictive maintenance also helps reduce waste by reducing the need for spare parts and minimizing the environmental impact due to any maintenance-related activity. This could be a way to save money on waste

disposal and lower the environmental footprint from your maintenance activities [68, 69].

• **Increased Efficiency:** By predicting how certain machines behave over time, operators can maximize the production process overall and save costs when a machine breaks while not in use. This leads to increased productivity and a reduction in the environmental footprints of industrial activity [70].

The future state of predictive maintenance in Industry 4.0 is optimistic, with a few up-and-coming trends and technologies that are destined to shape the future of this amazing domain. Embracing these trends and technologies, organizations can implement predictive maintenance successfully and enjoy its benefits, such as better productivity, minimum shutdowns, and a competitive edge.

CONCLUSION

This chapter gives the overall perspective of the fundamentals of data analytics and AI for predictive maintenance in Industry 4.0. The primary highlights are that data analytics has become an essential element in predictive maintenance, which helps organizations obtain insights from extensive datasets and make insightful decisions. AI, especially in machine learning and deep learning, changes predictive maintenance that allows them to analyze complex patterns and predict equipment failure. Collaboration between data analytics and AI has become a significant outcome for embracing predictive maintenance in every organization, which can use data analytics and AI responses as a tool for forecasting equipment failure optimization through proper maintenance schedules. There are some challenges associated with it, such as data quality (volume and veracity), scalability and speed of processing, cybersecurity issues and potential privacy in relation to the customer who uses the equipment, organizational behavioral challenges, and operational constraints. Innovations, including edge computing, digital twins, and explainable AI, will shape the future dynamic of what is possible with predictive maintenance. The key takeaways for organizations considering predictive maintenance are to start small, focus on data analytics and AI, make it seamless with existing systems, and tackle the cultural challenges involved. To sum up, Industry 4.0 predictive maintenance provides many advantages, like increased efficiency, decreased downtime, and improved competitiveness. Organizations that harness the power of data analytics and AI will be able to overhaul their maintenance practices and gain access to these benefits. The future of predictive maintenance finds great promise, and some emerging trends and technologies are sure to assist in the evolution. Given that the industry will continue to change, it is necessary for businesses to be aware and to adjust to keep up. However, predictive maintenance is more than a technology; it is a cultural shift to move away from reactive maintenance and use data predictively over time. It means development should desire to innovate, have a thirst for discovery, and should continuously improve. Predictive maintenance helps businesses stay efficient and remain competitive whilst reducing costs by ensuring the uptime of equipment and enhancing their use.

REFERENCES

[1] S. Vimal, M. Khari, N. Dey, R.G. Crespo, and Y. Harold Robinson, "Enhanced resource allocation in mobile edge computing using reinforcement learning based MOACO algorithm for IIOT", *Comput. Commun.*, vol. 151, pp. 355-364, 2020.
[http://dx.doi.org/10.1016/j.comcom.2020.01.018]

[2] S. Khan, M. Khari, and M. Azrour, "IoT in retail and e-commerce", In: *Electron. Commer. Res*, 2023, pp. 1-2.
[http://dx.doi.org/10.1007/s10660-023-09785-3]

[3] U. Sugandh, S. Nigam, M. Khari, and S. Misra, "An approach for risk traceability using blockchain technology for tracking, tracing, and authenticating food products", *Information (Basel)*, vol. 14, no. 11, p. 613, 2023.
[http://dx.doi.org/10.3390/info14110613]

[4] J.S. Dhatterwal, K.S. Kaswan, S. Saxena, and A. Panwar, "Big data for health data analytics and decision support", In: *in Computational Convergence and Interoperability in Electronic Health Records (EHR)*. IGI Global, 2024, pp. 93-116.

[5] S. Sinha, A. Panwar, P. Gupta, and V. Bhatnagar, "Evolution of business intelligence system: From ad-hoc report to decision support system to data lake based BI 3.0", In: *in Healthcare and Knowledge Management for Society 5.0: Trends, Issues, and Innovations*. CRC Press, 2022, pp. 255-269.
[http://dx.doi.org/10.1201/9781003168638-18]

[6] А. Ю. Горбовий, В. В. Лаговський, and А. А. Омельчук, "Штучний Інтелект У Текстильній Промисловості", *Appl. Quest. Math. Model.*, vol. 3, no. 2.2, pp. 123-132, 2023.
[http://dx.doi.org/10.32782/KNTU2618-0340/2020.3.2-2.11]

[7] Y. Kazancoglu, S.K. Mangla, Y. Berberoglu, C. Lafci, and J. Madaan, "Towards industry 5.0 challenges for the textile and apparel supply chain for the smart, sustainable, and collaborative industry in emerging economies", *Inf. Syst. Front.*, no. Sep, 2023.
[http://dx.doi.org/10.1007/s10796-023-10430-5]

[8] M. Khari, and A. Karar, "Analysis on intrusion detection by machine learning techniques : A review", *Int. J. Adv. Res. Comput. Sci. Softw. Eng.*, vol. 3, no. 4, pp. 545-548, 2013.

[9] E. Vyhmeister, and G.G. Castane, *Towards industry 5.0 by incorporation of trustworthy and human-centric approaches*. Springer Nature Switzerland, 2023, pp. 361-379.
[http://dx.doi.org/10.1007/978-3-031-46452-2_21]

[10] M.H. Rahman, M. Yaqot, and B.C. Menezes, "Towards circular economy in manufacturing industries based on industry 4.0 technologies", *2023 IEEE International Conference on Industrial Engineering and Engineering Management, IEEM 2023*, pp. 1502-1506, 2023.
[http://dx.doi.org/10.1109/IEEM58616.2023.10406739]

[11] P. Singh, K. Chaudhary, G. Chaudhary, M. Khari, and B. Rawal, "A machine learning approach to detecting deepfake videos: An investigation of feature extraction techniques", *Journal of Cybersecurity and Information Management*, vol. 9, no. 2, pp. 42-50, 2022.
[http://dx.doi.org/10.54216/JCIM.090204]

[12] Saurabh, C. Sharma, S. Khan, S. Mahajan, H.S. Alsagri, A. Almjally, B.I. Alabduallah, and A.A. Ansari, "Lightweight Security for IoT", *J. Intell. Fuzzy Syst.*, vol. 45, no. 4, pp. 5423-5439, 2023.
[http://dx.doi.org/10.3233/JIFS-232388]

[13]   S. Lahlou, M. Boulmalf, and K. Zkik, "Toward a secure industry 4.0: An SDN-assisted approach 'SSI4,'", In: *in Communications in Computer and Information Science. CCIS* vol. 1808. Springer Nature Switzerland: Germany, 2023, pp. 383-396.
[http://dx.doi.org/10.1007/978-3-031-40395-8_27]

[14]   M.M. Ismail, Z. Ahmed, A.F. Abdel-Gawad, and M. Mohamed, "Toward supply chain 5.0: An integrated multi-criteria decision-making models for sustainable and resilience enterprise", *Decision Making: Applications in Management and Engineering,* vol. 7, no. 1, pp. 160-186, 2023.
[http://dx.doi.org/10.31181/dmame712024955]

[15]   A. Agarwal, A. Verma, and M. Khari, "Comparative assessment of machine learning methods for early prediction of diseases using health indicators", In: *Approaches to Human-Centered AI in Healthcare.* IGI Global, 2024, pp. 160-186.
[http://dx.doi.org/10.4018/979-8-3693-2238-3.ch007]

[16]   N. Kashpruk, C. Piskor-Ignatowicz, and J. Baranowski, "Time series prediction in industry 4.0: A Comprehensive review and prospects for future advancements", *Appl. Sci. (Basel),* vol. 13, no. 22, p. 12374, 2023.
[http://dx.doi.org/10.3390/app132212374]

[17]   T.A.V. Nguyen, K.H. Nguyen, and D. Tucek, "Total quality management 4.0 framework: Present and future", *Operations and Supply Chain Management: An International Journal,* vol. 16, no. 3, pp. 311-322, 2023.
[http://dx.doi.org/10.31387/oscm0540391]

[18]   P. Singh, and M. Khari, "Necessity of time synchronization for IoT-based applications", In: *n Internet of Things: Technological Advances and New Applications.* Apple Academic Press, 2023, pp. 285-297.
[http://dx.doi.org/10.1201/9781003304609-15]

[19]   S.H. Reddy, H. Bathini, V.N. Ajmeera, R.S. Marella, T.V.V. Kumar, and M. Khari, "Startup unicorn success prediction using ensemble machine learning algorithm", In: *in Lecture Notes in Computer Science (including subseries Lecture Notes in Artificial Intelligence and Lecture Notes in Bioinformatics).* vol. 14532. LNCS, 2024, pp. 330-338.
[http://dx.doi.org/10.1007/978-3-031-53830-8_34]

[20]   U. Sakarya, "The visual-based robotic language for industry 4.0 applications: Robotic U language", *Signal Image Video Process.,* vol. 18, no. 1, pp. 91-98, 2024.
[http://dx.doi.org/10.1007/s11760-023-02713-w]

[21]   M. Khari, R. Dalal, A. Sharma, and B. Mehta, "Person identification in uav shot videos by using machine learning", In: *in Multimodal Biometric Systems.* CRC Press, 2021, pp. 45-60.
[http://dx.doi.org/10.1201/9781003138068-4]

[22]   F. Lamperti, K. Lavoratori, and D. Castellani, "The unequal implications of Industry 4.0 adoption: evidence on productivity growth and convergence across Europe", *Econ. Innov. New Technol.,* no. Oct, pp. 1-25, 2023.
[http://dx.doi.org/10.1080/10438599.2023.2269089]

[23]   H.A. Khan, and T.H. Walcott, "The role of Chatbots in Industry 4.0", *Proceedings - 2023 International Conference on Computing, Electronics and Communications Engineering, iCCECE 2023,* pp. 85-88, 2023.
[http://dx.doi.org/10.1109/iCCECE59400.2023.10238595]

[24]   P. Singh, M. Khari, and S. Vimal, "EESSMT: An energy efficient hybrid scheme for securing mobile ad hoc networks using IoT", *Wirel. Pers. Commun.,* vol. 126, no. 3, pp. 2149-2173, 2022.
[http://dx.doi.org/10.1007/s11277-021-08764-x]

[25]   U. Sugandh, M. Khari, and S. Nigam, "How blockchain technology can transfigure the indian agriculture sector", In: *Handb. Green Comput. Blockchain Technol,* 2021, pp. 69-88.
[http://dx.doi.org/10.1201/9781003107507-6]

[26]   T. Singh, A. Panwar, K.S. Kaswan, A. Jain, and U. Sugandh, "The datafication of everything: Challenges and opportunities in a hyperconnected world", *International Conference on Advancements in Smart Computing and Information Security,* pp. 254-268, 2024.
[http://dx.doi.org/10.1007/978-3-031-58604-0_18]

[27]   A. Panwar, V. Bhatnagar, S. Sinha, and R. Ranjan, "IoT security issues and solutions with blockchain", In: *in Industry 4.0 Technologies for Business Excellence: Frameworks, Practices, and Applications.* CRC Press, 2021, pp. 141-161.
[http://dx.doi.org/10.1201/9781003140474-8]

[28]   F. Arcidiacono, A. Ancarani, C. Di Mauro, and F. Schupp, "What drives I4.0 Adoption? Establishing the importance of strategy", *IEEE Eng. Manage. Rev.,* vol. 51, no. 3, pp. 33-41, 2023.
[http://dx.doi.org/10.1109/EMR.2023.3281549]

[29]   N. Muhammad, S.M. Ibrahim Yahaya, I.Y. Suleiman, F. Karim, and A.U. Sabo Ago, "The impact of industry 4.0 on digital marketing: Leveraging emerging technologies for business growth", *Int. J. Acad. Res. Bus. Soc. Sci.,* vol. 13, no. 12, 2023.
[http://dx.doi.org/10.6007/IJARBSS/v13-i12/19723]

[30]   S. Nigam, U. Sugandh, and M. Khari, "The integration of blockchain and IoT edge devices for smart agriculture: Challenges and use cases", In: *in Advances in Computers.* vol. 127. Elsevier, 2022, pp. 507-537.
[http://dx.doi.org/10.1016/bs.adcom.2022.02.015]

[31]   B. Najafi, A. Najafi, and A. Farahmandian, "The impact of artificial intelligence and blockchain on six sigma: A systematic literature review of the evidence and implications", *IEEE Trans. Eng. Manage.,* vol. 71, pp. 10261-10294, 2024.
[http://dx.doi.org/10.1109/TEM.2023.3324542]

[32]   G. Chaudhary, S. Srivastava, and M. Khari, "Generative edge intelligence for securing IoT-assisted smart grid against cyber-threats", *International Journal of Wireless and Ad Hoc Communication,* vol. 6, no. 1, pp. 38-49, 2023.
[http://dx.doi.org/10.54216/IJWAC.060104]

[33]   S. Saif, P. Das, S. Biswas, M. Khari, and V. Shanmuganathan, "HIIDS: Hybrid intelligent intrusion detection system empowered with machine learning and metaheuristic algorithms for application in IoT based healthcare", In: *Microprocess. Microsyst,* 2022, p. 104622.
[http://dx.doi.org/10.1016/j.micpro.2022.104622]

[34]   A.G. Ramírez-Gutiérrez, P. Solano García, O. Morales Matamoros, J.J. Moreno Escobar, and R. Tejeida-Padilla, "Systems approach for the adoption of new technologies in enterprises", *Systems (Basel),* vol. 11, no. 10, p. 494, 2023.
[http://dx.doi.org/10.3390/systems11100494]

[35]   G. Chaudhary, M. Khari, and A. Mahmoud, "Intelligent video moving target detection based on multi-attribute single value medium neutrosophic Method", *Journal of Intelligent Systems and Internet of Things,* vol. 5, no. 1, pp. 49-59, 2021.
[http://dx.doi.org/10.54216/JISIoT.050105]

[36]   P. Negi, R. Singh, A. Gehlot, S. Kathuria, A.K. Thakur, L.R. Gupta, and M. Abbas, "Specific soft computing strategies for the digitalization of infrastructure and its sustainability: A comprehensive analysis", *Arch. Comput. Methods Eng.,* vol. 31, no. 3, pp. 1341-1362, 2024.
[http://dx.doi.org/10.1007/s11831-023-10018-x]

[37]   M.U. Shoukat, L. Yan, J. Zhang, Y. Cheng, M.U. Raza, and A. Niaz, "Smart home for enhanced healthcare: exploring human machine interface oriented digital twin model", *Multimedia Tools Appl.,* vol. 83, no. 11, pp. 31297-31315, 2023.
[http://dx.doi.org/10.1007/s11042-023-16875-9]

[38]   J. Khan, G.A. Khan, J.P. Li, M.F. AlAjmi, A.U. Haq, S. Khan, N. Ahmad, S. Parveen, M. Shahid, S. Ahmad, M. Raji, B. Ahamad, A.A. Alghamdi, and A. Ali, "Secure smart healthcare monitoring in

industrial internet of things (IIoT) Ecosystem with cosine function hybrid chaotic map encryption",
Sci. Program., vol. 2022, no. 1, pp. 1-22, 2022.
[http://dx.doi.org/10.1155/2022/8853448]

[39]   V. Ellappan, "Sliding principal component and dynamic reward reinforcement learning based IIoT
attack detection", *Sci. Rep.,* vol. 13, no. 1, p. 20843, 2023.
[http://dx.doi.org/10.1038/s41598-023-46746-0]

[40]   A. Islam, and A. Naseem, "Role of Industry 4.0 tools in organizational performance of the IT sector",
Kybernetes, no. Dec, 2023.
[http://dx.doi.org/10.1108/K-09-2023-1697]

[41]   Y. Duan, O. Shuplat, V. Matsuka, S. Lukash, M. Horbashevska, and L. Kyslova, "Risk management
strategy for international investment projects of an innovative enterprise in the context of industry
4.0", *Econ. Aff.,* vol. 68, no. 4, pp. 2047-2056, 2023.
[http://dx.doi.org/10.46852/0424-2513.4.2023.16]

[42]   U. Sugandh, S. Nigam, S. Misra, and M. Khari, "A bibliometric analysis of the evolution of state-o-
-the-art blockchain technology (BCT) in the agrifood sector from 2014 to 2022", *Sensors (Basel),* vol.
23, no. 14, p. 6278, 2023.
[http://dx.doi.org/10.3390/s23146278] [PMID: 37514574]

[43]   A. Panwar, M. Khari, S. Misra, and U. Sugandh, "Blockchain in agriculture to ensure trust,
effectiveness, and traceability from farm fields to groceries", *Future Internet,* vol. 15, no. 12, p. 404,
2023.
[http://dx.doi.org/10.3390/fi15120404]

[44]   A. Panwar, and V. Bhatnagar, "Sentiment analysis of game review using machine learning in a hadoop
ecosystem", In: *in Handbook of Research on Engineering Innovations and Technology Management in
Organizations.* IGI Global, 2020, pp. 145-165.
[http://dx.doi.org/10.4018/978-1-7998-2772-6.ch008]

[45]   Molinié, K. Madani, and V. Amarger, "Unsupervised clustering at the service of automatic anomaly
detection in industry 4.0", In: *in Lecture Notes in Computer Science (including subseries Lecture
Notes in Artificial Intelligence and Lecture Notes in Bioinformatics)* vol. 14135. Springer Nature
Switzerland: Germany, 2023, pp. 435-450.
[http://dx.doi.org/10.1007/978-3-031-43078-7_36]

[46]   A.U. Haq, J.P. Li, B.L.Y. Agbley, A. Khan, I. Khan, M.I. Uddin, and S. Khan, "IIMFCBM: Intelligent
integrated model for feature extraction and classification of brain tumors using MRI clinical imaging
data in IoT-healthcare", *IEEE J. Biomed. Health Inform.,* vol. 26, no. 10, pp. 5004-5012, 2022.
[http://dx.doi.org/10.1109/JBHI.2022.3171663] [PMID: 35503847]

[47]   U. Sugandh, S. Nigam, and M. Khari, "Ecosystem of technologies for smart agriculture to improve the
efficiency and profitability of indian farmers", *Proceedings of the 17th INDIACom; 2023 10th
International Conference on Computing for Sustainable Global Development, INDIACom 2023,* pp.
1442-1449, 2023.

[48]   A.K. Dubey, A. Jain, A. Panwar, M. Kumar, H. Taneja, and P.S. Lamba, "UNet segmentation based
effective skin lesion detection using deep learning", *2023 International Conference on
Communication, Security and Artificial Intelligence, ICCSAI 2023,* pp. 470-474, 2023.
[http://dx.doi.org/10.1109/ICCSAI59793.2023.10421443]

[49]   A. Panwar, and V. Bhatnagar, "Scrutinize the idea of hadoop-based data lake for big data storage", In:
in Applications of Machine Learning. Algorithms for Intelligent Systems, First., S.P.P. Johri, J.K.
Verma, Eds., Springer, 2020, pp. 365-391.
[http://dx.doi.org/10.1007/978-981-15-3357-0_24]

[50]   M. Zulfiqar, M. Sony, S. Bhat, J. Antony, W. Salentijn, and O. McDermott, "Unlocking the potential:
Empirical analysis of enablers, barriers, benefits and technologies for integrating Industry 4.0 and
Lean Six Sigma in manufacturing organisations", *TQM J.,* no. Dec, 2023.

[http://dx.doi.org/10.1108/TQM-05-2023-0130]

[51] S. Vimal, M. Khari, R.G. Crespo, L. Kalaivani, N. Dey, and M. Kaliappan, "Energy enhancement using Multiobjective Ant colony optimization with Double Q learning algorithm for IoT based cognitive radio networks", *Comput. Commun.,* vol. 154, pp. 481-490, 2020.
[http://dx.doi.org/10.1016/j.comcom.2020.03.004]

[52] U. Sugandh, S. Nigam, and M. Khari, "Blockchain technology in agriculture for indian farmers: A systematic literature review, challenges, and solutions", *IEEE Syst. Man. Cybern. Mag.,* vol. 8, no. 4, pp. 36-43, 2022.
[http://dx.doi.org/10.1109/MSMC.2022.3197914]

[53] A.K. Dubey, A. Jain, A. Panwar, M. Kumar, H. Taneja, and P.S. Lamba, "Optimizing emotion recognition through weighted averaging in deep learning ensembles", *2023 International Conference on Communication, Security and Artificial Intelligence, ICCSAI 2023,* pp. 410-414, 2023.
[http://dx.doi.org/10.1109/ICCSAI59793.2023.10421386]

[54] M. Mohamed, K.M. Sallam, and A.W. Mohamed, "Transition supply chain 4.0 to supply chain 5.0: Innovations of industry 5.0 technologies toward smart supply chain partners", *Neutrosophic Systems with Applications,* vol. 10, pp. 1-11, 2023.
[http://dx.doi.org/10.61356/j.nswa.2023.74]

[55] S. Saif, P. Das, S. Biswas, S. Khan, M.A. Haq, and V. Kovtun, "A secure data transmission framework for IoT enabled healthcare", *Heliyon,* vol. 10, no. 16, p. e36269, 2024.
[http://dx.doi.org/10.1016/j.heliyon.2024.e36269] [PMID: 39224301]

[56] M. Azrour, J. Mabrouki, A. Guezzaz, S. Ahmad, S. Khan, and S. Benkirane, "IoT, machine learning and data analytics for smart healthcare", In: *IoT, Machine Learning and Data Analytics for Smart Healthcare.* CRC Press, 2024, pp. 1-94.
[http://dx.doi.org/10.1201/9781003430735]

[57] K. Kumari, S.K. Pahuja, and S. Kumar, "Machine learning implementations in COVID-19", In: *in Computational Modeling and Data Analysis in COVID-19 Research.* Apple Academic Press, 2021, pp. 1-16.
[http://dx.doi.org/10.1201/9781003137481-1]

[58] M.S. Rao, S. Modi, R. Singh, K.L. Prasanna, S. Khan, and C. Ushapriya, "Integration of cloud computing, IoT, and big data for the development of a novel smart agriculture model", *2023 3rd International Conference on Advance Computing and Innovative Technologies in Engineering, ICACITE 2023,* pp. 2779-2783, 2023.
[http://dx.doi.org/10.1109/ICACITE57410.2023.10182502]

[59] Z. Wang, "Digital twin technology", In: *Industry 4.0 - Impact on Intelligent Logistics and Manufacturing.* CRC Press, 2020.
[http://dx.doi.org/10.5772/intechopen.80974]

[60] A. Haq, J.P. Li, S. Khan, M.A. Alshara, R.M. Alotaibi, and C. Mawuli, "DACBT: Deep learning approach for classification of brain tumors using MRI data in IoT healthcare environment", *Sci. Rep.,* vol. 12, no. 1, p. 15331, 2022.
[http://dx.doi.org/10.1038/s41598-022-19465-1] [PMID: 36097024]

[61] Kanekar D. S., "Transforming indian industries through artificial intelligence and robotics in industry 4.0", *International Research Journal of Modernization in Engineering Technology and Science,* no. Oct, 2023.
[http://dx.doi.org/10.56726/IRJMETS45102]

[62] P. Chugh, M. Gupta, S. Indu, G. Chaudhary, M. Khari, and V. Shanmuganathan, "Advanced energy efficient pegasis based routing protocol for IoT applications", *Microprocess. Microsyst.,* vol. 103, p. 104727, 2023.
[http://dx.doi.org/10.1016/j.micpro.2022.104727]

[63] K. Kumar, and M. Khari, "Energy gaps and bacteriochlorophyll molecular graph representation based

on machine learning algorithm", In: *in Biomedical Research Developments for Improved Healthcare.* IGI Global, 2024, pp. 47-54.
[http://dx.doi.org/10.4018/979-8-3693-1922-2.ch003]

[64]   M. Khari, A.K. Garg, A.H. Gandomi, R. Gupta, R. Patan, and B. Balusamy, "Securing data in internet of things (IoT) using cryptography and steganography techniques", *IEEE Trans. Syst. Man Cybern. Syst.,* vol. 50, no. 1, pp. 73-80, 2020.
[http://dx.doi.org/10.1109/TSMC.2019.2903785]

[65]   R.O. Ogundokun, S. Misra, A.B. Adelodun, and M. Khari, "COVID-19 Detection System in a smart hospital setting using transfer learning and IoT-based model", In: *in Internet of Things, vol. Part F1201.* Springer International Publishing Cham, 2023, pp. 233-262.
[http://dx.doi.org/10.1007/978-3-031-28631-5_12]

[66]   W. Jian, J.P. Li, A.U. Haq, S. Khan, R.M. Alotaibi, S.A. Alajlan, and M.B.B. Heyat, "Feature elimination and stacking framework for accurate heart disease detection in IoT healthcare systems using clinical data", *Front. Med. (Lausanne),* vol. 11, p. 1362397, 2024.
[http://dx.doi.org/10.3389/fmed.2024.1362397] [PMID: 38841592]

[67]   A. Althabatah, M. Yaqot, B. Menezes, and L. Kerbache, "Transformative procurement trends: Integrating industry 4.0 technologies for enhanced procurement processes", *Logistics,* vol. 7, no. 3, p. 63, 2023.
[http://dx.doi.org/10.3390/logistics7030063]

[68]   M. Catalan, "Towards IoT ambient intelligence for industry 4.0", *Proceedings - 2023 International Conference on Future Internet of Things and Cloud, FiCloud 2023,* vol. 869, 2023pp. 142-148
[http://dx.doi.org/10.1109/FiCloud58648.2023.00029]

[69]   M. Jiménez-Partearroyo, A. Medina-López, and D. Juárez-Varón, "Towards industry 5.0: evolving the product-process matrix in the new paradigm", *J. Technol. Transf.,* vol. 49, no. 4, pp. 1496-1531, 2024.
[http://dx.doi.org/10.1007/s10961-023-10053-7]

[70]   N. Pritam, M. Khari, L. Hoang Son, R. Kumar, S. Jha, I. Priyadarshini, M. Abdel-Basset, and H. Viet Long, "Assessment of code smell for predicting class change proneness using machine learning", *IEEE Access,* vol. 7, pp. 37414-37425, 2019.
[http://dx.doi.org/10.1109/ACCESS.2019.2905133]

CHAPTER 2

AI-Enabled Industrial Intelligence: From Data Engineering to Predictive Modeling

Aditya Kejrewal[1,*]

UBS, Pune, India

Abstract: The application of artificial intelligence, combined with advanced data gathering, processing, and analytics, has revolutionized industrial operations and elevated predictive maintenance in Industry 4.0 to a new level. Cutting-edge big data analytics platforms, cloud computing, and IoT-enabled enhancements in data collection have made predictive machine learning models accessible, cost-effective, and feasible for industrial applications. The chapter illustrates the importance of a well-structured data architecture and details steps from data collection and pre-processing to training and deploying machine learning models. Integrating real-time data streams with historical data allows for a comprehensive view of equipment health, enabling timely and accurate maintenance decisions. These enhancements have improved accuracy and increased effectiveness in several central aspects. The key techniques discussed include supervised learning and unsupervised learning, deep neural networks, and time series forecasting. In this chapter, such developments are shown for the aerospace, manufacturing, and transportation industries. The chapter deals with issues like data collection, streaming, storing and processing large amounts of data, and construction of more sophisticated models based on contemporary AI and ML algorithms and, therefore, provides development towards enhancing predictive maintenance in the era of Industry 4.0.

Keywords: Cloud computing, Data streaming, Deep neural networks, Edge computing, ETL processes, IoT, Supervised learning, Time series analysis, Unsupervised learning.

INTRODUCTION

With advancements in industrial operations, predictive maintenance has come into play as a paradigm shift. It is an approach where technologies predict failures before they occur and thus improve the maintenance regimes. This chapter aims to elaborate on some of the cutting-edge analytic tools and methodologies, including machine learning, deep learning, pattern recognition, and others, that constitute a

---
[*] **Corresponding author Aditya Kejrewal:** UBS, Pune, India; E-mail: adityakejrewal2000@gmail.com

Tanu Singh, Vinod Patidar, Arvind Panwar & Urvashi Sugandh (Eds.)

critical part of the predictive maintenance revolution. The way predictive maintenance works includes performing data analysis to perform ML modeling to prevent breakdowns, Irregularities, and faults arising in industrial machinery based on patterns learned and monitored from data gathered from IoT sensors, environment, maintenance logs, and so forth [1]. Such forms of data analytics in predictive maintenance systems usually require a step-by-step combination of supervised, unsupervised, and deep learning, as well as anomaly detection and time series analysis methods to be used [2]. Equipment failure prediction and lifespan estimation are usually performed under supervised learning, and the former includes anomaly detection, which utilizes unsupervised learning and state machine modeling [3]. Deep learning models are utilized to analyze sensor data patterns, while time series analysis is applied to forecast equipment performance trends [4].

With the inclusion of these techniques, predictive maintenance systems achieve high accuracy and reliability, which enhances the effective utilization of operations and increases the reliability of equipment [5].

These complex models are trained on a high volume of datasets that are formed from the combination of operational data from equipment sensors that give monitored parameters such as vibrations, pressure, and temperature. Such big data analytics are useful in converting these insights into interventions [6]. It helps to manage the time-series data and facilitates the analysis of the data stream without restoring it; instead it identifies important features to guide data interpretation [7]. Advanced computing resources, especially those supported by cloud systems, can maintain the management of large amounts of data captured within a short time period and make accurate forecasts. Such a robust data processing architecture increases the accuracy of predictive maintenance models and enables their application efficiently and cost-effectively, which overall has a great impact on improving the efficiency of operations and reliability of the equipment. Apart from issuing alerts about impending failures, the models are also capable of forecasting the future state of the machinery. These forecasts improve maintenance through process improvement and re-engineering, supply chain control, Remaining Useful Lifetime (RUL) evaluation, and planning downtime properly. This chapter aims to demonstrate the trends in the field of predictive maintenance and management using AI systems in the context of Industry 4.0, highlighting advanced predictive maintenance methods, optimization strategies, risk management techniques, and big data technologies.

ARTIFICIAL INTELLIGENCE (AI) AND MACHINE LEARNING (ML) ALGORITHMS IN INDUSTRY 4.0

With the integration of the AI (Artificial Intelligence) models, the evolution and development of various techniques of predictive maintenance became faster and more efficient by making use of large volumes of operational data to foresee the drawbacks of the equipment and improve maintenance scheduling. It is possible to review the historical and current data obtained from sensors on IoT, data and control systems SCADA, and maintenance logs by using advanced techniques like supervised learning for predicting faults and unsupervised learning for detecting anomalies. These models identify trends and relationships, both of which are critical for predicting distress and the need for maintenance. The integration of Artificial Intelligence and Machine Learning (AI and ML) in predictive maintenance has a great impact on reducing unplanned equipment downtime, increasing the life span of the equipment, and facilitating effective operations. Additionally, the learning capabilities of these models are not static as they also evolve with time; thus, even as the environment changes, the maintenance approaches continue to be effective, which will, in turn, realize savings and improved performance in many sectors.

This section will discuss the main features of the ML approaches relevant to predictive maintenance, the usage of these methods for different tasks, and the description of real-world applications of these methods in multiple industrial sectors.

Supervised Learning Overview

In supervised learning, a model is trained with the help of labeled data. In such instances, the input data is related to the output that is already known. In various industries, supervised learning methods are widely deployed to forecast equipment breakdowns based on past records.

Applications

- **Failure Prediction:** Identifying when equipment is likely to fail.
- **Anomaly Detection:** Classifying normal *versus* anomalous behavior on the basis of historical patterns.

Example: Manufacturing Industry

Within the manufacturing factory, devices are used to monitor certain parameters such as temperature, vibration, and pressure of machines. There are certain devices in the manufacturing factory that serve the purpose of taking readings of parameters such as temperature, vibration, and pressure of the machines. The history, including breakdowns of equipment, is also included. This helps in applying and fitting supervised learning models to such data and to make predictions about failures based on the history of the equipment.

Implementation

- **Data Collection:** Sensor readings and maintenance logs.
- **Feature Engineering:** For instance, creating rolling averages of temperature and vibration.
- **Model Training:** Feeding data to ML algorithms like Decision Trees or Random Forests for learning.
- **Deployment:** Using the trained model for making predictions.

The following are some commonly used supervised learning algorithms and their applications:

Linear Regression

Overview: Linear regression (Fig. **1**) is a supervised learning algorithm used for estimating a linear relationship between an independent variable and a continuous dependent variable [8].

Application

- **Use Case:** Calculating the Remaining Useful Life (RUL) of machinery.
- **Example:** Using linear regression to predict when a car's engine could fail based on historical data of engine failures.

Logistic Regression

Overview: It is a statistical algorithm that analyzes the relationship between two data factors. It is used for binary classification problems. It predicts the probability of a given input data point belonging to a certain class (*e.g.*, failure or no failure).

Application

- **Use Case:** Predicting if equipment will fail during a certain time frame.
- **Example:** In the oil and gas industry, logistic regression can predict the probability of a pipeline leak based on pressure, temperature, and flow rate data.

Decision Trees

Overview: It uses a tree-like model of decisions and their consequences to predict the target variable's value.

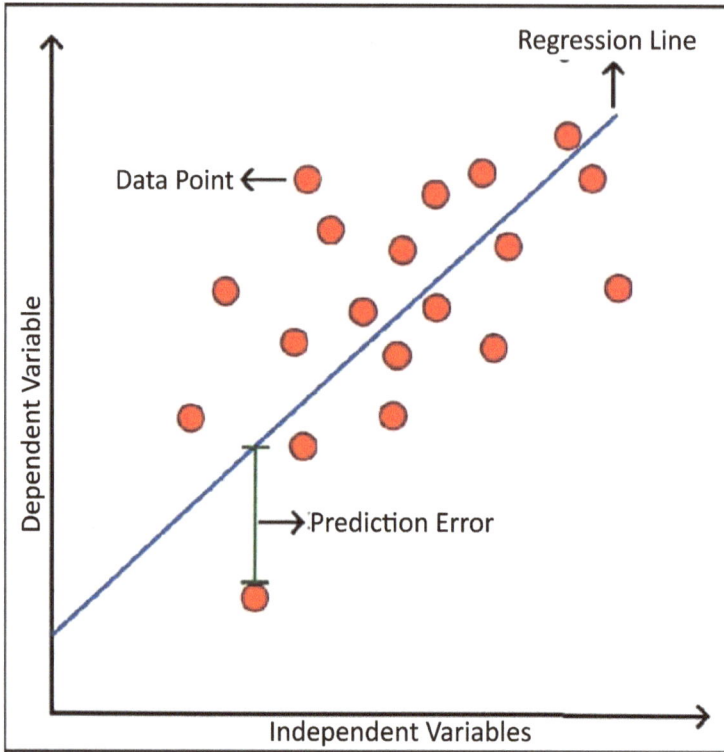

Fig. (1). Linear Regression.

Application

- **Use Case:** Classifying failure types based on sensor data.
- **Example:** Based on sensor inputs, decision trees classify whether a machine is likely to experience a mechanical, electrical, or thermal failure.

Support Vector Machines (SVM)

Overview: SVMs are supervised learning models used for linear or non-linear classification, outlier detection, and regression analysis [9, 10]. SVMs work by finding the optimal hyperplane in an N-dimensional hyperspace that can best separate the data points into different classes [11].

Application

- **Use Case:** Classifying normal *vs.* abnormal equipment behavior.
- **Example:** SVMs can classify network equipment status as normal or degraded on the basis of performance metrics like signal strength and error rates in the telecom industry.

Unsupervised Learning

Overview: Unsupervised learning is used when labeled data is unavailable. This technique helps identify hidden patterns in data, making it useful for anomaly detection.

- **Anomaly Detection:** Discovering unusual patterns that may indicate potential failures.
- **Clustering:** Grouping similar operating conditions to identify baseline behavior.
- **Example:** Equipment such as pumps and compressors generate data continuously. Unsupervised learning helps identify anomalies that could indicate impending failures.

Implementation

1. **Data Collection:** Continuous sensor data is gathered from equipment.
2. **Model Training:** Algorithms like K-Means [12] or DBSCAN cluster the data to identify normal *vs.* anomalous behavior.
3. **Monitoring:** Anomalies trigger alerts for further investigation.

Unsupervised learning algorithms help discover the underlying structure of the data. That makes them suitable for anomaly detection, pattern recognition, and clustering. Following are some commonly used unsupervised learning algorithms and their applications in predictive maintenance:

K-Means Clustering

Overview: K-Means is a clustering algorithm that groups unlabeled data into K-distinct clusters based on inferred underlying similarity [13].

Application

- **Use Case:** Grouping similar operational conditions to identify standard and abnormal states.
- **Example:** In the automotive industry, K-Means can cluster vehicle engine data to distinguish between normal and abnormal operating conditions.

DBSCAN (Density-Based Spatial Clustering of Applications with Noise)

Overview: DBSCAN (Fig. **2**) is a density-based clustering algorithm that maps data points into clusters of various shapes and sizes, including outliers as noise.

Application

- **Use Case:** Detecting anomalous operating conditions that differ from normal behavior.
- **Example:** In the energy sector, DBSCAN can identify unusual patterns in power consumption data from industrial machines.

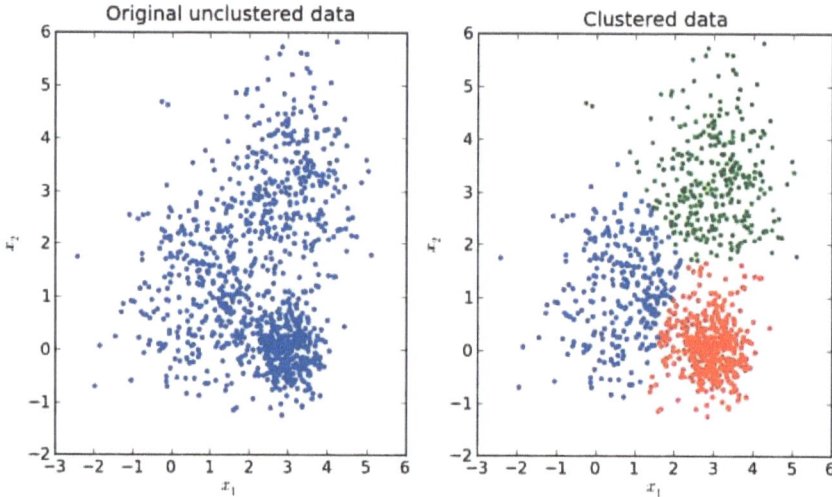

Fig. (2). Representation of clustering data points.

Principal Component Analysis (PCA)

Overview: It is a dimensionality reduction technique that is used for transforming correlated variables into principal components, thus reducing the number of features but retaining most of the original information [14].

Application

- **Use Case:** Simplifying high-dimensional sensor data to identify key indicators of equipment health.
- **Example:** In aerospace, PCA can be used to reduce the complexity of data collected from aircraft sensors.

Deep Learning

Overview: Deep learning, a subset of machine learning, uses multilayered neural networks to model complex relationships in data, which makes it a powerful technique for processing high-dimensional data such as time-series signals from IoT sensors and photographs captured from camera sensors [15].

Applications

- **Fault Detection:** Recognizing complex patterns in sensor data indicative of failure.
- **Predictive Analytics:** Predicting future equipment behavior based on historical trends.
- **Example: Aerospace Industry:** In aerospace, aircraft engines are equipped with numerous sensors that generate large volumes of data. Deep learning models analyze this data to predict maintenance needs.

Implementation

- **Data Collection:** High-dimensional data from engine sensors, including temperature and pressure readings.
- **Model Training:** Use of Convolutional Neural Networks (CNNs) or Long Short-Term Memory (LSTM) networks for learning from time series data.
- **Deployment:** Running models in real-time to monitor engine health and predict required maintenance when needed.

Here are some commonly used deep learning algorithms [16] and their applications in predictive maintenance:

Convolutional Neural Networks (CNN)

Overview: CNNs are a type of deep neural network used primarily to effectively process grid-like data, such as images (Fig. **3**). CNNs are trained on a large dataset of labeled images; the neural net then learns to recognize hierarchical patterns and spatial dependencies [17].

Application

- **Use Case:** Analyzing visual data from equipment to detect surface defects, wear, and tear.
- **Example:** CNNs are used in the manufacturing industry to analyze images of conveyor belts to detect misalignments or foreign objects.

Recurrent Neural Networks (RNNs) and Long Short-Term Memory Networks (LSTMs)

Overview: RNNs are designed for sequential data, efficiently capturing temporal dependencies. LSTMs, which are a variant of RNNs, are very capable of learning long-term dependencies, making them effective for time series forecasting.

Application

- **Use Case:** Predicting equipment failures in the future based on time-series data.
- **Example:** LSTMs can predict power transformer failures by analyzing historical as well as live sensor data.

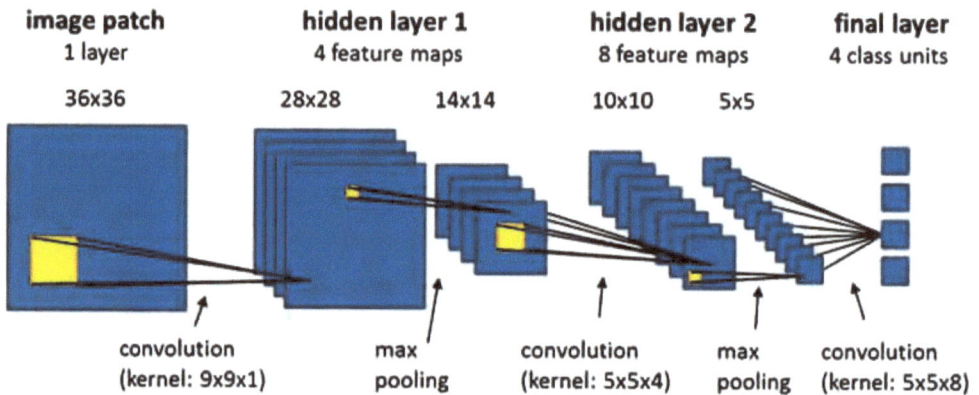

Fig. (3). CNN Architecture.

Time Series Analysis

Overview: Time series analysis is a crucial requirement of all kinds of predictive maintenance models since it involves data points recorded at discrete time intervals [18]. This methodology may help in determining the potential future stochastic patterns as well as the outputs and outcomes based onhistorical trends (Fig. **4**).

Applications

- **Trend Analysis:** Identifying long-term trends in equipment performance.
- **Forecasting:** Predicting future maintenance needs and equipment behavior.
- **Example: Transportation Industry:** In railways, time series analysis of locomotive data helps predict maintenance requirements and schedule repairs.

Implementation

- **Data Collection:** Monitoring data extracted from locomotives at standard intervals.
- **Model Training:** Time series forecasting methods like ARIMA or seasonal decomposition.
- **Monitoring:** Constantly analyze trends to make proactive adjustments to the schedule for maintenance.

Several algorithms are used in time series analysis, including ARIMA, STL (Seasonal Decomposition of Time Series), and Prophet.

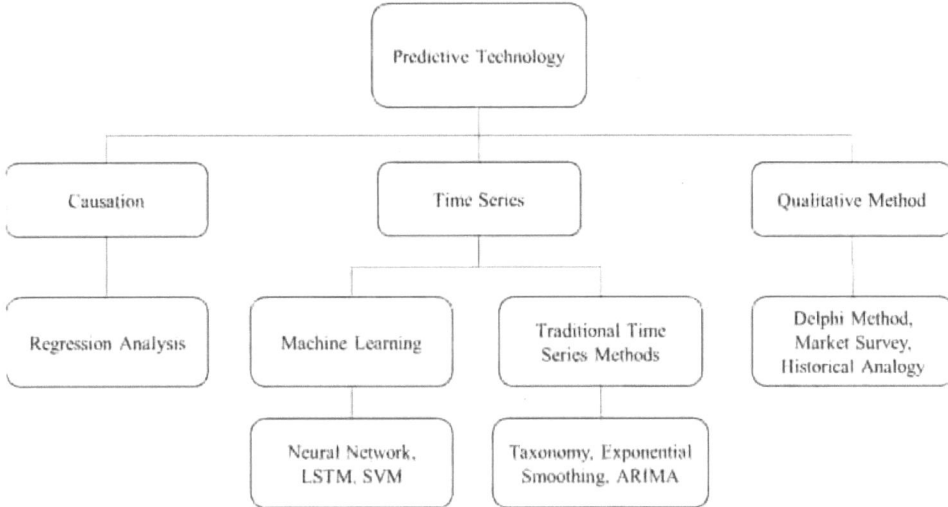

Fig. (4). Classification of Predictive Technologies.

ARIMA (Auto Regressive Integrated Moving Average)

Overview: ARIMA is a statistical method for forecasting time series data. These comprise AR (Autoregression), I (differencing), and MA (Moving Average), which are used to model and forecast further points in the series [19].

Application

- **Use Case:** Forecasting the future values of a time series to predict equipment failure.
- **Example:** ARIMA is used in the oil industry to predict the pressure levels in pipelines and identify potential leaks.

Prophet

Overview: Prophet is a forecasting tool developed by Meta (Facebook). It is used for handling time series data with missing data points and strong seasonal effects, making it robust for real-world applications [20].

Application

- **Use Case:** Forecasting time series data with daily, weekly, or yearly seasonality.
- **Example:** In the telecommunication business domain, Prophet can be used for

the prediction of network traffic for anomaly detection, which may lead to equipment failure.

ROLE OF BIG DATA ANALYTICS AND DATA ENGINEERING

In the case of predictive maintenance, big data analytics is quite essential as it changes the accumulated raw data to useful information aimed at forecasting equipment breakdowns and improving the maintenance process. In this context, the key importance of big data analytics is in resolving the issues associated with high speed and a high variety of data streams captured from heterogeneous sources such as IoT sensors, SCADA, and maintenance logs.

With the use of effective data processing and analysis techniques, including data mining, information processing, and visualization, which are characteristic of big data, industries are progressively taking up a proactive approach as opposed to the previous reactive maintenance approaches. This transformation allows for improving indicators of efficiency, reducing costs, and increasing reliability, which is why, today, heterogeneous systems for the analysis of large data sets are increasingly used in the framework of predictive maintenance.

This process begins with the analysis of the data acquired from numerous sources and advances through multiple stages, resulting in the creation of advanced predictive models [21]. We will go over the entire process from the very beginning and see how data is gathered and processed and what it is used for to make the maintenance processes more efficient (Fig. **5**).

Data Sources and Gathering

- **IoT Devices:** The data collection in predictive maintenance workflows is largely dependent on IoT devices containing sensors [22].

These devices are fixed on the machines to capture various operational variables. These include temperature sensors, which record the heat generated in motors; vibration sensors, which record imbalance in rotating equipment; pressure sensors, which record the movement of fluids in pipes; and humidity sensors, which determine the moisture levels in certain areas.

- **SCADA Systems:** Supervisory Control and Data Acquisition (SCADA) systems create continuous data streams about the status of operations along with performance metrics [23].
- **Maintenance Logs and ERP Systems:** The historical maintenance logs and the Enterprise Resource Planning (ERP) systems give context by recording past activities undertaken on the equipment. These types of records help to pinpoint

long-term patterns and trends.

- **Environmental Sensors:** Along with these devices, environmental sensors take other readings in peripheral parameters like humidity, temperature, and air quality that affect the performance of the equipment.

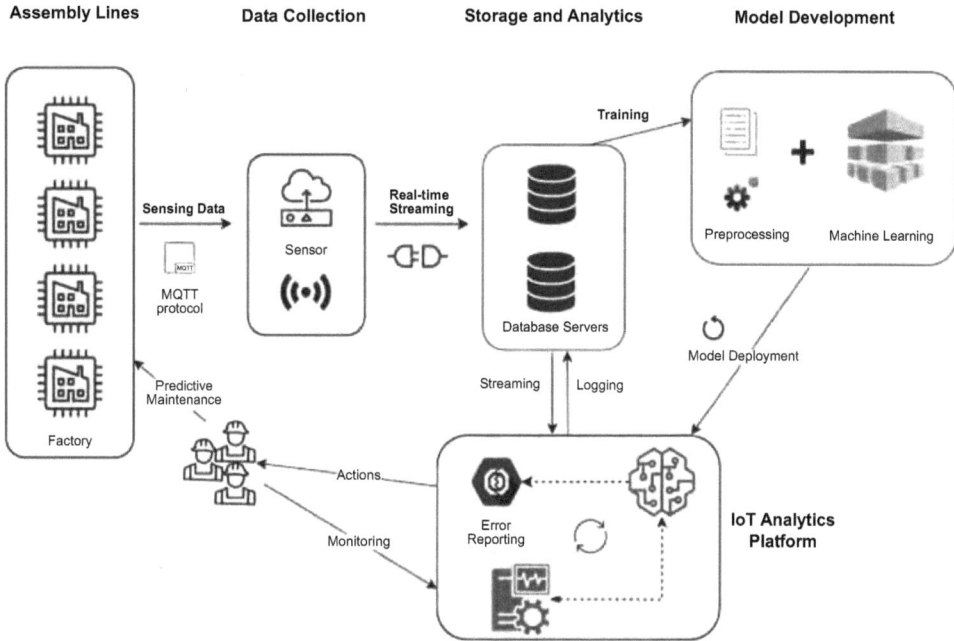

Fig. (5). IoT-Based Predictive Maintenance Workflow.

Types of Data Generated

- **Time-Series Data:** Continuous data points collected over a period, such as temperature and vibration.
- **Categorical Data:** A representation of states such as on/off.
- **Event Data:** Particular events or deviations, such as a drop or rise in pressure.

After collecting data from many sources, *e.g.*, IoT devices, SCADA systems, maintenance logs, and environmental sensors, the first step is to unite and concentrate this information into one place (Fig. **6**). It involves the first layer of processing done at the edge, where some data cleaning and massaging occurs before sending data to the central cloud infrastructure. Streams of data are cleansed, altered, compiled, and then fused to a single dataset optimal for analytics and forecasting purposes.

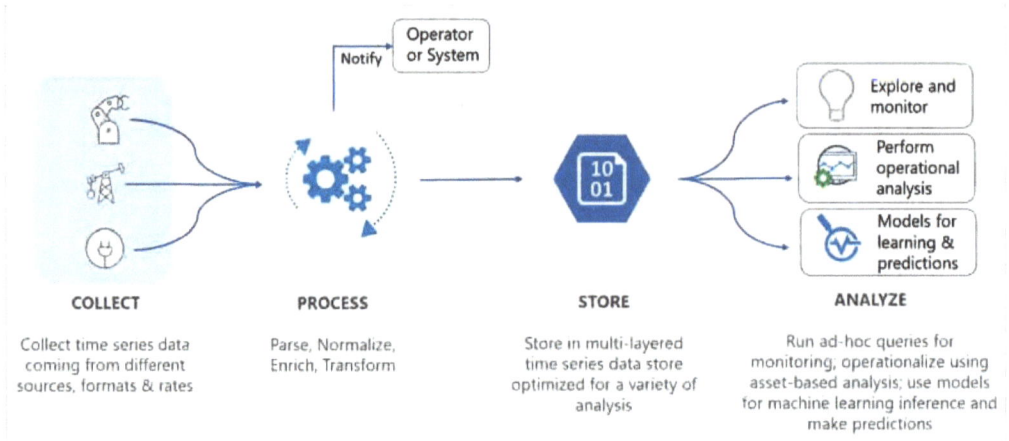

Fig. (6). Time Series Data Management and Analytics.

Data Aggregation and Initial Processing

Edge computing platforms like Azure IoT Edge (Fig. **7**) are used for initial processing close to the source. IoT Edge is a cloud intelligence platform that brings analytics and data processing closer to the source of the data and reduces bandwidth usage and latency [24]. This includes filtering noise, aggregating, and preliminary analytics. Azure services like Azure Machine Learning and Azure Stream Analytics [25] can be run on-premises through the use of Azure IoT Edge. For example, an edge device in a manufacturing factory collects data from IoT sensors and runs a module that removes noisy data and aggregates readings. By doing so, it reduces the amount of data that has to be sent to the cloud. It can aggregate the reading of temperature from every second to every minute and filter out any extreme outliers before converting it to a common format.

Some of the tasks for the initial data processing on the edge device are:

- **Data Filtering:** It refers to the elimination of erroneous or irrelevant data points.
- **Data Aggregation**: This represents the combination of data points over a given period with a view to reducing the frequency of transmission.
- **Data Transformation**: It standardizes data into a uniform format, ready and optimized for advanced processing.

Data Ingestion in IoT Hub

Once the data is processed preliminarily, the subsequent step involves information transfer to IoT Hub, which is a cloud-based managed service that can allow two-way interaction between IoT applications and devices. Data ingestion in the Azure

IoT hub is of paramount importance because it makes optimal use of the Internet of Things by helping move data from IoT devices to multiple Azure services for analysis, storage, and machine learning.

Data, which is consumed by the IoT Hub, is routed toward several endpoints based on predefined routing rules for thorough processing and analysis. The messages can be routed to several endpoints that vary with the content and the requirement of the use case. For instance, we may route all the sensor temperature data into a storage account for archiving and all the sensor vibration data to a real-time analytics service [26]. Several endpoints or services are used in the analysis, storage, and extraction of insights from data. The following are a few services offered in the Azure platform:

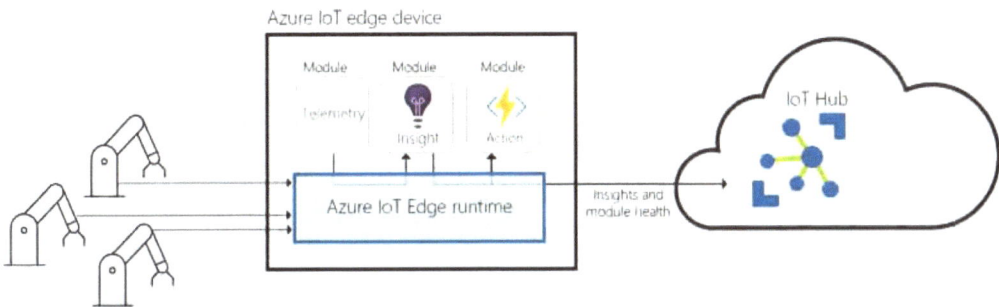

Fig. (7). IoT Edge Architecture.

Stream Analytics: Real-time data processing and complex event handling.

- **Azure Functions:** Serverless computing and custom data processing.
- **Blob Storage:** For scalable storage of raw and processed data.
- **Event Hubs:** For high-throughput data streaming and integration with other services.
- **Service Bus Queues/Topics:** For reliable message queuing and pub-sub messaging.
- **Azure Machine Learning**: Used for building, training, and subsequent deployment of machine learning models.

Data Processing and Transformation

Once data is ingested by a platform like Azure IoT Hub, it is routed to various services for real-time processing. The initial handling involves stream processing, which ensures that data is immediately available for analysis and action.

- **Stream Processing Engines:** The platforms, Apache Kafka, Apache Spark Streaming, and Apache Flink, are commonly used for real-time data processing.

They process incoming data streams by applying Complex Event Processing (CEP) rules to detect patterns and anomalies.

- **Real-Time Analytics:** Stream processing engines analyze data on-the-fly, enabling immediate detection of issues and triggering automated responses or alerts. For example, a stream processing engine analyzes real-time vibration data from machinery. If the vibration exceeds a certain threshold, an alert is triggered and maintenance is scheduled.

Data Storage

After initial processing, the data is directed to appropriate storage solutions for further analysis, historical record-keeping, and batch processing. For instance, temperature and vibration data are stored in a time-series database for immediate trend analysis, while raw data is archived in a data lake for long-term storage and detailed historical analysis.

ETL Processes

To prepare data for deeper analysis and machine learning, ETL (Extract, Transform, Load) pipelines are employed. For example, daily vibration data is extracted from the time-series database, cleaned to remove outliers, normalized to a common scale, and enriched with metadata about machine operating conditions. This transformed data is subsequently integrated into a data warehouse (Fig. **8**).

- **Extraction:** Data is extracted from multiple sources, such as IoT devices, SCADA systems, and historical databases.
- **Transformation:** The extracted data is cleaned to remove duplicates and errors, normalized to ensure consistency, and enriched with additional context. Feature engineering is also performed to create new variables from the raw data.
- **Loading:** The transformed data is loaded into centralized storage solutions like data warehouses or data lakes.

Training and Deploying Predictive Models

The areas of the predictive maintenance workflow that include the training of machine learning models as well as deploying them are very crucial. After the data has been collected and then processed and integrated, it is used to create predictive models. These models are trained on historical data, such as vibration and temperature readings, to detect patterns that signal impending equipment failures (Fig. **9**). Trained models use concepts such as neural networks, regression models, and decision trees to predict problems [27]. These models are used in real time to process streams of data and raise the alarm about impending equipment failure chances even before it happens; therefore, maintenance is performed preventively. This lessens the idle time of industrial resources, maximizes their optimum application, and increases the operational productivity of the factories, ensuring that the machinery systems work uninterrupted [28].

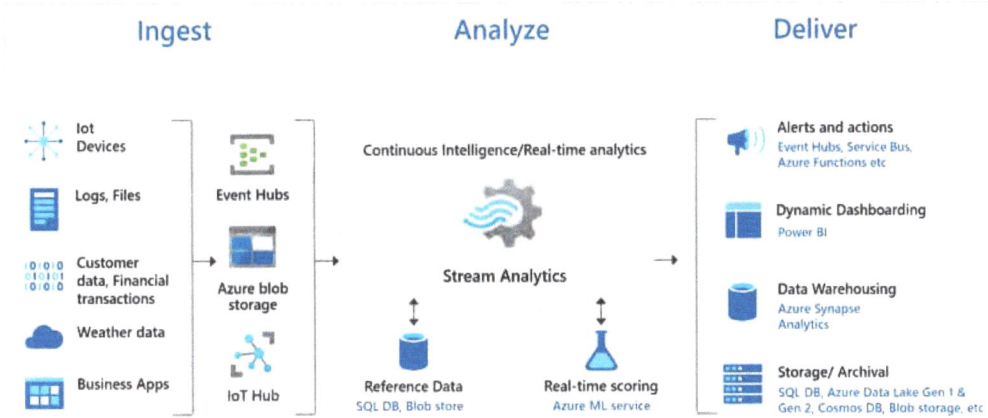

Fig. (8). End-to-End Real-time Data Processing Platform.

Model Development

- **Training Data Preparation:** The integrated and transformed data is split into training, validation, and test sets. Feature selection and engineering are performed to identify relevant predictors for the model.
- **Model Training:** Machine learning algorithms (regression models, decision trees, neural nets) are applied to the training data to develop predictive models.
- **Hyperparameter Tuning:** Techniques such as random search and grid search are leveraged to discover the optimal model parameters.

Model Deployment

- **Real-Time Predictions:** Deployed models are integrated with the data pipeline to make real-time predictions based on incoming data streams. Predictions trigger maintenance alerts or automated actions.
- **Continuous Learning:** Models are trained continuously on newly generated data to improve accuracy and adapt to changing conditions.

Data Visualization and Insights

A dashboard can show real-time equipment status, predictive maintenance alerts, and historical performance trends, helping stakeholders make informed decisions.

- **Visualization Tools (*e.g.*, Power BI, Tableau, Grafana):** Interactive dashboards and reports provide real-time and historical insights.
- **Real-Time Monitoring:** Dashboards display real-time data and predictions, enabling proactive maintenance and reducing downtime.

Steps to build Model

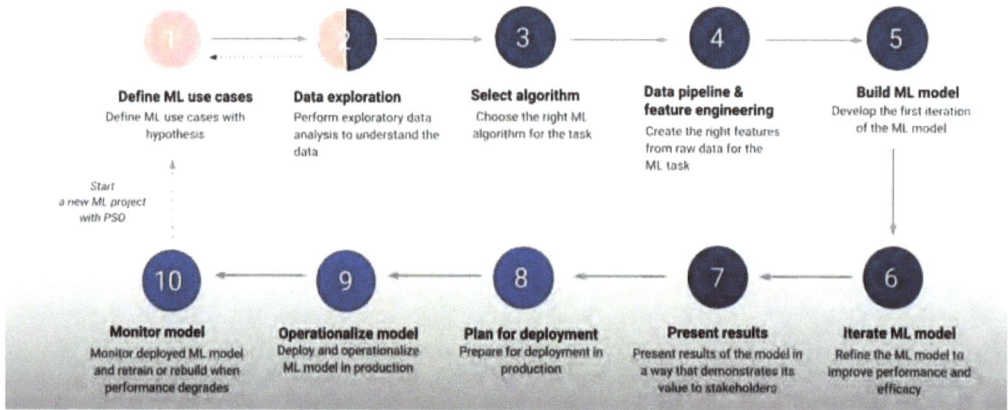

Fig. (9). Steps to Build a Machine Learning Model.

CONCLUSION

In this chapter, we have looked at the complex procedures that go into applying AI and ML techniques to predictive maintenance. There are processes, rather sophisticated and finely tuned ones, which have been carried out in the application of predictive maintenance technology and predictive maintenance management with the use of AI and ML techniques. Equipment downtime can be predicted with a good degree of accuracy using advanced algorithms like decision trees with neural networks and clustering techniques [29]. Collectively, these enable each other to strengthen the predictive maintenance abilities of the systems [30].

We further examined why it is important to pay attention to data architecture when trying to reach a practical solution. Every stage is necessary to provide high-quality predictions, from feature engineering and model deployment to data collecting and preparation. The combination of historical data and real-time data feeds enables us to get a complete picture of the condition of the equipment and to make effective and timely decisions regarding maintenance.

REFERENCES

[1]   IBM, "What is predictive maintenance? | IBM", 2023. Available from: www.ibm.com
https://www.ibm.com/topics/predictive-maintenance

[2]   A. Bousdekis, K. Lepenioti, D. Apostolou, and G. Mentzas, "Decision making in predictive maintenance: Literature review and research agenda for industry 4.0", *IFAC-PapersOnLine,* vol. 52, no. 13, pp. 607-612, 2019.
[http://dx.doi.org/10.1016/j.ifacol.2019.11.226]

[3]   S. Thudumu, P. Branch, J. Jin, and J. Singh, "A comprehensive survey of anomaly detection techniques for high dimensional big data", *J. Big Data,* vol. 7, no. 1, p. 42, 2020.
[http://dx.doi.org/10.1186/s40537-020-00320-x]

[4]   A. Jalil, and N. H. Rao, "Chapter 8 - Time series analysis (stationarity, cointegration, and causality)", *ScienceDirect,* 2019.

[5]   Available from: https://www.247software.com/blog/4-ways-to-leverage-predictive-maintenanc--data-analytics-in-your-venue-maintenance-strategy (accessed Sep. 18, 2024).

[6]   W. Lidong, and W. Guanghui, "Big data in cyber-physical systems, digital manufacturing and industry 4.0", *International Journal of Engineering and Manufacturing,* vol. 6, no. 4, pp. 1-8, 2016.
[http://dx.doi.org/10.5815/ijem.2016.04.01]

[7]   A. Almeida, S. Brás, S. Sargento, and Filipe Cabral Pinto, "Time series big data: a survey on data stream frameworks, analysis and algorithms", , vol. 10, no. 1, 2023.
[http://dx.doi.org/10.1186/s40537-023-00760-1]

[8]   D. Maulud, and A.M. Abdulazeez, "A review on linear regression comprehensive in machine learning", *Journal of Applied Science and Technology Trends,* vol. 1, no. 2, pp. 140-147, 2020.
[http://dx.doi.org/10.38094/jastt1457]

[9]   Available from: https://ieeexplore.ieee.org/document/708428

[10]   J. Cervantes, F. Garcia-Lamont, L. Rodríguez-Mazahua, and A. Lopez, "A comprehensive survey on support vector machine classification: Applications, challenges and trends", *Neurocomputing,* vol. 408, no. 1, pp. 189-215, 2020.
[http://dx.doi.org/10.1016/j.neucom.2019.10.118]

[11]   F. Ding, "Application of support vector machine for equipment reliability forecasting", *IEEE Xplore,* 2008. Available from: https://ieeexplore.ieee.org/document/4618157
[http://dx.doi.org/10.1109/INDIN.2008.4618157]

[12]   Niruhan Viswarupan, "K-means data clustering - towards data science", *Medium,* 2017. Available from: https://towardsdatascience.com/k-means-data-clustering-bce3335d2203

[13]   J.H. Yoo, Y.K. Park, and S.S. Han, "Predictive maintenance system for wafer transport robot using K-means algorithm and neural network model", *Electronics (Basel),* vol. 11, no. 9, pp. 1324-1324, 2022.
[http://dx.doi.org/10.3390/electronics11091324]

[14]   Available from: www.ibm.com
https://www.ibm.com/topics/principal-component-analysis

[15]   L. Alzubaidi, J. Zhang, A.J. Humaidi, A. Al-Dujaili, Y. Duan, O. Al-Shamma, J. Santamaría, M.A. Fadhel, M. Al-Amidie, and L. Farhan, "Review of deep learning: concepts, CNN architectures, challenges, applications, future directions", *J. Big Data,* vol. 8, no. 1, p. 53, 2021.
[http://dx.doi.org/10.1186/s40537-021-00444-8] [PMID: 33816053]

[16]   A. Moccardi, "Deep learning strategies for predictive maintenance", *Medium,* 2024. Available from: https://medium.com/@albertomoccardi/deep-learning-strategies-for-predictive-mainte-ance-9f1f40d8958a#:~:text=DBSCAN%20is%20particularly%20suited%20for

[17]   Keiron Teilo O'Shea and R. Nash, "An introduction to convolutional neural networks", *ResearchGate,* 2015.   Available   from:

https://www.researchgate.net/publication/285164623_An_Introduction_to_Convolutional_Neural_Net works

[18]   Tableau, "Time series analysis: Definition, types, techniques, and when it's used", *Tableau,* 2022. Available from: https://www.tableau.com/learn/articles/time-series-analysis

[19]   C.C. Wang, C.H. Chien, and A.J.C. Trappey, "On the application of ARIMA and LSTM to predict order demand based on short lead time and on-time delivery requirements", *Processes (Basel),* vol. 9, no. 7, p. 1157, 2021.
[http://dx.doi.org/10.3390/pr9071157]

[20]   Meta, "Prophet: Forecasting at scale", *Facebook Research.* Available from: https://facebook.github.io/prophet/

[21]   S. Pani, O. Pattnaik, and B.K. Pattanayak, "Predictive maintenance in industrial iot using machine learning approach", *International Journal of Intelligent Systems and Applications in Engineering,* vol. 12, no. 14s, pp. 521-534, 2024. Available from: https://ijisae.org/index.php/IJISAE/article/view/4689

[22]   M. Compare, P. Baraldi, and E. Zio, "Challenges to IoT-enabled predictive maintenance for industry 4.0", *IEEE Internet Things J.,* pp. 1-1, 2019.
[http://dx.doi.org/10.1109/JIOT.2019.2957029]

[23]   D.P.S. Telecom, "How SCADA systems work - data, sensors, networks, and RTUs", *Dpstele.com,* 2019. Available from: https://www.dpstele.com/scada/how-systems-work.php

[24]   PatAltimore, "What is Azure IoT Edge", 2023. Available from: learn.microsoft.com https://learn.microsoft.com/en-us/azure/iot-edge/about-iot-edge?view=iotedge-1.5

[25]   sidramadoss, "Introduction to Azure Stream Analytics", Available from: learn.microsoft.com https://learn.microsoft.com/en-us/azure/stream-analytics/stream-analytics-introduction

[26]   A. Pelaez, "Here's how IoT data collection works [complete guide]", *Ubidots Blog,* 2021. Available from: https://ubidots.com/blog/iot-data-collection/

[27]   A. Kanawaday, and A. Sane, "Machine learning for predictive maintenance of industrial machines using IoT sensor data", *IEEE Xplore,* 2017. Available from: https://ieeexplore.ieee.org/document/8342870
[http://dx.doi.org/10.1109/ICSESS.2017.8342870]

[28]   S. Elkateb, A. Métwalli, A. Shendy, and A.E.B. Abu-Elanien, "Machine learning and IoT – Based predictive maintenance approach for industrial applications", *Alex. Eng. J.,* vol. 88, pp. 298-309, 2024.
[http://dx.doi.org/10.1016/j.aej.2023.12.065]

[29]   R. Kumar, S. Rani, and Sehijpal Singh Khangura, "Machine learning for sustainable manufacturing in industry 4.0", *Informa,* 2023.
[http://dx.doi.org/10.1201/9781003453567]

[30]   O. Kovalenko, "Predictive maintenance with machine learning: A complete guide | SPD technology", *Software Product Development Company,* 2021. Available from: https://spd.tech/machine-learning/predictive-maintenance/

CHAPTER 3

Big Data Analytics for Predictive Maintenance in Industry 4.0.

Kiran Deep Singh[1], Harsh Taneja[2,*], Prabh Deep Singh[2] and **Jessica Singh Syal[3]**

[1] *Chitkara University Institute of Engineering and Technology, Chitkara University, Rajpura, Punjab, India*

[2] *Department of Computer Science and Engineering, Graphic Era Deemed to be University, Dehradun, India*

[3] *Bharati Vidyapeeth's College of Engineering, New Delhi, India*

Abstract: This chapter presents a design for a Situation-Based Maintenance Model (SBMM) that explains different statistical approaches to predict maintenance. It also gives some example applications to help grasp predictive maintenance before exploring the possible big data models that can predict when maintenance work is most needed. The high-level architecture that reflects the big data predictive maintenance model is presented for the proven potential of future industrial predictive maintenance systems. The growing interest in Industry 4.0 has driven the creation of systems that are capable of real-time data generation. Many different industrial areas can benefit from this grand concept, and analytics is an important area of Industry 4.0. Whether it is structured data from Enterprise Resource Planning (ERP) or Customer Relationship Management (CRM) systems, unstructured data from sensors and machines, or new types of data generated from Radio Frequency Identification (RFID) devices or the Internet of Things (IoT), processing and analyzing extremely large datasets is a challenge that needs to be mastered. This transformation can be achieved through Big Data Analytics. These analytics combine statistical data analysis techniques, models, and algorithms with human ingenuity to yield new insights and optimized decisions.

Keywords: Big data analytics, Industry 4.0, Internet of Things (IoT), Predictive maintenance, Predictive models.

INTRODUCTION

The term "Industry 4.0" was coined in Germany, and in recent years, it has been intensively used as a label for several technologies and trends in automation and data exchange in the manufacturing field, including industrial robotics, Internet of Things (IoT), digitally connected technologies, smart manufacturing, *etc.* The development of Industry 4.0 and smart manufacturing concepts is a result of technological advancements in several fields, including nanomaterials, regene-

---

[*] **Corresponding author Harsh Taneja**: Department of Computer Science and Engineering, Graphic Era Deemed to be University, Dehradun, India; E-mail: harshtaneja.cse@gmail.com

Tanu Singh, Vinod Patidar, Arvind Panwar & Urvashi Sugandh (Eds.)

rative and regenerable off-grid energy conversion systems and other products, automation engineering, cloud computing techniques, cyber-physical systems, cognition and decision-making processes, smart services, business models, and the need to increase competitiveness for profit maximization. The Industry 4.0 concept includes several major technological aspects. The major core, revealing the main technology and performance, is related to continuous information exchange among technologies, *i.e.*, cloud computing, Cyber-Physical Systems (CPS), the Internet of Things (IoT), and the related Digitization (DI) in a manufacturing context.

Big data has become the cornerstone of predictive maintenance technologies, and it can be said that all industries are somehow engaged with some kind of predictive maintenance research and development. Big data analytics technologies can allow the prediction of failures and breakdowns in an efficient manner, thus ensuring less downtime, anomalies reduction, and losses of the expected lifecycle as well as lower maintenance costs with spare parts and on-manpower. According to the Industry 4.0 quest, precision engineering of the spare part supply chain is also affecting the maintenance cost. At present, however, only a few industries can collect data regarding the equipment through their entire quality life cycle, from design to actual operation, selecting adequate predictive algorithms trained with the utilization data collected through the equipment in the operation phase and any additional relevant data. This subject aims to outline the most recent achievements in the field of predictive maintenance implementation in the Industry 4.0 context.

OVERVIEW OF BIG DATA ANALYTICS

Big data analytics refers to collecting, processing, analyzing, and interpreting a large number of data from different sources. The main challenges of big data analytics are data modeling and data processing in terms of volume, speed, timing, ingenuity, reliability, *etc.* These qualities are determined by what role big data plays in people and the value they can create. The realization of these values can help businesses make better decisions. Mobile Internet devices are also growing rapidly. The massive and increasing data sets generated by networked devices are the basis of big data. Big data and the powerful data mining methods developed by various disciplines, such as data analysis, database systems, data storage, information retrieval, machine learning, and pattern recognition, allow significant knowledge discovery in business and research.

In the era of digital transformation, various types of machines, electronically controlled devices, manufacturing facilities, and processes in manufacturing enterprises generate a great deal of structured and unstructured data, and the amount of this data becomes the key criterion for business success. Business success depends on the capability to cope and be profitable in an environment flooded with Industry 4.0 [1]. Technologies such as big data, the Internet of Things, cloud manufacturing, cloud computing, *etc.*, are the main driving forces of the transformation from traditional manufacturing to Industry 4.0. These technologies have a significant effect on predictive maintenance methods. More digital data-based work on predictive maintenance and related big data application models is the main direction for future KD machinery.

Importance of Predictive Maintenance in Industry 4.0

Predictive maintenance is also essential for high-value assets. The overview of predictive maintenance is shown in Fig. (**1**). If any of the production lines or equipment goes down, it can cause a loss of business. A given production line equipment will produce a large part of the production volume for a specific product. By performing predictive maintenance and making up time, equipment and/or machines can spend more time producing what they should have produced, leading to increased operational productivity. The maintenance planning and scheduling costs in the predictive application are significantly reduced. Because PdM relies on the predictability of a piece of equipment, PdM does not have timely interventions that are characteristic of new tools/trackers required for advanced asset failures, which also reduces the cost of the deferred repair schedule [2]. Fig. (**1**) shows the overview of predictive maintenance.

Efficiently managing a maintenance program with a large amount of data results in optimal efficiency and cost savings. Because the condition of the factory equipment is always desirable, Predictive Maintenance (PdM) is the maintenance of the physical condition and is not planned and performs maintenance according to the actual state of the piece of equipment to maximize the life of the equipment.

Minimize maintenance costs. There are significant benefits as follows: By properly maintaining the service life of parts, equipment, and machines, maintenance costs are minimized, which helps to minimize the all-inclusive manufacturing cost over time. Traditional maintenance programs can only estimate when the machine fails. By creating unnecessary replacements/parts maintenance costs, predictive maintenance eliminates the potential for poor performance/equipment reliability [3]. The steps for predictive maintenance in Industry 4.0 are shown in Fig. (**2**).

PREDICTIVE MAINTENANCE

REACTIVE MAINTENANCE	PREVENTIVE MAINTENANCE	PREDICTIVE MAINTENANCE	PRESPECTIVE MAINTENANCE
REACTIVE MAINTENANCE AFTER A BREAKDOWN	PREVENTIVE MAINTENANCE TO REDUCE BREAKDOWN	USE OF SENSORS AND SOFTWARE TO PREDICT BREAKDOWN	MACHINE LEARNING PREDICTS BREAKDOWNS AND IDENTIFIES SOLUTIONS

Fig. (1). Overview of predictive maintenance.

Fig. (2). Steps for predictive maintenance in industry 4.0.

The importance of predictive maintenance has been known for years, but a recent survey by Bsquare indicated that only 20% of its selected subjects have a fully implemented maintenance program. Bsquare notes that some 20% are in the planning stage, while 40% of managers are dissatisfied or unsure about their intelligence. There are many reasons other than resistance that are due to a lack of understanding.

Objectives of the Study

To compare the classification accuracy of predictive models, LSTM has been considered only in the high-quality ranked journal. Additionally, the classification accuracy of the predictive models can be compared to more than three predictive models. This conclusion can be constructed as follows. First, the fundamental definition of PM is reviewed, including the PM framework and PdM feature. They can analyze when to adopt PM and PM standards, such as the cost and availability of PM. Second, various AI techniques are introduced, for example, machine learning and deep learning-based prediction models, which have been recently implemented for PM in the current market [4]. Otherwise, the Internet of Things (IoT) that was introduced in 2012, as well as cloud technologies, have played an important role in the data acquisition part for building the predictive model. Then, machine learning and deep learning models were adopted to achieve that objective. At the same time, the performance of the models is insufficient. Therefore, the current research aims to utilize the PM standard within the latest AI techniques in the industry.

At the end of the study, a comparison framework is proposed to compare various predictive models in terms of classification accuracy. It can be concluded when to apply various advanced technologies for PM in advance. The IEEE journals from 1994 to 2011, which were published on data-driven predictive maintenance, discussed the prediction techniques, the result, and the difficulty degree factor. At the same time, it was developed in the current study to evaluate when machine learning and deep learning predictive models were utilized. For example, Random Forest (RF) (2019), Support Vector Machine (SVM) (2021), and K-Nearest Neighbor (KNN) (2018) were eagerly utilized from 2018 to 2019.

This paper aims to leverage influential research that adopts AI techniques such as machine learning, deep learning, and Internet of Things (IoT)-based big data analytics to predict the time when maintenance, which is known as PM, is needed. Multiple predictive models based on machine learning algorithms, such as Random Forest (RF), Support Vector Machine (SVM), and K-Nearest Neighbor (KNN), as well as the deep learning algorithm, which is Long Short-Term Memory (LSTM), are discussed in detail. Therefore, technical implementation issues may be addressed.

LITERATURE REVIEW

Industrial 4.0 and PdM are booming cross-disciplinary research areas, which not only focus on technical problems but also address the industry management, business, and application sectors. To summarize, PdM models and tools do not work until their models and tools bring performance advantages to real industry problems with tested industrial project data. The work on predictive maintenance in the literature consists of technical and application work in IIoT and data-driven models and approaches adapted in the technical work, performance assessment, and applications adapted in the application work.

The work focuses more on IIoT and cloud/fog/edge technical solutions for PDM in terms of management, business, application layer, strategy, system layers, and issues. Furthermore, more implementation experiences in different industry contexts and application scenarios are presented, and the associated performance metrics in diverse business contexts are also provided [5].

A survey describes PdM frameworks, problems, and trends in Industry 4.0. Cloud and fog computing, together with the Internet of Things (IoT), are adopted as processing platforms. Several methods are achievable. For example, edge computing is adopted for real-time processing and information filtering, and cloud and fog computing is employed for feature extraction, data dimension reduction, and PdM. In addition to the PdM framework, the study also describes several related problems, including energy consumption, security and privacy issues, performance measurement and evaluation, and testing and benchmarking procedures.

The study provides a recent review of PdM for Industry 4.0. It concludes that a variety of sensors are adopted in different industries. At individual sensor levels, there is a trend toward smart sensors and wireless technology. The authors classify PdM techniques into model-driven, signal-driven, and data-driven. By conducting a comparative analysis, they find that data-driven methods, especially deep learning-based methods, exhibit superior performance. Furthermore, the study demonstrates that cloud and edge computing play an important role in real-time monitoring and diagnostics [6].

Research on Predictive Maintenance (PdM) has thrived in the last few decades. The main distinguishing feature of PdM from traditional maintenance strategies is that no proactive maintenance is conducted. Instead, condition-monitoring data is streamed in real time, and prognostics is performed accordingly.

Definition of Industry 4.0

Within the framework of 4.0, data science became a new buzzword. "A full understanding and acceptance of current and new professions" is considered a central condition for successfully mastering the megatrend I4.0. Data scientists are considered to have the most exciting job. A recent study on the "labor market for data scientists" concluded that the data scientist's core competence is the acquisition, preparation, analysis, and interpretation of data—it requires a combination of knowledge in computer science, statistics, and the business context [7]. The idea is that data science will create a high number of online markets for the labor market in the business and will become a mainstream topic.

According to the German Federal Government, Industry 4.0 not only automates industry but also " changes it fundamentally." The automation experts believe that "I4.0 is the path to intelligent automation and the use of state-of-the-art information and communication technology. According to Kagermann, "I4.0 is based on several technological trends and their combination, *e.g.*, Internet of Things (IoT), Advanced Analytics, Cyber-Physical Systems (CPS), Smart Factory and Industrial Internet. This will make automation more flexible and products more customizable while reducing design time, lead times, and time to market.

Role of Big Data Analytics in Industry 4.0

In Industry 4.0, the Internet of Things (IoT) generates a dramatic amount of big data, which is associated with the search for an effective PdM maintenance policy. At first, traditional PdM begins with the implementation of Condition Monitoring (CM) systems, which are achieved by vibration monitoring, ultrasound monitoring, thermography monitoring, and oil analysis. Based on sensing technologies, the collected signals are then dispatched to the control center, which inherits manual procedures or employs rule-based algorithms to interpret the status information. Recently, big data has been generated from modern CM systems and conveyed to cloud technology. Since the cloud platform can handle real-time monitoring data, a big data analytics strategy is capable of being introduced. Both maintenance and prediction models are treated by machine learning algorithms executed in cloud technology. With the support of a cloud platform, big data analytics can analyze a large amount of operational data [8]. Fig. (**3**) shows the role of big data in Industry 4.0.

Due to the emerging trend of Industry 4.0, manufacturing environments are gradually being equipped with smart sensing technologies and big data analytics tools. Thereby, factories can accumulate a large amount of big data not only to improve their productivity but also to achieve the goal of effective maintenance. The maintenance strategy without considering the current status of machines is referred to as "blind or dumb maintenance". Outdated maintenance method leads to many drawbacks, including low or high maintenance costs, decreasing machinery availability, and uncertainty in maintenance scheduling. In contrast to the redundant maintenance strategy, the Predictive Maintenance (PdM) policy is capable of providing better solutions in terms of preserving the value of maintenance for machines by utilizing real-time data.

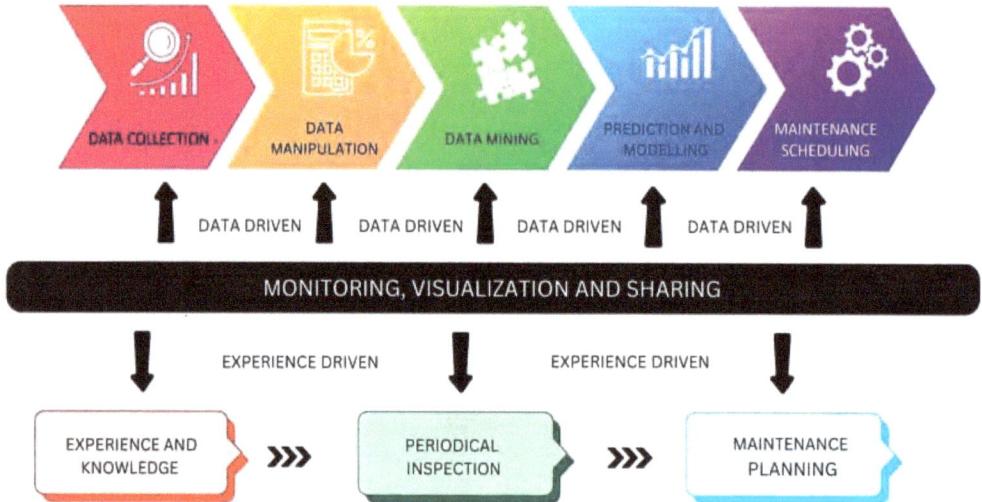

Fig. (3). Responsiveness, Reliability, and Security.

Applications of Predictive Maintenance in Industry 4.0

The main objective of data-driven maintenance is to explain how big data can be used to maintain and provide essential support in a digital plant for innovative help. From an Industry 4.0 viewpoint, real-time predictive maintenance transforms the lifecycle progresses into a sovereign approach based on the so-called "p" value (predictive, more agile, preventive, and peculiar) to increase our knowledge. The prediction model also reduces engine wear and carbon footprint and improves machinery resources manageability to implement sustainable and energy-efficient implementations and digital plant buildings. Workers' protection and seeds' quality & availability can also be increased.

Predictive maintenance is a cornerstone of the fourth industrial revolution (Industry 4.0). It uses big data analytics that combines edge computing with artificial intelligence or cloud-based for monitoring systems and equipment, making predictions, and preventing any risk or shutdown whenever there is any catastrophic failure. Advanced industrial solutions powered with various real-time data sources such as accelerometer, ultrasound, vibration, infrared thermal images, motor current, or voltage signature detect, predict, and suggest the health of a machine, component, or system. Digital transformation can take place using high-performance big data analytics. Real-time analytics data can report potential anomalies before the system has been pushed for replacement or even if corrective replacements are necessary, helping plant operators with zero-unplanned redundancy of machinery and to adopt Industry 4.0. Predictive technologies, such as analysis for failure and destructive prediction, are helping in the development of new adapt sets and decision techniques [9].

Challenges in Implementing Big Data Analytics for Predictive Maintenance

The volume of data from heterogeneous in-house and external sources can be overwhelming, and it can suffer from data silos present within organizations, especially in traditional manufacturing, energy, and utilities industries. Data from each process, from various systems and plants, and from different domain types, such as process control, time series, sensor, and network data, need to be integrated [10]. To meet these requirements, the chosen analytics technology should support the training and execution of parallel processing algorithms so that the system does not become the throughput bottleneck. Processing can still be slow if the number of servers required are not available promptly.

Challenges in implementing big data analytics for predictive maintenance: Surveys have pointed out some technical and organizational challenges that can slow down the implementation of predictive maintenance and advanced supporting technologies, including big data analytics. The most often listed challenges in implementing big data analytics in domains such as predictive maintenance are related to data volume, data velocity, difficulties in data capturing, and requirements for both IT and personnel. The volume of data has been regarded as one of the major challenges in big data analytics [11].

Methodology

To use big data for predictive maintenance, several big data technologies can be employed, such as platforms, data formats, algorithms, tools, and associated hardware and software. A typical workflow involves several tasks, such as data acquisition, data analysis, modeling, deployment, and validation of the industry. However, implementation is an important step in the selected architecture to fulfill all the requirements described earlier. Thanks to the onset of various Industry 4.0 technologies, not only do IT companies integrate advanced analytics to provide predictive, preventive, and prescriptive maintenance techniques, but they also use smart HMI HSI and AR technology to provide even more powerful diagnostics. This is a challenge for the industry that should also consider asset health.

The planned maintenance can be designed by monitoring the components used in the equipment in general. In predictive maintenance, sensors attached to the machines provide continuous information on the operating parameters, along with a history of equipment operating data, to predict a potential failure and then replace the equipment accordingly. Predictive maintenance schedules eliminate the distribution of lubricants, filter changes, and other small, healthy components that may still work efficiently because the equipment needs to be running. This is achieved by taking data from all equipment and evaluating it under trained analytical algorithms, collectively referred to as predictive maintenance. These algorithms enable companies to recognize subtle signs, discover behavioral patterns, and discover deviations that indicate a problem or closely correlate with equipment failure.

Research Design

As stated in the section "Introduction", the main goal of this work is to provide an architecture for big data predictive maintenance in Industry 4.0. Therefore, before addressing this issue in depth, the research should obtain knowledge background concerning maintenance strategies, condition monitoring techniques, big data technologies, and models that are included in the final model. This objective should be accomplished through a general review of the state of the art. This review aims to understand and clarify the main methods and key concepts that other researchers have used to address similar problems. That is why a systematic literature review must be established.

Data Collection and Analysis

An intelligent choice of the most significant aspects decreases the number of monitored features, computationally lessening the recognition complexity. A simple sensor concentration analysis implementation is done by showing a time trend linked to the appearance and the worsening of a problem where the threshold on an individual instant level's repetition would be difficult to set at the beginning. It is necessary to understand that real-world data do not resemble the cleaned datasets used in the training of medical and military equipment. MME and MMIRE are performed in various environmental conditions. Baseline and operational data distributions are centered and spread in terms of a chemical 'pH' for a physiological variable that must be monitored.

The production roadmap of a maintenance 4.0 system begins with the connection to data sources. Prognostic solutions need imbalanced labeled data. These data require annotated events caused by system failures, which occur infrequently, and for this, an averaged historical event is too inconclusive. Also, event capture requires commonly expensive actions. This rationalizes an error in the choice of the data to be recorded. Moreover, without monitoring systems, these expensive actions are made onto completely healthy systems, implicitly causing aging. The longer the time duration from the last event, the less accurate the prediction.

Selection of Predictive Maintenance Techniques

There are several monitoring techniques for predictive maintenance. The most practical technique is through the direct inspection of the machine tools. With the advancement of technology, sensors have been utilized to perform machine tools condition monitoring. Non-sensor-based or data-driven-based condition monitoring techniques have a high accuracy in the prediction of early damage detection and can provide a quantitative tool for life assessment of the cutting tools. Neural networks, support vector regression, decision trees, principal component analysis, Bayesian network, and polynomial fitting are widely used to forecast the critical components or tools using these data-driven-based condition monitoring techniques. Input parameters that have an effect on training the model for classification and prediction are machining parameters, tool wear, and cutting force.

Predictive maintenance intends to predict a defective component in advance so that action can be taken to avoid failure. In the selection of predictive maintenance technique, the user may consider the durability of the component or the mean time to repair by using some quantitative methods such as Weibull distribution, time-driven replacement, or block-based maintenance. The difficulty in obtaining these parameters may also incur a significant concern to involve these models in critical operations. The most common technique in the predictive maintenance lifecycle that starts the diagnosis stage of the machine tools is the monitoring and testing of the internal or external parameters of the components.

DATA COLLECTION AND PREPROCESSING

Most of the factories today (approx 80%) have one or more kinds of sensors that generate data. These data can be of different types: temperature, size, mass, pressure, rate, velocity, *etc.* Each of these types has its own units. Some data can be categorical or have different time stamps: temperature, pressure, and other data can be collected per second. Some data can be operated in real-time or at scheduled times and are collected from diverse sources. As shown in Fig. (**4**), it can be from either a) Different components, b) similar components, or c) from the system as a whole.

PREDICTIVE MAINTENANCE

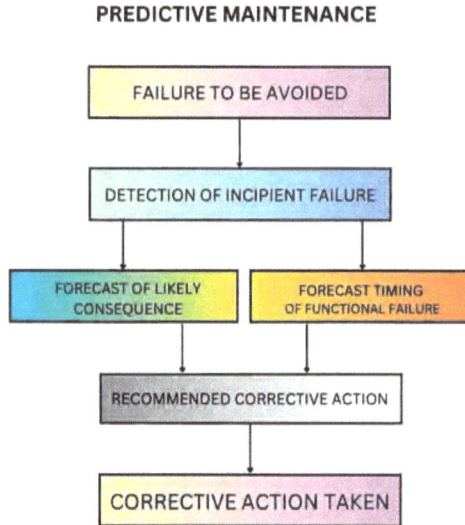

Fig. (4). Monitoring, Visualization, and Sharing the data.

Data Sources for Predictive Maintenance

The sensor data of the equipment is obtained through some real-time monitoring systems. Traditionally, they are usually installed on the equipment to objectively reflect the various status and conditions of the device, such as the equipment's temperature, vibration, acoustic emission, spectral information, and mechanical wear conditions. Mostly due to the high expense of these sensors, industrial users always turned to various consultants and third-party vendors to support the design, installation, setup, calibration, and validation of the machine monitoring systems, as well as the presentation and integration of this machine condition data into their broader IT infrastructures, given the development of vibration sensors supporting machine monitoring systems, which are more feasible and easier than ever to be used by industrial customers. For example, some specialized vendors can provide online information, both about the machine's operational status and sensor performance quality, to end users to support their predictive maintenance approach.

Real-time sensor data: It reflects the running status of the equipment in the physical world and is generated by different sensors (*e.g.*, vibration sensors, temperature sensors, pressure sensors, current sensors). Recently, with sensing technology experiencing rapid development, sensors have not only become more accurate and sensitive but also cheaper and smarter. Furthermore, condition monitoring technology has also developed greatly, involving non-contact technology (*e.g.*, monitoring the temperature rise in the device by infrared imaging technology), Internet of Things technology (*e.g.*, automatically predicting the device health according to vibration signal and temperature signal by wireless network sensors), and so on. Nowadays, the concept "Internet of Things" (IoT) has almost penetrated every aspect of people's lives, and this is no exception to the industry domain, especially in the context of Industry 4.0. It is now possible to monitor the status of the device anywhere, anytime through IoT technology in a vast number of sensors and measurement equipment.

Data Preprocessing Techniques

Some traditional feature extraction methods for equipment failure diagnostic decision-making consist of discrete Fourier transform and representation of power spectrum density or short-term Fourier transform. To improve the traditional methods, its implementation will take into account the equipment failure spectral patterns, and therefore, it may conduct over-segmentation or under-segmentation issues because the unit's fragility affects the standard feature extraction processing and limits interpretability. Furthermore, its implementation will consider the device codes, including machinery health status and even the preprocessing settings and kind of failure features that lead to equipment indications. Next, noise will be added that may reveal the nature of the machinery's response to various types of faults. Even more, the type of offshore wind farm turbine failure indication may vary according to the aspect.

In predictive failure analysis, raw time-series data about machinery are preprocessed. Accurate production line forecasts and diagnoses are highly reliant on these processed time-series data sets. It mainly includes three main steps: acquisition of raw data, pre-processing with noise, drift and outliers, and feature extraction. Different techniques are applied to perform these steps. The overall process begins with data acquisition. After cleaning, the missing values are deleted and less relevant variables are removed. Then, feature extraction procedures are used to scale each measurement and transform it into signal-based features. Finally, the features are aggregated over their entire lines of the manufacturing table.

Data Quality Assessment

Big data analytics is the application of advanced analytic techniques to very large, diverse, rapidly changing data sets. For big data analytics to yield accurate and timely valuable information, the data should be of the highest quality. The suggestions to deal with these challenges are mainly divided into two categories:

cost of data pre-processing and challenges related to feature derivation and feature engineering. The feature manufacturing process is very important because "the products are as valuable as the features chosen for use and the processing of these features are relevant". Another important feature of this feature is to know in advance the characteristics that have a maximum impact on predictive performance.

Data quality assessment: Problems related to data quality have been highlighted by researchers to be a major challenge in big data analytics. The need for a reliable data-driven approach is emphasized using big data analytics, but it was noted that the biggest obstacle in the application of big data in this field is poor data quality. Data quality is most critical in the first stages of predictive modeling, such as data pre-processing and feature engineering. Industrial big data have their peculiarities, which are mainly due to the variety of data, and the main problems generally associated with it are the heterogeneity, diversity, and complexity of the respective management. This heterogeneity of data is due to the number and diversity, both in structure and type, associated with acquisition systems.

Predictive Maintenance Models

There are four types of predictive maintenance models for voltage sags: extreme learning machine, support vector machine, extended local binary pattern, and adaptive neuro-fuzzy. The experimental result shows that the SVM and ELBP-SVM model achieves the highest accuracy rate for both sorting algorithm-based classification and optical material-based classification. In the welding traffic scenario, using a combination of deep learning and recurrent neural networks can improve the predictive accuracy of RNN. Electric vehicle platform predictive maintenance incorporating deep learning models can support the diagnosis. The long short-term memory network-based deep learning model shows the prognostic ability for predictive maintenance. In conclusion, predictive maintenance of a smart manufacturing system can use the LSTM-based time series model. The deep feature extraction with CNN can demonstrate the predictive performance in predictive maintenance.

Classification is an approach to separating data points that are categorized according to the different characteristics and evaluating or assigning labels to new observations whose characteristics are unknown. Regression is the statistical analysis that estimates relationships or the value of an arbitrary variable that depends on the corresponding input value. Time series analysis explores the history of a given series to forecast its future behavior. Cluster analysis refers to grouping the objects in such a way that the objects in the same group (cluster) are more distinctive than those in other groups. Based on the type of failure using unsupervised learning and directed toward a broader analysis of failure patterns, the usage of a consensus clustering algorithm applied to aggregated features is adopted. The clustering approach produces better results than the k-nearest neighbors classifier, decision tree, SVM, and random forest classifiers.

Predictive Maintenance (PdM) is designed to help determine the condition of in-service equipment to be subsequently serviced according to their predicted failure time. Unlike other maintenance strategies, predictive maintenance requires the disclosure condition of in-service equipment, and the maintenance time can be reduced. The condition-based model is the most commonly used technique in predictive maintenance. The predictive models in predictive maintenance primarily include four categories: classification, regression, time series analysis, and clustering.

Overview of Predictive Maintenance Models

PM models can also be categorized based on the characteristics of their underlying inputs. Sensors and other devices are used to collect various types of data from machines. Depending on the type of sensors and other devices used to collect the data, as well as the way the data is collected, different types of data such as vibration data, ultrasonic data, oil analysis data, infrared data, current data, sound data, temperature data, and shaft speed data can be collected. Each of these data types is unique in terms of fault detection and type, as well as data characteristics such as linearity, stationarity, non-stationarity, *etc.* Data that each type of sensor or device generates from machines has different characteristics. PM models that are built using each of these types of sensor data are expected to have a different correlation level with specific failure modes. Furthermore, each machine generates data of different forms and characteristics depending on the type, size, use, where and how it is installed, and how and for what it is being used. Different diagnostic tools and approaches are required to relate machine problems to data opportunities.

Predictive maintenance is not a new concept, and its importance is increasingly being recognized. In predictive maintenance, instead of performing preventive maintenance tasks at regular intervals regardless of their need, the condition of the equipment is monitored, and maintenance is performed when defined criteria are met. Because one can predict potential equipment problems, corrective maintenance can be scheduled to be done during non-working hours, avoiding negative effects on production. In retrospective and predictive PM, equipment problems are diagnosed first. Retrospective PM models are built using historical run-to-failure maintenance records and fault-specific equipment parameters. These models are then used to identify impending equipment problems. By contrast, predictive PM models are built solely based on historical equipment parameters. Hence, predictive PM models do not benefit from the knowledge of what a specific equipment fault looks like. They can be more generalizable to various types of faults and magnitudes of degradation conditions.

Statistical Models for Predictive Maintenance

Several prognostic techniques employing artificial neural networks have been proposed for modeling the state of degradation of engineering systems like automotive engine bearings. Most of these involve training a feed-forward neural network to predict the time at which a specified condition will be reached in the machine using current or previous sensor measurements. One issue with this is that often, the desired future condition of the machine is unknown. As such, the approach of training a separate network for each possible end of life for all units is generally not suitable. Kordon and Tomar, for instance, proposed an architecture for a neural network that can be used to determine the machine's prognostic health index, which can be used as an indication of the remaining useful life of the machine. The device utilizes multiple features extracted from the vibration signal of the machine and consists of three main parts: an embedding layer with Long Short-Term Memory (LSTM) units for handling the sequential nature of the data used in the feature extraction process using three separate sliding windows, an attention layer that emphasizes the relevant features, and a third layer that calibrates the results and conducts averaging of the three used windows before emitting the final value of the machine's generated prognostic health index value. This would denote the level of machine degradation and can be used as a scalar label for initial onset detection or in computational clusters for various optimal maintenance decision techniques [12].

There are many models in statistics for forecasting machine failures. However, they can all be divided into two major classes, which are the physics-based methods and data-driven methods. The physics-based methods involve a good understanding of the processes leading to failure and then performing some analysis to identify critical conditions that will lead to the end of life of the machine. Subsequently, these conditions are monitored and used to predict the time at which the machine might fail. Data-driven methods, on the other hand, mainly involve employing machine learning or other data mining techniques to process the information contained in data. Unlike the physics-based methods, they require no a priori knowledge of the processes that might lead to failure. Popular survival analysis techniques like the exponential smoothing and hazard-type models are included in a more detailed review of statistical models for predictive maintenance.

Machine Learning Models for Predictive Maintenance

Do *et al.* presented various machine learning models used in predictive maintenance. They proposed the most common machine learning models for maintenance with the consideration of domain knowledge, feature space, and the targeted problem/services. The models are classified based on physical model variables and include physical models, semi-empirical data-driven models, completely driven data models, unsupervised learning, and supervised learning. Unsupervised learning is the optimization of the machine learning models using no class label, where the learning algorithm is implemented to identify patterns and features within the input data. Meanwhile, supervised learning is a learning algorithm that uses class labels to supervise the actual guidance or predictors toward the optimum result. An adaptive hybrid-controller-damage statistical-based predictive algorithm for predictive maintenance on FDM devices in the Internet of manufacturing things encompasses predictions with unsupervised learning and supervised learning. Fig. (5) shows the categorization of machine learning models in PDM.

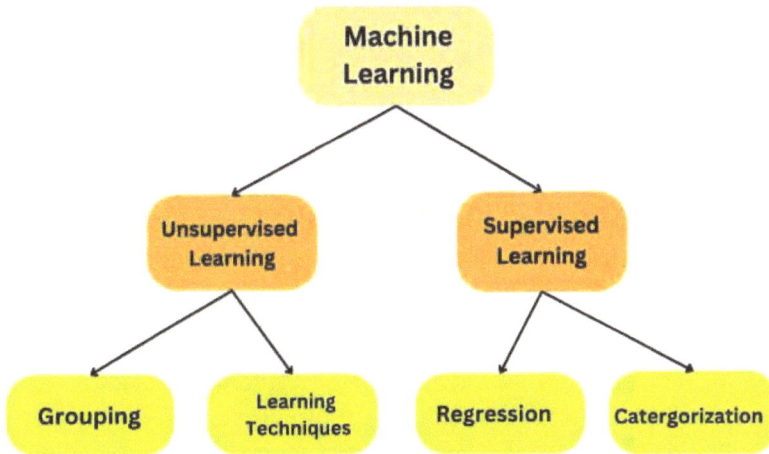

Fig. (5). Categorization of Machine Learning Models in PDM.

In contrast to physical models, machine learning models are also capable of modeling the system either in the absence of physics knowledge or beyond physics knowledge. Since the relations in physical models are formalized using mathematical operators, it is hard to interpret. While in machine learning models, they are easier to interpret as most of the features can be explained in the model.

Learning a machine model is also faster and can be implemented relatively flexibly. Nowadays, machine learning has gained huge interest in predictive maintenance due to its interpretability, fast learning and implementation, and its flexibility. A variety of models in machine learning can be used for maintenance. Some of the popular ones are decision trees, neural networks, random forest, gradient boosting, extreme gradient boosting, support vector machine, k-nearest neighbor, Gaussian process, naïve Bayes, *etc.*

Implementation and Evaluation

To evaluate the proposed framework based on the PI System, a prototype is developed using vehicles as the experimental platform. The fleet is jointly developed by a collaborative team composed of a domestic automotive manufacturer and the research group, with the data collected from vehicles pre-installed with telematics systems. This system can obtain long-distance flight data from different autonomous vehicles and upload the data to the PI System for advanced analysis. The parameters mainly include 4 classes: the airborne state, axis centerline, speed profile, and temperature environment.

Implementation of Big Data Analytics for Predictive Maintenance

A big data architecture is needed when organizations decide to implement big data analytics. The architecture that is implemented within the scope of this research connects easily with the organization's existing IT environment. The set of possible modern analytics tools is checked to see if they can perform hard rules for decision-making and a soft rule by supporting the process of defining hard rules. This helps the maintenance organization use its extensive yet scattered knowledge to look for hidden patterns in the big data available to the organization. If hidden patterns are found, an organization can begin to predict the best time to start a certain action based on predictive maintenance. There is a lot of work that needs to be done before an organization can start with predictive maintenance. In the research, the organization needs to be creative in different analytical techniques, models, or combinations of models that are available to support the maintenance domain with the research prototype.

Many companies that manufacture, maintain, or sell complex equipment will be able to derive real value from implementing big data analytics for predictive maintenance. To apply big data analytics in the maintenance domain, several technologies need to be combined. A concrete plan and architecture are necessary for the introduction or implementation of big data analytics in a maintenance organization. With the test case of ProRail, a railway infrastructure manager, as a central case, a SAP HANA data model and a Hadoop data model are designed and implemented to collect all the necessary data. The data is cleaned, pre-processed, and loaded in a SAP HANA and Hadoop environment, which will be used to test the designed maintenance model. The actual consumption data is compared with data extracted from different maintenance and material stock databases. The results can be visualized in a real-time management dashboard.

Evaluation of Predictive Maintenance Models

There are several relevant factors when evaluating the maintenance strategy for multi-component systems, both from the system point of view, such as machine configuration, failure distribution, and machine operation, and from the maintenance point of view, such as repair capacity, shortage costs, and overtime costs.

In addition, it must respect the limitations of the maintenance strategy to be considered. The main goals when evaluating maintenance policies are the minimization of costs or the maximization of production. The most common metric in maintenance analysis is Maintenance Overtime Percentage (MOP), which is different from Corrective Overdue Percentage (COP) because MOP provides an over-time information percentage, and the machines' service is no longer at risk.

Three main types of maintenance planning activities can be applied within a maintenance plan: run-time (or corrective) maintenance, preventive maintenance, and condition-based monitoring or predictive maintenance. Maintenance control has four principal maintenance strategies: corrective, preventive, predictive, and reliability-centered maintenance. Evaluation of predictive maintenance models must function in diverse long-term scenarios, taking into account inputs such as uncertainties.

Maintenance management involves three basic tasks: maintenance planning, maintenance execution, and maintenance control. The planning assigns the maintenance activities to the specific equipment component and sets the work start time, and it is based on information regarding the maintenance action, the material, and the capacity. The maintenance execution includes activities such as providing information about the maintenance activity, feedback, and the completion of maintenance. The control involves work orders created by maintenance planning, activities to prevent and correct failures, and suitable long-term strategies.

RESULTS AND DISCUSSION

This study was elaborated, taking into account the augmented requirements of Industry 4.0, which include flexibility, autonomy, and self-regulation of the manufacturing processes, as laid out by a more sustainable, economically driven, socially integrated, and technologically advanced fourth revolution. Within this brittle scenario, what is at stake is the so-called intimacy needed within the complex information and communication technology perspective, as well as the necessary semantics, accuracy, or authenticity of the information related to equipment states required by the big data approach in today's techno-savvy architectures. The study was based on a collection of real industrial data, which, beyond the interest from an academic and industrial perspective, has posed significant challenges related to the signal treatment, dimensionality reduction, and cyclo-stationary identification and tracking, which tangled and entangled the initial contributions stemming from such sophisticated data.

Analysis of Predictive Maintenance Outcomes

In these and many other success stories for predictive maintenance, dominantly predictive models are used. The main focus of PdM currently is prediction rather than explanation or insight. This is problematic from both a technical and an organizational perspective. From a technical point of view, generating effective and reliable predictions without a suitable hypothesis is known to be hard and sometimes unreliable. To ensure that the filters in the PdM system are capable of understanding the underlying physical process, current switch-based diagnostics can be improved by probabilistic representations of the failure modes. From an organizational perspective, Friedman (1997) notes that machine models can be overpowering. Organizational learning often occurs at the periphery of a company. More junior employees are involved in less centralized decisions and, therefore, provide the grist for the mill. Expert models should be designed based on all these insights.

Many success stories exist for predictive maintenance. A well-known example is the deployment of PdM in paper manufacturing processes by the Kimberly-Clark Corporation. The availability of their machines in some processes improved by 25%. In a series of webinars on predictive maintenance, various end-user companies presented their success stories. One interesting example was a producer of grinding wheels. The performance of this product significantly depends on the properties of the material being used. Therefore, the company wanted to increase the material quality, whilst keeping the material costs at the same level. This kind of finesse in the manufacturing process can only be obtained by an optimal control of the process conditions. The company developed a model to predict material quality based on process parameters and implemented the model in a predictive maintenance system. They achieved the desired product quality increase, which resulted in an increase of 300% in yield.

Discussion of Findings

The study shows that data quality and communication governance affect the predictive maintenance process. Although data analytics, including big data analytics, are applied to identify predictive features to make good maintenance decisions that allow companies to successfully preempt potential equipment failures, sub-standard results are likely to be obtained when big data from inside and outside an organization are used to address predictive features and predictive modeling for manufacturing predictive maintenance because of data quality deterioration. Particularly, internal data of maintenance includes large volumes of diverse data sources such as equipment design documents, maintenance documents, work orders, historical equipment performance data, internal sensor data, and external equipment's operating data, thanks to the substantial amount of connected equipment assets through the Internet of Things for Industry 4.0. Furthermore, external data of maintenance that interacts with internal structured equipment data such as equipment's attributes, like make, manufacturer, machine ID, and installation date, also deteriorate.

Our study offers several insights into industrial equipment maintenance. Firstly, it informs how data analytics, particularly big data analytics, are used for predictive maintenance in the manufacturing sector. Analyzing manufacturing companies in multiple countries such as the UK, USA, Sweden, India, and China, the study shows that big data analytics are extensively used to identify predictive features and predictive models. This suggests that even though many companies publicly highlight the employment of big data analytics for various types of predictive modeling, the manufacturing industry stands as an early adopter of big data analytics in decision-making for predictive maintenance. By highlighting the strong reliance on big data analytics, it is observed that the information obtained from the use of big data analytics endorses good maintenance decisions to successfully preempt potential equipment failures as well as to reduce maintenance costs.

Advantages and Disadvantages of Predictive Maintenance Models

It gives a comparison of their performances in various industrial environments. For example, certain models may provide increased accuracy of the calculated outcomes but may be sensitive to different datasets, and on the other hand, certain models can be very robust, but their work requires a great many calculations. By pointing out such trade-offs to the reader, the suitability of each model to a particular purpose should become clearer to the reader.

Several of the models' more impressive attributes include their ability to withstand fluctuations in supply shortage data, as well as their generalized performance with other similar datasets.

Robustness and Generalization Capabilities

The model's accuracy and its ability to maintain the appropriate level of performance on a variety of scenarios and data is defined by the robustness and generalization criteria. Robustness may be defined as a model's ability to perform with little change when faced with changes in input data values, changes to the environment, or the presence of noisy data. This attribute is critical, especially in the industrial environment, because sensor values, working parameters, and equipment states are usually different. A good model can handle such variations so that the frequency of false alarms or wrong classifications that may cause production interruptions is reduced. Some of the approaches applied in this class are stress testing, noise addition, and adversarial learning.

Generalization, on the other hand, defines how well a model can do in other scenarios and, therefore, performance on unseen data. There is a lot of variance because of the equipment and the operational conditions of the industry, the type of sensors, *etc.*, in an actual setting. This variability can be easily addressed by a model with good generalization capacity, able to deliver similar performance across a wide variety of use cases. The procedures that help to gain a generalization function are producing models regarding various and varied sets of data, implementing cross-validation, and avoiding overfitting utilizing methods that contribute towards the reduction of the coefficients.

While considering the applicability of predictive maintenance models, it is necessary to consider such criteria. As one may achieve very good results on training sets on certain data, the ability of a model to generalize and keep high robustness is the decisive factor for reliability and applicability in practice.

Comparative Evaluation of Models

An evaluation of predictive maintenance models should not only be based on the accuracy of the models but also consider other attributes such as robustness, generalization support, scalability, and computational cost. Accuracy, albeit being an important performance measurement, merely captures a relative indication of how well an existing model performs, just fine-tuned for a given dataset, and does not present a true picture of the model's performance robustness in various or fluctuating scenarios. Robustness quantifies how a model behaves when the data it needs to use is noisy or contains outliers. This is crucially important in working environments based on machinery where fluctuations in machine performance or sensor quality are possible.

Generalization, another important performance measure, measures how well the established model performs on other new data sets hence clarifying whether the data set is over-customized to the model or is capable of adapting to variability across other operating conditions. For example, a model learned on data getting from one type of machine should be good if it is implemented in similar machines but in different conditions.

Comparative evaluation also focuses on the efficiency of computations. There can be an issue with resource availability since some models may be computationally complex. Such trade-offs are likely conveyed by performance graphs or a table that makes model selection more informative.

Through incorporating these multi-dimensional assessments, suggested predictive maintenance models are chosen to be not only effective in providing optimal accuracy but also reliable in terms of robustness, applicability to other systems, and optimality in terms of time and computational resources necessary for long-term real-world application.

CONCLUSION

In future works, some challenges and improvements might be achieved. In detail, the mechanics of how to use data-driven models to predict when a fault might occur are not yet well understood. Our paper explained the data quality in four challenges (*e.g.*, missing, duplicated, noise, and so on) and the methods to solve them. On the one hand, plenty of methods for particular problems can be found, such as the Markov theory, Taylor Decomposition, and signal reconstruction. More methods are easily expanded. Due to the different characteristics, such as different industries, facilities, operating environments, data, and so on, the PM process derived from big data is complex. It might take a long time to conduct the PM for both empirical motivation reasons and a lack of capability. Although the predictive maintenance study is a part of the economic perspective, the economic issues involved in PM practice have also been a topic of increasing research interest. However, there are still potential issues that need to be addressed. In summary, big data analytics for predictive maintenance can be used in Industry 4.0.

In this study, the aim is to modify the current predictive model quality comparison techniques to suit processing industry conditions. A novel approach to predictive model evaluation is proposed to start with, classifying them both into two broad categories: supervised and unsupervised methods. Under each type, these models have been tested under traditional artificial setups and also empirical datasets obtained from a major industrial refrigeration process of 120 months of data. Moreover, amongst the unsupervised models, the proposed approach has also been validated using severity-based assignments, *i.e.*, a scenario where a variation of the outputs results in different penalty payouts. Encouraging results in these lines instill belief in the proposed approach. Furthermore, this study is unique by not only applying these models in real-time but also statistically verifying the goodness of the models, thereby promulgating the choice for a potential user. The insights from this study can thus help in addressing the prevailing predictive maintenance-related challenges to a great extent.

REFERENCES

[1]   J. Yan, Y. Meng, L. Lu, and L. Li, "Industrial big data in an industry 4.0 environment: Challenges, schemes, and applications for predictive maintenance", *IEEE Access,* vol. 5, pp. 23484-23491, 2017. [http://dx.doi.org/10.1109/ACCESS.2017.2765544]

[2]   R. Rosati, L. Romeo, G. Cecchini, F. Tonetto, P. Viti, A. Mancini, and E. Frontoni, "From knowledge-based to big data analytic model: a novel IoT and machine learning based decision support system for predictive maintenance in Industry 4.0", *J. Intell. Manuf.,* vol. 34, no. 1, pp. 107-121, 2023. [http://dx.doi.org/10.1007/s10845-022-01960-x]

[3]   G.M. Sang, L. Xu, P. De Vrieze, Y. Bai, and F. Pan, "Predictive maintenance in industry 4.0", *Proceedings of the 10th International Conference on Information Systems and Technologies,* pp. 1-11, 2020.

[4]   R. Sahal, J.G. Breslin, and M.I. Ali, "Big data and stream processing platforms for Industry 4.0 requirements mapping for a predictive maintenance use case", *J. Manuf. Syst.,* vol. 54, pp. 138-151, 2020.
[http://dx.doi.org/10.1016/j.jmsy.2019.11.004]

[5]   S. Sajid, A. Haleem, S. Bahl, M. Javaid, T. Goyal, and M. Mittal, "Data science applications for predictive maintenance and materials science in context to Industry 4.0", *Mater. Today Proc.,* vol. 45, pp. 4898-4905, 2021.
[http://dx.doi.org/10.1016/j.matpr.2021.01.357]

[6]   A. Cachada, J. Barbosa, P. Leitño, C.A. Gcraldcs, L. Deusdado, J. Costa, C. Teixeira, J. Teixeira, A.H. Moreira, P.M. Moreira, and L. Romero, "Maintenance 4.0: Intelligent and predictive maintenance system architecture", *2018 IEEE 23rd International Conference on Emerging Technologies and Factory Automation (ETFA) 2018,* vol. 1, IEEE, pp. 139-146, 2018.

[7]   C. Kaur, P. Singh, and S.S. Kang, "A business intelligence based novel framework for big data analysis", *International Journal of Advanced Research in Computer Science.,* vol. 7, no. 6, 2016.

[8]   D. Uike, S. Agarwalla, V. Bansal, M.K. Chakravarthi, R. Singh, and P. Singh, "Investigating the role of blockchain to secure identity in IoT for industrial automation", *2022 11th International Conference on System Modeling & Advancement in Research Trends (SMART) 2022,* IEEE, pp. 837-841, 2022. [http://dx.doi.org/10.1109/SMART55829.2022.10047385]

[9]   R. Verma, H. Taneja, K.D. Singh, and P.D. Singh, "Enhancing data analytics in environmental sensing through cloud IoT integration", *Journal of Climate Change,* vol. 10, no. 2, pp. 41-45, 2024. [http://dx.doi.org/10.3233/JCC240013]

[10]   M.S. Guru Prasad, P. Singh, H. Taneja, A.K. Jain, and S. Chandrappa, "Statistical analysis of multi job processing in Hadoop environment using schedulers", *Journal of Information and Optimization Sciences,* vol. 43, no. 3, pp. 497-504, 2022. [http://dx.doi.org/10.1080/02522667.2022.2042087]

[11]   A Panwar, and V Bhatnagar, "Scrutinize the idea of Hadoop-based data Lake for big data storage", *Applications of Machine Learning,* pp. 365-391, 2020.
[http://dx.doi.org/10.1007/978-981-15-3357-0_24]

[12]   N. Sharma, A. Panwar, and U. Sugandh, "Big data analytics in health care: A literature survey", *International Journal of Recent Research Aspects.,* vol. 5, no. 1, 2018.

CHAPTER 4

Hardware Security Enhancement with Generative Artificial Intelligence

Phey Phey Lim¹, Kim Ho Yeap²,*, Veerendra Dakulagi³ and **Yu Jen Lee²**

¹ Intel Corporation, Penang, Malaysia

² Department of Electronic Engineering, Universiti Tunku Abdul Rahman, 31900 Kampar, Malaysia

³ Department of CSE (Data Science), Guru Nanak Dev Engineering College, Bidar, Karnataka, India

Abstract: In today's society, which is heavily influenced by technology, it is crucial to prioritize the security and integrity of computer systems and their underlying hardware components. As advancements in hardware technologies continue to progress rapidly, new vulnerabilities emerge, posing significant risks to the confidentiality and integrity of sensitive information. Therefore, it is essential to proactively identify and mitigate potential threats to hardware. Traditionally, threat modeling tools have primarily focused on software vulnerabilities, neglecting the exploration of hardware vulnerabilities. However, with the increasing complexity of hardware architectures, there is an urgent need for effective methodologies to assess and address potential threats at the hardware level. Currently, state-of-the-art approaches in hardware threat modeling rely on static analysis techniques and knowledge of known hardware vulnerabilities. The existing approaches are considered cumbersome since they require computer validation experts and engineers to perform manual inspection, simulation-based testing, and formal verification. These approaches face increasingly difficult challenges these days when hardware architectures continuously evolve, rendering them more advanced and complicated. In order to cope with these challenges, it is therefore essential to seek alternative and more reliable approaches that are capable of improving the efficacy and accuracy of threat identification and analysis. Since generative Artificial Intelligence (AI) is equipped with the tool to model and generate complex data patterns, it can be considered an alternative approach for hardware threat modeling. With the aid of generative AI, the restricted scope faced by threat modeling can, therefore, be expanded. By incorporating generative AI into hardware threat modeling, hardware vulnerabilities that are hard to be detected and analyzed by conventional approaches can be identified. Hence, the overall security and integrity of computer systems can also be significantly enhanced, resulting in the formation of a more secure environment for protecting sensitive information.

---

* Corresponding author Kim Ho Yeap: Department of Electronic Engineering, Universiti Tunku Abdul Rahman, 31900 Kampar, Malaysia; E-mail: yeapkh@utar.edu.my

Tanu Singh, Vinod Patidar, Arvind Panwar & Urvashi Sugandh (Eds.)
All rights reserved-© 2025 Bentham Science Publishers

Keywords: Artificial intelligence, Hardware security, RAG approach, RISC-V architecture, Threat modeling.

INTRODUCTION

The lifestyle of mankind has been interwoven seamlessly with advanced and ever-evolving technology nowadays. As such, computer systems and their corresponding auxiliaries have become an indispensable asset to society. For this reason, it is important to safeguard the security and reliability of computer systems and their hardware components. As the technology continues to evolve, more atrocious threats that defy the confidentiality and integrity of data are deemed to emerge. There is thus an urgent need to develop hardware security enhancement approaches to suppress the potential threats.

In order to develop approaches that can effectively mitigate threats, the security issues inherently associated with computer systems are to be identified and understood. Throughout the years, computer validation aficionados have focused their efforts and resources on coping with software threats and vulnerabilities. As technology continues to march inexorably towards a whole new realm, there exist threats in hardware architectures that have turned out to be a critical issue that can no longer be neglected.

Indeed, all of the latest hardware threat modeling approaches were developed on the basis of established hardware vulnerabilities, and they also emphasize primarily static analysis. Some of these popular approaches include manual inspection of hardware designs, testing *via* simulation, and formal verification. Though effective in certain aspects, all these approaches possess inherent limitations. In particular, these approaches have a high possibility of failing to detect threats that fall beyond the scope of well-recognized hardware vulnerabilities and static analysis.

It is apparent that there is a pressing need to look into existing hardware threat modeling approaches and find ways to cover the deficiencies in them. One of the solutions is to adopt generative Artificial Intelligence (AI) and to fuse it with existing approaches. The incorporation of AI technology may introduce a quantum leap in existing hardware threat modeling approaches, increasing their efficiencies and accuracies considerably. By using generative AI as a catalyst in threat modeling, new and subtle threats and vulnerabilities that are not archived in existing databases and are also undetectable by static analysis may be identified. This is because generative AI is capable of self-learning. By feeding it with an extensive amount of datasets, it can then study and recognize patterns and subsequently generate synthetic scenarios that emulate potential attack vectors. In other words, generative AI provides an avenue for threat modeling approaches to iteratively enhance their efficiencies and develop more sturdy countermeasure strategies.

Taking the RISC-V architecture as an example for proof-of concept, this chapter shall delineate how generative AI can be incorporated into current approaches to identify and mitigate threats and vulnerabilities in the hardware framework. Python programming language shall be used as the tool for embedding generative AI into the approaches.

LITERATURE REVIEW

In a paper [1], a study to gauge the impact of few-shot prompting on Codex was conducted. The study made use of the CodeXGLUE code and it incorporated cross-project and same-project datasets. The results strongly suggested that Codex was superior over fine-tuned foundational models such as CodeBERT, CodeT5, GraphCodeBert, *etc.*, in cross-project scenarios. It is worthwhile noting that Codex achieved a 12.56% increase in the BLEU-4 score in comparison with the foundational models.

In a study [2], Khadija, Aziz, and Nurharjadmo proposed an automated approach for information retrieval *via* a chatbot. Their approach classified PDF documents according to characters, headers, and tokens and subsequently stored segmented classes into a Pinecone vector database. The chatbot made use of cosine similarity to evaluate the similarities between the user prompt and document classes within the vector database when responding to users' queries. The efficacy of this approach is convincingly reflected in the measured metrics – it attained a unigram BLEU score of 0.84, a bigram BLEU score of 0.87, and a low negative log-likelihood ratio loss of 0.19.

Zhang *et al.* introduced a customized framework designed for resolving code queries named EcoAssistant [3]. EcoAssistant parsed code compiler outputs, unsuccessful execution traces, and error messages. EcoAssistant utilized various types of Large Language Model (LLM) assistants and implemented a response-reference mechanism—successful queries and responses were saved for future reference. By employing these strategies, the success rate allegedly surpassed that attained by GPT-4 by 10 points.

In another study [4], an expand-guess-refine approach was used to develop an LLM specifically tailored to answer medical-related queries. The USMLE dataset was used in the LLM, and Multiple-Choice Questions (MCQs) were employed in interactions with users. The LLM used zero-shot prompting, and the received document was segmented *via* a recursive text splitter. Its embeddings were saved in the Facebook AI Similarity Search (FAISS) vector database. When providing an answer to a user query, the LLM went through three stages:

i. **Expansion:** In this first stage, the original text is expanded with keywords or points. The enriched texts are then modified into a direct query format.
ii. **Guessing:** The LLM makes predictions based on the retrieved documents.
iii. **Refinement:** In this final stage, the enriched texts, the predicted answers, and the MCQ options are integrated so as to form a final output prompt.

An assessment of the USMLE dataset revealed that the accuracy of the LLM was 70.63%. The figure outperformed ChatGPT, which achieved only 59.44% for the same questions.

Du *et al.* in [5] introduced Tree-GPT as a framework for remote sensing data workflows in the areas pertaining to forestry. Tree-GPT split input data into 4000 tokens per segment, and these tokens were subsequently saved in the Chroma vector database. When attempting to respond to users' queries, the LLM resorted to FAISS to obtain the outcomes. This is then followed by classifying and selecting the data segments in which the similarity threshold exceeded 0.6. The selected data is used to form the final responses. This framework was found to produce accurate responses. Tree-GPT was also capable of providing accurate graphical images and producing basic machine learning codes.

In a paper [6], a comparative analysis was performed to investigate the effectiveness and efficiency of various types of LLMs. The analysis was mainly focused on chain-of-thought and standard promptings. The researchers [6] concluded that the former prompting technique is superior, especially when handling cases related to common sense, arithmetic, and symbolic reasoning. Even so, however, Zhou *et al.* claimed that the prompting approach that they developed was able to supersede the chain-of-thought prompting [7]. The new prompting, named least-to-most prompting, constitutes two stages, as summarized below:

i. **Decomposition:** The prompt provides examples that illustrate how decomposition works. It then asks the user to provide a breakdown of the problem.
ii. **Sub-problem Solving:** In this second stage, solution examples, a list of sub-questions and their corresponding solutions, and the query that requires responses are provided.

The assessment suggested that the least-to-most performed much better than the standard and chain-of-thought prompting methods. In a parallel effort, Wang *et al.* introduced the self-consistency prompting method. Least-to-most prompting is meant to replace the chain-of-thought prompting method. This LLM generated multiple problem-solving pathways, which resulted in different final answers. The final solution given to the user is chosen based on the one with the most consistent answer.

METHODOLOGY

LLMs such as ChatGPT and Perplexity come in handy when a user requires solutions to tackle different situations. Some of the features that LLMs are capable of performing include writing emails and codes, such as algorithms written in C, C++, MATLAB, or Python programming languages and Verilog or System Verilog Hardware Description Language (HDL) and VHDL. Unfortunately, they have their own constraints as well – their efficacy in solving a problem is rather domain-specific. To cope with this limitation, the LLM can either be trained to cater to a specific domain from scratch or a pre-trained LLM can be fed with domain-specific data [9]. The former modus operandi is usually less popular since it is rather costly [10]. Hence, the research work described in this chapter employs the latter approach, *i.e.*, a pre-trained LLM is leveraged with RISC-V-specific data. In this case, the retrieve, augment, and generate or RAG methodology is manipulated to improve the LLMs [11].

Fig. (**1**) graphically depicts the project methodology. In essence, this project can be categorized into two stages – the preparation and stage detection stages. In the preparation stage, the source code for an architecture is analyzed; in the threat detection stage, the architecture specification is processed in PDF format. Doing so, the project aims to identify stubborn and hard-to-detect vulnerable source codes, compile them, and produce the compiled result as the final output.

Preparation

In the initial stage, the input is extracted from a repository, which consists of the Register Transfer Level (RTL) source code pertaining to the architecture. In order to break the files into smaller chunks, the RecursiveCharacterTextSplitter module from the Python LangChain library is used. The segmented file is saved into the PostgreSQL vector database, as shown in Fig. (**2**). The segments are encapsulated as embeddings. The step to encapsulate the segments is important because the embeddings serve as numerical representations of words, sentences, or documents. The embeddings, therefore, allow easier understanding of the LLMs. Here, the text-embedding-ada-002 model is utilized to generate these embeddings.

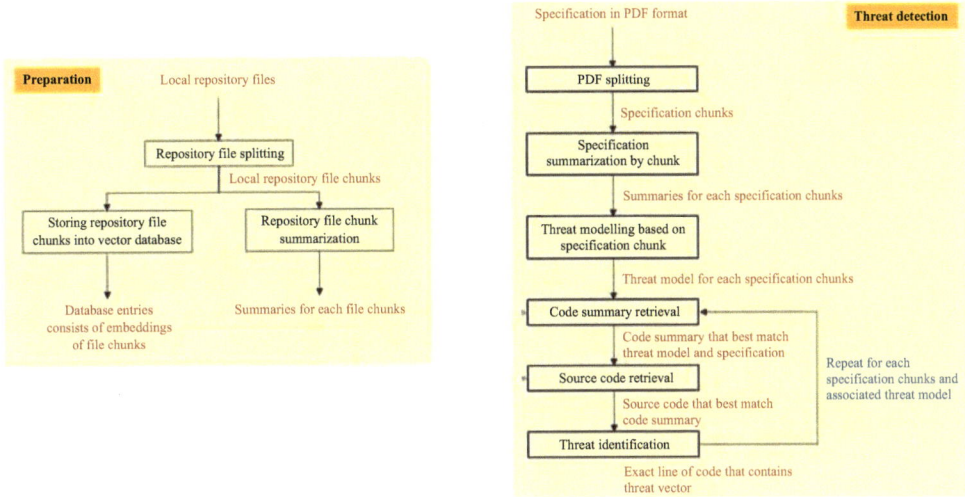

Fig. (1). Methodology for domain-specific LLM augmentation.

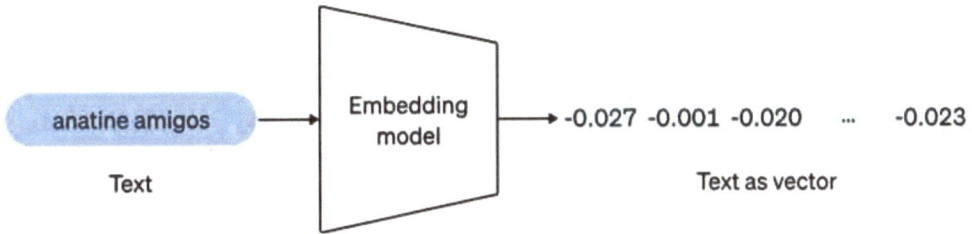

Fig. (2). Illustration of Text-to-Vector Conversion by the Embedding Model.

To provide the convenience of future references, the file segments are concised into one-sentence summaries. The python source code for generating the one-sentence summaries and an example of the one-sentence summary are shown in Figs. (**3 and 4**), respectively. The summarization process is performed using the StuffDocumentsChain module from Python LangChain.

```
prompt_template = """Summarize the code below into one sentence
according to RISC-V architecture:
"{chunk}"
CONCISE SUMMARY:"""
```

Fig. (3). Example prompt used for generating summaries.

```
`include "config.sv"
`include "constants.sv"

module adder #(
    parameter  WIDTH = 1
) (
    input  [WIDTH-1:0] operand_a,
    input  [WIDTH-1:0] operand_b,
    output [WIDTH-1:0] result
);

    assign result = operand_a + operand_b;

endmodule
```

(a)

```
This code defines a module in the RISC-V architecture that
performs addition on two operands and outputs the result.
```

(b)

Fig. (4). (a) Original code snippet summarized by the LLM into a single sentence in **(b)**.

In an RAG-based LLM application, the original query is combined with the document chunk retrieved from the database and passed to the LLM for generating the response [4]. However, it must be noted that if the prompt length is longer than the token limit, the LLM will fail to answer the question [12].

As the prompt serves as an instruction to the LLM, it has a significant impact on the output generated by the LLM. In particular, the prompt provides rules and guidelines to the LLM by setting the context of the conversation to control the output generated [13]. Therefore, it is important to craft the prompt according to application needs to get the most out of the LLM.

Threat Detection

In the threat detection stage, the architectural specification in PDF format is consumed and split into chunks using RecursiveCharacterTextSplitter from Python LangChain. The threat vectors for each specification chunk are then identified with the help of LLM. The LLM used here is the gpt-35-turbo- 16k-0613 model offered by Azure OpenAI. Compared to baseline LLM, this model offers up to 16,385 tokens in a single request [14]. This is needed to accommodate the use case here where the LLM needs to consume some code in the prompt while still needing some token for returning the response. Fig. (5) describes the prompt used for threat detection.

```
messages = [{"role": "system",
             "content": f"You are a helpful assistant that "
                        f"help to identify security threat "
                        f"from sections specification "
                        f"provided. To be more precise, "
                        f"the specification provided is "
                        f"RISC-V specification. Here is the "
                        f"specification: "
                        f"{chunk}"
                        f"Provide only threat vectors in a "
                        f"numbered list in your answer. "
                        f"Do not include anything else, not "
                        f"even some general statement or "
                        f"suggestion."}]
```

Fig. (5). Example prompt used for threat detection model.

Once the threat vectors are identified, together with the specification chunk, the LLM will select the most relevant code summary from the list of code summaries generated earlier. This task is performed using the gpt-35-turbo-16k-0613 model by the LLM. The prompt related to this process is illustrated in Fig. (**6**).

```
messages = [{"role": "system",
             "content": f"Given a summary of a section of "
                        f"RISC-V specification and the "
                        f"associated threat vector, pick "
                        f"and return the most relevant code "
                        f"summary from a list of summaries "
                        f"given."
                        f"[Specification]: {spec}"
                        f"[Associated threats]: {threat}"
                        f"[Code summaries]: {summaries}"}]
```

Fig. (6). Prompt example for selecting relevant code summary.

The chosen code summary is used to extract the most relevant source code from the vector database. This is achieved by utilizing the PGVector library in Python LangChain. PGVector is an extension for Postgres that allows for vector similarity search within the database. It retrieves the source code that best matches the description provided by the one-line summary, leveraging the earlier stored embeddings.

Afterward, the LLM (Language Model) is instructed to identify the vulnerable line of code based on the identified threat vectors and specifications. In this process, the gpt-35-turbo-16k-0613 model is employed as the LLM. The corresponding prompt can be seen in Fig. (**7**).

```
messages = [{"role": "system",
             "content": f"You are a helpful assistant that "
                        f"help to pinpoint the line of code "
                        f"that is vulnerable according to "
                        f"the threat vectors provided. Tell "
                        f"the exact line that is vulnerable."
                        f"[Source code]: {code}"
                        f"[Threat]: {threat}"}]
```

Fig. (7). Prompt example for identifying vulnerable code lines.

PREPARATION OF TEST DATA

The inputs of the system are the RISC-V source code and specification, as previously indicated. The source code employed in this endeavor is derived from the GitHub repository: https://github.com/tilk/riscv-simple-sv. The specification conforms to the RISC-V Unprivileged ISA version 20191213. To ensure comprehensive threat detection, existing threat vectors within the source code are initially identified through manual inspection. Moreover, new threat vectors are intentionally introduced into the code for detection by this project.

Analysis of Test Data

The code excerpts displayed in Figs. (8-13) bring attention to potential threats identified in a variety of SystemVerilog files, which include adder.sv, regfile.sv, data_memory_interface.sv, example_data_memory.sv, control_transfer.sv, and singlecycle_datapath.sv.

The adder module in adder.sv, as shown in Fig. (8), exposes a vulnerability in Line 14 where it fails to handle overflow situations. This omission leaves the module susceptible to exploitation and may lead to inaccurate outcomes.

Fig. (9) illustrates that Line 28 of the regfile module in regfile.sv permits write operations to the register file without any form of validation or limitations. This poses a significant threat as it exposes the system to potential control flow manipulation or unauthorized access to sensitive data.

In Fig. (10), Line 24 of the data_memor_interface module in data_memory_interface.sv directly connects the input address to the output bus_address without any validation, posing a risk of unauthorized memory access. Moreover, Line 27 is open to potential data corruption or manipulation due to memory store instructions.

```systemverilog
01 `include "config.sv"
02 `include "constants.sv"
03
04 module adder #(
05     parameter  WIDTH = 32
06 ) (
07     input  [WIDTH-1:0] operand_a,
08     input  [WIDTH-1:0] operand_b,
09     output [WIDTH-1:0] result
10 );
11
12     assign result = operand_a + operand_b;
13
14 endmodule
```

Fig. (8). Excerpt of adder.sv code highlighting vulnerability in overflow handling.

```systemverilog
01 `include "config.sv"
02 `include "constants.sv"
03
04 module regfile (
05     input  clock,
06     input  write_enable,
07     input  [4:0] rd_address,
08     input  [4:0] rs1_address,
09     input  [4:0] rs2_address,
10     input  [31:0] rd_data,
11     output [31:0] rs1_data,
12     output [31:0] rs2_data
13 );
14
15     // 32 registers of 32-bit width
16     logic [31:0] register [0:31];
17
18     // Read ports for rs1 and rs2
19     assign rs1_data = register[rs1_address];
20     assign rs2_data = register[rs2_address];
21
22     // Register x0 is always 0
23     initial register[0] = 32'b0;
24
25     // Write port for rd
26     always_ff @(posedge clock)
27         if (write_enable)
28             if (rd_address != 5'b0)
register[rd_address] <= rd_data;
29
30 endmodule
```

Fig. (9). Vulnerability in write operation handling within regfile.sv.

```
01  `include "config.sv"
02  `include "constants.sv"
03
04  module data_memory_interface (
05      input   clock,
06      input   read_enable,
07      input   write_enable,
08      input   [2:0]  data_format,
09      input   [31:0] address,
10      input   [31:0] write_data,
11      output  [31:0] read_data,
12
13      output         [31:0] bus_address,
14      input          [31:0] bus_read_data,
15      output         [31:0] bus_write_data,
16      output logic   [3:0]  bus_byte_enable,
17      output                bus_read_enable,
18      output                bus_write_enable
19  );
20
21      logic [31:0] position_fix;
22      logic [31:0] sign_fix;
23
24      assign bus_address       = address;
25      assign bus_write_enable = write_enable;
26      assign bus_read_enable  = read_enable;
27      assign bus_write_data    = write_data << (8*address[1:0]);
28
29      // calculate byte enable
30      always_comb begin
31          bus_byte_enable = 4'b0000;
32          case (data_format[1:0])
33              2'b00:  bus_byte_enable = 4'b0001 <<
address[1:0];
34              2'b01:  bus_byte_enable = 4'h0011 <<
address[1:0];
35              2'b10:  bus_byte_enable = 4'b1111 <<
address[1:0];
36              default: bus_byte_enable = 4'b0000;
37          endcase
38      end
39
40      // correct for unaligned accesses
41      always_comb begin
42          position_fix = bus_read_data >> (8*address[1:0]);
43      end
44
45      // sign-extend if necessary
46      always_comb begin
47          case (data_format[1:0])
48              2'b00:  sign_fix = {{24{~data_format[2] &
position_fix[7]}}, position_fix[7:0]};
49              2'b01:  sign_fix = {{16{~data_format[2] &
position_fix[15]}}, position_fix[15:0]};
50              2'b10:  sign_fix = position_fix[31:0];
51              default: sign_fix = 32'bx;
52          endcase
53      end
54
55      assign read_data = sign_fix;
56
57  endmodule
```

Fig. (10). Lack of validation in address assignment in data_memory_interface.sv.

In Fig. (**11**), Line 16 of the example_data_memory module located in example_data_memory.sv makes use of the memory array mem by utilizing the address input, which can potentially create vulnerabilities if the address is not correctly aligned.

```
01 `include "config.sv"
02 `include "constants.sv"
03
04 module example_data_memory (
05    input [`DATA_BITS-3:0] address,
06    input [3:0] byteena,
07    input clock,
08    input [31:0] data,
09    input wren,
10    output [31:0] q
11 );
12
13      (* nomem2reg *)
14      logic [31:0] mem[0:2**(`DATA_BITS-2)-1];
15
16      assign q = mem[address];
17
18      always_ff @(posedge clock)
19          if (wren) begin
20              if (byteena[0]) mem[address][0+:8] <=
data[0+:8];
21              if (byteena[1]) mem[address][8+:8] <=
data[8+:8];
22              if (byteena[2]) mem[address][16+:8] <=
data[16+:8];
23              if (byteena[3]) mem[address][24+:8] <=
data[24+:8];
24          end
25
26 `ifdef DATA_HEX
27      initial $readmemh(`DATA_HEX, mem);
28 `endif
29
30 endmodule
```

Fig. (11). Potential vulnerability in memory access alignment within example_data_memory.sv.

In Fig. (**12**), Lines 10 to 19 within the control_transfer module in control_transfer.sv are responsible for making branch decisions based on the values of inst_funct3. An issue may occur if inst_funct3 does not align with the specified constants, resulting in unpredictable behavior.

```
01  `include "config.sv"
02  `include "constants.sv"
03
04  module control_transfer (
05      input        result_equal_zero,
06      input [2:0]  inst_funct3,
07      output logic take_branch
08  );
09
10      always_comb
11          case (inst_funct3)
12              `FUNCT3_BRANCH_EQ:  take_branch
= !result_equal_zero;
13              `FUNCT3_BRANCH_NE:  take_branch =
result_equal_zero;
14              `FUNCT3_BRANCH_LT:  take_branch
= !result_equal_zero;
15              `FUNCT3_BRANCH_GE:  take_branch =
result_equal_zero;
16              `FUNCT3_BRANCH_LTU: take_branch
= !result_equal_zero;
17              `FUNCT3_BRANCH_GEU: take_branch =
result_equal_zero;
18              default: take_branch = 1'bx;
19          endcase
20
21  endmodule
```

Fig. (12). Risk of unauthorized jumps in control_transfer.sv due to default case handling.

Lines 65 to 69 of the singlecycle_datapath module in singlecycle_datapath.sv, as depicted in Fig. (**13**), pose a vulnerability. This vulnerability arises from the execution of addition operations that involve immediate values. Consequently, it opens up the possibility of manipulation and alteration of control flow.

```systemverilog
001  `include "config.sv"                                081  ) mux_next_pc_select (
002  `include "constants.sv"                             082      .in0 (pc_plus_4),
003                                                       083      .in1 (pc_plus_immediate),
004  module singlecycle_datapath (                       084      .in2 ({alu_result[31:1], 1'b0}),
005      input  clock,                                    085      .in3 (32'b0),
006      input  reset,                                    086      .sel (next_pc_select),
007                                                       087      .out (next_pc)
008      input  [31:0] data_mem_read_data,               088  );
009      output [31:0] data_mem_address,                 089
010      output [31:0] data_mem_write_data,              090  multiplexer2 #(
011                                                       091      .WIDTH(32)
012      input  [31:0] inst,                              092  ) mux_operand_a (
013      output [31:0] pc,                                093      .in0 (rs1_data),
014                                                       094      .in1 (pc),
015      output [6:0] inst_opcode,                        095      .sel (alu_operand_a_select),
016      output [2:0] inst_funct3,                        096      .out (alu_operand_a)
017      output [6:0] inst_funct7,                        097  );
018      output alu_result_equal_zero,                    098
019                                                       099  multiplexer2 #(
020      // control signals                               100      .WIDTH(32)
021      input pc_write_enable,                           101  ) mux_operand_b (
022      input regfile_write_enable,                      102      .in0 (rs2_data),
023      input alu_operand_a_select,                      103      .in1 (immediate),
024      input alu_operand_b_select,                      104      .sel (alu_operand_b_select),
025      input [2:0] reg_writeback_select,               105      .out (alu_operand_b)
026      input [1:0] next_pc_select,                      106  );
027      input [4:0] alu_function                         107
028  );                                                   108  multiplexer8 #(
029                                                       109      .WIDTH(32)
030      // register file inputs and outputs              110  ) mux_reg_writeback (
031      logic [31:0] rd_data;                            111      .in0 (alu_result),
032      logic [31:0] rs1_data;                           112      .in1 (data_mem_read_data),
033      logic [31:0] rs2_data;                           113      .in2 (pc_plus_4),
034      logic [4:0]  inst_rd;                            114      .in3 (immediate),
035      logic [4:0]  inst_rs1;                           115      .in4 (32'b0),
036      logic [4:0]  inst_rs2;                           116      .in5 (32'b0),
037                                                       117      .in6 (32'b0),
038      // program counter signals                       118      .in7 (32'b0),
039      logic [31:0] pc_plus_4;                          119      .sel (reg_writeback_select),
040      logic [31:0] pc_plus_immediate;                 120      .out (rd_data)
041      logic [31:0] next_pc;                            121  );
042                                                       122
043      // ALU signals                                   123  register #(
044      logic [31:0] alu_operand_a;                      124      .WIDTH(32),
045      logic [31:0] alu_operand_b;                      125      .INITIAL(`INITIAL_PC)
046      logic [31:0] alu_result;                         126  ) program_counter(
047                                                       127      .clock         (clock),
048      // immediate                                     128      .reset         (reset),
049      logic [31:0] immediate;                          129      .write_enable  (pc_write_enable),
050                                                       130      .next          (next_pc),
051      // memory signals                                131      .value         (pc)
052      assign data_mem_address    = alu_result;        132  );
053      assign data_mem_write_data = rs2_data;          133
054                                                       134  regfile regfile(
055      adder #(                                         135      .clock         (clock),
056          .WIDTH(32)                                   136      .write_enable  (regfile_write_enable),
057      ) adder_pc_plus_4 (                              137      .rd_address    (inst_rd),
058          .operand_a  (32'h004),                       138      .rs1_address   (inst_rs1),
059          .operand_b  (pc),                            139      .rs2_address   (inst_rs2),
060          .result     (pc_plus_4)                      140      .rd_data       (rd_data),
061      );                                               141      .rs1_data      (rs1_data),
062                                                       142      .rs2_data      (rs2_data)
063      adder #(                                         143  );
064          .WIDTH(32)                                   144
065      ) adder_pc_plus_immediate (                      145  instruction_decoder instruction_decoder(
066          .operand_a  (pc),                            146      .inst          (inst),
067          .operand_b  (immediate),                     147      .inst_opcode   (inst_opcode),
068          .result     (pc_plus_immediate)             148      .inst_funct7   (inst_funct7),
069      );                                               149      .inst_funct3   (inst_funct3),
070                                                       150      .inst_rd       (inst_rd),
071      alu alu(                                         151      .inst_rs1      (inst_rs1),
072          .alu_function       (alu_function),          152      .inst_rs2      (inst_rs2)
073          .operand_a          (alu_operand_a),         153  );
074          .operand_b          (alu_operand_b),         154
075          .result             (alu_result),           155  immediate_generator immediate_generator(
076          .result_equal_zero  (alu_result_equal_zero) 156      .inst          (inst),
077      );                                               157      .immediate     (immediate)
078                                                       158  );
079      multiplexer4 #(                                  159
080          .WIDTH(32)                                   160  endmodule
```

Fig. (13).   Vulnerable addition operation handling in singlecycle_datapath.sv.

Threat Vectors Injection

The ALU.sv System Verilog source code has been manipulated to introduce a threat by modifying lines 39 to 50, as shown in Fig. (**14**). The alterations made to the code involve eliminating the checks for division by zero, consequently leading to the creation of vulnerabilities, as depicted in Fig. (**15**).

```
04 module alu (
05     input          [4:0]  alu_function,
06     input signed [31:0] operand_a,
07     input signed [31:0] operand_b,
08     output logic [31:0] result,
09     output               result_equal_zero
10 );
11
12     ifdef M_MODULE
13         logic [63:0] signed_multiplication;
14         logic [63:0] unsigned_multiplication;
15         logic [63:0] signed_unsigned_multiplication;
16     endif
17
18     assign result_equal_zero = (result == 32'd0);
19
20     always_comb begin
21         result = 'ZERO;
22         case (alu_function)
23             'ALU_ADD:   result = operand_a +   operand_b;
24             'ALU_SUB:   result = operand_a -   operand_b;
25             'ALU_SLL:   result = operand_a <<  operand_b[4:0];
26             'ALU_SRL:   result = operand_a >>  operand_b[4:0];
27             'ALU_SRA:   result = operand_a >>> operand_b[4:0];
28             'ALU_SEQ:   result = {31'b0, operand_a == operand_b};
29             'ALU_SLT:   result = {31'b0, operand_a < operand_b};
30             'ALU_SLTU:  result = {31'b0, $unsigned(operand_a) <
$unsigned(operand_b)};
31             'ALU_XOR:   result = operand_a ^   operand_b;
32             'ALU_OR:    result = operand_a |   operand_b;
33             'ALU_AND:   result = operand_a &   operand_b;
34     ifdef M_MODULE
35             'ALU_MUL:   result = signed_multiplication[31:0];
36             'ALU_MULH:  result = signed_multiplication[63:32];
37             'ALU_MULHSU:    result = signed_unsigned_multiplication[63:32];
38             'ALU_MULHU: result = unsigned_multiplication[63:32];
39             'ALU_DIV:
40                 if (operand_b == 'ZERO)
41                     result = 32'b1;
42                 else if ((operand_a == 32'h80) && (operand_b == 32'b1))
43                     result = 32'h80;
44                 else
45                     result = operand_a / operand_b;
46             'ALU_DIVU:
47                 if (operand_b == 'ZERO)
48                     result = 32'b1;
49                 else
50                     result = $unsigned(operand_a) / $unsigned(operand_b);
51             'ALU_REM:
52                 if (operand_b == 'ZERO)
53                     result = operand_a;
54                 else if ((operand_a == 32'h80) && (operand_b == 32'b1))
55                     result = 'ZERO;
56                 else
57                     result = operand_a % operand_b;
58             'ALU_REMU:
59                 if (operand_b == 'ZERO)
60                     result = operand_a;
61                 else
62                     result = $unsigned(operand_a) % $unsigned(operand_b);
63     endif
64             default:
65                 result = 'ZERO;
66         endcase
67     end
68
69     ifdef M_MODULE
70         always_comb begin
71             signed_multiplication   = operand_a * operand_b;
72             unsigned_multiplication = $unsigned(operand_a) * $unsigned(operand_b);
73             signed_unsigned_multiplication = $signed(operand_a) *
$unsigned(operand_b);
74         end
75     endif
76
77 endmodule
```

Fig. (14). Original ALU.sv SystemVerilog Source Code.

```
`ALU_DIV:
      result = operand_a / operand_b;
`ALU_DIVU:
      result = $unsigned(operand_a) /
$unsigned(operand_b);
```

Fig. (15). Modified ALU.sv source code highlighting vulnerabilities introduced through threat injection.

RESULTS AND DISCUSSION

Table **1** displays the identified threats in the source code along with the corresponding detection results. A total of 11 threats are identified in the source code, comprising both inherent vulnerabilities and injected threats. Among these, eight threats are accurately detected. However, one of the detected threats (threat #4) is deemed invalid since the flagged code is located within a testbench, which does not constitute a threat vector within the architecture. Additionally, one injected threat remains undetected, while another is successfully identified. This underscores a limitation of the tool in detecting threats beyond those explicitly outlined in the specification. Overall, the detected threat vectors yield an accuracy rate of 81.82% (nine out of 11 threats detected are correct).

Table 1. Test result.

No.	Line of Code	Detected/Not Detected	Valid/Invalid Threat
1	assign result = operand_a + operand_b;	Detected	Valid threat
2	if (rd_address != 5'b0) register[rd_address] <= rd_data;	Detected	Valid threat
3	assign inst_opcode = inst[6:0];	Detected	Valid threat
4	jalr t0, t1, 0	Detected	Invalid threat. This line of code is in a testbench which is irrelevant for threat detection.
5	assign bus_address = address;	Detected	Valid threat
6	`assign bus_write_data = write_data << (8*address[1:0]);`	Detected	Valid threat
7	assign q = mem[address];	Detected	Valid threat

(Table 1) cont.....

No.	Line of Code	Detected/Not Detected	Valid/Invalid Threat
8	`always_comb case (inst_funct3) `FUNCT3_BRANCH_EQ: take_branch = !result_equal_zero; `FUNCT3_BRANCH_NE: take_branch = result_equal_zero; `FUNCT3_BRANCH_LT: take_branch = !result_equal_zero; `FUNCT3_BRANCH_GE: take_branch = result_equal_zero; `FUNCT3_BRANCH_LTU: take_branch = !result_equal_zero; `FUNCT3_BRANCH_GEU: take_branch = result_equal_zero; default: take_branch = 1'bx; endcase	Detected	Valid threat
9	result = operand_a / operand_b;	Detected	Valid threat
10	result = $unsigned(operand_a) / $unsigned(operand_b);	Not detected	Valid threat
11	`adder_pc_plus_immediate ( .operand_a (pc), .operand_b (immediate), .result (pc_plus_immediate) );`	Detected	Valid threat

CONCLUSION

At the conclusion of this project, a command line interface enabling users to input local repository paths and specification document paths has been developed. This project is equipped with the capability to preprocess inputs to generate threat vectors. During testing with test data, the tool successfully detected a total of 11 threat vectors, with nine of them confirmed as valid threats. Among these threat vectors, two were injected into the source code in addition to those inherent to it. However, the tool exhibited inconsistent performance when detecting threat vectors not explicitly documented in the specification, only identifying one out of two artificial threat vectors. Nonetheless, the tool's accuracy of 81.82% surpasses the expected 75% accuracy outlined in the project objectives. In summary, both objectives of the project have been achieved successfully.

Throughout the course of this project, individual threat vectors have been identified for each file or section of the specification without taking into account the interactions and relationships between all components within the architecture. However, it is often the interactions between components that play a crucial role in determining the presence of a threat vector. To enhance future iterations, it is advised to include an analysis of the data flow between multiple source code files during threat modeling. This could entail the implementation of an extra phase to identify the files associated with a particular file and evaluate their interactions using LLM prior to conducting threat modeling.

Moreover, the results of the testing phase indicated that the tool exhibited subpar performance in detecting artificial threat vectors. This deficiency could be attributed to the initial identification of threat vectors solely based on the specification before the tool identifies the faulty code. In scenarios where threat vectors are not explicitly outlined in the documentation, the tool may encounter challenges in detecting them. To tackle this issue, it is suggested to introduce an additional phase dedicated to identifying threat vectors by scrutinizing the source code itself.

REFERENCES

[1]   T. Ahmed, and P. Devanbu, "Few-shot training LLMs for project-specific code-summarization", *Proceedings of the 37th IEEE/ACM International Conference on Automated Software Engineering,* pp. 1-5, 2022.

[2]   M.A. Khadija, A. Aziz, and W. Nurharjadmo, "Automating information retrieval from faculty guidelines: Designing a PDF-driven chatbot powered by OpenAI ChatGPT", *IEEE International Conference on Computer, Control, Informatics and its Applications,* pp. 394-399, 2023. [http://dx.doi.org/10.1109/IC3INA60834.2023.10285808]

[3]   J. Zhang, R. Krishna, A.H. Awadallah, and C. Wang, "EcoAssistant: Using LLM assistant more affordably and accurately", arXiv preprint arXiv:2310.03046, 2023.

[4]   S. Manathunga, and I. Hettigoda, "Aligning large language models for clinical tasks", arXiv preprint arXiv:2309.02884, 2023.

[5]   S.Q. Du, S.J. Tang, W.X. Wang, X.M. Li, and R.Z. Guo, "Tree-GPT: Modular large lanaguage model expert system for forest remote sensing image understanding and interactive analysis", *Int. Arch. Photogramm. Remote Sens. Spat. Inf. Sci,* vol. XLVIII-1/W2-2023, pp. 1729-1736, 2023. [http://dx.doi.org/10.5194/isprs-archives-XLVIII-1-W2-2023-1729-2023]

[6]   J. Wei, X. Wang, D. Schuurmans, M. Bosma, F. Xia, E. Chi, Q.V. Le, and D. Zhou, "Chain-of-thought prompting elicits reasoning in large language models", *Adv. Neural Inf. Process. Syst.,* vol. 35, pp. 24824-24837, 2022.

[7]   D. Zhou, N. Schärli, I. Hou, J. Wei, N. Scales, X. Wang, D. Schuurmans, C. Cui, O. Bousquet, Q.V. Le, and E.H. Chi, "Least-to-most prompting enables complex reasoning in large language models", *in the 11th International Conference on Learning Representations,* 2022.

[8]   X. Wang, J. Wei, D. Schuurmans, Q. Le, E. Chi, S. Narang, A. Chowdhery, and D. Zhou, "Self-consistency improves chain of thought reasoning in language models", arXiv preprint arXiv:2203.11171, 2022.

[9]   Y. Xie, K. Aggarwal, and A. Ahmad, "Efficient continual pre-training for building domain specific large language models". arXiv preprint arXiv:2311.08545, 2023.

[10] X. Li, Y. Yao, X. Jiang, X. Fang, X. Meng, S. Fan, P. Han, J. Li, L. Du, B. Qin, and Z. Zhang, "Flm-101b: An open llm and how to train it with $100 k budget", arXiv preprint arXiv:2309.03852, 2023.

[11] C. de Souza, J.B. Neto, A. de Souza, T. Gotto, and E. Monteiro, "Lessons from building CodeBuddy:

A contextualized AI coding assistant", arXiv preprint arXiv:2311.18450, 2023.

[12] M.A. Arefeen, B. Debnath, and S. Chakradhar, "Leancontext: Cost-efficient domain-specific question answering using llms", In: *Natural Language Processing Journal*, 2024, p. 100065.

[13] J. White, Q. Fu, S. Hays, M. Sandborn, C. Olea, H. Gilbert, A. Elnashar, J. Spencer-Smith, and D.C. Schmidt, "A prompt pattern catalog to enhance prompt engineering with chatgpt", arXiv preprint arXiv:2302.11382, 2023.

[14] "Azure OpenAI Service models", Available from: https://learn.microsoft.com/en-us/azure/a--services/openai/concepts/models

Fundamentals of Predictive Maintenance Using Machine Learning, Deep Learning, and IoT in Industry 4.0

Sunakshi Mehra[1,*], **Varun Kumar Singh**[1] and **Ashif Ali**[2]

[1] *Galgotias College of Engineering and Technology, Greater Noida, Uttar Pradesh, India*

[2] *Noida Institute of Engineering and Technology, Greater Noida, Uttar Pradesh, India*

Abstract: The term "digital age" refers to the 21st century, characterized by the widespread use of digital platforms for data and information sharing. This era is marked by critical technologies such as sensor networks, Machine Learning (ML), Deep Learning (DL), Predictive Maintenance (PDM), and the Internet of Things (IoT), which are pivotal in driving the Industry 4.0 revolution. Today, industrial operations encompass pre- and post-production, quality control, and supply chain management, all fully automated. Physical tasks are handled by intelligent robots equipped with machine learning capabilities, freeing humans to focus on cognitive activities. These robots perform diverse tasks while real-time sensor networks collect environmental data, ensuring efficient and adaptable industrial operations 3.5. This study aims to highlight the pivotal roles of ML, DL, and IoT within the framework of Industry 4.0, leveraging historical performance data for real-time decision-making. The chapter critically evaluates a multitude of tools, models, protocols, and cutting-edge technologies deployed in Industry 4.0 settings. It identifies areas requiring further investigation and provides recommendations to steer future advancements in Industry 4.0.

Keywords: Deep learning, Internet of Things, Industry 4.0, Machine learning, Predictive maintenance.

INTRODUCTION

The latest industrial revolution is termed Industry 4.0, commonly known as the Industrial Internet of Things (IIoT) and smart manufacturing. It primarily focuses on automation, interconnection, cyber-physical systems, machine learning, and big data [1, 2], as well as smart manufacturing and the Industrial Internet of

* **Corresponding author Sunakshi Mehra:** Galgotias College of Engineering and Technology, Greater Noida, Uttar Pradesh, India; E-mail: mehra.sunakshi623@gmail.com

Tanu Singh, Vinod Patidar, Arvind Panwar & Urvashi Sugandh (Eds.)

Things (IIoT) [3, 4]. Additionally, it incorporates both physical operations and smart procedures that are guided by artificial intelligence and automation. Here, instead of using their bodies to operate industries, people use their intellect. Industry 4.0 has transformed into a cutting-edge production system that ensures efficient output while keeping costs to a minimum. Furthermore, blockchain technology is essential for establishing a safe, interconnected, and competitive environment, facilitating swift societal development. A shift in production away from rural areas and toward urban centers was ushered in with the invention of the steam engine in 1760, starting the first industrial revolution [5, 6].

Trains were the main means of transportation, and coal became the main source of energy. The introduction of combustion engines and the widespread use of oil marked the beginning of the Second Industrial Revolution, which promoted mass manufacturing and quick industrialization [7, 8]. Global industry automation was a result of the Third Industrial Revolution, which began in the 1960s with advances in electronics and information technology [9, 10]. The German government started a project in 2011 that served as the inspiration for Industry 4.0 [11]. The main objectives of this revolution are decentralized decision-making, technology decisions, information transparency, and interconnection.

Computing power, computational resources, cyber-physical systems, and the Internet of Things are driving this change [12]. These advanced technologies enable seamless communication and efficient operations by integrating IoT nodes with cyber-physical infrastructure. In this new era, humans remain essential for monitoring and controlling every operation [13, 14]. Moreover, it enables the real-time detection of any problems with machinery or their early detection to prevent total failure and save maintenance costs [15, 16]. Fig. (**1**) depicts the revolutions in industry. Because 3D printing technology makes product design more efficient, it is a major force behind the Fourth Industrial Revolution. It enables customized manufacturing, enhances flexibility, and promotes ecological sustainability [17 - 19]. Intelligent machinery and automated enterprises rely on smart sensors for their operations. These sensors are crucial components in automated control systems and monitoring devices within the context of Industry 4.0 [20 - 22]. In agriculture, they revolutionize practices by enabling real-time crop monitoring, leading to savings in labor, costs, and time [23]. These sensors are highly accurate in identifying damage and pests, and they are also crucial to irrigation control [24, 25]. However, Industry 4.0 presents several challenges. The most critical factor is security [26 - 28]. Companies can mitigate the burden of higher initial costs by adopting low-cost machinery and equipment designs [29, 30]. Continuous surveillance in some companies raises privacy concerns [31, 32]. The convergence of ML with the IoT has enabled a significant industry shift. Cost containment must be a top priority across all industries without compromising product quality. Human error remains a constant risk in manual industries.

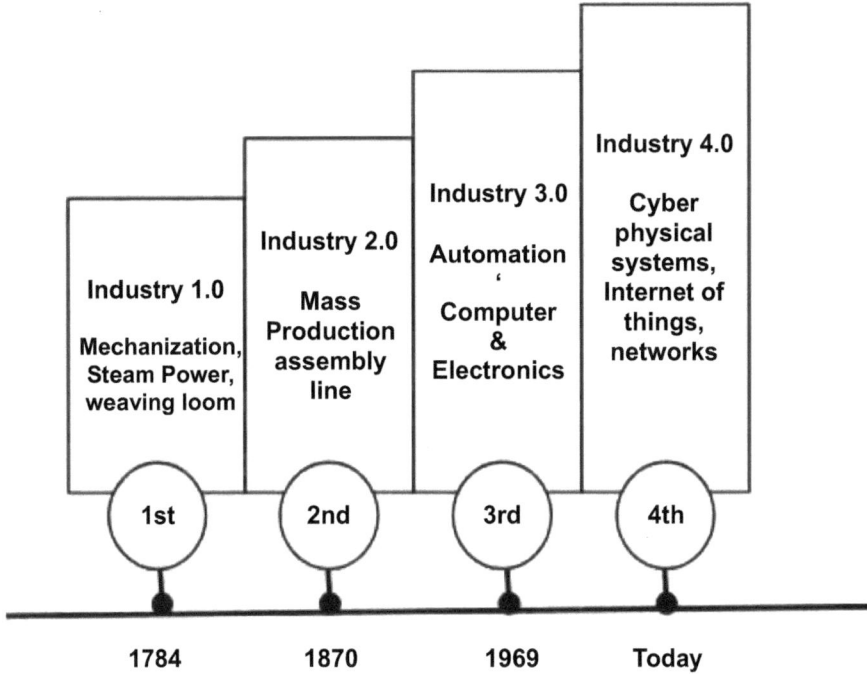

Fig. (1). Revolutions in industry. It illustrates the changes and their primary causes from Industry 1.0 to Industry 4.0.

The integration of ML and IoT devices has elevated system automation to unprecedented levels. Tasks such as post-manufacturing quality checks and equipment maintenance are now efficiently managed by these technologies. IoT sensor nodes monitor product and equipment performance during manufacturing, while machine learning algorithms detect potential anomalies [33]. Moreover, the requirement for human work may be greatly decreased by this automation. Machines have developed into extremely intelligent beings with the capacity to see their environment and make judgments based on past data. IoT devices are used to inspect products after they are manufactured. These devices track and label things, and they frequently contain ML-powered sensors like cameras. Furthermore, AI techniques are combined with IoT sensors and devices. Studies on ML and the Internet of Things (IoT) in the context of Industry 4.0 frequently omit protocols, technology, sensors, and algorithms as they pertain to the IoT [34, 35].

However, review journals often overlook protocols, technologies, sensors, and algorithms relevant to the Internet of Things (IoT) when evaluating research on Machine Learning (ML) to support Industry 4.0. This oversight can hinder academics involved in initial work from pinpointing areas requiring additional research. Our research addresses this gap by focusing on the specific intersection of ML and IoT in Industry 4.0. This book serves as a comprehensive resource that assists researchers in refining their findings and identifying areas for further investigation by contrasting current research on the use of ML and IoT in Industry 4.0. Critically, by highlighting trends and information gaps, the study contributes to the corpus of knowledge. The goal of our research is to determine which sensors, technologies, protocols, and algorithms are most frequently utilized in Industry 4.0 IoT and machine learning applications. This study offers a thorough analysis, examining these components' efficacy and appeal in a range of industrial scenarios.

Section 2 of our study reviews the literature and outlines our article selection process. Our goal is to assess the long-term effects of IoT and ML applications in Industry 4.0 by critically evaluating the most recent research findings and projecting them out over the next twenty to thirty years. We give a detailed description of the protocols used in automated systems in this aspect in Section 3. Important suggestions for future lines of inquiry and possible uses of ML and IoT in Industry 4.0 are provided in Section 4. Finally, our conclusions from this thorough investigation are summarized in Section 5.

LITERATURE REVIEW

This article examines a number of machine learning and Internet of Things research projects, focusing on the potential effects these projects may have on different businesses during the Fourth Industrial Revolution. Additionally, it aims to assist students in discovering a range of employment choices relating to creative disciplines. Numerous studies have thoroughly investigated a range of aspects related to Industry 4.0. As an illustration [36], a thorough examination of the Internet of Things in the context of the fourth industrial revolution was carried out. Their analysis sheds light on the real-world uses, difficulties, and open research questions around Industry 4.0 and IoT. The study also looks at the factors that contributed to Industry 4.0's development and importance. Industry 4.0's ability to collect enormous volumes of data from production and manufacturing processes presents issues for businesses trying to optimize their solutions [37]. A workable solution to these problems is to make use of bio-inspired algorithms, which provide insightful information with less computation and data usage [38].

Using data gathered from sensors, real-time process monitoring makes use of sophisticated computing techniques, including AI, ML, and DL [39]. Technologies associated with Industry 4.0 have a favorable impact on sustainability on a number of levels, including systems, processes, and products [40]. Recent academic attention has focused on 'smart manufacturing', where machines are interconnected *via* wireless networks [41]. This trend highlights the growing reliance on IoT, artificial intelligence, and autonomous vehicles by businesses, employees, and society as a whole. Another analysis discusses cybersecurity threats associated with Industry 4.0 [42], proposing measures to mitigate these risks. The rise of blockchain technology has heightened concerns regarding cybersecurity [43], exploring its applications in Industry 4.0, identifying areas requiring further research, and offering practical examples. Furthermore [44], a study clarified how Industry 4.0, cloud computing, big data, IoT, and cyber-physical systems are integrated, demonstrating how intertwined these elements are in contemporary industrial settings.

Innovation in manufacturing companies is being driven by advancements in Artificial Intelligence (AI), Deep Learning (DL), Blockchain Technology (BT), Cyber-Physical Systems (CPS), Decentralized Manufacturing Systems (DMS), Cloud Computing (CC), and the Internet of Things [45 - 47]. From the extraction of raw materials to the disposal of the product, these technologies allow producers to collect, process, and manage data across the whole product lifecycle [48]. The recent academic focus has shifted toward 'smart manufacturing', involving interconnected machines through wireless networks [49]. This development highlights how industry practices and social reliance are being impacted by the increasing integration of IoT, AI, and other technologies at the system, process, and product levels.

Machine and Deep Learning

Deep learning is a branch of machine learning that focuses on neural network layers and allows large amounts of data to be analyzed at different levels of abstraction [49, 103 - 105]. In recent years, these techniques have significantly enhanced decision-making in manufacturing, as well as capabilities in object detection and speech recognition [50]. DL-based networks offer diverse applications, such as autonomous information processing and predictive maintenance, operating independently of human intervention [51]. Fig. (**2**) shows deep learning and its approaches used in Industrial Revolution 4.0.

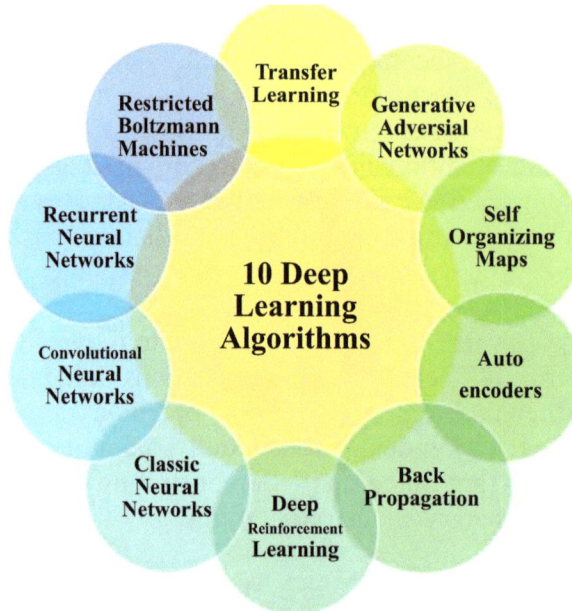

Fig. (2). The methods of deep learning employed in Industrial Revolutions 4.0.

Initially introduced by Frank Rosenblatt in 1957 for basic pattern recognition with two layers, neural networks faced skepticism after MIT researchers in 1969 questioned their ability to learn basic XOR operations, which temporarily dampened research enthusiasm [52, 53]. However, subsequent exploration demonstrated the potential for even a single hidden layer to address any continuous problem, validated by the universal approximation theorem [54]. Despite initial doubts, the effectiveness of DNN algorithms in feature extraction sets them apart from other ML techniques [55]. Multilayer perceptrons, or DNNs, are trained to interpret and evaluate representations from extensive datasets [56]. Their ability to extract insights without manual design makes DL-based techniques crucial in modern manufacturing [57]. The evolution of deep learning has enabled industries to tackle complex nonlinear challenges more efficiently, leveraging advancements in data availability and computing power. According to Vinuesa *et al.* (2020) [58], AI-driven strategies will continue to transform sustainability efforts across the banking, manufacturing, and healthcare sectors [59]. A study demonstrates the growing integration of deep learning algorithms and traditional machine learning within Industry 4.0 frameworks by manufacturing organizations. These systems aim to enhance production efficiency through functions such as predictive maintenance and condition monitoring. Such methods are integral components of data-driven tools designed to simulate intricate interactions between input and output variables in various processes [60]. ML and DL, often discussed in conjunction in the literature, are pivotal for advancing Industry 4.0 [61]. The distinctions and similarities between ML and DL terms have not been thoroughly explored or emphasized in research [62]. Deep learning approaches, more advanced versions of ML algorithms, excel in handling large-scale unstructured data, making them superior for addressing complex challenges [63]. Unlike ML, DL techniques exhibit a hierarchical structure and vary in terms of feature learning, training methods, and model construction [64]. DL techniques streamline model development and feature learning into a single step through end-to-end optimization, involving the selection of multiple kernels or adjustment of input variables and parameters [65].

AI-based tools, such as DL and ML algorithms, are essential for promoting sustainable development and providing direction for future generations in terms of planning and implementation [66]. Modern AI-driven data analytics technology enables industries to reduce waste and carbon emissions while enhancing resource efficiency [67]. Integrating AI improves supply chain sustainability by lowering carbon footprints and increasing operational efficiency [68]. AI-optimized supply chain designs minimize environmental impact by reducing overall mobility and its associated negative effects [69].

Introducing the single relaxation parameter τ [35] the collision operator can be approximated by the following expression [33, 34]:

$$\Omega_i = -\frac{f_i - f_i^{eq}}{\tau} \quad ; \quad i = 0,...,8 \tag{1}$$

where f_i^{eq} is the Equilibrium Distribution Function (EDF). The EDF is expanded around the local velocity [35 - 38] as follows:

$$f_i^{eq} = w_i \rho \left(1 + \frac{1}{c_s^2} (\mathbf{e}_i \cdot \mathbf{v}) + \frac{1}{2c_s^4} (\mathbf{e}_i \cdot \mathbf{v})^2 - \frac{1}{2c_s^2} v^2 \right); \tag{2}$$

Aligned with the United Nations' 2030 sustainability goals, industries are increasingly adopting renewable energy sources despite their efficiency challenges compared to non-renewable alternatives [70]. In order to tackle this challenge, the manufacturing industry is employing Artificial Intelligence (AI) techniques to maximize the effectiveness of renewable energy sources [71], with a particular emphasis on predicting energy output and identifying facility problems [72]. Data-driven technologies are essential in today's industrial environment. Raj *et al.* (2020) [73] emphasize that Industry 4.0's advanced data-driven technologies are fostering innovation and sustainability in a variety of manufacturing sectors.

In this section, we conduct a comprehensive literature review on Internet of Things security and conclude that additional research is necessary to comprehend IoT security in relation to the 4.0 Industrial Revolution.

FRAMEWORKS AND TOOLS

This section provides an overview of significant technology and techniques employed in various studies.

According to a study, the MQTT protocol, also known as MQ Telemetry Transport, is a messaging system designed for devices with limited bandwidth and high latency [74]. MQTT, a publish/subscribe communication protocol, is essential for the Internet of Things and machine-to-machine communication scenarios. It excels particularly on wireless networks where capacity limitations and unstable connections may lead to latency issues. The protocol comprises two primary components: brokers and clients. An intermediary central MQTT broker facilitates the efficient flow of messages from a publisher (client) to a subscriber (client).

CoAP, according to another study [75], is based on the client-server architecture and is stateless. CoAP differs from HTTP in that the former makes use of the request/response technique and then transfers over UDP to relay the message. The protocol follows the principles of REST by making use of URIs for enabling GET, POST, PUT, and DELETE operations. Two layers divide CoAP: the message layer provides message redundancy and consistency, while the request/response layer focuses on managing connectivity and communication. CoAP has four kinds of messages. Firstly, confirmable and non-confirmable are designed differently. Then, acknowledge and reset. A wide and robust key agreement mechanism accompanied by a mutual authentication system is based on XOR, concatenation hashing, Elliptic Curve Cryptography (ECC), and physically Unclonable Functions (PUFs) that form the main support of authentication systems in successful acquisition.

A good system for agreement on keys as well as mutual authentication is based on XOR, concatenation, hashing, Elliptic Curve Cryptography (ECC), and Physically Unclonable Functions (PUFs), which form the cornerstone of robust authentication mechanisms [76]. These two components, when combined, allow for secure data transmission between servers and Internet of Things nodes. The protocol consists of three phases: (i) System Initialization Phase: By using publicly available cryptographic key information, this phase initializes the Internet of Things ecosystem. (ii) Registration Phase: IoT nodes and trustworthy servers begin a secure connection for the purposes of registration. In this step, every IoT node produces multiple identifications as (ID_i), challenge-response pairs as CRPs, and public-private key pairs as and public-private key pairs (PPPs; *Qi, di*), which are generated by each IoT node. (iii) Key Agreement and Mutual Authentication Phase: In this phase, an Internet of Things node (the i-th node) engages with another node (the j-th node) to establish mutual authentication and agree on cryptographic keys.

LoRaWANs, or wide-area networks optimized for long-range communication, allow devices to transmit small data payloads efficiently, conserving battery power [77]. End nodes engage in bidirectional communication with several gateways, transmitting data packets across the network. The network server gathers packets from each gateway, removes duplicates, and forwards processed data to the appropriate application server for sensor data management. When the network server receives replies, it chooses the best gateway to retransmit data to the end computers. This overview encapsulates the operational core of the LoRaWAN technology. As a wireless personal area network, Bluetooth Low Energy (BLE), also referred to as BLE [78], is widely used in home appliances, security, healthcare, and Internet of Things applications. It excels in efficiently transmitting small data packets while minimizing energy consumption. BLE operates with two primary roles: peripherals and central devices, referred to as Slave and Master once connected. Peripherals initiate the connection process by broadcasting advertisement packets to central devices, which can only be initiated by the latter. Upon recognizing advertisements, the central device sends a connection request packet to establish a link. The connection interval defines the duration between data packet transmissions from the Master (formerly the Central) to the Slave.

Advanced Encryption Standard, or AES, is a symmetric block cipher that can use key lengths of 192, 256, or 128 bits [79]. It operates through a series of operations involving byte computations. AES employs ten rounds of operations for 128-bit keys, with each round generating a new key from the original AES key. Every decryption round consists of four subprocesses: Add Round Key, Mix Columns, Shift Rows, and Byte Substitution, all of which are carried out in reverse order. To decrypt the encrypted data and recover the original plaintext, these procedures are sequentially carried out.

Types of Sensors

The two primary parts of high-frequency RFID (Radio Frequency Identification) technology—an RFID reader and an RFID tag—are utilized to track and identify products through the utilization of radio waves [80]. Through its antenna, the reader continuously emits radio waves. A feedback signal is sent by the tag in response to an approaching tag. Inductive coupling, in which the reader's field creates a voltage across the tag's coil, provides the basis for this interaction. The tag's memory and controller are powered by rectified and stored portions of this induced voltage.

Effective object tracking is made possible by the tag's modulation of the load in response to recorded data, which modifies the induced voltage measured by the reader. RFID technology is widely employed in common items and improves supply chain management by speeding up and lowering the cost-effectiveness of decision support systems [81].

LEDs, short for light-emitting diodes, are semiconductor devices centered around a specialized p-n junction diode [82]. They emit light when an electric current passes through them. When the LED is forward-biased, electron-hole recombination at the junction causes this emission. Photons are released when holes in the p-type material are combined with electrons from the n-type material. Light is released as a result of this event.

Raspberry Pi: With integrated Wi-Fi and Bluetooth modules, this tiny, inexpensive single-board computer [83] enables the internet-based transfer of digital data collected and stored in cloud storage. These data can be examined and monitored further as necessary. The Raspberry Pi is capable of engaging with the outside world and carrying out tasks similar to those of a desktop computer. A major surge in its utilization has occurred during the Industry 4.0 revolution. For instance, emphasizes how it is used in the food industry to replace specialized labor and proprietary architectures, handle data security issues, cut costs, and create opportunities for the provision of high-quality food.

A spectrometer [84] is a device used to measure the intensity of radiation across a range of electromagnetic frequencies using wavelengths. It functions by dispersing a light beam into its component colors through a diffraction grating, which is then detected by a sensor. There are various types of spectrometers available, with compact and affordable microspectrometers being particularly popular. These small spectrometers find widespread use across industries such as food safety, color analysis, and agriculture.

Accelerometer: An accelerometer [85] gauges an object's acceleration or vibration forces. Piezoelectric, piezoresistive, and capacitive are some of the types. Piezoresistive ones increase resistance to pressure, while piezoelectric ones use physical stress to measure shock and vibration. The most popular type of accelerometers employ capacitance to measure acceleration. They are useful in motion analysis, fall detection, and activity recognition.

Automated systems extensively utilize machine learning and deep learning techniques to identify patterns in data, enabling informed decision-making. These algorithms are crucial for demand estimation and price forecasting. This section discusses and provides an overview of the algorithms used in recent studies. The details about the methodology and practical applications are also included. The GMDH algorithm uses a network of NNs to produce a self-organizing network from a set of specific input neurons [86]. The entire structure is built towards the output by neurons in the top layer, which convey signals downward. This design adaptively changes the layer count in order to avoid overfitting and increase accuracy. It includes genetic algorithms so that upper-layer neurons can help lower-layer neurons evolve into new configurations.

Pareto multi-objective optimization: When making judgments that need balancing numerous competing goals, achieving one goal sometimes means sacrificing another. Pareto multi-objective optimization finds the optimum trade-offs among several possibilities when no one solution can accomplish all goals [87] without sacrificing some. The approach identifies the ideal answer by evaluating several perspectives to attain the most satisfactory equilibrium among all objectives.

A vital method for tackling significant uncertainty in data tables is Monte Carlo simulation [88]. In industries where achieving precise data is challenging due to multiple contributing factors, it is essential to consider uncertainties when building robust models. Monte Carlo simulation models the probability of various unpredictable outcomes, effectively illustrating the inherent risks and uncertainties in prediction and forecasting models. By iteratively simulating scenarios and introducing random values to unknown variables, Monte Carlo simulation generates insights that enhance the resilience of the model architecture.

The Unscented Kalman Filter (UKF) efficiently optimizes weights to reduce both the average and variability of network errors [89]. It is particularly effective for fine-tuning neuron weights, improving prediction accuracy, and handling nonlinear processes. UKF significantly lowers overall network errors by adjusting error averages and variations. Recent applications include its use in 60 GHz radar systems for person localization and activity monitoring (discussed in Ref [90]). Additionally, UKF has shown superior performance compared to other methods in accurately predicting low-speed induction motor speeds, as shown in a study [91].

Fuzzy logic (FL) technique Fuzzy Logic (FL), which employs linguistic terms for easier comprehension, accommodates values beyond true or false. Through fuzzification, inputs are transformed into fuzzy sets with membership functions that represent degrees of truth, enabling the translation of domain knowledge into measurable values. Using rules applied to these fuzzy sets, an inference engine processes the data and produces crisp values through defuzzification, often employing methods such as Graded Mean Integration. FL finds practical application in agricultural systems; for instance, it can regulate greenhouse conditions for tulip production, as illustrated in a study [92]. LabVIEW and fuzzy logic are employed to adjust irrigation and temperature in response to environmental fluctuations.

The Bird-Mating Optimization (BMO) algorithm [93] draws inspiration from the mating strategy of birds. In this meta-heuristic approach, birds with higher gene quality tend to have longer lifespans compared to those with lower gene quality. Consequently, each bird seeks a superior partner to enhance the genetic strength of their offspring and potentially increase longevity. In the context of the algorithm, bird species represent the search space, and finding a superior mate signifies improved conditions. The algorithm identifies the chick with the highest fitness value, determined by an objective function that evaluates the quality of each brood based on a decision variable.

The Bagged Decision Tree (BDT) [94] employs a bagging technique to reduce the variance of a Decision Tree (DT). It achieves this by dividing the training data into multiple subsets, training distinct decision trees on each subset, and then aggregating their results for predictions. Compared to using a single decision tree, Bayesian Decision Trees (BDT) improve prediction accuracy by averaging outcomes across multiple trees.

OperaBLE is a Bluetooth Low Energy (BLE) wearable designed to improve efficiency in Industry 4.0 settings. As described in the prototype [95], it ensures reliability and sustainability in industrial operations, facilitating interaction between humans and machines. This low-power wearable predicts and prevents potential accidents. Additionally, OperaBLE enhances the performance of fog repositories. At its core, the device features an integrated BLE for efficient data transmission. It employs an algorithm to analyze human movement in workplace environments.

An Artificial Neural Network (ANN) is a computing system engineered to replicate the operations of the human brain [96]. Known for its ability to self-learn, it can produce highly accurate results, especially with large datasets. All of the input and output layers of an ANN are comprised of several interconnected processing units. To train a neural network to produce the expected results based on input attributes, data is fed into these units using a weighted approach. Artificial Neural Networks (ANNs) proficiently reduce errors and improve performance using methods like backpropagation, enabling iterative adjustments to their outputs.

Decision Trees (DT) are among the most effective techniques for addressing classification, decision-making, and predictive challenges [97]. Fig. (**3**) illustrates machine learning and its types.

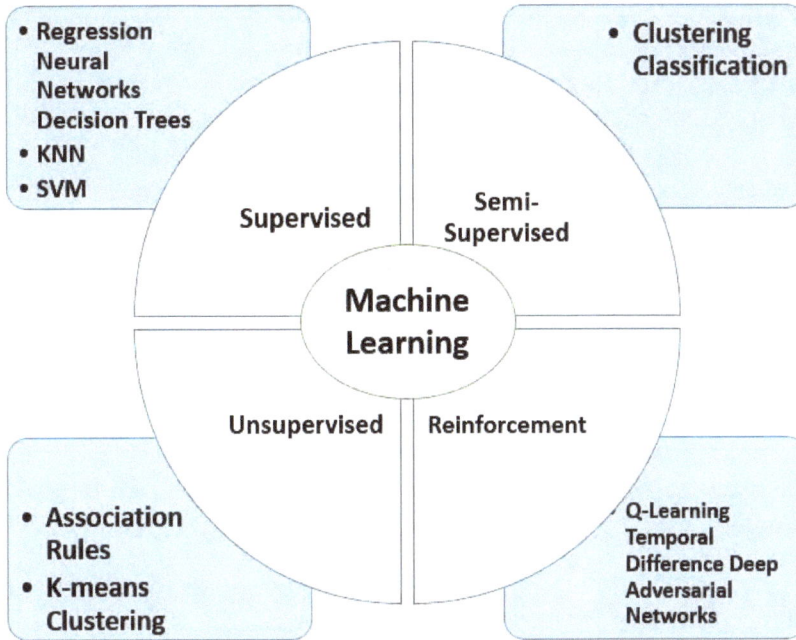

Fig. (3). Machine learning models for use in Industrial applications.

They possess a hierarchical structure in which child nodes or branches originate from a root node according to specific rules or criteria. At each node or decision point, there is a branch that indicates the result of a test that was run using these criteria. This framework allows for clearly explained and transparent decision-making.

A widely used probabilistic machine learning method for classification tasks is Naïve Bayes [98]. It works on the Bayes theorem with naive independence that assumes features in a dataset are unrelated to each other. Naive Bayes is useful in several applications, such as document categorization, sentiment analysis, and spam detection, but this assumption certainly may not hold in reality. The method then assigns the input to the class having the maximum likelihood after calculating the probability of each class with respect to the input features. Naive Bayes is still preferred for many classification problems because of its simplicity, effectiveness, and efficiency.

Another popular supervised machine learning technique used for classification problems is the Support Vector Machine (SVM) [99]. Its objective is to find the border, often known as the decision boundary that separates the n-dimensional space into different classes or classes. In doing so, SVM achieves the correct classification of new points into their target classes. The hyperplane in the role of the decision border is optimal because it maximizes the margin between the classes, hence very effectively structuring and classifying data points. This feature makes SVM particularly good for a lot of classification tasks.

K-Nearest Neighbors, or KNN, is a popular supervised learning machine algorithm to be applied to classification and regression problems [100]. It relies on the fact that data points, which are alike, stand closer to each other.

A distance measure between data points is Euclidean distance. K-Nearest Neighbor, KNN, is a slow, non-parametric learning algorithm that makes no assumptions regarding the distribution of data and requires minimal training. Its applications include flexibility, such as currency rate forecastings, object detections, prediction for the stock market, and credit rating. KNN is quite extensively used for many predictive jobs because it proves to be effective and does not require hard labor.

Random Forest is a very popular and successful supervised algorithm in machine learning that can be used for classification and regression. It forms an ensemble of many decision trees each one of them predicting the class or output. For classification tasks, the class that receives the highest count of votes from all the trees will be selected by the forest. For regression problems, it calculates the average of all predictions produced by each one of the trees. The more trees in the ensemble, the better Random Forest's forecast accuracy and dependability. The adaptability and robustness of Random Forest provide it a favored option for various predictive modeling applications.

The remarkable effectiveness of Convolutional Neural Networks (CNNs) at extracting high-level features from images makes them a popular choice for applications such as object detection and classification [101, 102].

Rectified Linear Unit (ReLU) layers, input, convolutional, pooling, and fully connected layers make up these networks. Important aspects of the image are extracted by the convolutional layers, while the ReLU layers introduce non-linearity [103, 104]. Unlike fully connected layers that utilize the analyzed data to generate class labels through probability assignments, pooling layers diminish the spatial dimensions of the data.

Because of their remarkable effectiveness in image processing tasks, CNNs continue to be widely used in many applications despite their high CPU requirements and need for big datasets during training.

SUGGESTION AND PROSPECTIVE HORIZONS

Industry 4.0 combines state-of-the-art technologies customized for each industry to guarantee safe, effective, and sustainable operations with the least amount of human involvement. Utilizing IoT, machine learning, and sensor networks facilitates automatic cold storage, mitigates risks, and employs predictive algorithms tailored to various industrial requirements. Industry 4.0 is a new approach to current industrial practices that improves quality control, reduces energy consumption, and maximizes output. Industry 4.0 utilizes the advanced technology uniquely created for the sector with which it operates, ensuring efficiency, security, and sustainability with minimal human interaction. The fourth industrial revolution, or Industry 4.0, includes the use of the Internet of Things, machine learning, and sensor networks to help automate cold storage, reduce risk, and solve other industrial problems [105]. Industry 4.0 becomes a transformative power in the development of industrial processes by maximizing output, using less energy, and improving quality control.

1. **Predictive Maintenance:** Machine learning models leverage data from IoT sensors to predict equipment breakdowns before they occur, enabling proactive maintenance and minimizing downtime.
2. **Quality Control**: DL algorithms can inspect products on the assembly line, detecting defects with higher accuracy than human inspection to improve the quality of products.
3. **Supply Chain Optimization:** Machine learning algorithms optimize supply chain efficiency through effective inventory control, precise demand forecasting, and cheaper transportation costs, thus resulting in significant cost savings.
4. **Autonomous Robots:** DL equips the robots to autonomously drive complex tasks such as material handling, assembly, and instantaneous decision-making.
5. **Energy Efficiency:** Machine learning can increase energy usage in manufacturing plants by analyzing patterns and adjusting activities in real time to reduce energy consumption.
6. **Customization and Personalization:** DL allows mass customization by analyzing client data and modifying the production processes for specific needs.
7. **Cyber security:** ML algorithms can detect anomalies and potential cyber threats within interconnected systems, enhancing cybersecurity measures in

smart factories.

8. **Human Machine Interaction**: DL improves safer and easier human-machine interfaces, such as the cooperative robots "cobots," which can work directly with human workers.

9. **Data-driven Insights:** ML and DL algorithms make sense of large data sets created by IoT devices to deliver insights apt for process optimization and decision-making.

10. **Citizen Perception and Citizen Rule:** Citizen rule can further be enhanced by themselves by changing their perception and understanding how the systems should be in relation to them.

Besides the bumps on the ends of production and efficiency, these advances have opened more doors for creative and sustainable manufacturing and industrial processes.

The applications of artificial intelligence in the context of the Fourth Industrial Revolution are illustrated in Fig. (**4**).

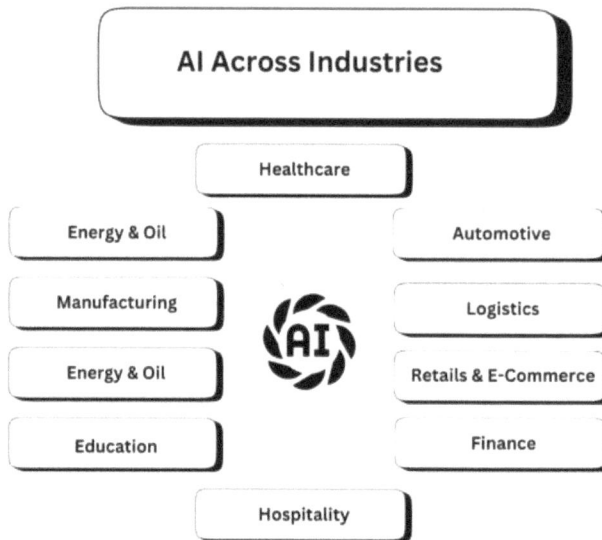

Fig. (4). The Fourth Industrial Revolution and the applications of artificial intelligence.

KEY APPLICATIONS IN THE ERA OF DEEP LEARNING

1. **Manufacturing and Automation:** Deep learning algorithms are used to predict equipment failures by analyzing sensor data. For instance, companies like Siemens and General Electric apply deep learning to detect anomalies in

machine performance, reducing downtime and improving operational efficiency [106]. In industries like automotive manufacturing, deep learning-based image recognition systems are used for inspecting products on assembly lines. For example, Tesla uses deep learning algorithms in its production lines to detect defects in vehicles, ensuring high-quality standards.

2. **Supply Chain Optimization:** Retailers like Walmart and Amazon use deep learning for accurate demand forecasting, optimizing inventory levels and improving supply chain management. The algorithms analyze historical sales data, weather patterns, and consumer behavior to predict future demand with greater precision. Deep learning models are employed to optimize delivery routes for logistics companies such as FedEx and UPS. By analyzing traffic patterns, weather conditions, and other variables, these systems can suggest the most efficient delivery routes, reducing fuel consumption and delivery time.

3. **Healthcare and Medical Diagnostics:** In healthcare, deep learning models are extensively used to analyze medical images like X-rays, MRIs, and CT scans for early detection of diseases such as cancer. Companies like Zebra Medical Vision and Google Health have developed AI systems that assist doctors in diagnosing diseases by detecting anomalies in medical images. Deep learning algorithms analyze patient data (*e.g.*, genetic information, medical history) to recommend personalized treatment plans. IBM's Watson Health is an example of using AI to assist doctors in making more informed treatment decisions based on vast amounts of medical literature and data.

4. **Automotive Industry (Autonomous Vehicles):** Companies like Waymo (a subsidiary of Alphabet) and Tesla are at the forefront of integrating deep learning for autonomous driving. Deep learning models process vast amounts of sensor data (such as LiDAR, radar, and cameras) to enable vehicles to make real-time driving decisions, including navigation, obstacle avoidance, and route optimization.

5. **Retail and Customer Experience:** E-commerce platforms like Amazon, Netflix, and Spotify use deep learning to power their recommendation engines. By analyzing user behavior, preferences, and purchase history, deep learning algorithms provide personalized recommendations, increasing sales and customer satisfaction. Companies like Walmart and Bank of America use AI-powered chatbots to handle customer inquiries. Deep learning-based Natural Language Processing (NLP) allows these systems to understand and respond to customer queries efficiently, reducing the need for human customer service representatives.

These examples showcase how deep learning is revolutionizing a wide range of industries, driving automation, efficiency, and innovation in various sectors.

CONCLUSION

Industry 4.0 is generally known as the smart factory, which increases efficiency and productivity in the production process with minimal errors and lead time and a better way to satisfy the demands of consumers. It needs full automation with the use of machine learning along with the Internet of Things, as it constitutes very essential parts. Major activities of Industry 4.0 include demand forecasting, supply chain optimization, data analysis, and process management that is being performed by machines and otherwise supporting aspects, such as autonomous production and manufacturing, made possible by smart sensors and devices, which in turn allows for automation. Recent research has revealed the growing importance of Machine Learning (ML) and the Internet of Things (IoT) in industrial applications. A few of the highlighted applications of these involved cybersecurity, efficient warehouse operations, proper energy efficiency, and data modeling.

REFERENCES

[1]   H. Lasi, P. Fettke, H.G. Kemper, T. Feld, and M. Hoffmann, "Industry 4.0", *Bus. Inf. Syst. Eng.,* vol. 6, no. 4, pp. 239-242, 2014.
        [http://dx.doi.org/10.1007/s12599-014-0334-4]

[2]   S. Vaidya, P. Ambad, and S. Bhosle, "Industry 4.0 a glimpse", *Procedia Manuf.,* vol. 20, 2018pp. 233-238. 2nd International Conference on Materials, Manufacturing and Design Engineering (iCMMD2017), 11-12 December 2017, MIT Aurangabad, Maharashtra, India. Available from: http://www.sciencedirect.com/science/article/pii/S2351978918300672
        [http://dx.doi.org/10.1016/j.promfg.2018.02.034]

[3]   S. Munirathinam, "Chapter six - industry 4.0: industrial internet of things (iiot), of Advances in Computers", In: *The Digital Twin Paradigm for Smarter Systems and Environments: the Industry Use Cases* in: P. Raj, P. Evangeline (Eds.), Elsevier, 2020, pp. 129-164.
        [http://dx.doi.org/10.1016/bs. adcom.2019.10.010]

[4]   M. McKnight, "IoT, Industry 4.0, Industrial IoT. Why connected devices are the future of design", *KnE Eng.,* vol. 2, no. 1, pp. 197-202, 2017.

[5]   A. Trew, "Spatial takeoff in the first industrial revolution", *Rev. Econ. Dyn.,* vol. 17, no. 4, pp. 707-725, 2014.
        [http://dx.doi.org/10.1016/j.red.2014.01.002]

[6]   Available from: http://www.sci encedirect.com/science/article/pii/S1094202514000039

[7]   N. Crafts, "The first industrial revolution: resolving the slow growth/rapid industrialization paradox", *J. Eur. Econ. Assoc.,* vol. 3, no. 2-3, pp. 525-534, 2005.
        [http://dx.doi.org/10.1162/jeea.2005.3.2-3.525]

[8]   P.J. Atkeson, and Kehoe, "The transition to a new economy after the second industrial revolution", *Working Paper 8676, National Bureau of Economic Research,* 2001.
        [http://dx.doi.org/10.3386/w8676]

[9]   J. Mokyr, and R. H. Strotz, "The second industrial revolution, 1870-1914", *Storia Dell'economia Mondiale,* 1945.

[10]   J. Greenwood, *The Third Industrial Revolution: Technology, Productivity, and Income Inequality, No. 435.* American Enterprise Institute, 1997.

[11]   J. Rifkin, "The third industrial revolution: how the internet, green electricity, and 3-d printing are ushering in a sustainable era of distributed capitalism", *World Fin. Rev.,* vol. 1, no. 1, pp. 4052-4057, 2012.

[12]   C. Fuchs, "Fuchs, Industry 4.0: the digital German ideology", *TripleC,* vol. 16, no. 1, pp. 280-289, 2018.
[http://dx.doi.org/10.31269/triplec.v16i1.1010]

[13]   G. Li, Y. Hou, and A. Wu, "Fourth Industrial Revolution: technological drivers, impacts and coping methods", *Chin. Geogr. Sci.,* vol. 27, no. 4, pp. 626-637, 2017.
[http://dx.doi.org/10.1007/s11769-017-0890-x]

[14]   M. Hermann, T. Pentek, and B. Otto, "Design principles for Industrie 4.0 scenarios", *2016 49th Hawaii Int. Conf. Syst. Sci. (HICSS),* pp. 3928-3937, 2016.
[http://dx.doi.org/10.1109/HICSS.2016.488]

[15]   S. Wang, J. Wan, D. Li, and C. Zhang, "Implementing smart factory of industrie 4.0: an outlook", *Int. J. Distrib. Sens. Netw.,* vol. 12, no. 1, p. 3159805, 2016.
[http://dx.doi.org/10.1155/2016/3159805]

[16]   T. Zonta, C.A. da Costa, R. da Rosa Righi, M.J. de Lima, E.S. da Trindade, and G.P. Li, "Predictive maintenance in the Industry 4.0: A systematic literature review", *Comput. Ind. Eng.,* vol. 150, p. 106889, 2020.
[http://dx.doi.org/10.1016/j.cie.2020.106889]

[17]   Z. Li, K. Wang, and Y. He, Z. Li, K. Wang, and Y. He, "Industry 4.0 - potentials for predictive maintenance", *Proceedings of the 6th International Workshop of Advanced Manufacturing and Automation,* pp. 42-46.
[http://dx.doi.org/10.2991/iwama-16.2016.8]

[18]   S. Chong, G.T. Pan, J. Chin, P.L. Show, T.C.K. Yang, and C.M. Huang, "Integration of 3d printing and industry 4.0 into engineering teaching", *Sustainability (Basel),* vol. 10, no. 11, p. 3960, 2018.
[http://dx.doi.org/10.3390/su10113960]

[19]   M. Niemeläinen, A. Shi, S. Shirowzhan, S. Sepasgozar, and C. Liu, "3D printing architectural freeform elements: challenges and opportunities in manufacturing for Industry 4.0", *Proc. 36th Int. Symp. Autom. Robot. Constr. (ISARC),* M. Al-Hussein (Ed.), Canada, Banff, pp. 1298-1304, 2019.
[http://dx.doi.org/10.22260/ISARC2019/0174]

[20]   A. Schütze, N. Helwig, and T. Schneider, "Sensors 4.0–smart sensors and measurement technology enable Industry 4.0", *Journal of Sensors and Sensor Systems,* vol. 7, no. 1, pp. 359-371, 2018.

[21]   A.G. Frank, L.S. Dalenogare, and N.F. Ayala, "Industry 4.0 technologies: Implementation patterns in manufacturing companies", *Int. J. Prod. Econ.,* vol. 210, pp. 15-26, 2019.
[http://dx.doi.org/10.1016/j.ijpe.2019.01.004]

[22]   Available from: edirect.com/science/article/pii/S0925527319300040

[23]   S. Aheleroff, X. Xu, Y. Lu, M. Aristizabal, J. Pablo Velásquez, B. Joa, and Y. Valencia, "IoT-enabled smart appliances under industry 4.0: A case study", *Adv. Eng. Inform.,* vol. 43, p. 101043, 2020.
[http://dx.doi.org/10.1016/j.aei.2020.101043]

[24]   P. Ferreira, J. Corista, S. Gião, J. Ghimire, R. Sarraipa, and R. Jardim-Gonçalves, "Towards smart agriculture using fiware enablers", *2017 International Conference on Engineering, Technology and Innovation (ICE/ITMC),* pp. 1544-1551, 2017.
[http://dx.doi.org/10.1109/ICE.2017.8280066]

[25]   S. Otles, and A. Sakalli, "15 - industry 4.0: the smart factory of the future in beverage industry", In: *Production and Management of Beverages.,* A.M. Grumezescu, A.M. Holban, Eds., Woodhead Publishing, 2019, pp. 439-469.
[http://dx.doi.org/10.1016/B978-0-12-815260-7.00015-8]

[26]   C. Adley, "Past, present and future of sensors in food production", *Foods,* vol. 3, no. 3, pp. 491-510, 2014.
[http://dx.doi.org/10.3390/foods3030491] [PMID: 28234333]

[27]   M.M. Alani, and M. Alloghani, "Security challenges in the industry 4.0 era", In: *Industry 4.0 and Engineering for a Sustainable Future.* Springer, 2019, pp. 117-136.
[http://dx.doi.org/10.1007/978-3-030-12953-8_8]

[28]   L. Jamai, L.A. Ben Azzouz, and L. Saïdane, *Security issues in industry 4.0, in: 2020 International Wireless Communications and Mobile Computing.* IWCMC, 2020, pp. 481-488.
[http://dx.doi.org/10.1109/IWCMC48107.2020.9148447]

[29]   T. Pereira, L. Barreto, and A. Amaral, "Network and information security challenges within Industry 4.0 paradigm", *Procedia Manuf.,* vol. 13, pp. 1253-1260, 2017.
[http://dx.doi.org/10.1016/j.promfg.2017.09.047]

[30]   B. Albers, T. Gladysz, V. Pinner, T. Butenko, and T. Stärmlinger, "Procedure for defining the system of objectives in the initial phase of an Industry 4.0 project focusing on intelligent quality control systems", *Procedia CIRP,* vol. 52, 2016pp. 262-267 the Sixth International Conference on Changeable, Agile, Reconfigurable and Virtual Production (CARV2016).
[http://dx.doi.org/10.1016/j.procir.2016.07.067]

[31]   D. Sezer, F. Romero, M. Guedea, C. Macchi, and Emmanouilidis, "An Industry 4.0-enabled low cost predictive maintenance approach for SMEs", *2018 IEEE Int. Conf. Eng. Technol. Innov. (ICE/ITMC),* pp. 1-8, 2018.
[http://dx.doi.org/10.1109/ICE.2018.8436307]

[32]   M.M.H. Onik, C. Kim, and J. Yang, "Personal data privacy challenges of the fourth industrial revolution", *2019 21st Int. Conf. Adv. Commun. Technol. (ICACT),* pp. 635-638, 2019.
[http://dx.doi.org/10.23919/ICACT.2019.8701932]

[33]   C. Sadeghi, M. Wachsmann, and M. Waidner, *Security and privacy challenges in industrial internet of things, in: 2015 52nd ACM/EDAC/IEEE Design Automation Conference.* DAC, 2015, pp. 1-6. Available from: https://dl.acm.org/doi/10.1145/2744769.2747942

[34]   M.W. Condry, and C.B. Nelson, "Using smart edge iot devices for safer, rapid response with industry iot control operations", *Proc. IEEE,* vol. 104, no. 5, pp. 938-946, 2016.
[http://dx.doi.org/10.1109/JPROC.2015.2513672]

[35]   N.N. Misra, Y. Dixit, A. Al-Mallahi, M.S. Bhullar, R. Upadhyay, and A. Martynenko, "IoT, big data, and artificial intelligence in agriculture and food industry", *IEEE Internet of Things Journal,* vol. 9, no. 9, pp. 6305-6324, 2022.
[http://dx.doi.org/10.1109/JIOT.2020.2998584]

[36]   Z. Ge, Z. Song, S.X. Ding, and B. Huang, "Data mining and analytics in the process industry: the role of machine learning", *IEEE Access,* vol. 5, pp. 20590-20616, 2017.
[http://dx.doi.org/10.1109/ACCESS.2017.2756872]

[37]   D.C. Villagran-Vizcarra, D. Luviano-Cruz, L.A. Pérez-Domínguez, L.C. Méndez-González, and F. Garcia-Luna, "Applications analyses, challenges and development of augmented reality in education, industry, marketing, medicine, and entertainment", *Appl. Sci. (Basel),* vol. 13, no. 5, p. 2766, 2023.
[http://dx.doi.org/10.3390/app13052766]

[38]   S.B. Kotsiantis, I.D. Zaharakis, and P.E. Pintelas, "Machine learning: a review of classification and combining techniques", *Artif. Intell. Rev.,* vol. 26, no. 3, pp. 159-190, 2006.
[http://dx.doi.org/10.1007/s10462-007-9052-3]

[39]   A.K. Kushwaha, A.K. Kar, and Y.K. Dwivedi, "Applications of big data in emerging management disciplines: A literature review using text mining", *International Journal of Information Management Data Insights,* vol. 1, no. 2, p. 100017, 2021.
[http://dx.doi.org/10.1016/j.jjimei.2021.100017]

[40]   M. Liu, S. Fang, H. Dong, and C. Xu, "Review of digital twin about concepts, technologies, and industrial applications", *J. Manuf. Syst.,* vol. 58, pp. 346-361, 2021.
[http://dx.doi.org/10.1016/j.jmsy.2020.06.017]

[41]   C. Enyoghasi, and F. Badurdeen, "Industry 4.0 for sustainable manufacturing: Opportunities at the product, process, and system levels", *Resour. Conserv. Recycling,* vol. 166, p. 105362, 2021.
[http://dx.doi.org/10.1016/j.resconrec.2020.105362]

[42]   J. Wang, Y. Ma, L. Zhang, R.X. Gao, and D. Wu, "Deep learning for smart manufacturing: Methods and applications", *J. Manuf. Syst.,* vol. 48, pp. 144-156, 2018.
[http://dx.doi.org/10.1016/j.jmsy.2018.01.003]

[43]   J. Prinsloo, S. Sinha, and B. von Solms, "A review of industry 4.0 manufacturing process security risks", *Appl. Sci. (Basel),* vol. 9, no. 23, p. 5105, 2019.
[http://dx.doi.org/10.3390/app9235105]

[44]   M. Javaid, A. Haleem, R. Pratap Singh, S. Khan, and R. Suman, "Blockchain technology applications for Industry 4.0: A literature-based review", *Blockchain: Research and Applications,* vol. 2, no. 4, p. 100027, 2021.
[http://dx.doi.org/10.1016/j.bcra.2021.100027]

[45]   J. H. Kim, "A review of cyber-physical system research relevant to the emerging IT trends: industry 4.0, IoT, big data, and cloud computing", *J. Ind. Integr. Manag.,* vol. 2, no. 03, p. 1750011, 2017.
[http://dx.doi.org/10.1142/S2424862217500117]

[46]   M. Javaid, A. Haleem, R.P. Singh, and R. Suman, "Substantial capabilities of robotics in enhancing industry 4.0 implementation", *Cognitive Robotics,* vol. 1, pp. 58-75, 2021.
[http://dx.doi.org/10.1016/j.cogr.2021.06.001]

[47]   M. Javaid, A. Haleem, R.P. Singh, S. Rab, and R. Suman, "Significance of sensors for industry 4.0: Roles, capabilities, and applications", *Sens. Int.,* vol. 2, p. 100110, 2021.
[http://dx.doi.org/10.1016/j.sintl.2021.100110]

[48]   T. Ahmad, R. Madonski, D. Zhang, C. Huang, and A. Mujeeb, "Data-driven probabilistic machine learning in sustainable smart energy/smart energy systems: Key developments, challenges, and future research opportunities in the context of smart grid paradigm", *Renew. Sustain. Energy Rev.,* vol. 160, p. 112128, 2022.
[http://dx.doi.org/10.1016/j.rser.2022.112128]

[49]   A.M. Ferrari, L. Volpi, D. Settembre-Blundo, and F.E. García-Muiña, "Dynamic life cycle assessment (LCA) integrating life cycle inventory (LCI) and Enterprise resource planning (ERP) in an industry 4.0 environment", *J. Clean. Prod.,* vol. 286, p. 125314, 2021.
[http://dx.doi.org/10.1016/j.jclepro.2020.125314]

[50]   J. Chai, H. Zeng, A. Li, and E.W.T. Ngai, "Deep learning in computer vision: A critical review of emerging techniques and application scenarios", *Mach. Learn. Appl.,* vol. 6, p. 100134, 2021.
[http://dx.doi.org/10.1016/j.mlwa.2021.100134]

[51]   Z. Qin, and Y. Lu, "Self-organizing manufacturing network: A paradigm towards smart manufacturing in mass personalization", *J. Manuf. Syst.,* vol. 60, pp. 35-47, 2021.
[http://dx.doi.org/10.1016/j.jmsy.2021.04.016]

[52]   N. Nikolakis, G. Siaterlis, and K. Alexopoulos, "A machine learning approach for improved shop-floor operator support using a two-level collaborative filtering and gamification features", *Procedia CIRP,* vol. 93, pp. 455-460, 2020.
[http://dx.doi.org/10.1016/j.procir.2020.05.160]

[53]   Y. LeCun, Y. Bengio, and G. Hinton, "Deep learning", *Nature,* vol. 521, no. 7553, pp. 436-444, 2015.
[http://dx.doi.org/10.1038/nature14539]

[54]   Z.Q. Zhao, P. Zheng, S.T. Xu, and X. Wu, "Object detection with deep learning: A review", *IEEE Trans. Neural Netw. Learn. Syst.,* vol. 30, no. 11, pp. 3212-3232, 2019.

[http://dx.doi.org/10.1109/TNNLS.2018.2876865] [PMID: 30703038]

[55]   L. Alzubaidi, J. Zhang, A.J. Humaidi, A. Al-Dujaili, Y. Duan, O. Al-Shamma, J. Santamaría, M.A. Fadhel, M. Al-Amidie, and L. Farhan, "Review of deep learning: concepts, CNN architectures, challenges, applications, future directions", *J. Big Data,* vol. 8, no. 1, p. 53, 2021.
[http://dx.doi.org/10.1186/s40537-021-00444-8] [PMID: 33816053]

[56]   M. Javaid, A. Haleem, R. Pratap Singh, R. Suman, and S. Rab, "Significance of machine learning in healthcare: Features, pillars and applications", *International Journal of Intelligent Networks,* vol. 3, pp. 58-73, 2022.
[http://dx.doi.org/10.1016/j.ijin.2022.05.002]

[57]   A. Voulodimos, N. Doulamis, A. Doulamis, and E. Protopapadakis, "Deep learning for computer vision: A brief review", *Comput. Intell. Neurosci.,* vol. 2018, no. 1, pp. 1-13, 2018.
[http://dx.doi.org/10.1155/2018/7068349] [PMID: 29487619]

[58]   C. Zhang, and Y. Lu, "Study on artificial intelligence: The state of the art and future prospects", *J. Ind. Inf. Integr.,* vol. 23, p. 100224, 2021.
[http://dx.doi.org/10.1016/j.jii.2021.100224]

[59]   R. Vinuesa, H. Azizpour, I. Leite, M. Balaam, V. Dignum, S. Domisch, A. Felländer, S.D. Langhans, M. Tegmark, and F. Fuso Nerini, "The role of artificial intelligence in achieving the Sustainable Development Goals", *Nat. Commun.,* vol. 11, no. 1, p. 233, 2020.
[http://dx.doi.org/10.1038/s41467-019-14108-y] [PMID: 31932590]

[60]   A. Di Vaio, R. Palladino, R. Hassan, and O. Escobar, "Artificial intelligence and business models in the sustainable development goals perspective: A systematic literature review", *J. Bus. Res.,* vol. 121, pp. 283-314, 2020.
[http://dx.doi.org/10.1016/j.jbusres.2020.08.019]

[61]   X. Yao, J. Zhou, J. Zhang, and C.R. Boër, "From intelligent manufacturing to smart manufacturing for Industry 4.0 driven by next generation artificial intelligence and further on", *In 2017 5th Int. Conf. Enterprise Syst. (ES),* IEEE., pp. 311-318, 20172017.
[http://dx.doi.org/10.1109/ES.2017.58]

[62]   M. Bellandi, and L. De Propris, "Local productive systems' transitions to industry 4.0+", *Sustainability (Basel),* vol. 13, no. 23, p. 13052, 2021.
[http://dx.doi.org/10.3390/su132313052]

[63]   P.P. Shinde, and S. Shah, "A review of machine learning and deep learning applications", *2018 4th Int. Conf. Comput. Commun. Control Autom. (ICCUBEA),* IEEE., pp. 1-6, 2018.
[http://dx.doi.org/10.1109/ICCUBEA.2018.8697857]

[64]   S.A. Salloum, M. Alshurideh, A. Elnagar, and K. Shaalan, "Machine learning and deep learning techniques for cybersecurity: a review", *The International Conference on Artificial Intelligence and Computer Vision,* Springer International Publishing: Cham, pp. 50-57, 2020.
[http://dx.doi.org/10.1007/978-3-030-44289-7_5]

[65]   M.C. Zizic, M. Mladineo, N. Gjeldum, and L. Celent, "From industry 4.0 towards industry 5.0: A review and analysis of paradigm shift for the people, organization and technology", *Energies,* vol. 15, no. 14, p. 5221, 2022.
[http://dx.doi.org/10.3390/en15145221]

[66]   S. Nosratabadi, A. Mosavi, P. Duan, P. Ghamisi, F. Filip, S. Band, U. Reuter, J. Gama, and A. Gandomi, "Data science in economics: comprehensive review of advanced machine learning and deep learning methods", *Mathematics,* vol. 8, no. 10, p. 1799, 2020.
[http://dx.doi.org/10.3390/math8101799]

[67]   A. Di Vaio, R. Palladino, R. Hassan, and O. Escobar, "Artificial intelligence and business models in the sustainable development goals perspective: A systematic literature review", *J. Bus. Res.,* vol. 121, pp. 283-314, 2020.
[http://dx.doi.org/10.1016/j.jbusres.2020.08.019]

[68]   T. Zonta, C.A. da Costa, R. da Rosa Righi, M.J. de Lima, E.S. da Trindade, and G.P. Li, "Predictive maintenance in the Industry 4.0: A systematic literature review", *Comput. Ind. Eng.,* vol. 150, p. 106889, 2020.
[http://dx.doi.org/10.1016/j.cie.2020.106889]

[69]   A. Deiva Ganesh, and P. Kalpana, "Future of artificial intelligence and its influence on supply chain risk management – A systematic review", *Comput. Ind. Eng.,* vol. 169, p. 108206, 2022.
[http://dx.doi.org/10.1016/j.cie.2022.108206]

[70]   M. Abdirad, and K. Krishnan, "Industry 4.0 in logistics and supply chain management: a systematic literature review", *Eng. Manag. J.,* vol. 33, no. 3, pp. 187-201, 2021.
[http://dx.doi.org/10.1080/10429247.2020.1783935]

[71]   T.E.T. Dantas, E.D. de-Souza, I.R. Destro, G. Hammes, C.M.T. Rodriguez, and S.R. Soares, "How the combination of Circular Economy and Industry 4.0 can contribute towards achieving the Sustainable Development Goals", *Sustain. Prod. Consum.,* vol. 26, pp. 213-227, 2021.
[http://dx.doi.org/10.1016/j.spc.2020.10.005]

[72]   N.T. Ching, M. Ghobakhloo, M. Iranmanesh, P. Maroufkhani, and S. Asadi, "Industry 4.0 applications for sustainable manufacturing: A systematic literature review and a roadmap to sustainable development", *J. Clean. Prod.,* vol. 334, p. 130133, 2022.
[http://dx.doi.org/10.1016/j.jclepro.2021.130133]

[73]   M. Pech, J. Vrchota, and J. Bednář, "Predictive maintenance and intelligent sensors in smart factory", *Sensors (Basel),* vol. 21, no. 4, p. 1470, 2021.
[http://dx.doi.org/10.3390/s21041470] [PMID: 33672479]

[74]   A. Raj, G. Dwivedi, A. Sharma, A.B. Lopes de Sousa Jabbour, and S. Rajak, "Barriers to the adoption of industry 4.0 technologies in the manufacturing sector: An inter-country comparative perspective", *Int. J. Prod. Econ.,* vol. 224, p. 107546, 2020.
[http://dx.doi.org/10.1016/j.ijpe.2019.107546]

[75]   P.K. Donta, S.N. Srirama, T. Amgoth, and C.S.R. Annavarapu, "Survey on recent advances in IoT application layer protocols and machine learning scope for research directions", *Digit. Commun. Netw.,* vol. 8, no. 5, pp. 727-744, 2022.
[http://dx.doi.org/10.1016/j.dcan.2021.10.004]

[76]   F.A. Alhaidari, and E.J. Alqahtani, "Securing communication between fog computing and IoT using constrained application protocol (CoAP): A survey", *J. Commun.,* vol. 15, no. 1, pp. 14-30, 2020.
[http://dx.doi.org/10.12720/jcm.15.1.14-30]

[77]   S. Garg, K. Kaur, G. Kaddoum, and K.K.R. Choo, "Toward secure and provable authentication for Internet of Things: Realizing industry 4.0", *IEEE Internet Things J.,* vol. 7, no. 5, pp. 4598-4606, 2020.
[http://dx.doi.org/10.1109/JIOT.2019.2942271]

[78]   A. Lavric, and V. Popa, "A LoRaWAN: Long range wide area networks study", *2017 International Conference on Electromechanical and Power Systems (SIELMEN),* IEEE., pp. 417-420, 2017.
[http://dx.doi.org/10.1109/SIELMEN.2017.8123360]

[79]   G.A. Akpakwu, B.J. Silva, G.P. Hancke, and A.M. Abu-Mahfouz, "A survey on 5G networks for the Internet of Things: Communication technologies and challenges", *IEEE Access,* vol. 6, pp. 3619-3647, 2018.
[http://dx.doi.org/10.1109/ACCESS.2017.2779844]

[80]   K.L. Tsai, F.Y. Leu, L.L. Hung, and C.Y. Ko, "Secure session key generation method for LoRaWAN servers", *IEEE Access,* vol. 8, pp. 54631-54640, 2020.
[http://dx.doi.org/10.1109/ACCESS.2020.2978100]

[81]   S. Suresh, and G. Chakaravarthi, "RFID technology and its diverse applications: A brief exposition with a proposed Machine Learning approach", *Measurement,* vol. 195, p. 111197, 2022.

[http://dx.doi.org/10.1016/j.measurement.2022.111197]

[82]   S. Joshi, M. Sharma, and A. Barve, "Implementation Challenges of Blockchain technology in Closed-loop supply chain: A Waste Electrical and Electronic Equipment (WEEE) Management perspective in developing countries", *In Supply Chain Forum: An Int. J.,* vol. 24, 2023no. 1, pp. 59-80
[http://dx.doi.org/10.1080/16258312.2022.2135972]

[83]   S. Li, S.C. Tan, C.K. Lee, E. Waffenschmidt, S.Y. Hui, and C.K. Tse, "A survey, classification, and critical review of light-emitting diode drivers", *IEEE Trans. Power Electron.,* vol. 31, no. 2, pp. 1503-1516, 2016.
[http://dx.doi.org/10.1109/TPEL.2015.2417563]

[84]   H. Zhang, R. Srinivasan, and V. Ganesan, "Low cost, multi-pollutant sensing system using raspberry pi for indoor air quality monitoring", *Sustainability (Basel),* vol. 13, no. 1, p. 370, 2021.
[http://dx.doi.org/10.3390/su13010370]

[85]   A. Vasiliev, M. Muneeb, J. Allaert, J. Van Campenhout, R. Baets, and G. Roelkens, "Integrated silicon-on-insulator spectrometer with single pixel readout for mid-infrared spectroscopy", *IEEE J. Sel. Top. Quantum Electron.,* vol. 24, no. 6, pp. 1-7, 2018.
[http://dx.doi.org/10.1109/JSTQE.2018.2820169]

[86]   A. D'Alessandro, S. Scudero, and G. Vitale, "A review of the capacitive MEMS for seismology", *Sensors (Basel),* vol. 19, no. 14, p. 3093, 2019.
[http://dx.doi.org/10.3390/s19143093] [PMID: 31336990]

[87]   I. Ebtehaj, H. Bonakdari, A. H. Zaji, H. Azimi, and F. Khoshbin, "GMDH-type neural network approach for modeling the discharge coefficient of rectangular sharp-crested side weirs", *Eng. Sci. Technol., Int. J.,* vol. 18, no. 4, pp. 746-757, 2015.
[http://dx.doi.org/10.1016/j.jestch.2015.04.012]

[88]   S. Raychaudhuri, "Introduction to Monte Carlo simulation", *Winter Simul. Conf.,* pp. 91-100, 2008.*Introduction to monte carlo simulation.,* pp. 91-100, 2008.
[http://dx.doi.org/10.1109/WSC.2008.4736059]

[89]   R. Lei, and Y. Cheng, "A pareto-based differential evolution algorithm for multi-objective optimization problems", *2010 Chinese Control and Decision Conference,* IEEE., pp. 1608-1613, 2010.
[http://dx.doi.org/10.1109/CCDC.2010.5498305]

[90]   G. Revach, N. Shlezinger, X. Ni, A.L. Escoriza, R.J.G. van Sloun, and Y.C. Eldar, "KalmanNet: Neural network aided Kalman filtering for partially known dynamics", *IEEE Trans. Signal Process.,* vol. 70, pp. 1532-1547, 2022.
[http://dx.doi.org/10.1109/TSP.2022.3158588]

[91]   P. Vaishnav, and A. Santra, "Continuous human activity classification with unscented Kalman filter tracking using FMCW radar", *IEEE Sens. Lett.,* vol. 4, no. 5, pp. 1-4, 2020.
[http://dx.doi.org/10.1109/LSENS.2020.2991367]

[92]   S. Jafarzadeh, C. Lascu, and M.S. Fadali, "State estimation of induction motor drives using the unscented Kalman filter", *IEEE Trans. Ind. Electron.,* vol. 59, no. 11, pp. 4207-4216, 2012.
[http://dx.doi.org/10.1109/TIE.2011.2174533]

[93]   N. Chukhrova, and A. Johannssen, "Fuzzy regression analysis: Systematic review and bibliography", *Appl. Soft Comput.,* vol. 84, p. 105708, 2019.
[http://dx.doi.org/10.1016/j.asoc.2019.105708]

[94]   S. Corde, V.R. Chifu, I. Salomie, E.S. Chifu, and A. Iepure, "Bird mating optimization method for one-to-n skill matching", *In 2016 IEEE 12th Int. Conf. Intell. Comput. Commun. Process. (ICCP),* IEEE., pp. 155-162, 2016.
[http://dx.doi.org/10.1109/ICCP.2016.7737139]

[95]   R.E. Banfield, L.O. Hall, K.W. Bowyer, and W.P. Kegelmeyer, "A comparison of decision tree ensemble creation techniques", *IEEE Trans. Pattern Anal. Mach. Intell.,* vol. 29, no. 1, pp. 173-180,

2007.
[http://dx.doi.org/10.1109/TPAMI.2007.250609] [PMID: 17108393]

[96]   X. Xiaoyan, W. Feng, W. Liang, and Q. Tailong, "Structural damage detection using PCA and improved FRF curvature method", *2011 Fourth International Conference on Intelligent Computation Technology and Automation,* vol. 1, IEEE., pp. 723-726, 2011.
[http://dx.doi.org/10.1109/ICICTA.2011.188]

[97]   P.J. Braspenning, F. Thuijsman, and A.J.M.M. Weijters, *Artificial neural networks: an introduction to ANN theory and practice.,* Springer Verlag, 1995. Available from: http://www.ncbi.nlm.nih.gov/pubmed/22047867

[98]   H. Sharma, and S. Kumar, "A survey on decision tree algorithms of classification in data mining", *Int. J. Sci. Res. (Raipur),* vol. 5, no. 4, pp. 2094-2097, 2016. [IJSR].
[http://dx.doi.org/10.21275/v5i4.NOV162954]

[99]   M. Granik, and V. Mesyura, "Fake news detection using naive Bayes classifier", *2017 IEEE 1st Ukraine Conf. Electr. Comput. Eng. (UKRCON),* IEEE., pp. 900-903, 2017.
[http://dx.doi.org/10.1109/UKRCON.2017.8100379]

[100]   S. Yue, P. Li, and P. Hao, "SVM classification:Its contents and challenges", *Appl. Math. J. Chin. Univ.,* vol. 18, no. 3, pp. 332-342, 2003.
[http://dx.doi.org/10.1007/s11766-003-0059-5]

[101]   S.R. Sannasi Chakravarthy, N. Bharanidharan, and H. Rajaguru, "Deep learning-based metaheuristic weighted k-nearest neighbor algorithm for the severity classification of breast cancer", *IRBM,* vol. 44, no. 3, p. 100749, 2023.
[http://dx.doi.org/10.1016/j.irbm.2022.100749]

[102]   A. Wahid, J.G. Breslin, and M.A. Intizar, "Prediction of machine failure in industry 4.0: a hybrid CNN-LSTM framework", *Appl. Sci. (Basel),* vol. 12, no. 9, p. 4221, 2022.
[http://dx.doi.org/10.3390/app12094221]

[103]   S. Mehra, and S. Susan, "Early fusion of phone embeddings for recognition of low-resourced accented speech", *In 2022 4th Int. Conf. Artif. Intell. Speech Technol. (AIST),* IEEE., pp. 1-5, 2022.
[http://dx.doi.org/10.1109/AIST55798.2022.10064735]

[104]   S. Mehra, V. Ranga, and R. Agarwal, "Multimodal integration of mel spectrograms and text transcripts for enhanced automatic speech recognition: Leveragingextractive transformer-based approaches and late fusion strategies", *Comput. Intell.,* vol. 40, no. 6, p. e70012, 2024.
[http://dx.doi.org/10.1111/coin.70012]

[105]   S. Mehra, V. Ranga, R. Agarwal, and S. Susan, "Speaker independent recognition of low-resourced multilingual Arabic spoken words through hybrid fusion", *Multimedia Tools Appl.,* vol. 83, no. 35, pp. 82533-82561, 2024.
[http://dx.doi.org/10.1007/s11042-024-18804-w]

[106]   V.K. Singh, S. Mehra, and A. Ali, "Edge computing integration with 5G for IoT: Framework, challenges, and future directions", *Challenges, and Future Directions,* 2024.
[http://dx.doi.org/10.2139/ssrn.5001181]

CHAPTER 6

Predictive Maintenance for Enhanced Resilience in Natural Disasters

Vaswati Gogoi[1]**, Tanu Singh**[1,*]**, Vinod Patidar**[1] **and Manu Singh**[2]

[1] *School of Computer Science, University of Petroleum and Energy Studies, Dehradun, Uttarakhand, India*

[2] *School of Computing Science and Engineering, Galgotias University, Gr. Noida, Uttar Pradesh, India*

Abstract: Disasters occur frequently around the world, affecting structures and people, thus resulting in massive disruption of services. This is particularly the case with the increasing frequency and intensity of disasters, leading to the necessity of more proactive steps to improve the critical systems' resiliency. Predictive maintenance (PM), which uses data to predict when equipment might fail, provides a solution in this sense as it enables organizations to plan for repairs that will prevent major failures. This chapter aims to discuss how PM can be incorporated into disaster management plans to mitigate the impact of natural disasters and enhance the durability of structures. This chapter provides an overview of applications of information methods mentioned previously, including descriptive, diagnostic, predictive, and prescriptive analytics. It also reveals the issues of data quality, data accessibility, and multidisciplinary data fusion from weather forecasts, seismic data, and Internet of Things (IoT) sensor data. Besides, it also describes how PM can improve risk evaluation and assessment solutions, early warning systems, infrastructure health, and disaster management solutions. The chapter outlines how predictive maintenance redefines disaster planning and management based on real-life case studies. The relevance of data integration and availability can be a barrier, but PM is a strong positive lever for enhancing the protection of critical infrastructure in disaster-sensitive areas.

Keywords: Climate change, Climatological disasters, Data analytics, Data integration, Disaster management, Geophysical disasters, Hydrological disasters, Meteorological disasters, Predictive maintenance.

INTRODUCTION

A natural disaster is a catastrophic occurrence caused by natural processes or events that lead to the loss of lives, property, and structures [1]. In light of the

---

* **Corresponding author Tanu Singh:** School of Computer Science, University of Petroleum and Energy Studies, Dehradun, Uttarakhand, India; E-mail: tanu.singh@ddn.upes.ac.in

Tanu Singh, Vinod Patidar, Arvind Panwar & Urvashi Sugandh (Eds.)

effect of global warming and climate change that has contributed to the rise in the frequency and intensity of occurrence of natural disasters, there has never been a greater need to embrace innovation in managing such disasters [2]. Disaster management paradigms in the past have largely been of a reactive nature, in which the response to catastrophic disasters is to restore and reconstruct after the occurrence [3]. However, this approach always has a profound consequence of causing vast destruction, loss of lives, and high costs of repairing in society caused by the destruction. Thus, in recent years, there has been more concentration on risk assessment, risk prevention, and ways to minimize the effects of natural disasters [3].

Predictive maintenance (PM) is one approach that uses dated technologies to check the functionality and health of infrastructure or equipment before a failure happens [4]. Traditionally practiced in specific fields like manufacturing and aviation, this concept is now in focus to be an excellent mode of tackling disasters. Besides mitigating the likelihood of infrastructure failure during a catastrophe, PM improves the ability of essential systems to compensate for change and uncertainty in the environment [5, 6]. Consequently, this chapter focuses on explaining what PM is and why it is necessary for natural disaster management in data analytics to integrate PM in the management of natural disasters.

PM - AN OVERVIEW

PM is a preventive maintenance technique that involves the assessment of the status of a given asset, equipment, structure, or machine with the intention of assessing when they should be maintained [7]. This method depends on the acquisition of real-time data that enables organizations to decide the appropriate time to conduct maintenance, thus minimizing incidences of downtime due to equipment failure. The concept of PM revolves around the condition or state evaluation of infrastructures with real-time monitoring. It includes gathering information from various sources, which include sensors, records, and the environment, among others, to forecast future breakdowns. PM involves the following, as shown in Fig. (**1**).

- **Data Collection:** This is achieved through the use of IoT sensors, smart gadgets, and other devices that constantly check the conditions of infrastructure.
- **Data Transmission:** Once collected, the data is either stored in centralized storage or, more specifically, in cloud servers for processing. Relaying this data through dependable means, such as Wi-Fi and Bluetooth, is done effectively and without much interference in the PM cycle.

- **Data Analysis:** The gathered data undergo flow analysis with sophisticated algorithms, such as machine learning (ML) algorithms for pattern recognition, to forecast risks.
- **Prediction and Failures:** The predictive models simulate possible equipment breakdowns according to current and previous conditions. Such predictions allow organizations to schedule maintenance activities so that unnecessary idle time is eliminated, thereby guaranteeing the continuity of operations. In other words, it is possible to use ML to elaborate forecasts regarding certain values changing over time.
- **Decision-Making:** If a possible problem is observed, the maintenance crew plans the correction or overhaul when they make their decisions, hence reducing interference.
- **Maintenance and Feedback:** After maintenance, the system always receives feedback, which enhances the next predictions. This way, the algorithms are continuously educated and supplemented by the input that makes the PM and, consequently, the accuracy of the algorithms a constant learning process.

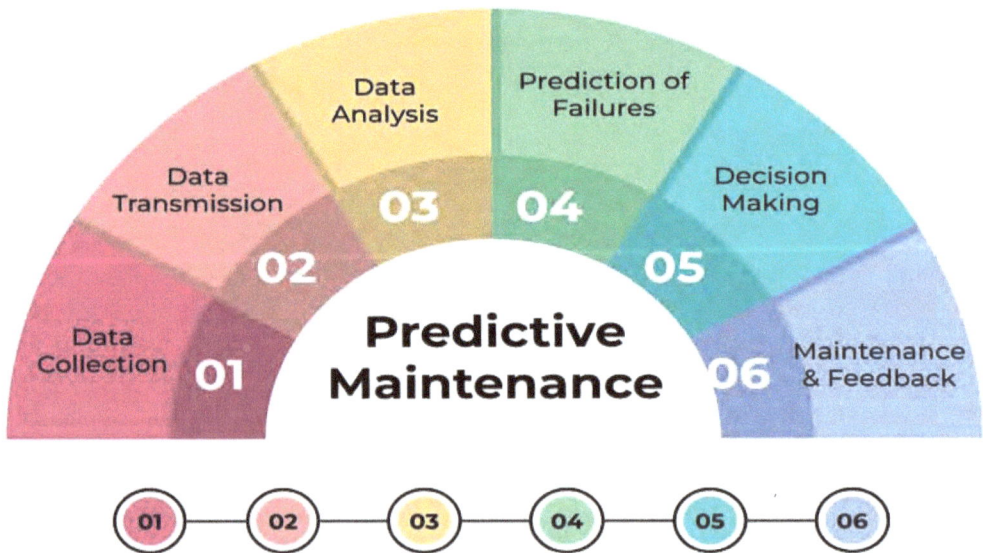

Fig. (1). Steps of PM.

In the aspect of disasters, through constant assessment of structures like bridges, power, and water companies, this concept of performing regular check-ups, especially on the mechanical structures, will prevent them from failing during disasters. Surveillance of the state of the structure in a bridge before an earthquake might help prevent the bridge from collapsing during the earthquake [8]. The concept of PM can be adopted where vehicles like firefighting trucks, ambulances, and rescue equipment are used to always be in good working conditions. Hence, in disaster response, PM helps improve the response effort by avoiding equipment breakdowns at that time.

Importance of PM in Natural Disaster Management

Most natural disasters are sensitive to predict when they will occur, and thus communities can be left highly fragile to suffer severe infrastructure losses [8]. The importance of PM in disaster management is well illustrated when assessing the unpredictability and the size of the destruction caused by disasters. Whether quakes, hurricanes, floods, or wildfires, critical infrastructure functions can worsen the consequences of such disasters, hamper the response, and protract the recovery efforts [9]. PM is, therefore, very beneficial to such disaster-prone areas since potential disasters can be prevented or minimized through protective and reinforcement measures.

- **Preventing Catastrophic Failures:** This indeed is quite disastrous, particularly at a time of natural disasters when structures collapse, causing significant losses in terms of human lives and property. For example, a flood may cause a dam to burst, or hurricanes can cause electrical grids to malfunction and thus result in devastation. PM also addresses such infrastructure issues, which allows for the determination of the areas that contain weaknesses that may cause failure.
- **Reducing Recovery Costs and Time:** Disaster impacts infrastructures a lot. When they are destroyed, it may take a lot of time and financial power to renew them [9]. As compared with rectifying large failures, which cause severe damage, PM helps minimize the level of failure, which is beneficial in terms of time and repair costs.
- **Supporting Early Warning Systems:** In some circumstances, PM may complement conventional early warning systems, making it possible to approach disaster management in its entirety [10].

DATA ANALYTICS IN PM - ROLE AND PURPOSE

One of the key reasons why the application of PM is practical is the integration of data analytics. These PM systems that are based on the latest data gathering and analysis methodologies offer a more accurate projection regarding overall state of the current infrastructure, as well as future breakdowns [11, 12]. PM systems that would be able to define some behavior based on considerable amount of data coming from the sensors, records, and other factors can be developed with the help of algorithms and ML [12]. It may stop or reduce the chances of failure that maintenance teams may not be able to detect early enough since the analysis gives a pattern and trends of what may fail next [10]. This is a strength since real-time data processing is essential to PM when it involves significant amounts of data.

Objectives of Data Analytics

The main goal of data analytics in the context of PM is to identify failure before it occurs. This is achieved through a combination of descriptive, diagnostic, and predictive analytics, as explained below [6]:

- **Descriptive Analytics:** It entails studying data accumulated over a certain period to establish trends and patterns related to infrastructure performance.
- **Diagnostic Analytics:** In contrast, it relies on causality, which assists the maintenance teams in understanding the main reasons for their failures.
- **Predictive Analytics:** This approach employs data in ML algorithms to predict the best time for an intervention in anticipation of a failure.
- **Prescriptive Analytics:** This is intended to recommend the best course of action if a certain part requires replacement. This will improve maintenance work and the appropriate time when it needs to be done.

This chapter provides an overview of applications of information methods mentioned previously, including descriptive, diagnostic, predictive, and prescriptive analytics. It also reveals the issues of data quality, data accessibility, and multi-disciplinary data fusion from weather forecasts, seismic data, and IoT sensor data. Besides, it also describes how PM can improve risk evaluation and assessment solutions, early warning systems, infrastructure health, and disaster management solutions. The chapter outlines how PM redefines disaster planning and management based on real-life case studies. The relevance of data integration and availability can be barriers, but PM is a strong positive lever for enhancing the protection of critical infrastructure in disaster-sensitive areas.

To ensure effectiveness in presenting the various details of how PM can improve the resilience in natural disaster management, this chapter is organized as follow:

- **Natural Disasters—Understanding and Background:** This section focuses on the background of natural disasters, their types, and their impact on infrastructure and communities.
- **Data Collection for PM:** This section examines the sources and techniques used in data acquisition for PM. It looks at the data on weather conditions, seismic data on earth or structures, satellite imagery, or IoT sensors.
- **Data Analytics Techniques:** This section gives a clearer understanding of the various data analytics methods that can be applied to PM. It includes historical

analysis, diagnostic analysis, prediction, and prescriptive analysis to elaborate more on how each of these techniques enhances the efficiency of PM systems.

- **Integrating PM for Natural Disasters:** In this section of the chapter, the author looks at how the approach of using PM can be incorporated.
- **Challenges and Limitations:** This section discusses the challenges and limitations of the data analytics and PM approach.
- **Conclusion:** This section concludes the data analytics and PM applied to the natural disaster.

NATURAL DISASTERS: UNDERSTANDING AND BACKGROUND

Natural disasters are unanticipated calamities and, in most cases, devastating ones that occur because of the forces of nature. These disasters are catastrophic, affecting entire communities and economies and even claiming so many lives as well as destroying properties [13]. The occurrence and frequency of these disasters also differ across the different geographical locations due to geographical, climatic, and ecological factors. Natural disasters in the present world of climate change/disaster change, which affect the vulnerability of the regions, particularly in urban areas, require more knowledge and understanding for response and preparedness rather than a reactive response. In the past, individuals worldwide have gone through disastrous events that include large-scale earthquakes, hurricanes, and others [9]. Human activities exacerbate the impact of disasters through practices like urban planning, deforestation, and environmental pollution. For example, flood risks are associated with deforestation of the land, which in turn augments the susceptibility of communities in flooding regions combined with increasing precipitation. There is a need to know the causes of natural disasters and how such calamities affect infrastructure and civilizations to enable one to design coping mechanisms.

Natural Disasters: Types and Characteristics

There are different types of natural disasters, and all have different features, reasons, and effects that occur. To evaluate the breadth of disaster management and resilience, it is necessary to highlight the main kinds of natural disasters. These include:

- Geophysical disasters are natural disasters resulting from geophysical activities within the earth's surface. This category may entail earthquakes, volcanic activities, tsunamis, and landslides [14]. Of all the geophysical events, earthquakes are some of the most catastrophic; these events occur because of the movement of tectonic plates. These waves result in the collapse of structures and the destruction of transport infrastructure and lead to other disasters, including tsunamis or fires.

- Hydrological Disasters: Floods are the dominant events in the occurrence of hydrological disasters. Flooding is caused by rainwater, rivers that overflow, burst dams, or storm surges that originate from cyclones [15]. The extent of flooding is because of geographic features, the amount of precipitation it receives, deforestation, and poor water management. Although it can also be categorized as a geophysical event, a landslide usually results from the effects of water, especially from rainfall in regions with sandy grounds. Some of the elements of hydrological disasters are magnitude and velocity. This is the rate at which hydrological disasters occur, and this largely determines the level of damage that is caused.

- Meteorological disasters are those events that are caused by atmospheric conditions, such as hurricanes, tornadoes, and storms. These disasters are marked by strong winds, torrential rain, and, in some cases, hail, thunder, or lightning [9]. These are enormous types of storms that occur over warm sea water and differ only in the geographical locations in which they occur, *i.e.*, hurricanes in the Americas, typhoons in Asia, and cyclones in the Indian Ocean. These are categorized according to their wind speeds, and the effects of these natural phenomena are not just confined to the coastal region where they occur. Storm flooding and storm surges are major threats from hurricanes. While the former is widespread but comparatively moderate, the latter is highly circumscribed but very severe. Mesoscale vortexes of air that originate from a thunderstorm and curve to the ground are mesoscale convective vortexes.

- Climatological disasters are linked to climate variability in the atmosphere that are long-term, which include droughts and heat waves [13]. Most of them take several months, if not years, to unfold themselves, and they manifest in series that cause detrimental impacts on ecosystems and human societies. A drought is a situation where there is limited rainfall for an extended period, causing water deficiency, crop failure, and, in some cases, famine. The drought measures include the drought's duration and severity and the geographical area it covers.

All these natural disasters and their types with the global distributions are diagrammatically depicted in Fig. (**2**).

Impact of Natural Disasters on Infrastructure and Communities

Natural disasters continue to cause severe destruction to the infrastructure and communities [9]. Natural disasters, therefore, bring social and economic shocks with long-standing impacts that affect the regions' physical, social, and financial lives for years. These disasters affect critical infrastructure, including transport systems, power, water, and healthcare sectors, bearing the worst of the impacts, which worsens the effects of the disaster in an affected community. Knowledge of how and when disasters occur and their effects on infrastructure and communities is key in implementing approaches to minimize losses and to fast-track rebuilding efforts.

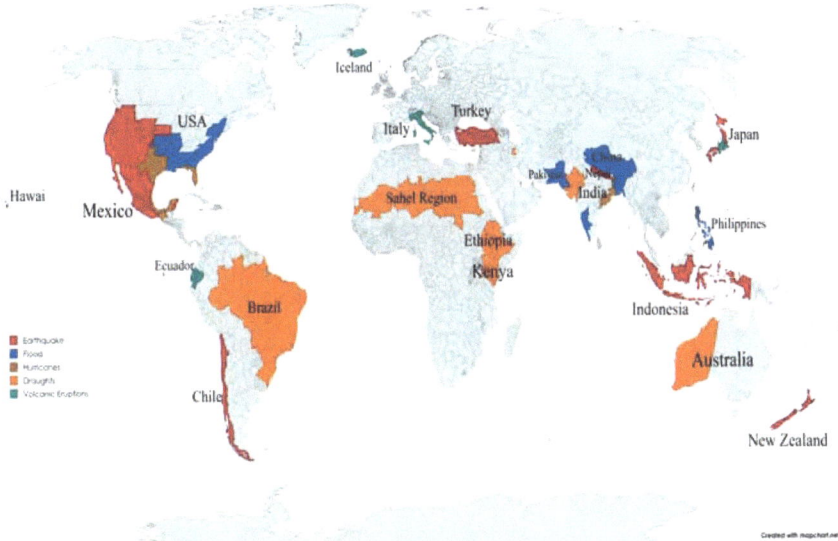

Fig. (2). Global Distribution of Natural Disasters by its type (Data Source: UNDRR, EM-DAT, World Bank).

Impact on Infrastructure

Natural disasters often target the weakest points in a region's infrastructure, leading to widespread damage and service disruption [13]. Earthquakes, for example, can cause buildings to collapse, bridges to buckle, and roads to crack, making it difficult for emergency services to reach affected areas. The damage to transportation infrastructure hampers rescue efforts and disrupts the flow of goods and services, causing shortages and delaying recovery. In many cases, the destruction of critical infrastructure, such as hospitals or emergency response centers, severely limits the ability to provide medical care and other essential services [14]. Floods are particularly destructive to infrastructure, as they erode roads and foundations and damage underground systems like sewage and water pipes. The water damage caused by floods can lead to long-term issues such as mold growth, weakening the structural integrity of buildings. Additionally, floods often result in power outages by submerging electrical grids and transformers [15]. This can leave entire regions without power for days or even weeks, exacerbating the effects of the disaster. Similar impacts are seen in hurricanes, where the combination of high winds and storm surges can devastate coastal infrastructure, leading to the displacement of communities and significant economic losses.

Here, Fig. (**3**) depicts the infrastructure damage chart for various regions.

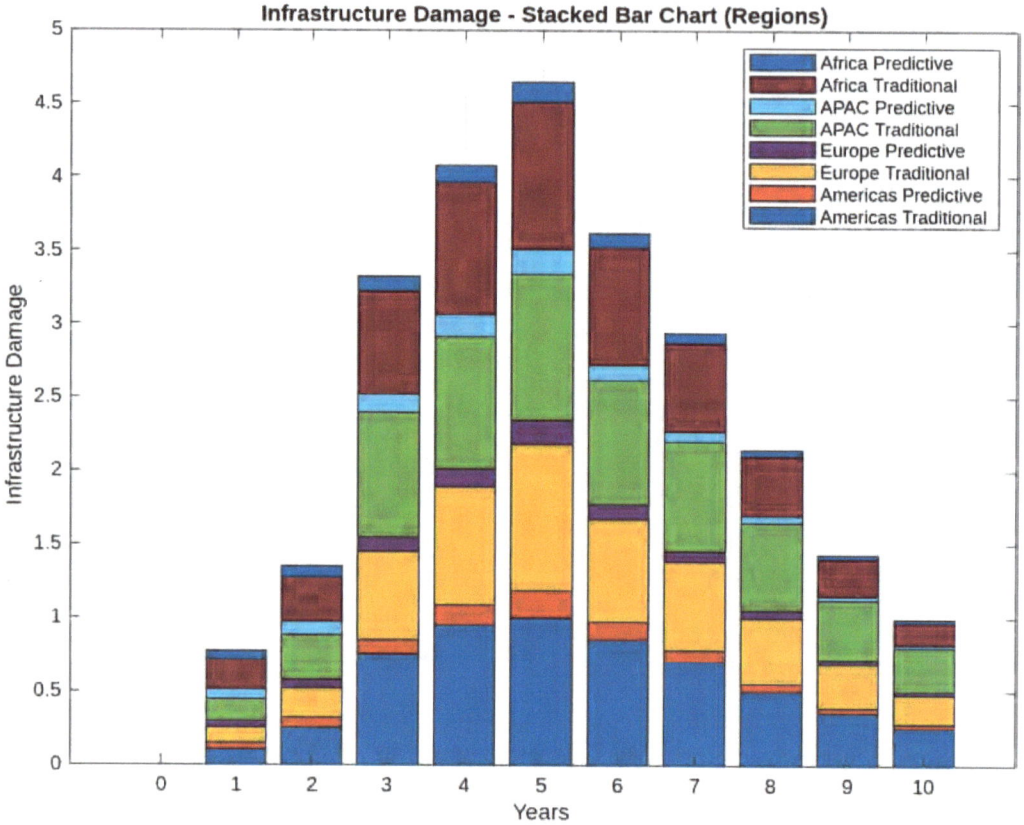

Fig. (3). Comparative analysis of infrastructure damage in various regions (Data Source: UNEP, UNDRR, EM-DAT, World Bank).

Impact on Communities

The human toll of natural disasters is equally significant. Beyond the immediate loss of life, injuries, and displacement, natural disasters have long-term effects on communities' social and economic well-being [9]. Vulnerable populations—such as older people, low-income groups, and those living in high-risk areas—are disproportionately affected by natural disasters. Displacement from homes and communities can lead to social dislocation, with families separated and communities fragmented. Additionally, natural disasters often trigger a cascade of secondary effects, including spreading diseases due to contaminated water supplies or disrupting healthcare services. The economic impact of natural disasters is also severe, with both short-term and long-term consequences [9]. In the immediate aftermath, businesses are forced to shut down, transportation and supply chains are disrupted, and significant resources are diverted to emergency response efforts. Long-term economic impacts include the cost of rebuilding damaged infrastructure, which can strain government budgets and divert funds from other critical areas such as education and healthcare. In some cases, the economic toll can set back development efforts by years, particularly in developing countries. Socially, the psychological impact of natural disasters on affected communities is often overlooked. The trauma of losing loved ones, homes, and livelihoods can lead to long-term mental health issues such as depression, anxiety, and Post-Traumatic Stress Disorder (PTSD) [9]. Moreover, losing a community's social fabric can result in weakened support networks, making recovery even more challenging. In many cases, communities must rebuild their infrastructure and sense of identity and belonging. Here, Fig. (**4**) depicts the community damage chart for various regions.

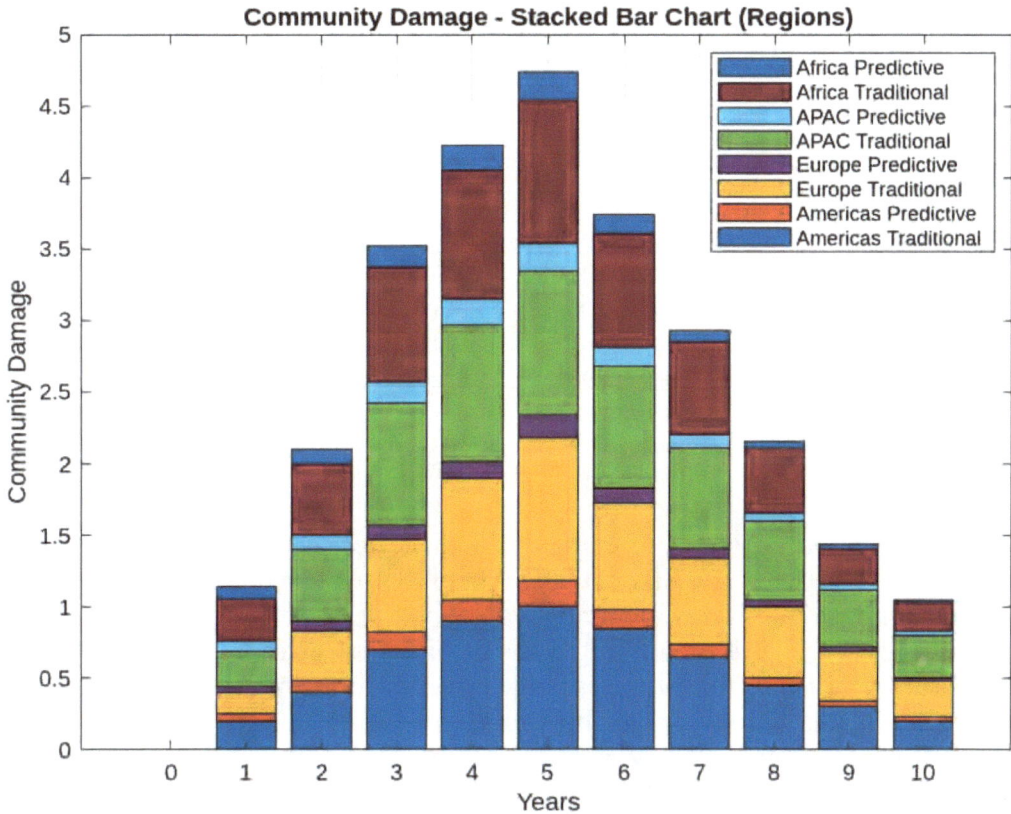

Fig. (4). Comparative Analysis of communities' damage in various regions (Data Source: UNDRR, GFDRR, IFRC, FEMA, ECHO, NDMA).

Historical Data and Patterns of Natural Disasters

Forecasting and evaluating natural disasters and studying their periodicity are significant in forming preconditions for effective disaster risk reduction [14]. Archival data is useful in identifying the occurrence, magnitude, and distribution of disasters to prepare the government, organizations, and people for the future. Analyzing the former catastrophes, the scientists determine the tendencies and regularities that can become the basis of interference and predictive models. These serve as a means of worked-out warning systems and allow organizing prevention measures and necessary actions for potential catastrophes [10].

Importance of Historical Data

Therefore, archival information on natural disasters is the fundamental base used when assessing the threats linked to various kinds of disasters. For instance, past earthquake occurrences can be useful in that they enable researchers to locate areas with a high probability of future earthquakes. In the same way, previous information on floods can help identify more vulnerable areas so that governments can introduce barriers in the form of levees, dams, and early warning systems.

Identifying Patterns and Trends

Researchers can use historical disasters to establish patterns that are useful in planning and managing disasters [5]. For instance, some areas are flooded all year round because of a favorable climate for rainfall, while others are more prone to being burnt during a dry season. Identifying these patterns enables the government to put preventive measures in place early, such as making firebreaks in regions that are susceptible to fires or strengthening flood barriers before the onset of the rainy season.

Regarding the backgrounds of earthquakes, historical data is used to determine areas of the fault lines and hike up the probabilities of seismic activity occurring. Even though the occurrence of earthquakes cannot be determined, historical data may become crucial in identifying areas of high risk, making it possible to put down safety measures that will lessen the effect of forthcoming earthquakes [14]. Likewise, volcanic activity can be evaluated over historical periods, and the probability of future activity can be estimated for regions; this may help authorities develop contingency plans and other protective measures against such activities.

In the case of floods, archaeological and historical data show the variation of floodplain margins to forecast how rivers and coastal zones behave in the presence of varied amounts of rainfall or several meters of surge. All this data is essential for urban planning because it reveals where flood defenses need to be constructed and how structures in these regions should be adapted for withstanding floods.

DATA COLLECTION FOR PM

Data collection is among the most important processes for developing any PM strategy. PM is a process that requires constant and timely collection of information from different sources of essential structures and equipment [16]. It is necessary to identify and gather real-time data that enables the systems to anticipate failure situations. This is especially important in disaster risk management since any infrastructure collapse, such as the power, transport, or communication infrastructure, can lead to catastrophic disasters.

It includes, but is not limited to, data gathered from radio frequency identification (RFID) tags placed on physical assets using outside sources such as weather prediction, seismic activity, satellite images, *etc.* All these data source feeds provide necessary and relevant insights about the environment, the health of the infrastructure, and the threats that can be encountered. However, data acquisition is just a part of the process; data received must be processed, stored, and managed properly to give results. In this section, we discuss the key sources of data, data acquisition, and ways of storing and managing this data for improved prediction of the time required to perform maintenance tasks.

Sources of Data

The overall effectiveness of the PM concept, therefore, highly depends on the diversity and quality of the data pieces that are fed to the mechanism [5]. All sorts of data are fed into the predictive models, including internal and external factors that affect the performance of infrastructures. Here is a detailed look at some of the primary sources of data used in PM:

- **Weather Data:** Weather conditions are some of the factors that influence the viability and efficiency of infrastructure [17]. For instance, temperature, particularly excess temperature, rain, humidity, and wind can wear out materials and thus fail at an early stage. Whereas in natural disasters, coordinates of lightning become very important to predict the probability of storms, floods, or any other natural calamities that can cause damage to structures.
- **Seismic Data:** Seismographic records are obtained through wired networks of machines that record ground shifts and earthquakes. This data is critical in assessing the stability of structures such as buildings, bridges, and other structures in regions prone to earthquakes [8]. On the other hand, seismic

activity allows using PM systems to identify the primary signs of the object's stress and organize an inspection or additional strengthening before the critical point. Seismic data is procured from various government bodies involved in studying geological structures like the U. S. Geological Survey (USGS) or Japan's National Research Institute for Earth Science and Disaster Prevention and is a part of the PM systems.

- **Satellite Imagery:** Satellite imagery is an invaluable tool for monitoring large-scale infrastructure and environmental conditions [17]. Satellites equipped with high-resolution cameras and sensors capture images of the Earth's surface can assess damage following a disaster, monitor environmental changes, or track infrastructure conditions over time. For example, satellite imagery can detect changes in land elevation, which may indicate subsidence or landslides.
- **IoT Sensors:** The Internet of Things (IoT) has revolutionized PM by allowing infrastructure and equipment to be continuously monitored in real time. IoT sensors are embedded in machinery, buildings, bridges, roads, and other critical infrastructure to measure various performance indicators, such as temperature, pressure, vibration, humidity, and more. These sensors provide real-time data on the health of physical assets, enabling maintenance teams to detect anomalies and predict when failures might occur [8].
- **SCADA Systems:** Supervisory Control and Data Acquisition (SCADA) systems are widely used in manufacturing, energy, and transportation industries. SCADA systems collect data from industrial processes and infrastructure components, such as pipelines, electrical grids, and water treatment plants. This data is crucial for monitoring system performance, detecting issues, and coordinating maintenance activities. By integrating SCADA data into PM models, organizations can predict when critical components may fail, preventing service interruptions and costly repairs.
- **Drones:** Drones, or Unmanned Aerial Vehicles (UAVs), have become essential for inspecting infrastructure in hard-to-reach or dangerous areas [17]. With cameras, sensors, and LiDAR (Light Detection and Ranging) technology, drones can capture high-resolution images and data from infrastructure such as bridges, tall buildings, wind turbines, or power lines. This data can be used to assess structural integrity, detect damage, and inform PM strategies.
- **Environmental Data:** Environmental data, including information on soil conditions, water levels, and air quality, plays a crucial role in PM for a certain type of infrastructure [17]. For instance, soil moisture data can help predict landslides or flooding risks, while air quality data can inform maintenance schedules for air filtration systems in extensive industrial facilities. Environmental sensors in the field collect this data and provide insights into how changing environmental conditions might affect infrastructure performance. Table 1 shows the data sources with their applications in PM.

Table 1. Key data sources and their applications in PM.

Data Source	Description	Application in Predictive Maintenance
Weather Data	Real-time weather conditions, including temperature, humidity, and wind speed	Used to predict material degradation or potential environmental hazards [13].
Seismic Data	Information from seismic sensors that detect ground movement and earthquake activity.	Assesses the structural stability of buildings and infrastructure in seismic zones.
Satellite Imagery	High-resolution images of the Earth's surface from satellites.	Monitors large-scale changes, such as subsidence, and tracks infrastructure health over time.
IoT Sensors	Devices embedded in machines or structures that monitor parameters like vibration, pressure, *etc.*	Provides real-time monitoring of asset health, helping predict failures.
SCADA Systems	Systems that collect and control data from industrial processes like power grids or pipelines.	Used to monitor performance and predict the failure of critical infrastructure components.
Drones	Unmanned aerial vehicles that collect visual and sensor data from hard-to-reach infrastructure.	Inspects infrastructure like bridges or power lines for defects and damage.
Environmental Data	Data on soil, water levels, and air quality collected from various environmental monitoring tools.	Predicts risks such as flooding or landslides and their impact on infrastructure.

DATA ACQUISITION TECHNIQUES

Collecting data for PM involves various acquisition techniques that ensure that correct data is captured at the right time [8]. The quality and reliability of the data are crucial for making accurate predictions and maintaining the integrity of critical infrastructure. Data acquisition can be active or passive, with techniques varying based on the type of infrastructure, environmental conditions, and the data source. Here are some standard data acquisition methods used in PM:

- **Sensor Deployment and Calibration:** Sensor deployment is the most direct method of data acquisition in PM [18]. Sensors can be placed on machinery, buildings, bridges, roads, and other critical infrastructure to collect real-time data on temperature, pressure, humidity, vibration, and other performance indicators. These sensors must be strategically placed in areas most susceptible to wear and tear, such as joints, motors, or load-bearing points. Moreover, sensor calibration is essential to ensure data accuracy.
- **Remote Sensing:** Remote sensing involves collecting data from a distance using satellite, airborne, or ground-based sensors. Satellite remote sensing is useful for capturing large-scale environmental data, such as weather patterns, land use, or

changes in terrain. Remote sensing data can be integrated with IoT sensor data to provide a comprehensive view of infrastructure health, especially in areas prone to natural disasters like floods or landslides. Airborne remote sensing, often done with drones, provides high-resolution images and 3D infrastructure, allowing for detailed inspections and early detection of potential issues.

- **Data from SCADA Systems:** SCADA systems are designed to automate the control and monitoring of industrial processes and infrastructure systems [11]. SCADA data is continuously collected from sensors and actuators embedded in critical infrastructure, such as power grids, pipelines, and water treatment facilities. This data is transmitted to centralized control centers, which are processed and analyzed for performance monitoring and fault detection.

- **Wireless Sensor Networks (WSNs):** Wireless Sensor Networks (WSNs) consist of spatially distributed sensors that communicate wirelessly to collect and transmit data. WSNs are particularly useful for monitoring large or remote infrastructure, such as dams, pipelines, or transportation networks, where traditional wired systems are impractical [13]. These networks can be configured to collect data on environmental conditions, structural health, and system performance, which is then transmitted to a central database for analysis [12].

- **IoT Integration:** Real-time monitoring of infrastructure and machinery is emerging in the PM field through IoT technology in data acquisition. Smart sensors placed in assets continuously record different parameters like temperature, pressure, or vibration, which define the equipment's state. This data is communicated through wireless networks to cloud environments, where it is processed by ML techniques to foretell possible failures [19].

- **Acoustic Emission Monitoring:** Acoustic emission testing is carried out on materials and machinery to establish their structural faults. This technique involves using devices that can detect ultrasonic vibrations that emanate from fractures that may exist in structures. The acoustic data is used to discover probable failures before they assume severe forms. This technique is widely adopted in aerospace, oil & gas, and transportation industries where structure strength is very important. With acoustic emission monitoring, PM is used in identifying signs of wear and damage to arrange for repair or strengthening before it happens [20].

- **Visual and Thermal Imaging:** Such uses include the Indian Remote Sensing Satellite (IRS), which offers an enhanced view of the usual data acquisition methods to give a detailed status of an infrastructure's health through visual and thermal imaging methods. Visual imaging helps in surface-level defect inspection, such as cracks, corrosion, or displacement, where cameras or drones are mostly used. Thermal imaging, on the other hand, identifies heat patterns that may suggest problems such as increased thermal activity of machines or electrical problems. These imaging techniques are helpful in areas that are large or contain structures that are difficult to access, such as power lines, wind turbines, and high-rise buildings.

Data Storage and Management

After data has been gathered, the subsequent major challenge in PM is to analyze and properly archive the data. In typical large organizations, the amount of information produced by PM systems can be overwhelming, especially when handling real-time actual data provided by IoT sensors, SCADA systems, or even satellite images [19]. Data management includes the appropriate storage of data so it can be easily accessed, protected, and made ready for use, and a few are listed below:

- **Cloud-Based Storage Solutions:** Computing services that use cloud technology have brought drastic changes and improvements to how data is stored today due to their ability to offer large, scalable, and flexible storage solutions that do not cost much. AWS, Microsoft Azure, or Google's cloud system allows organizations to store large-scale data generated from IoT sensors, drones, and other sources without requiring an organization to build its own physical data centers.
- **Edge Computing:** In some of the PM applications, real-time analysis is required [20]. For example, in motorized systems or smart productions, delays in the communication of data to the cloud and from the cloud can cause problems or failures. This problem is rectified by edge computing, where data is processed locally or at the edge near its source before being transferred to the cloud as a storage facility. Edge computing found a promising use case in PM where high amounts of sensor data are collected and real-time response is expected, predominantly expressed in industrial use cases.
- **Big Data Management Systems:** Due to the sheer volume of data produced by PM systems, it can be classified as big data, one of the key characteristics of which is its sheer size and another is its inherent complexity. Big data management systems, such as Hadoop and Apache Spark, are designed to handle the three Vs of big data: volume, velocity, and variety [20]. These systems can perform calculations time simultaneously over several subnetworks, making it easier to store large data inputs and compile them for analysis. In PM, specific big data tools used for processing sensor data, historical archives of other upstream maintenance activities, environmental information, and others are indispensable so that the predictive algorithms can have all the necessary information for making proper forecasts.
- **Data Lakes and Warehouses:** Apart from cloud storage solutions and big data platforms, data lakes or data warehouses are commonly employed by organizations to store their PM data [20]. Data lakes retain raw data in its

original form and structure, which makes the data very flexible in the analysis process. This is especially applicable in areas such as PM, whereby information from different fronts (*e.g.*, sensors, seismic activity, satellite images, *etc.*) may require a different approach for analysis. Data warehouses, in contrast, contain pre-aggregated and transformed data, and the data is in a structured format and can easily be used in querying and reporting. Both data lakes and warehouses serve as a data storage repository for all the PM data, thus making it easily accessible for analysis.

- **Data Security and Compliance:** It should be noted, however, that data security always plays an important role in any applications based on big data implementation, and PM is no exception [21]. The security and privacy of data can, therefore, be defined as key concerns for organizations since data can be accessed, modified, or destroyed by unauthorized individuals or incidents. This comprises the use of mechanisms such as encryption, restricted access, and authentication to the information to be protected. In industries, for example, energy, transportation, and healthcare, where PM is a big issue in terms of infrastructure, one is bound to consider the issue of regulation.

- **Data Lifecycle Management:** PM data includes data collected or generated, stored, processed, and analyzed in managing the maintenance lifecycle and conclusions that must be accurate and unadulterated [6]. Data lifecycle management includes setting up policies on storage, archiving, and disposal of the data needed to develop PM models to ensure that the data used is relevant and up-to-date. In some industries with compliance requirements, legal demands may require organizations to keep some data for a longer time. This also falls under lifecycle management since it is a routine where data is reviewed to ensure that the data set used is up-to-date and accurate.

- **Data Governance and Quality Control:** The policies of data governance should have strong measures put in place so that the data is credible, accurate, and coherent [22]. Data governance can, therefore, be described as the way in which data is collected, managed, and used in compliance with laid-down principles and guidelines. This entails providing guidelines for data integrity checks with the objective of checking data before using it in the models. The lack of quality data in PM entails wrong forecasts on the equipment that may either undergo unnecessary maintenance or fail at the wrong times [6]. If not checked from time to time, errors may arise, compromising the quality of the data collected.

Data Analytics Techniques

Analytical tools are central to the effective implementation of condition monitoring and maintenance, thereby helping organizations predict future problems with certain assets [16]. Applying a huge amount of data gathered by sensors, machines, and other objects, data analytics enables maintenance teams to make wise decisions regarding asset availability and lifecycle. At the core of PM, there are several analytical methods, each of which targets different stages of the maintenance process, from past data analysis to real-time decision-making on future actions. These techniques are typically divided into four main categories: descriptive analytics, diagnostic analytics, predictive analytics, and prescriptive analytics [23]. All those types are of maintaining a facility, and their use creates the foundation of a quantitative decision-making paradigm and is explained in the next sub-sections.

Historical Data - Descriptive Analytics

Descriptive analytics is a core database in analyzing PM since it focuses on what has happened before. Descriptive analytics mainly deals with the study of past events and patterns of performance to enable maintenance teams to develop a foundation base for comparison and analysis [23]. Concisely, in consideration of PM, historical data may contain data on prior equipment breakdown, maintenance history, performance indicators, and operating conditions such as temperature, pressure, and humidity. For instance, organizations can discover conventional failure modes for given equipment, identify the average time between failures, and evaluate the previous maintenance performed. Specific analytical methods used in descriptive analytics, such as trend analysis and time series analysis, are crucial for uncovering patterns in disaster-related data, including equipment failure trends over time or seasonal variations in maintenance requirements. Spatial mapping is employed to visualize affected regions, enabling organizations to pinpoint geographic areas frequently impacted by disasters and requiring focused attention. Frequency distribution helps identify the recurrence of certain failure modes or disaster events, providing a clearer understanding of their intensity and frequency. Furthermore, clustering techniques can group similar types of equipment, failure patterns, or disaster-prone regions, facilitating targeted maintenance and resilience planning strategies.

Descriptive analytics can also be applied to sort the assets in terms of their condition and performance, which in turn assists an organization in order maintenance activities. They preserve historical data that is very useful, especially in the process of making decisions because of descriptive analytics [23]. Maintenance teams can then set baseline data in assets to help them recognize variations from normal operations that may be suggestive of a growing problem.

Descriptive analytics help organizations unlock the past data on equipment. Through that historical consideration, decision-makers are better placed to understand the cause of failure and make appropriate decisions for future actions.

Nevertheless, descriptive analytics is just the first form of analysis that can be performed on the data. However, it paints a picture of implementation failure and who is responsible for it. Still, it lacks information on why it happened or what needs to be done to avoid it recurring. This is where diagnostic and predictive analytics were introduced.

Identify Failure Modes - Diagnostic Analytics

Where descriptive analytics finds out what has happened, diagnostic analytics aims at establishing why a particular equipment or a performance has failed [22]. Diagnostic analytics in the case of PM is, therefore, the use of data to ascertain the causes of failures and hence allow an organization to combat the specific factors that are likely to cause the degradation of equipment. Unlike simple regression, this type of analysis can further specify the connections between variables, for instance, between external conditions, performance outcomes, and equipment characteristics [6]. Diagnostic analytics is one of the most significant objectives for determining the failure modes, which refers to how equipment may fail. It should also be noted that failure modes can be triggered by many factors, such as mechanical abrasion, material fatigue, inadequate maintenance, effects on the environment, and operators' mistakes. Using historical performance data dealing with previous failures and poor performances, diagnostic analytics offers insights to the maintenance teams that enable them to improve on past performances and avoid repeat failures.

There are various approaches to diagnostic analytics, one of which is the root cause analysis (RCA), which is a search for a root cause of how a failure occurred to establish the inherent reason for it. For instance, if a piece of machinery were to break down because it had overheated, then the diagnostic analytics may show that the actual problem was in the cooling system or that the temperatures in the surrounding environment were rising. This way, organizations eliminate the recurrence of a problem and enhance the dependable and improved use of equipment in the future. Besides, the diagnostic analytics used can be applied to measure the efficiency of past maintenance actions and identify failure modes [22]. For example, using data gathered before and after a repair, the maintenance teams are able to know if the repair corrected the issue or if other actions are required. This feedback loop lets the organizations store information about their strategies and maintain the asset reliability over time.

In general, diagnostic analytics should be considered one of the most valuable tools in the PM framework since it helps identify the causes of equipment malfunction and prevents future problems. Failure mode analysis also comes as an added advantage given that it allows organizations to identify the root causes of failure, hence providing preventative measures that help in the extension of asset durability and, therefore, the reduction of chances of complete failure.

Forecast Failures: Predictive Analytics

The essence of PM is therefore anchored on predictive analysis since this provides a means to anticipate when equipment is most likely to fail and correct this before the occurrence of a failure. Using real-time data that is received from sensors in the equipment, archive records of similar performances, and external parameters like weather conditions, *etc.*, predictive analytics can leverage ML models and statistical methods to identify the chances of failure in the future with considerable accuracy [15].

The major objective of every predictive analysis is to predict failures with a view to having the maintenance teams do their work at the most opportune time. On the other hand, preventive maintenance mainly focuses on time-based planning for repair and inspection, and maintenance is required only when the evidence calls for it. This eliminates useless maintenance activities and decreases the time of inoperability and physical breakdowns that would warrant expensive repair or cause a hazard.

Using software applications, the following steps are involved in predictive analytics: First, data is gathered from multiple sources such as IoT sensors, SCADA, or other data sources, and weather data can be included as an example of an external data source [11]. These data are then passed through other processes to identify patterns of equipment degradation, which predictive models then analyze. According to the example, a predictive model can assess the patterns in vibration data obtained from a motor and decide whether signs of wear exist. Once the model identifies a potential failure area, it also determines when the failure will occur, enabling maintenance to organize for repairs and replacement before they occur.

Another strength of predictive analytics is that the organization can consider condition-based maintenance. Instead of carrying out maintenance at random intervals, organizations can do it based on the real condition of the equipment. In the process, they can cut costs and the time taken for the exercise [19]. For instance, looking at the predictive analytics results, it is possible to speak about the well-being of some equipment; thus, it can be left until the signs of deterioration appear. On the other hand, if a failure is possible, the maintenance can be done even before the failure occurs.

Therefore, the deployment of predictive analytics can also be used in other areas for managing resources and inventories, such as inventory control. This way the organization can anticipate when particular elements or parts are going to break down, hence anticipate the spare parts and get the maintenance crews ready for the fix. It reduces the possibility of supply chain interruptions and shortens equipment's duration before they are back to full functionality [11].

Prescriptive Analytics for Decision-Making

While predictive analytics mainly deals with forecasting failures, prescriptive analytics goes further by providing recommendations. When it comes to maintenance, the data's prescriptive analytics allows for choosing the right maintenance tasks and the right time for them in the PM case [23]. Prescriptive analytics thus leverages information obtained from predictive models to provide remedies that are likely to help maintenance teams pick the right approach towards averting failures, lowering costs, and boosting the efficiency of their assets.

This analytics uses machine learning, optimization algorithms, and simulations to infer the most suitable maintenance strategies [15]. For instance, if the predictive system shows that an automotive part is likely to degrade in the next month, the prescriptive system may suggest that it should be repaired within one week to curb auto failure. Further, prescriptive analytics can help offer advice on the best way to maintain an element, whether it is cheaper to repair the component or replace it.

Most prescriptive analytics have the advantage of making automatic decisions. Sometimes, prescriptive analytics can be complemented by autonomous systems, which initiate maintenance processes based on the information found [21]. For instance, in a smart factory, prescriptive analytics can recommend ordering new spare parts or calling the maintenance team based on streams of data received from IoT sensors in real time. They also help reduce the workload on human operators and guarantee that maintenance work is done at the appropriate times. Prescriptive analytics not only helps in predictive maintenance decisions but also in deciding the utilization of resources and controlling the costs to the minimum level [11]. For instance, prescriptive models can use data concerning equipment usage, schedules, the frequency of maintenance, and costs incurred towards recommendations of the best practice. This may require performing maintenance during off-peak production to avoid interruption of the workflow process or doing the repairs on the most vital machines that are necessary for the production process, among others.

Prescriptive analytics avoids guesswork, offering concrete advice for improving how different organizations manage their maintenance programs. It also guarantees that the right activities are executed at the right time, thus reducing times when equipment will fail at the wrong time [23].

INTEGRATING PM FOR NATURAL DISASTERS

Identifying areas and integrating PM into disaster preparedness and response containers is one way of increasing the strength of infrastructure and communities. Disasters may include things like earthquakes, floods, and hurricanes, and these often result in disaster to the important essential facilities, which often lead to discontinuation of service provision, loss of property, and even a threat to human life [10]. When applied in frameworks for disaster risk management solutions, PM delivers methods that allow organizations to identify critical risks, their effects on facility systems, and ways to prevent severe damage in a disaster so that line operations and those maintaining facility systems are protected by taking exceptional care not to hamper the basic operations of the business [24].

Risk Assessment Models

Risk evaluation is one of the critical steps inherent in disaster management, and the Project Monitoring and Evaluation Committee (PMC) can help assess risks connected with natural disasters. The risk assessment models use information on the health condition of infrastructures, environment, and disasters to estimate the probability of failure and the impact that they may cause [2]. These models assist organizations in planning maintenance activities to identify areas that require reinforcement to relieve the impact of a catastrophe before it happens. It also assists in risk assessment since it offers up-to-date information on the performance of assets and levels of risk, which enables a quicker evaluation of risks.

Risk assessment models are usually developed from historical data, setting up a simulation environment, and continuous monitoring. Historical data gives better and more detailed information about past disaster events and how such a disaster affected structures and other physical [6]. IoT sensors and other remote sensing technologies allow for the updates of risks in real time as data becomes available on the risks because of the occurrence of different events.

Using PM in risk analysis, key areas of risk can be noted and adequate measures are taken to strengthen structures, minimizing chances of losing structures during disaster [25].

Early Warning System

Early warning systems based on information technology help give warning before a particular natural disaster occurs, so that necessary measures to protect the people and assets affected by the disaster can be taken. PM can also improve the reliability of early warning systems to maintain the critical infrastructures needed during disaster incidences [22]. For instance, methods used to give early warning of hurricanes require, among other things, weather prediction and tools for reaching the public. These communication networks may be ineffective if there is a problem with the infrastructure in handling the communication of the warning system.

In the case of disaster early warning, it supports the robust operation of overall infrastructure that supports the early warning systems, such as the telephone and telecommunication towers, power and electricity, and data centers, among others, through the prediction of failure and thus timely fixing [21]. Applying PM, the potential failure of these systems is detected, and a repair is initiated before a disaster occurs due to constant checkups of the health status of these systems. For instance, if a telecommunications tower has fatigue or wear or is structurally unsound, then the PM systems can also alert maintenance crews, ensuring that the tower is serviceable during a hurricane or flood. Besides building the background of the early warning system, the PM can be integrated into the flow of warnings. Data generated by PM sensors may be combined with the data used for disaster predictions. Meters on dams, levees, or other structures that hold water can measure the water level and its pressure in real time for flood alerts.

Combining methodologies of PM with early warning systems enables organizations to ensure the proper working of the critical infrastructures and make the preparedness for disaster more effective [10, 26].

Infrastructure Health Monitoring

Supervision of component health is a critical disaster protection practice because a breakdown in infrastructural systems during a disaster adds to the consequences. PM makes management of infrastructure health possible and may include bridges, roads, power plants, water systems, and telecommunication networks [2]. This data gives organizations signs of fatigue, corrosion, or environmental effects that call for pre-emptive measures to avoid failure during a disaster. Infrastructural health monitoring includes the use of diverse sensors and data acquisition systems. For instance, strain technologies on bridges record how much stress is applied on the structural members, while velocity sensors on equipment identify unevenness that can cause mechanical breakdowns. Exterior measuring devices measure conditions outside the structure, such as temperatures, humidity levels, and air quality, indicating how these external factors impact the structure's performance. When such data streams are incorporated into the prevention and correction systems, then the health status of an organization's infrastructure is constantly evaluated, and precautions to counter arising problems are taken.

An essential feature of the PM approach to monitoring the health of infrastructures is that it can identify some changes that are not especially startling at first sight [19]. For instance, the initial signs, which may encompass tiny cracks at the support beams of a bridge or minuscule shearing off the building's foundation, can easily be sensed by the given devices before they worsen. The above detection means that the maintenance teams can identify problems that require attention before they get out of hand, thus decreasing the chances of failure during natural disasters. Besides the assessment of single assets, it is possible to use the PM systems to commence with geospatial data to check the state of certain network infrastructures.

Disaster Recovery Planning

Disaster recovery planning refers to a process of identifying strategies and a set of measures that would have to be taken to reconstruct critical facilities and continuing services that were interrupted as the result of certain catastrophes [9]. The other application of PM in disaster recovery is to maintain and prepare business-critical systems in advance, thereby reducing the time and costs that may be required to rehabilitate them back to the standard operating position after a disaster. PM means systematic and regular checks on the health of infrastructures to prevent and mitigate the risks of encountering challenges that may hinder the continuity of operations during phases of recovery [13].

However, the mobilization of resources remains a challenge in disaster recovery, more so if they are to be used in a coordinated manner. The maintenance teams, which are assigned the task of repairing the site, must work with a bottleneck or allocate most resources to areas that have been destroyed. The actual value of these PM systems is in these mean-time decisions, where an organization can know which asset needs immediate attention and which assets they can deal with later [6]. Apart from providing a basis for identifying management, PM can be used to establish prior results for disaster response contingency [27]. For instance, if the predictive models show that a central bridge is likely to collapse during an earthquake, members of an organization can work on a smaller network of roads that the ambulances and fire brigades can access in the event of an earthquake. The use of PM in disaster recovery planning can help reduce the time taken to restore infrastructure and services, reduce costs, and enhance communities' resiliency [22].

Some real-life case studies of several disasters with their PM integration are explained below:

Flood Management in Kerala

- **Disaster:** The state of Kerala was flooded in 2018, and this led to damage to so many properties, people having to be evacuated from their homes, and many lost their lives. Causes of the flood are not just limited to water rainfall and inadequate control of water holding ponds.
- **PM Implementation:** After the disaster, there were IoT sensors and remote monitoring systems installed in the dams and reservoirs of the Kerala flood management system. These systems monitor amounts of water, velocities, and conditions of flood defense constructions in real time. It can be used to reduce cases of dam failure, and it can also provide early warning on floods. The authorities have adjusted the time for water release during the rainy season using simulation models to determine when water should be let into the rivers to reduce flooding downstream.

Seismic Monitoring in Gujarat

- **Disaster:** Gujarat is most vulnerable to earthquakes, one of which took place in 2001, the Bhuj Train Earthquake, which left thousands of people dead and several buildings wrecked.
- **PM Integration:** Post the earthquake, Gujarat was successful in establishing a seismic monitoring system along with IoT-based structural health monitoring of structures like bridges, dams, and buildings. Stress, vibration, and crack sensors provide permanent monitoring of the structures and allow for the identification of possible failures in advance. Current models then predict the effects of prospective future earthquakes to enable the preservation of structures weakened by the disasters.

Wildfire Preparedness in California

- **Disaster:** With droughts and heat waves, fire incidents affect many homes, power lines, and forests in California due to wildfires. The Camp Fire of 2018 was one of the most fatal fires that caused lots of casualties and property destruction.
- **PM Strategy:** Utilities such as Pacific Gas and Electric (PG&E) use predictive maintenance to inspect power lines in fire-susceptible zones. Heat and vibration IoT sensors help identify damage to even some lines that could lead to fires. This system allows utilities to avoid turning off the power and repairing it to lessen the wildfire hazard.

Hurricane Response in the United States

- **Disaster:** Hurricanes have destroyed several facilities, especially in coastal states, and affected services such as power and transportation, for example, in Florida and Louisiana. A tropical cyclone in 2005 called Hurricane Katrina affected so many people and overpowered the levee system in New Orleans.
- **PM and Early Warning:** Since then, the U.S. has incorporated predictive maintenance in its electricity infrastructure and flood protection. Not only do IoT sensors keep track of electrical substations, but they can also predict equipment failure before a storm occurs. Drones and remote sensing are used to determine the state of these infrastructures before the storms and to avoid physically having to access some of these locations.

CHALLENGES AND LIMITATIONS

Challenges: This section focuses on the challenges of PM in natural disasters.

- **Data Quality and Availability:** It is clear that the success of PM depends on the three A's, accurate and complete data [7]. Some of the challenges to prediction include sensor failure, partial data acquisition, and data corruption, such as sensor drift [17]. Hence, it is often routine to maintain, employ backups, and validate the sensors to obtain accurate data.
- **Data Timeliness:** Real-time monitoring of such situations requires proper time-bound data collection since it is essential for disaster-prone regions. Transferring data (for instance, during floods or earthquakes) may be slowed down by communication barriers [19]. Initiatives such as edge computing and reliable interconnectivity are needed.
- **Data Management:** Handling large amounts of data from sensors, SCADA systems, and satellite images is a challenge. Media cloud storage and large-volume hosting platforms such as Hadoop and other big data solutions are helpful in handling such data [16].
- **Multidisciplinary Data Integration:** Combining different types of information (weather, seismic, structural) in one system poses data heterogeneity and interoperability issues [14]. It is crucial to maintain cooperative relationships among the fields and make use of open data formats in this case.
- **Data Privacy and Security:** Any confidential information in fields such as healthcare or energy is at risk of cyberattacks. Data must be protected by using potent encryption, access control, and the law in protecting data, such as GDPR [21, 24, 28].

When considering these challenges, it is possible to apply PM to improve disaster and infrastructure systems.

Limitations

This section focuses on the limitations of PM in natural.

- **High Initial Setup Costs:** With the adoption of PM systems, there is a need for the extensive use of IoT sensors, storage of data, and analytic tools; these are capital-intensive and thus cannot be implemented in all firms or localities.
- **Complex Data Integration:** PM depends on a combination of different types of data (weather, seismic, structural health), which can be problematic due to different formats, standards, and sources. Managing multidisciplinary information is challenging and demands the use of appropriate technologies.
- **Data Quality Issues:** Prediction errors can occur due to wrong or partial information resulting from faulty sensors or the wrong way of data acquisition. The sensors need to be cleaned every now and then, and validation processes must be extremely rigid to appreciate data quality.
- **Technological Infrastructure Requirements:** PM systems require strong internet, power, and communications provisions for zero interface delay. Where there is constrained infrastructure, such as in disaster-prone or remote areas, the above issues defeat PM.
- **Limited Human Resources and Expertise:** PM success depends on knowledge of data storage and analysis, machine learning, and maintenance planning. Technical expertise is scarce, and in the areas where it is available, full utilization of PM is not easy.
- **Data Privacy and Security Concerns:** The information that PM systems collect characteristically belongs to a class of sensitive data. Maintaining data confidentiality and integrity in sensitive fields such as energy or health is vital to avoid failure or data leaks.

CONCLUSION

This chapter discusses the PM, which helps in guaranteeing efficient infrastructure upgrades where necessary, especially in vulnerable areas vulnerable to disasters. Collecting and analyzing real-time IoT data from sensors, weather, and seismic data on PM allow organizations to predict equipment failure before it happens. These preventive measures are effective in facilitating continuous delivery of essential services during and after disasters, minimal business disruptions and recovery periods, and less expensive repair seasons. PM also sustains early warning systems as much as it preserves basic structures required for organizational communication as well as disaster response. However, PM comes with the following risks: it has high implementation costs, has quality issues with data, and may take a lot of technical effort to merge distinct data sets. In the context of the current chapter, these inhibitors affect PM in areas with scarce or no technological equipment or human resources. Preserving data integrity and confidentiality is also an issue, as data from SCADA of critical infrastructure companies can be very sensitive. Nevertheless, PM has the potential to be a handy tool in disaster management. Focusing on failures is useful for predicting them and optimizing the recovery process; thus, it is a critical tool for enhancing organizational disaster resilience in risky locations. Through effective data integration, improved policies, and more infrastructure investment, PM can make a considerable contribution to reducing the impacts of disasters and enhancing asset recovery times.

REFERENCES

[1]   D.E. Alexander, *Disaster and emergency planning for preparedness, response, and recovery.* Oxford Research Encyclopedia of Natural Hazard Science, 2015.
       [http://dx.doi.org/10.1093/acrefore/9780199389407.013.12]

[2]   A.K.S. Jardine, D. Lin, and D. Banjevic, "A review on machinery diagnostics and prognostics implementing condition-based maintenance", *Mech. Syst. Signal Process.*, vol. 20, no. 7, pp. 1483-1510, 2006.
       [http://dx.doi.org/10.1016/j.ymssp.2005.09.012]

[3]   G.D. Haddow, J.A. Bullock, and D.P. Coppola, *Introduction to emergency management.* Butterworth-Heinemann, 2017.

[4]   R. Ghosh, D. Roy, and N.K. Das, "Predictive maintenance through Internet of Things: A machine learning-based approach", *Procedia Comput. Sci.*, vol. 170, pp. 846-851, 2020.

[5]   C.S. Holling, "Resilience and stability of ecological systems", *Annu. Rev. Ecol. Syst.*, vol. 4, no. 1, pp. 1-23, 1973.
       [http://dx.doi.org/10.1146/annurev.es.04.110173.000245]

[6]   X. Wang, Y. Zhang, J. Liu, Y. Wang, and X. Zhou, "Data-driven predictive maintenance for intelligent systems", *Industrial Electronics Technology Handbook,* pp. 1049-1061, 2017.

[7]   Y. Lei, N. Li, L. Guo, N. Li, T. Yan, and J. Lin, "Machinery health prognostics: A systematic review from data acquisition to RUL prediction", *Mech. Syst. Signal Process.*, vol. 104, pp. 799-834, 2018.
       [http://dx.doi.org/10.1016/j.ymssp.2017.11.016]

[8]   N.A. Hoult, P.R. Fidler, P.G. Hill, and C.R. Middleton, "Long-term wireless structural health monitoring of the Ferriby Road Bridge", *J. Bridge Eng.*, vol. 13, no. 6, pp. 618-625, 2008.

[9]   S.L. Cutter, L. Barnes, M. Berry, C. Burton, E. Evans, E. Tate, and J. Webb, "A place-based model for understanding community resilience to natural disasters", *Glob. Environ. Change,* vol. 18, no. 4, pp. 598-606, 2008.
       [http://dx.doi.org/10.1016/j.gloenvcha.2008.07.013]

[10]   J.H. Sorensen, "Hazard warning systems: Review of 20 years of progress", *Nat. Hazards Rev.*, vol. 1, no. 2, pp. 119-125, 2000.
       [http://dx.doi.org/10.1061/(ASCE)1527-6988(2000)1:2(119)]

[11]   J. Wan, S. Tang, D. Li, S. Wang, C. Liu, H. Abbas, and A.V. Vasilakos, "A manufacturing big data solution for active preventive maintenance", *IEEE Trans. Industr. Inform.*, vol. 13, no. 4, pp. 2039-2047, 2017.
       [http://dx.doi.org/10.1109/TII.2017.2670505]

[12]   J.P. Lynch, and K.J. Loh, "A summary review of wireless sensors and sensor networks for structural health monitoring", *Shock and Vibration Digest,* vol. 38, no. 2, pp. 91-128, 2006.
       [http://dx.doi.org/10.1177/0583102406061499]

[13]   K. Smith, and D.N. Petley, *Environmental hazards: Assessing risk and reducing disaster.* Routledge, 2009.
[http://dx.doi.org/10.4324/9780203884805]

[14]   R.J. Geller, "Earthquake prediction: a critical review", *Geophys. J. Int.,* vol. 131, no. 3, pp. 425-450, 1997.
[http://dx.doi.org/10.1111/j.1365-246X.1997.tb06588.x]

[15]   A. Mosavi, P. Ozturk, and K. Chau, "Flood prediction using machine learning models: Literature review", *Water,* vol. 10, no. 11, p. 1536, 2018.
[http://dx.doi.org/10.3390/w10111536]

[16]   Z. Wu, M. Ma, D. Yang, Y. Huang, and X. He, "Data-driven approaches for predictive maintenance of industrial equipment: A survey", *IEEE Access,* vol. 8, pp. 149864-149881, 2020.

[17]   S. Manfreda, M.F. McCabe, P.E. Miller, R. Lucas, V. Pajuelo Madrigal, G. Mallinis, E. Ben Dor, D. Helman, L. Estes, G. Ciraolo, J. Müllerová, F. Tauro, M.I. De Lima, J.L.M.P. De Lima, A. Maltese, F. Frances, K. Caylor, M. Kohv, M. Perks, G. Ruiz-Pérez, Z. Su, G. Vico, and B. Toth, "On the use of unmanned aerial systems for environmental monitoring", *Remote Sens. (Basel),* vol. 10, no. 4, p. 641, 2018.
[http://dx.doi.org/10.3390/rs10040641]

[18]   A.M. Abu-Mahfouz, and G.P. Hancke, "Design and deployment of wireless sensor networks for health monitoring systems in asset management and disaster management applications", *IEEE Access,* vol. 6, pp. 5300-5307, 2018.

[19]   Y. Kang, and O. Mirza, "Artificial intelligence and machine learning applications in predictive maintenance and asset management: A review", *Energy Rep.,* vol. 7, pp. 2657-2670, 2021.

[20]   P.C. Zikopoulos, C. Eaton, D. deRoos, T. Deutsch, and G. Lapis, *Understanding big data: Analytics for enterprise class Hadoop and streaming data.* McGraw-Hill Osborne Media, 2012.

[21]   A. Humayed, J. Lin, F. Li, and B. Luo, "Cyber-physical systems security—A survey", *IEEE Internet Things J.,* vol. 4, no. 6, pp. 1802-1831, 2017.
[http://dx.doi.org/10.1109/JIOT.2017.2703172]

[22]   C.E. Ebeling, *An introduction to reliability and maintainability engineering.* McGraw-Hill Education, 2019.

[23]   M. Chen, S. Mao, and Y. Liu, "Big data: A survey", *Mob. Netw. Appl.,* vol. 19, no. 2, pp. 171-209, 2014.
[http://dx.doi.org/10.1007/s11036-013-0489-0]

[24]   G.P. Cimellaro, A.M. Reinhorn, and M. Bruneau, "Framework for analytical quantification of disaster resilience", *Eng. Struct.,* vol. 32, no. 11, pp. 3639-3649, 2010.
[http://dx.doi.org/10.1016/j.engstruct.2010.08.008]

[25]   S. Kaplan, and B.J. Garrick, "On the quantitative definition of risk", *Risk Anal.,* vol. 1, no. 1, pp. 11-27, 1981.
[http://dx.doi.org/10.1111/j.1539-6924.1981.tb01350.x] [PMID: 11798118]

[26]   H.A. Saleh, and H. Eschenauer, "Multidisciplinary optimization in engineering disaster preparedness and prevention", *Eng. Optim.,* vol. 42, no. 9, pp. 807-815, 2010.

[27]   M.A. Deodhar, and C.W. de Silva, "Multidisciplinary design and optimization of disaster relief shelters", *J. Aerosp. Eng.,* vol. 16, no. 3, pp. 104-111, 2003.

[28]   Q. Yan, and L. Huang, "Cybersecurity challenges in smart grids and IoT networks: Emerging vulnerabilities, attack surface, and mitigation techniques", *IEEE Internet Things J.,* vol. 8, no. 13, pp. 10491-10512, 2021.

CHAPTER 7

Advancing Agriculture 4.0 through Federated Learning Techniques: Collaborative Analysis of Distributed Agricultural Data

Ankush Kumar Gaur[1,*] and **Joseph Arul Valan**[2]

[1] *UPES, Dehradun, Uttarakhand 248007, India*

[2] *National Institute of Technology Nagaland, Chumukedima, Dimapur, Nagaland, India*

Abstract: Agriculture 4.0 is evolving by combining traditional farming methods with advanced technologies from Industry 4.0, offering farmers new opportunities to improve their agricultural practices. However, implementing Agriculture 4.0 through the incorporation of these innovative technologies and evidence-based strategies is facing challenges. Moreover, data is proven as one of the most significant assets in the era of big data. Analyzing massively distributed agricultural data while ensuring its privacy, security, and scalability concerns is also an important challenge. This chapter presents the state-of-the-art by leveraging the applications of federated learning methods to handle the aforementioned challenges and promote collaborative analysis of distributed agricultural data. In this work, we utilize the publicly accessible Rice Dataset Cammeo and Osmancik, which comprises 3,810 instances, with 2180 instances of Osmancik and 1,630 instances of Cammeo. This study presents a federated learning-based rice variety classification (AgriFedClassifier) framework for analyzing distributed agricultural data while safeguarding the privacy and security of clients' local data. We simulate the framework with Multilayer Perceptron models at each client, training the models for a fixed number of local epochs using local data and aggregating model updates at the server employing Federated Averaging (FedAvg) and Federated Proximal (FedProx) methods. We evaluate the effectiveness of federated learning techniques on horizontally distributed agricultural data under two scenarios: IID and non-IID datasets. Experimental results demonstrate that in non-IID data distributions with 80% of stragglers (nodes encountering delays), FedProx achieved a classification accuracy of 89.33%, whereas FedAvg achieved only 50% accuracy. The results section presents an analysis of the effectiveness of federated and centralized models. Overall, we observe that FedProx effectively managed data heterogeneity, mitigated delays, and improved efficiency compared to FedAvg.

---

* **Corresponding author Ankush Kumar Gaur:** UPES, Dehradun, Uttarakhand 248007, India;
E-mail: ankushkumardddm@gmail.com

Tanu Singh, Vinod Patidar, Arvind Panwar & Urvashi Sugandh (Eds.)

Keywords: Aggregation methods, Agriculture 4.0, Collaborative machine learning, Distributed machine learning, Federated learning, Federated optimization, IID, Industry 4.0, Non-IID.

INTRODUCTION

The evolution from Industry 4.0 to Agriculture 4.0 [1, 2] investigates the incorporation of innovative, cutting-edge solutions, including IoT, big data processing, AI-driven systems, and robotics into agricultural activities, enhancing crop productivity, efficient resource utilization, and sustainable development. This emphasizes essential technologies such as IoT for real-time monitoring [3], AI and big data for predictive analytics [4], robotics for automation [5, 6], and blockchain for ensuring supply chain transparency [7]. Although these advantages exist, there are barriers that hinder the practical implementation of Agriculture 4.0 [8 - 10], such as small-scale farmers investing a high-cost technology, gap between farmers and AI researchers, managing and analyzing the vast amount of heterogeneous agricultural data, and need for robust infrastructure and expertise. Moreover, there is a lack of skills, as farmers need training to use these advanced technologies [11]. Ensuring data security and addressing security are other significant challenges.

Federated learning (FL) has the capacity to offer practical approaches to many of the problems encountered in Agriculture 4.0. FL [12] is a distributed machine learning approach that enables decentralized data processing. It promises benefits to micro farmers by allowing them to leverage advanced AI and machine learning applications without investing in high-cost infrastructure [13, 14]. This approach utilizes the computational power of client machines, which may reduce the need for expensive centralized data centers. Additionally, FL is capable of promoting collaboration between farmers and AI researchers, filling the skill gap by allowing farmers to use refined models developed from a wide pool of agricultural data. This decentralized method also promises data privacy and security, as data remains local, mitigating the risk of data theft [15]. Moreover, FL has the ability to handle heterogeneous data from various sources, which helps manage and analyze vast amounts of distributed agricultural data. Distributing the processing workload makes AI more accessible, promoting the larger adoption of innovative technologies like big data and IoT [16 - 18] in agriculture and empowering the sustainable development of Agriculture 4.0.

This work aims to analyze the performance of federated learning techniques [19, 20] for distributed agricultural data analysis. We introduce a federated learning-based rice variety classification (AgriFedClassifier) framework to demonstrate the practical implementation of FL. To verify the stability of the proposed framework in defiance of heterogeneous agricultural data and stragglers, we distribute the data in two scenarios: IID and non-IID datasets. We also compare the effectiveness of federated and non-federated models. Based on the analysis

results, we observe that FedProx effectively manages data heterogeneity, mitigates delays, and outperforms FedAvg.

FEDERATED LEARNING APPROACH

FL involves a ML method where several decentralized devices jointly train a common model void of transferring their data off local devices [21 - 23]. This feature allows us to perform machine learning in those locations where previously it was not possible. To implement this client server approach in agriculture, several steps will need to be followed sequentially. Firstly, the server establishes a global machine learning model and transmits it to all engaged clients. Secondly, each client trains this commonly received model locally using their own data. Once local training has been concluded after several iterations, the clients revert the revised model parameters relayed to the server to complete the third step. In the fourth step, the server aggregates these parameters using aggregation techniques to update the global model. Steps 1 to 4 continue iteratively until the model converges to an optimal state. Throughout this process, raw data remains local, maintaining its privacy and reducing the risk of data theft [24, 25]. It also promotes collaboration among remote clients without revealing their identities to one another.

Federated Learning Methods: Federated Averaging (FedAvg)

This method in federated learning is used to train a global model by averaging the model updates from multiple client devices. In the kth communication round, the server does global aggregation by applying the rule:

$$\bar{\omega}k = \frac{1}{N}\sum_{i=1}^{N} w_i^k \qquad\qquad (1)$$

where $w_i^k, \bar{\omega}k$ represents a client's local weight as well as the aggregated weight.

Generally, the aim of this method is to minimize the global loss for which the following global loss function will be utilized.

$$F(\overline{\omega}k) = \frac{1}{N}\sum_{i=1}^{N} F_i(\overline{\omega}k) \tag{2}$$

where Fi ($\cdot$) represents the local loss function for the i-th client.

In standard FL, learning goals can be specified as finite sum objectives:

$$\min_{w \in R^d} f(w) \ where \ f(w) \overset{def}{=} \frac{1}{n}\sum_{i=1}^{n} f_i(w) \tag{3}$$

Here, data is divided across 'K' clients, along with 'Pk', which is the collection of data point indexes for client k, together with nk = | Pk |. As a result, we can change objective (3) to:

$$f(w) = \sum_{k=1}^{K} \frac{n_k}{n} F_k(w) \, , \text{where } F_k(w) = \frac{1}{n_k} \sum_{i \in P_k} f_i(w) \tag{4}$$

However, FedAvg assumes that all participating devices or clients will finish all training iterations (*i.e.*, epochs). In practice, devices often vary in their hardware capabilities, leading to discrepancies where devices completing fewer epochs may hinder the convergence rate [26 - 28]. Additionally, FedAvg computes a weighted average based on the quantity of data each device holds, potentially favoring devices with larger datasets. This limitation opens the door for further research to improve the aggregation method.

Federated Proximal (FedProx)

FedProx improves upon FedAvg by effectively managing the system heterogeneity among participating devices. While FedAvg assumes uniform computational capabilities and excludes devices that cannot complete the required number of epochs, FedProx incorporates a proximal term into the local objective function. This addition stabilizes the optimization process, enabling devices to execute differing levels of local tasks based on their specific system limitations without significantly disrupting the global model's convergence. By accommodating a range of computational capabilities, FedProx facilitates more robust and efficient model training in heterogeneous environments, making it a superior choice for federated learning scenarios with diverse device capabilities. The following equation represents the procedure for calculating weights under FedProx:

$$w_{new} = \frac{1}{K} \sum_{k=1}^{K} w_k + \lambda \sum_{k=1}^{K} \frac{\mu}{2} \| w_k - w_{old} \| \qquad (5)$$

Where w_{new} represents the updated global model weights after one round of federated learning. K shows the total count of involved devices or clients in the federated learning process. wkare the model weights from the k-th client. λ is a regularization factor that regulates the contribution of the proximal term. μ is another regularization parameter that scales the impact of the difference between the new and old weights. $\| w_k - w_{old} \|$ represents the difference between the k-th client's weights and the old global weights.

Average of Clients Weights

The term $\frac{1}{K} \sum_{k=1}^{K} w_k$ of equation (5) calculates the simple average of the weights from all K clients. This is similar to the FedAvg approach, where the global model is refined through the averaging of local models.

Proximal Term

The term $\lambda \sum_{k=1}^{K} \frac{\mu}{2} \| w_k - w_{old} \|$ of equation (5) represents an additional regularization that FedProx introduces. This term penalizes large deviations in the client weights wk from the old global weights wold. The parameters λ and μ control the strength of this penalization.

Combined Effect

Incorporating the proximal term helps stabilize the optimization process by discouraging drastic changes in the local models. This is especially useful in heterogeneous environments where different devices may have varying amounts of computational power and data, leading to inconsistent updates. By adding this regularization, FedProx can achieve more stable and efficient convergence compared to FedAvg. Thus, the given equation reflects how FedProx modifies the standard FedAvg approach by adding a term that accounts for the incongruity between the current local weights and the previous global weights, controlled by regularization parameters λ and μ. This modification aims to improve the robustness and convergence of the FL process in diverse settings.

MATERIALS AND METHODS

Dataset Description

To address the requirements for agricultural data, we acquired the Rice Dataset (Cammeo and Osmancik) [29] accessed through the UCI Machine Learning Repository database. The dataset includes 3,810 images of rice grains from two species with 2180 instances of Osmancik and 1,630 instances of Cammeo, which were processed to extract features. For each grain of rice, 7 morphological features were derived.

Data Preprocessing

In the tabular dataset of Cammeo and Osmancik, significant diversity among samples within classes was noted. To mitigate this, we used a random oversampling technique to create additional instances for the underrepresented class. Additionally, we standardized the input feature data to ensure each feature contributes uniformly during the learning process, averting any disproportionate influence due to varying scales. Fig. (**1**) demonstrates the process of generating additional instances using the oversampling method. Fig. (**2**) shows the standardization of input features data.

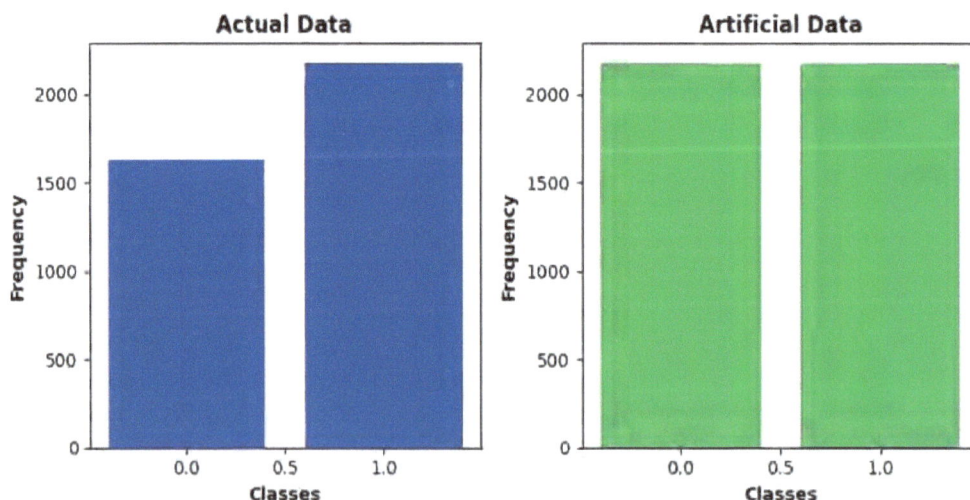

Fig. (1). Number of samples per class before and after preprocessing.

Data Distribution: IID *vs* non-IID

In this research study, we employ the Cammeo and Osmancik Dataset for classification in a Federated Learning (FL) setup involving 10 clients. It is essential to grasp the data distribution in FL situations as it impacts model effectiveness and client simplification. We consider two key setups: IID data distribution and non-IID data distribution.

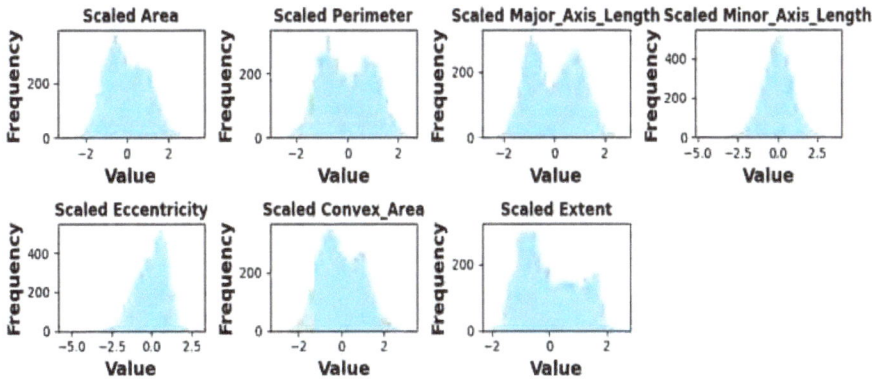

Fig. (2). Normalized input feature data.

Within the IID framework, data belonging to each client is presumed to be autonomously drawn from a similar distribution, enabling easier model consolidation. Primarily, the dataset comprises 3,810 instances of two different types of rice. Post-preprocessing, the dataset expands to 4,360 samples. Following an 80-20 train-test split, the training set consists of 3,488 samples, with the test set containing 872 samples. Each client in the IID scenario receives 348 distinct samples for local training, ensuring no overlap between clients. Additionally, 87 samples are designated for testing purposes per client, as visualized in Fig. (**3**).

The presence of non-IID features in data from different clients in agriculture can arise from differences in soil types, environmental conditions, and farming techniques. Because of the non-IID data distribution, models must be trained and aggregated with care, taking into account client variability while maintaining security and privacy.

In non-IID data distribution, each client is randomly assigned 50% of the total labels in order to address data heterogeneity. As shown in Fig. (**4**), each client's average train sample length is roughly 174.0, while each client's average test sample length is 43.5.

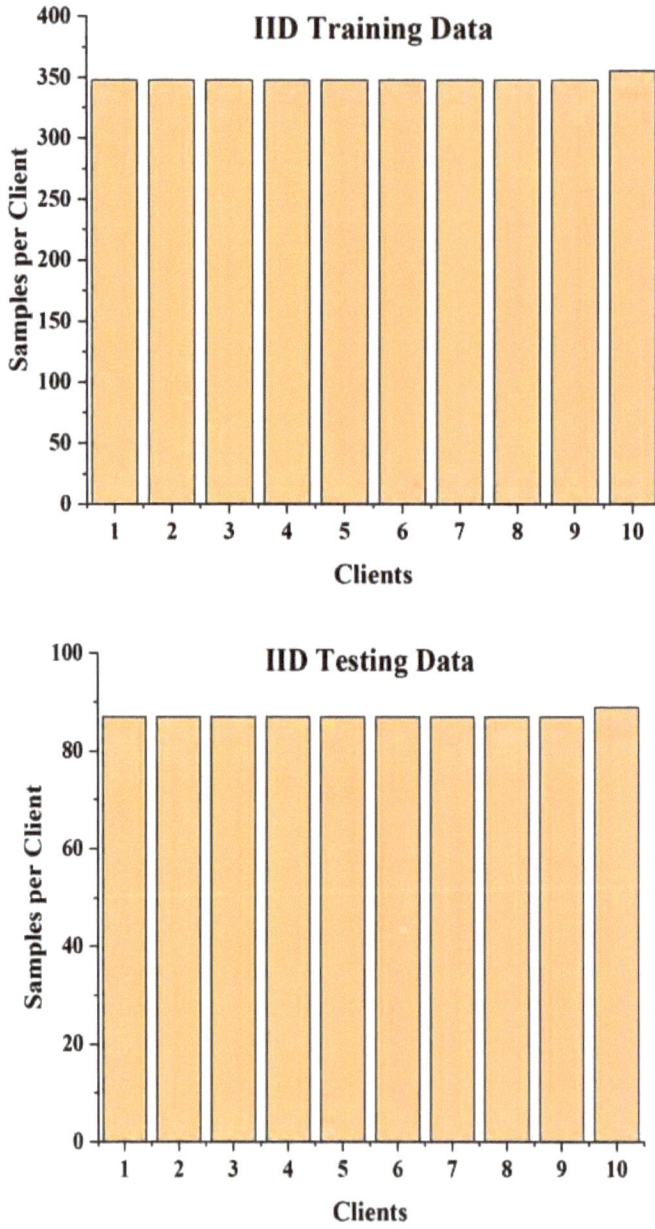

Fig. (3). Client-specific train and test data distributed in an IID fashion.

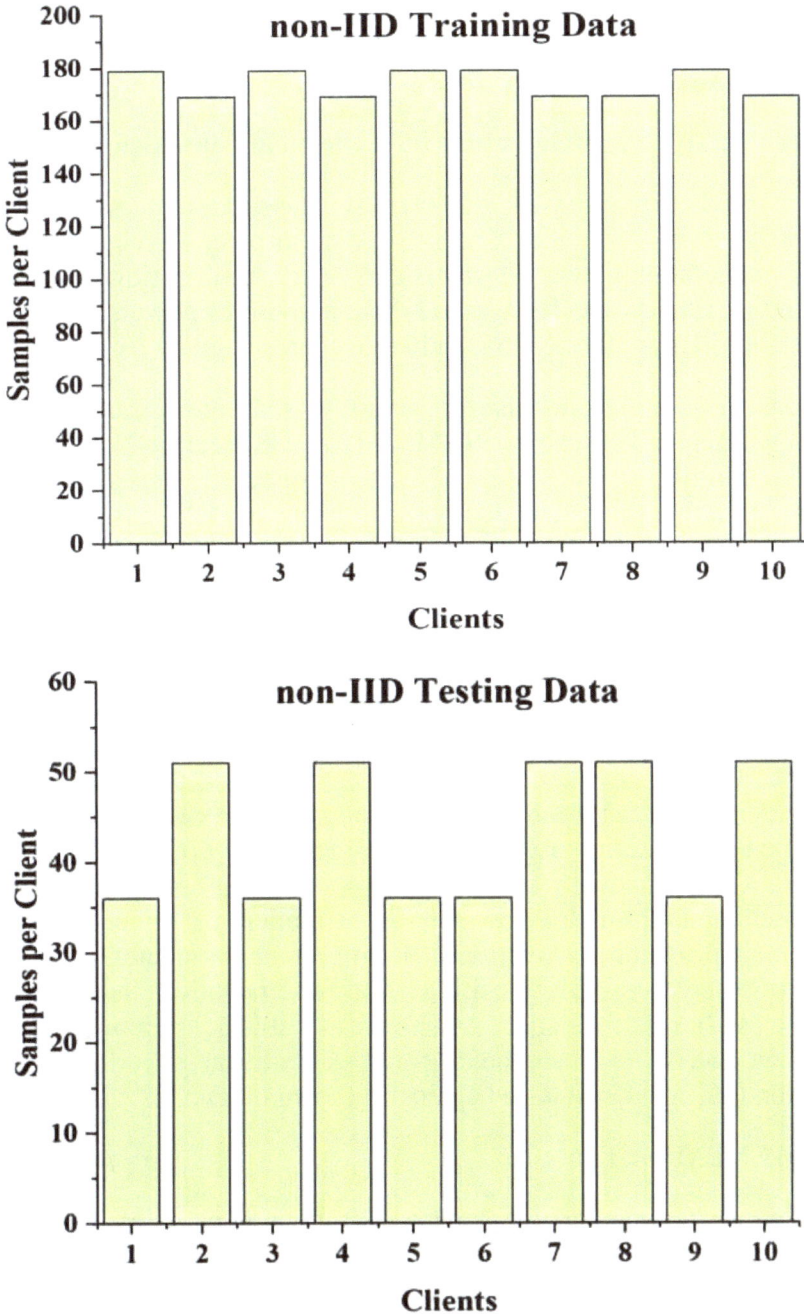

Fig. (4). Client-specific train and test data distributed in a non-IID fashion.

By analyzing the impact of both independent and identically distributed (IID) and non-uniform data distribution distributions on the model effectiveness and convergence within the framework of FL, this research endeavors to offer valuable perspectives on how to effectively utilize diverse data sources in agricultural classification assignments.

Framework and Model architecture for Federated Classification

The Federated Learning-based rice variety classification (AgriFedClassifier) framework used in this study was created to protect farmers' privacy while promoting cooperation between farmers and agricultural institutions, as shown in Fig. (**5**). In this framework, farmers are the autonomous players, and agricultural research institutions are the servers; a client is represented by i.

While there exist other models for feature-based rice variety classification, including Multilayer Perceptron, SVM, DT, and K-nearest Neighbor, we only address the Multilayer Perceptron (MLP) architecture presented in Fig. (**6**). Instead of evaluating the exact accuracy of various models, our research seeks to assess the difference in performance between federated and standalone models. This comparison study provides insightful information about how well federated learning protects data privacy and fosters cooperative learning among distributed data sources. These kinds of findings help to enhance decentralized machine learning techniques.

Performance Metrics

The accuracy with which a model predicts outcomes in comparison to the actual results is the usual criterion used to evaluate the efficacy of a model developed or assessed for a classification task. However, considering only prediction accuracy might not deliver a thorough assessment of the model's performance. A confusion matrix, which provides an overview of important parameters, including true positives, true negatives, false positives, and false negatives, is a useful tool for analyzing classifier performance. As shown in Table **1**, these metrics—forming the confusion matrix—evaluate the classifier's effectiveness, particularly in binary classification [30, 31], when tested against a known dataset.

EXPERIMENTAL SETUP

We validate the suggested approach with PyTorch. The experiment uses particular packages and libraries and is run on Google Colab. Several replicas of the MLP model are created using deep copy, and data imbalance is handled *via* RandomOverSampler. Matplotlib.Plotting real and synthetic data is done with pyplot; feature scaling is done with StandardScaler, and data splitting is done with train_test_split, *etc*.

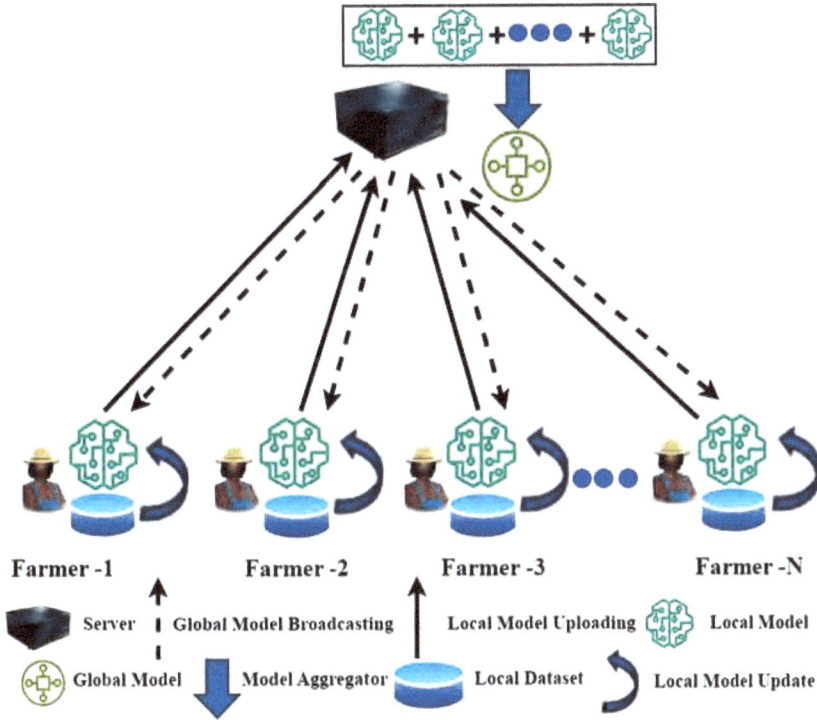

Fig. (5). AgriFed Classifier.

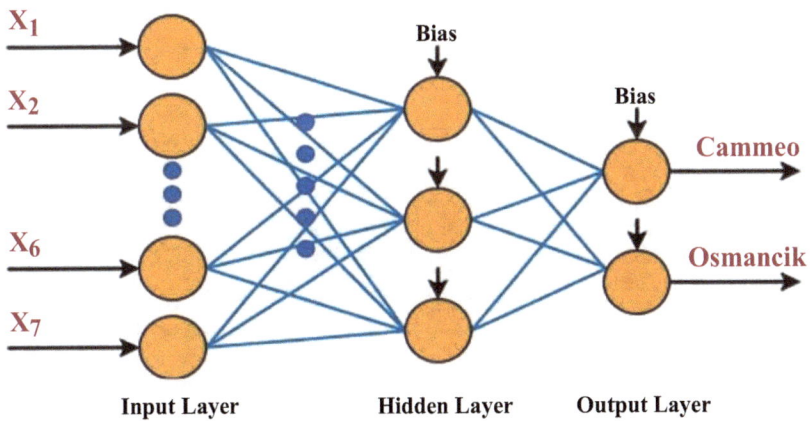

Fig. (6). MLP model architecture.

Table 1. Confusion matrix to classify binary classes.

		Predicted	
	-	Positive C $^+$	Negative C $^-$
Actual	Positive C $^+$	True positive (TP) / Positive cases correctly classified	False negative (FN) examples inaccurately identified as negative but actually positive
-	Negative C $^-$	False positive (FP) examples inaccurately classified as positive but actually negative	True negative (TN) / Correctly predicted negative outcomes

Using the training sets of ten clients, we mimicked AgriFedClassifier. For each of the first 20 communication rounds, we set the batch size to 10 and the learning rate to 0.35 and executed 10 local training sessions to train MLP models in AgriFedClassifier. The MLP network architecture's parameters are displayed in Table **2**, and the AgriFedClassifier's parameters are shown in Table **3**. FedAvg and FedProx federated learning approaches are used to aggregate the model updates.

Table 2. Hyperparameters of the MLP model.

Parameter Identifiers	Parameters
Count of hidden layers	1
Hidden layers' activation function	Sigmoid
Output layer's activation function	Sigmoid
Training rate	0.35
Optimal epoch count for local training	10

Table 3. Parameters of AgriFedClassifier.

Parameter Identifiers	Parameters
Server and Client architectures	MLP
Number of participating clients	10
Round count	20
Fraction of clients	1
Stragglers fraction	0 (0 to 1)
Forms of aggregation	Average and Proximal
mu (Regularization factor)	0 and >0

RESULTS: IID *VS* NON-IID

To collaboratively categorize rice types, we used the distributed classification technique in this section. Implementing the Federated Averaging and FedProx strategies in federated learning, we first examined the classification conclusions of rice varieties underneath two diverse data distribution circumstances (*i.e.*, IID and non-IID). Furthermore, we examined the effects on categorization accuracy of different client participation percentages in the federation (*e.g.*, 0%, 40%, and 80%). Lastly, we contrasted the results of models that were federated with those that were not.

In this experiment, ten clients participated in the federated categorization procedure. To explore communication challenges such as poor internet connection, electricity blackouts, and resource shortages, we modified the client count, sending model revisions transmitted to the server for assembling the universal model. Moreover, non-IID data was used for addressing data heterogeneity, with local training occurring on different samples from various classes. Both aggregation methods performed as expected under favorable conditions, as shown by the training error rates and test accuracy levels presented in Fig. (**7a-f**) across different scenarios. Moreover, we found a trend in the non-IID data, as shown in Fig. (**8a-f**). A rise in the straggler count was correlated with a fall in the global MLP model's performance.

Comparative Analysis of Performance in Federated *versus* Non-federated Environments

This study's primary focus is not on directly comparing exact accuracies. In lieu of this, it aims to assess the relative operational success of federated and centralized models. To provide a comprehensive evaluation, a range of metrics—including Correctness Rate, Error Rate, Precision, Recall Rate, Specificity, and F1 Performance —were used for benchmarking. The traditional categorization model achieved high accuracy due to the unified storage for the full dataset. In contrast, when employing the federated classification approach, where all clients participated in federated modeling without sharing their local data, the results showed minimal loss compared to the centralized scenario. Tables **4** (**a**) and (**b**) present the assessment of the federated MLP model's performance on IID datasets employing FedAvg and FedProx aggregation protocols, respectively. Table **5** provides a performance comparison of federated and centralized models under optimal circumstances. Meanwhile, Table **6** highlights the strength of federated learning techniques when handling non-IID data and varying straggler percentages.

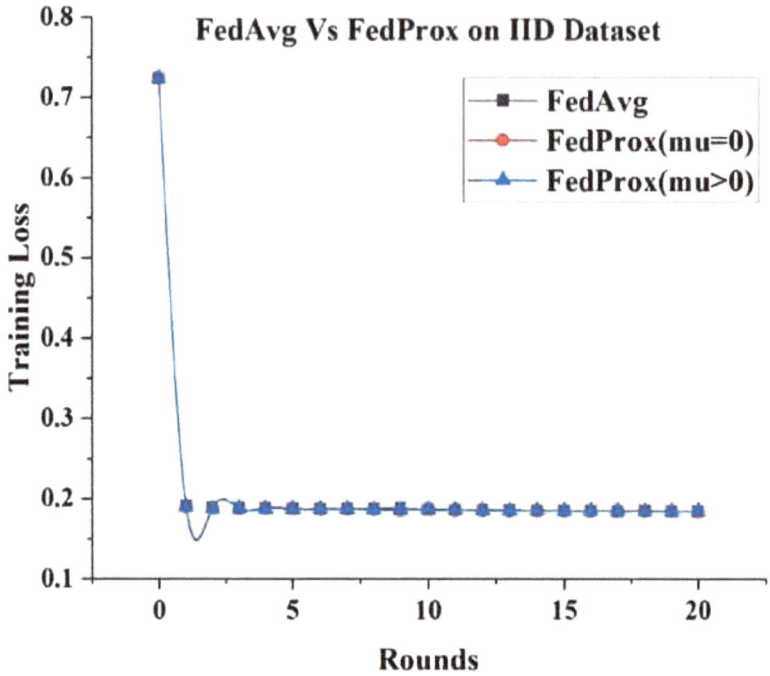

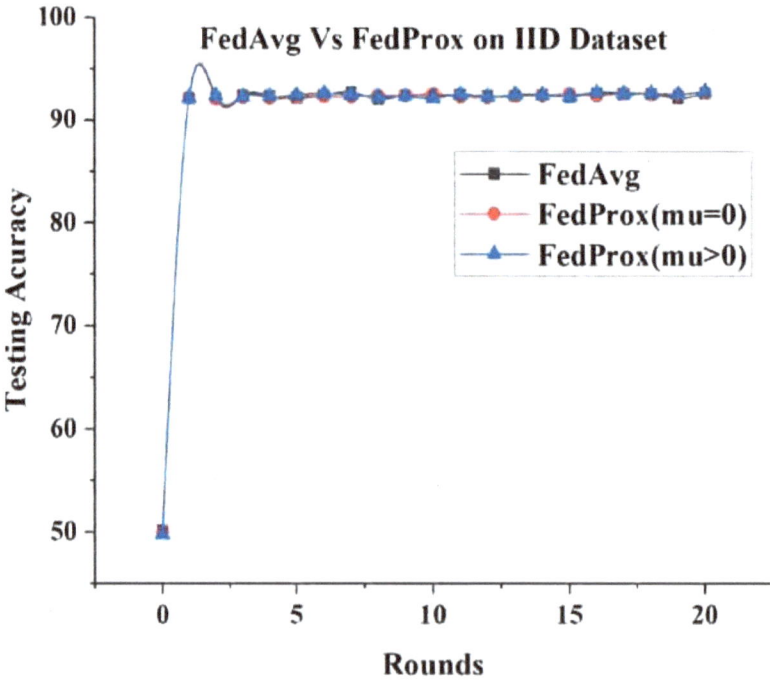

(Fig. 7) contd.....

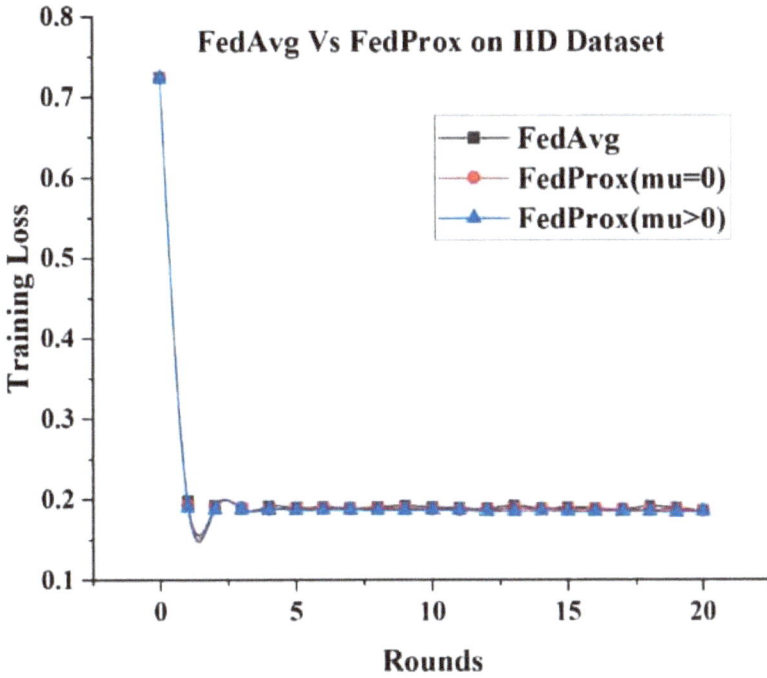

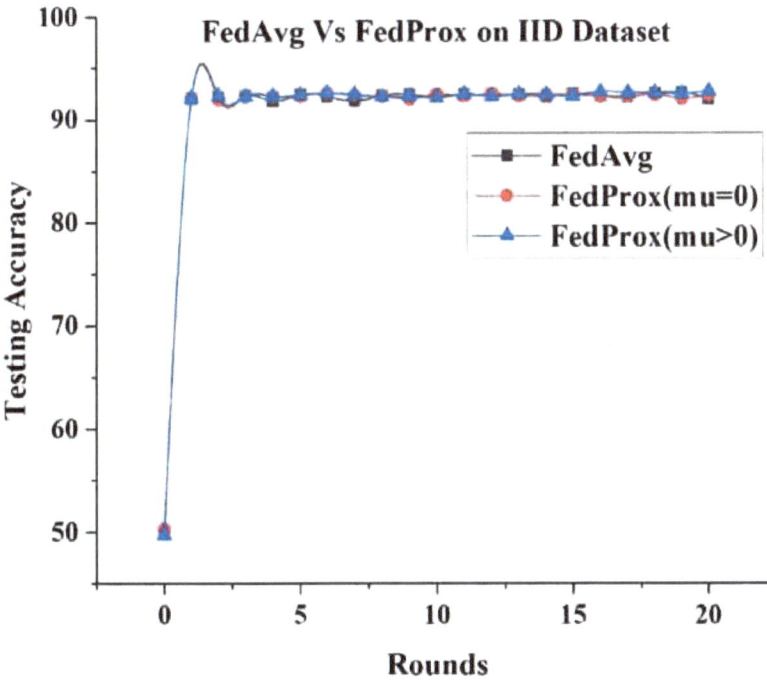

(Fig. 7) contd.....

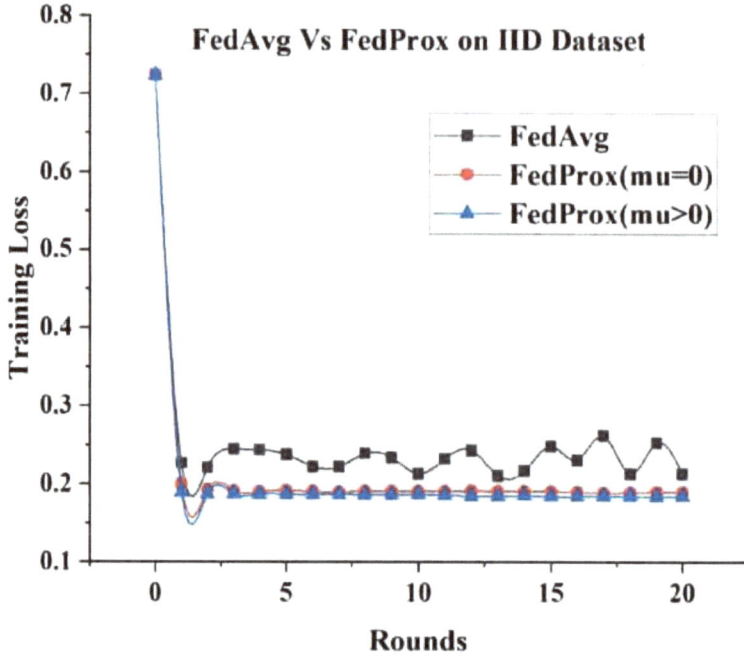

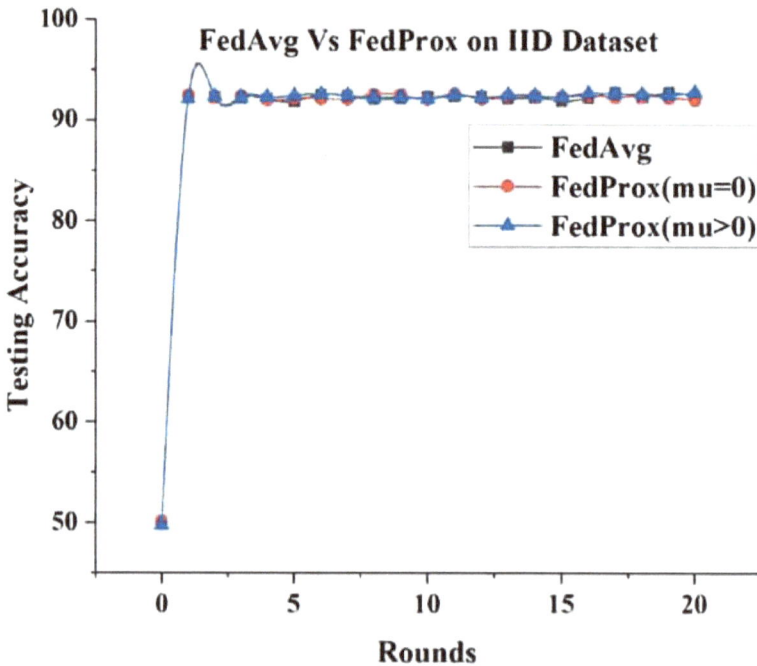

Fig. (7). (**a**) and (**b**) illustrate the training loss metrics and accuracy on test data under conditions with no stragglers, while (**c**) and (**d**) depict the same benchmarks with 40% stragglers and (**e**) and (**f**) with 80% stragglers.

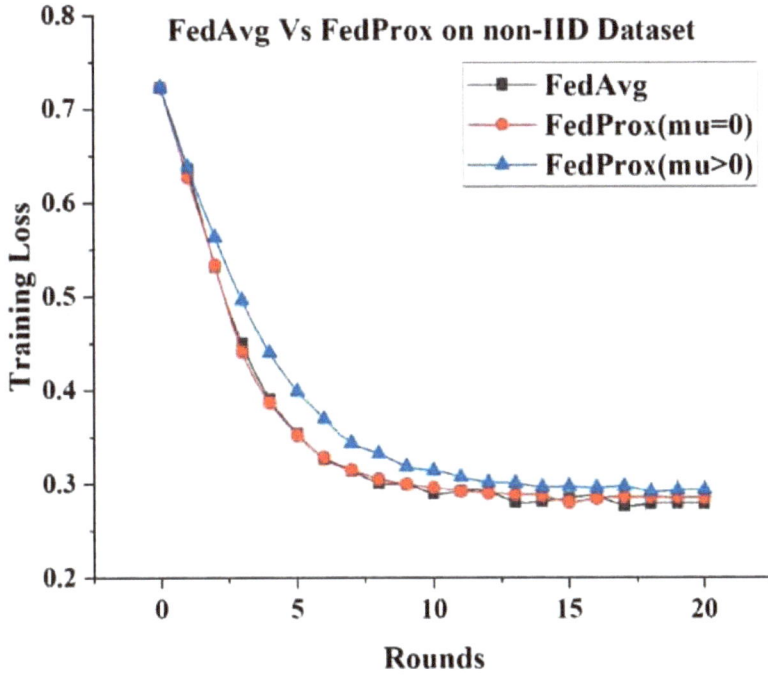

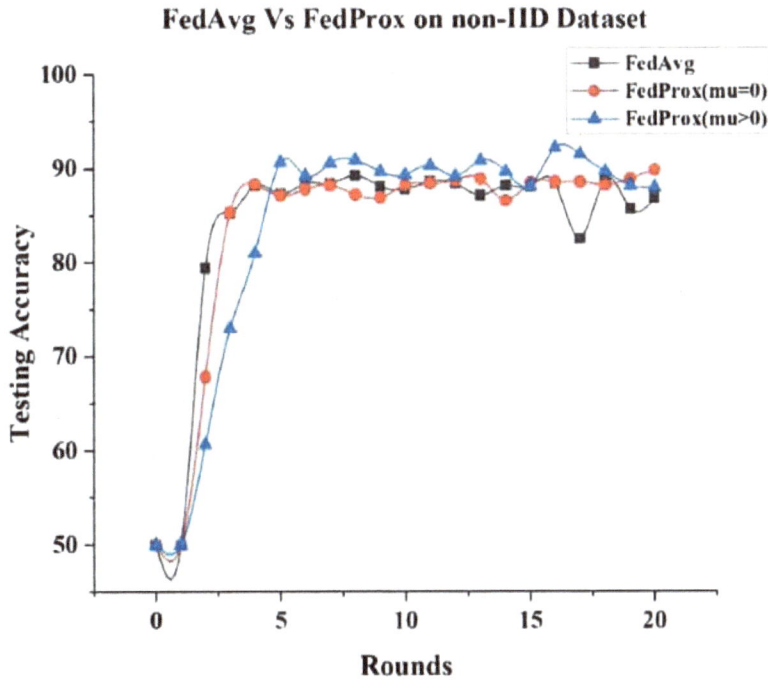

(Fig. 8) contd.....

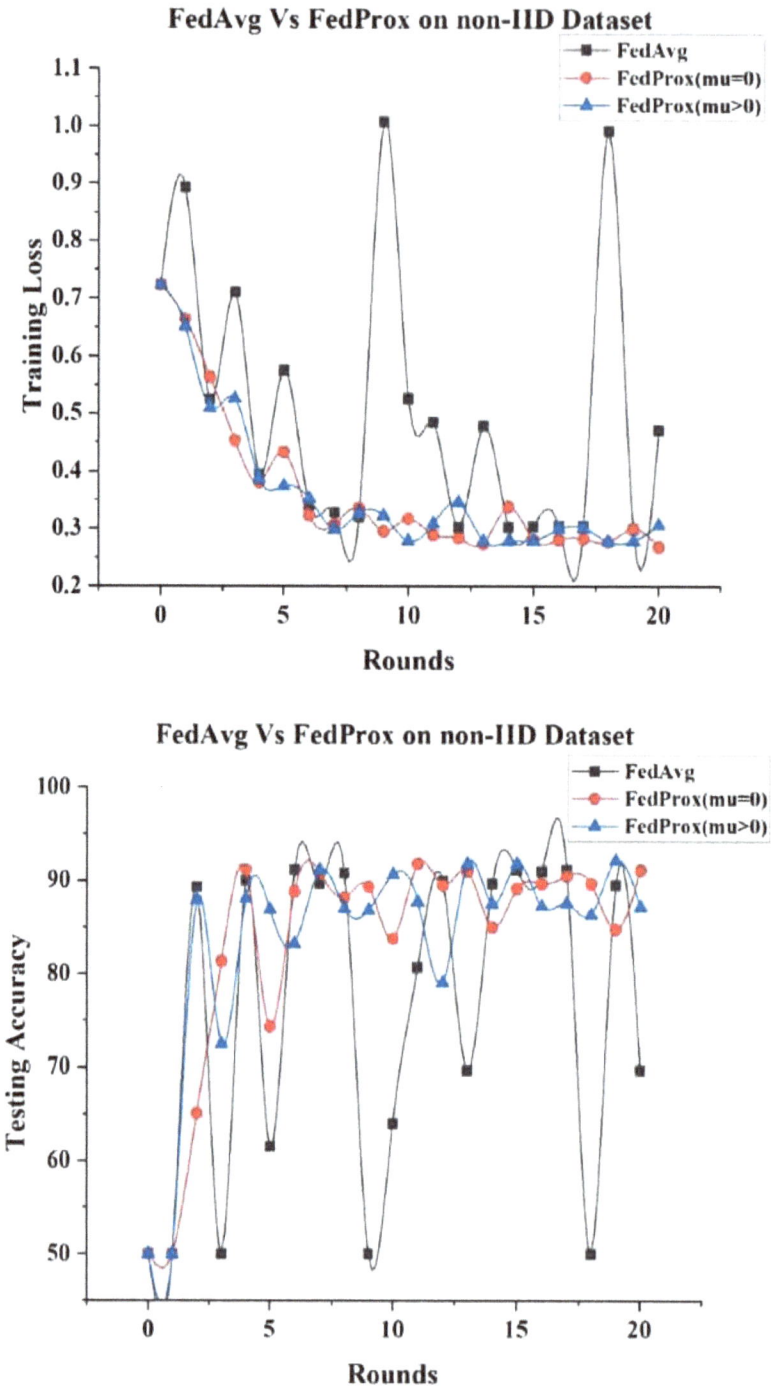

FedAvg Vs FedProx on non-IID Dataset

FedAvg Vs FedProx on non-IID Dataset

(Fig. 8) contd.....

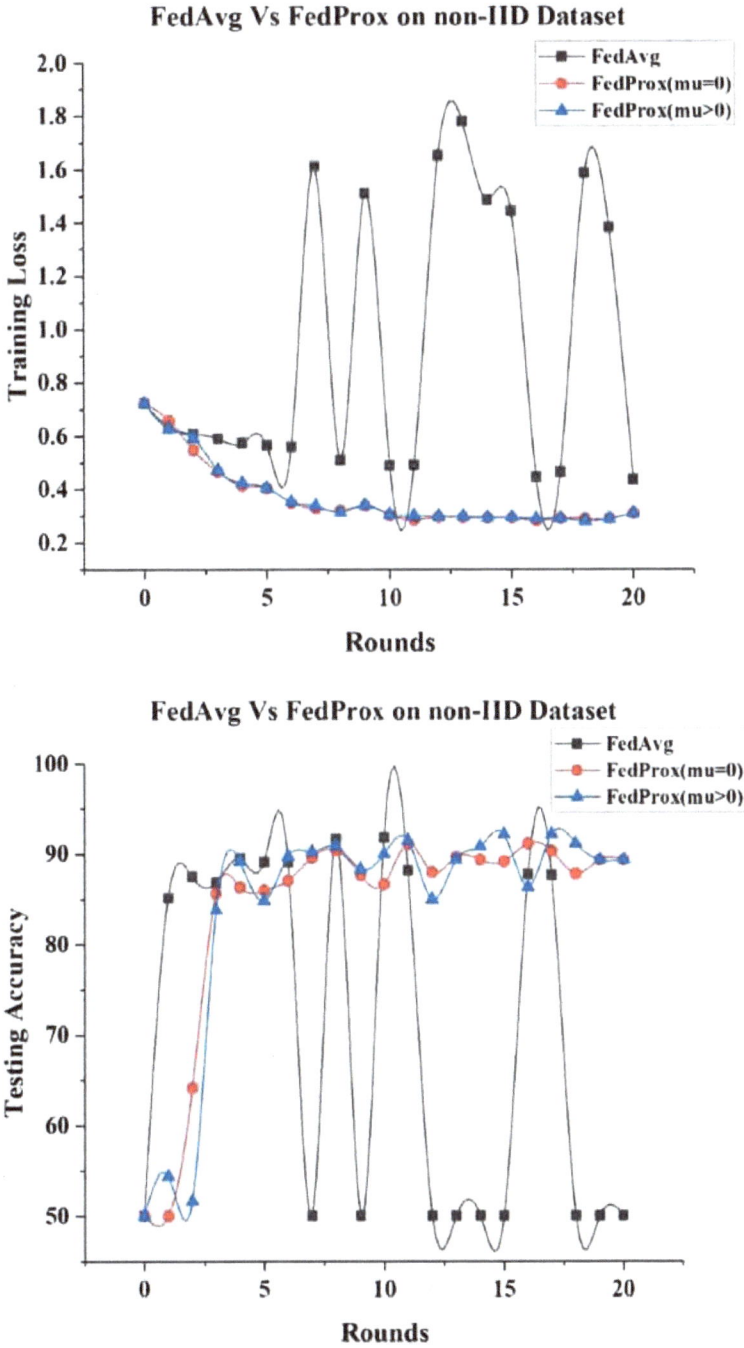

Fig. (8). In (**a**) and (**b**), training loss and testing accuracy are displayed without stragglers, while (**c**) and (**d**) show results with 40% stragglers, and (**e**) and (**f**) reflect conditions with 80% stragglers.

Table 4(a). FedAvg-based Confusion Analysis for the MLP Model at a Global Level.

Actual	Predict	
-	Cammeo	Osmancik
Cammeo	404	32
Osmancik	33	403

Table 4(b). FedProx-Enhanced Confusion Analysis for the MLP Model at a Global Level (mu>0).

Actual	Predict	
-	Cammeo	Osmancik
Cammeo	405	31
Osmancik	33	403

Table 5. Analysis of classification findings for centralized and federated models under an IID distribution with no straggler presence.

Assessment Measures	Centralized MLP Model Performance without Federated Learning	FedAvg-based Federated MLP Model Performance	FedProx-based Federated MLP Model Performance (mu > 0)
Accuracy (%)	92.86	92.63	92.78
Error Rate (%)	7.14	7.37	7.22
Precision (%)	91.04	92.54	92.66
Recall (%)	91.04	92.54	92.66
Specificity (%)	93.36	93.06	93.16
F1 Score (%)	91.60	92.54	92.66

Table 6. Stability of federated models when facing non-IID data and varying straggler proportions.

-	0% Stragglers		
Assessment Measures	Fed-Avg	Fed-Prox (mu=0)	Fed-Prox (mu>0)
Accuracy (%)	86.83	89.83	88.00
Error Rate (%)	13.17	10.17	12.00
Precision (%)	87.68	91.01	88.68
Recall (%)	87.35	90.80	88.50
Specificity (%)	88.96	90.97	89.73
F1 Score (%)	87.41	90.70	88.54
-	40% Stragglers		
Assessment Measures	Fed-Avg	Fed-Prox (mu=0)	Fed-Prox (mu>0)
Accuracy (%)	69.66	91.16	87.16

(Table 6) cont.....

Error Rate (%)	30.34	8.84	12.84
Precision (%)	80.85	90.80	89.01
Recall (%)	64.36	90.80	88.50
Specificity (%)	81.09	91.36	89.02
F1 Score (%)	61.95	90.80	88.30
-		**80% Stragglers**	
Assessment Measures	**Fed-Avg**	**Fed-Prox (mu=0)**	**Fed-Prox (mu>0)**
Accuracy (%)	50.00	89.33	89.33
Error Rate (%)	50.00	10.67	10.67
Precision (%)	34.36	89.01	86.38
Recall (%)	58.62	88.50	85.05
Specificity (%)	75.00	89.02	87.95
F1 Score (%)	43.32	88.30	85.16

CONCLUDING REMARKS

To enhance production, sustainability, and data confidentiality in agriculture, this chapter contributes to the ongoing modernization of agricultural practices through the integration of advanced technologies. This study's findings contribute to the ongoing voyage and development of federated learning applications within various agricultural domains. Further investigations can delve into this research by incorporating a wider range of computational models and data repositories, thus enhancing the reach and impact of federated learning in the agricultural sector.

REFERENCES

[1]   Y. Liu, X. Ma, L. Shu, G.P. Hancke, and A.M. Abu-Mahfouz, "From industry 4.0 to agriculture 4.0: Current status, enabling technologies, and research challenges", *IEEE Trans. Industr. Inform.,* vol. 17, no. 6, pp. 4322-4334, 2021.
[http://dx.doi.org/10.1109/TII.2020.3003910]

[2]   G. Aceto, V. Persico, and A. Pescapé, "A survey on information and communication technologies for industry 4.0: State-of-the-art, taxonomies, perspectives, and challenges", *Institute of Electrical and Electronics Engineers Inc.,* 2019.
[http://dx.doi.org/10.1109/COMST.2019.2938259]

[3]   A.S.P. Pamula, A. Ravilla, and S.V.H. Madiraju, "Applications of the internet of things (IoT) in real-time monitoring of contaminants in the air, water, and soil †", *Eng. Proc.,* vol. 27, no. 1, p. 26, 2022.
[http://dx.doi.org/10.3390/ecsa-9-13335]

[4]   E.D. Zamani, C. Smyth, S. Gupta, and D. Dennehy, "Artificial intelligence and big data analytics for supply chain resilience: a systematic literature review", *Ann. Oper. Res.,* vol. 327, no. 2, pp. 605-632, 2023.
[http://dx.doi.org/10.1007/s10479-022-04983-y] [PMID: 36212520]

[5] C. Cheng, J. Fu, H. Su, and L. Ren, "Recent advancements in agriculture robots: Benefits and challenges", *MDPI.*, 2023.
[http://dx.doi.org/10.3390/machines11010048]

[6] K. Bazargani, and T. Deemyad, "Automation's impact on agriculture: Opportunities, challenges, and economic effects", *Multidisciplinary Digital Publishing Institute (MDPI).*, 2024.
[http://dx.doi.org/10.3390/robotics13020033]

[7] S. Menon, and K. Jain, "Blockchain technology for transparency in agri-food supply chain: Use cases, limitations, and future directions", *IEEE Trans. Eng. Manage.*, vol. 71, pp. 106-120, 2024.
[http://dx.doi.org/10.1109/TEM.2021.3110903]

[8] D.C. Rose, R. Wheeler, M. Winter, M. Lobley, and C.A. Chivers, "Agriculture 4.0: Making it work for people, production, and the planet", *Land Use Policy*, vol. 100, p. 104933, 2021.
[http://dx.doi.org/10.1016/j.landusepol.2020.104933]

[9] F. da Silveira, S.L.C. da Silva, F.M. Machado, J.G.A. Barbedo, and F.G. Amaral, "Farmers' perception of the barriers that hinder the implementation of agriculture 4.0", *Agric. Syst.*, vol. 208, p. 103656, 2023.
[http://dx.doi.org/10.1016/j.agsy.2023.103656]

[10] R. Abbasi, P. Martinez, and R. Ahmad, "The digitization of agricultural industry – a systematic literature review on agriculture 4.0", *Elsevier B.V.*, 2022.
[http://dx.doi.org/10.1016/j.atech.2022.100042]

[11] F. da Silveira, F. H. Lermen, and F. G. Amaral, "An overview of agriculture 4.0 development: Systematic review of descriptions, technologies, barriers, advantages, and disadvantages", *Elsevier B.V*, 2021.
[http://dx.doi.org/10.1016/j.compag.2021.106405]

[12] Q. Yang, Y. Liu, T. Chen, and Y. Tong, "Federated machine learning: Concept and applications", *ACM Trans. Intell. Syst. Technol.*, vol. 10, no. 2, pp. 1-19, 2019.
[http://dx.doi.org/10.1145/3298981]

[13] E. M. B. M. Karunathilake, A. T. Le, S. Heo, Y. S. Chung, and S. Mansoor, "The path to smart farming: Innovations and opportunities in precision agriculture", *Multidisciplinary Digital Publishing Institute (MDPI).*, 2023.
[http://dx.doi.org/10.3390/agriculture13081593]

[14] R. Chandra, and S. Collis, "Digital agriculture for small-scale producers", *Commun. ACM*, vol. 64, no. 12, pp. 75-84, 2021.
[http://dx.doi.org/10.1145/3454008]

[15] S. Shen, T. Zhu, D. Wu, W. Wang, and W. Zhou, "From distributed machine learning to federated learning: In the view of data privacy and security", In: *Concurrency and Computation: Practice and Experience*. John Wiley and Sons Ltd, 2022.
[http://dx.doi.org/10.1002/cpe.6002]

[16] N. Chamara, M. D. Islam, G. (Frank) Bai, Y. Shi, and Y. Ge, "Ag-IoT for crop and environment monitoring: Past, present, and future", *Elsevier Ltd.*, 2022.
[http://dx.doi.org/10.1016/j.agsy.2022.103497]

[17] S. Wolfert, L. Ge, C. Verdouw, and M. J. Bogaardt, "Big data in smart farming – a review", *Elsevier Ltd.*, 2017.
[http://dx.doi.org/10.1016/j.agsy.2017.01.023]

[18] S. Fielke, B. Taylor, and E. Jakku, "Digitalisation of agricultural knowledge and advice networks: A state-of-the-art review", *Elsevier Ltd.*, 2020.
[http://dx.doi.org/10.1016/j.agsy.2019.102763]

[19] H. B. McMahan, E. Moore, D. Ramage, S. Hampson, B. Agüera y Arcas,, *Communication-Efficient Learning of Deep Networks from Decentralized Data*, 2017.

[20]   T. Li, A.K. Sahu, M. Zaheer, M. Sanjabi, A. Talwalkar, and V. Smith, "Federated optimization in heterogeneous networks", 2018. Available from: http://arxiv.org/abs/1812.06127

[21]   D. C. Nguyen, M. Ding, P. N. Pathirana, A. Seneviratne, J. Li, and H. Vincent Poor, "Federated learning for internet of things: A comprehensive survey", *Institute of Electrical and Electronics Engineers Inc.,* 2021.
[http://dx.doi.org/10.1109/COMST.2021.3075439]

[22]   W.Y.B. Lim, N.C. Luong, D.T. Hoang, Y. Jiao, Y-C. Liang, Q. Yang, D. Niyato, and C. Miao, "Federated learning in mobile edge networks: A comprehensive survey", *IEEE Commun. Surv. Tutor.,* vol. 22, no. 3, pp. 2031-2063, 2020.
[http://dx.doi.org/10.1109/COMST.2020.2986024]

[23]   S. Banabilah, M. Aloqaily, E. Alsayed, N. Malik, and Y. Jararweh, "Federated learning review: Fundamentals, enabling technologies, and future applications", *Inf. Process. Manage.,* vol. 59, no. 6, p. 103061, 2022.
[http://dx.doi.org/10.1016/j.ipm.2022.103061]

[24]   V. Mothukuri, R.M. Parizi, S. Pouriyeh, Y. Huang, A. Dehghantanha, and G. Srivastava, "A survey on security and privacy of federated learning", *Future Gener. Comput. Syst.,* vol. 115, pp. 619-640, 2021.
[http://dx.doi.org/10.1016/j.future.2020.10.007]

[25]   S. Truex, "A hybrid approach to privacy-preserving federated learning", *Proceedings of the ACM Conference on Computer and Communications Security,* Association for Computing Machinery, pp. 1-11, 2019.
[http://dx.doi.org/10.1145/3338501.3357370]

[26]   X. Gu, K. Huang, J. Zhang, and L. Huang, Fast Federated Learning in the Presence of Arbitrary Device Unavailability. 12052 - 12064, 2021.

[27]   R. Taiello, M. Önen, C. Gritti, and M. Lorenzi, "Let them drop: Scalable and efficient federated learning solutions agnostic to stragglers", *ACM International Conference Proceeding Series,* Association for Computing Machinery, 2024.
[http://dx.doi.org/10.1145/3664476.3664488]

[28]   A. Imteaj, U. Thakker, S. Wang, J. Li, and M.H. Amini, "A survey on federated learning for resource-constrained IoT devices", *IEEE Internet Things J.,* vol. 9, no. 1, pp. 1-24, 2022.
[http://dx.doi.org/10.1109/JIOT.2021.3095077]

[29]   I. Cinar, and M. Koklu, "Classification of rice varieties using artificial intelligence methods", *Int. J. Intell. Syst. Appl. Eng.,* vol. 7, no. 3, pp. 188-194, 2019.

[30]   H. M, and S. M. MN, "A review on evaluation metrics for data classification evaluations", *Int. J. Data Mining & Knowledge Manag. Process,* vol. 5, no. 2, pp. 01-11, 2015.
[http://dx.doi.org/10.5121/ijdkp.2015.5201]

[31]   M. Sokolova, and G. Lapalme, "A systematic analysis of performance measures for classification tasks", *Inf. Process. Manage.,* vol. 45, no. 4, pp. 427-437, 2009.
[http://dx.doi.org/10.1016/j.ipm.2009.03.002]

CHAPTER 8

From Data to Insights: A Bibliometric Exploration of AI Innovations in the Fourth Industrial Revolution

Arvind Panwar[1,*], **Urvashi Sugandh**[2], **Achin Jain**[3], **Kuldeep Singh Kaswan**[1] and **Harsh Taneja**[4]

[1] *School of Computing Science and Engineering, Galgotias University, Gr. Noida, Uttar Pradesh India*

[2] *School of Computer Science and Engineering, Bennett University, Greater Noida, India*

[3] *Department of Information Technology, Bharati Vidyapeeth's College of Engineering, New Delhi, India*

[4] *Department of CSE, Graphic Era Deemed to be University, Dehradun, India*

Abstract: The Fourth Industrial Revolution, which is hallmarked by the convergence of digital, biological, and physical systems, has placed AI at the heart of all technological advancements. In turn, this chapter uses bibliometric techniques to provide an in-depth analysis of AI innovations in such a transformative era. Moreover, due to the use of the Len.org database, we have an opportunity to highlight various trends in the field of AI, determine research areas that require more profound analysis, and identify the emergent topics within the domain. To provide a more sophisticated review of bibliometric data, one may apply different techniques of analysis, such as co-citation analysis and network mapping. Together, the implemented methods expose an intricate web of knowledge that impacts current developments in AI research. In this study, the authors search for the links between technological advancements and changes in the role of AI. It is of paramount importance to identify the influence of certain regions, institutions, and scholars on the AI field of study. For this reason, the reflection on the latest trends allows the authors to compare different studies, note the difficulties in the field, such as data availability and methodology, and derive new insights for other researchers. The latter is critically vital since it is essential to comprehend a path researchers may follow to understand the implications of technological advancement in different periods. In such a way, bibliometric techniques may also determine the current path of AI research and outline emergent trends of future studies.

---

[*] **Corresponding author Arvind Panwar:** School of Computing Science and Engineering, Galgotias University, Gr. Noida, Uttar Pradesh India; E-mail: arvind.nice3@gmail.com

Tanu Singh, Vinod Patidar, Arvind Panwar & Urvashi Sugandh (Eds.)

Keywords: Artificial Intelligence (AI), Bibliometric analysis, Emerging trends, Fourth industrial revolution, Industry 4.0, Innovation ecosystem, Len.org database.

INTRODUCTION

Background of Industry 4.0 and AI

The Fourth Industrial Revolution, also known as Industry 4.0, is a transformative era in the ever-evolving history of industries. The central premise of the Fourth Industrial Revolution is that it is fundamentally different from how other industrial epochs worked and continue to function [1, 2]. The convergence of the physical, digital, and biological spheres of life and the advent of new computational paradigms have marked the establishment of Industry 4.0. Implementing the new model is Artificial Intelligence, self-evidently, with its main characteristic, which is the simulation of the human mind [3, 4]. The guideline function of AI in the Fourth Industrial Revolution is immutable; it powers automation, produces vast amounts of data as a result, and facilitates progress across industries, from healthcare and finance to transportation and manufacturing [5, 6].

Industry 4.0 makes it evident that AI is not only a tool to advance it but, essentially, a cause of its continuance [7, 8]. Moreover, AI increases the number of tasks the machines can carry out autonomously and is used to monitor, track, and observe details of machine performance. Thus, notions such as the "smart factory" have become a reality with the guidance of AI. The movement toward innovative products is opposite to the stagnant products of the earlier Industrial Revolutions, which could not interact with or respond to their environment. Last but not least, the use of AI in industrial processes leads to a significant increase in efficiency, productivity, and ability to customize products [9, 10].

Importance of Bibliometric Analysis in Understanding Research Trends

The bibliometric analysis represents an effective tool for understanding the development and future tendencies of AI and Industry 4.0. With the development of AI, its study has also developed. As a result of this, the number of publications devoted to the development and application of AI has reached its peak [11]. In this regard, it has become somewhat problematic to trace common tendencies or to understand in what directions it is possible to expect further development in this sphere of studies. Bibliometric analysis represents a quantitative approach to studying academic literature that presents information about the structure and dynamics peculiar to a particular field of study [12, 13]. As a result, by analyzing the information contained by citing references, the network of co-authors, and the keywords, it is possible to understand the intellectual space of the sphere of studies [14]. This article presents the importance of bibliometric analysis for understanding AI and Industry 4.0 development and tendencies.

Drawing attention to the above, one should admit that bibliometric analysis helps to understand AI and Industry 4.0 as instruments that are aimed at fostering the development of certain spheres interested in supporting productivity, effectiveness, and quality [15 - 17]. Additionally, the information presented in this article presupposes that bibliometric analysis helps researchers, policymakers, and industry representatives to understand which way AI is used in separate sectors and which common tendencies can be followed in the future [18 - 20]. Furthermore, conducting such analysis helps to understand which aspects need to be additionally studied to facilitate the development of certain spheres using AI and Industry 4.0.

Objectives of the Chapter

The aim of this chapter is to provide a detailed bibliometric examination of the artificial intelligence innovations in the context of the 4th Industrial Revolution. By drawing on data from the Len.org database, the chapter has the following objectives:

- **Explore Publication Trends:** Examine the rising pace of AI publications, identify the period when AI publications experienced the most significant growth, and draw some inferences from these trends.
- **Identify Key Research Areas:** Map the major themes within AI and the topics of its publication. It will shed light on the AI research focus and potentially hot *topics* in development in the future.
- **Analyse Geographic and Institutional Contributions:** Explore which countries and *especially* institutions were leading in the particular publication years. It will help to identify implicit regional specializations.
- **Identify Emerging Trends:** Specify those papers/areas that are relatively new in AI research, are gaining attention, and have the potential to rapidly develop in the future.
- **Discuss Implications for Future Research:** Discussing implications for future research and providing recommendations. It is a very crucial part of the chapter in which the future development of the study is discussed.

The central recommendation is the necessity of further research in the areas thathave not been studied well, supported by inferences based on the completed bibliometric analysis results. Overall, the data in the chapter aims to provide a deeply elaborated insight into the impact of AI on the 4th Industrial Revolution, which is of interest to researchers, industry professionals, and decision-makers.

THEORETICAL FRAMEWORK

AI in the Fourth Industrial Revolution

The dawn of the Fourth Industrial Revolution marks a profound shift in how societies and industries work, propelled by the merging of digital, physical, and biological spheres. Central to this change is Artificial Intelligence, a technology that has become pivotal for innovation by enabling machines to perform tasks generally requiring human cognition [21, 22]. Integrating AI into Industry 4.0 reshapes sectors, amplifies automation, improves decision-making processes, and cultivates innovative systems with the ability to learn and adapt to their surroundings [23, 24].

AI's role in Industry 4.0 permeates diverse fields, including manufacturing, healthcare, finance, and transportation. In manufacturing, AI facilitates smart factories where interconnected machinery communicates autonomously to optimize production in real time, decreasing downtime while augmenting customization [25, 26]. Within healthcare, AI aids precision medicine by inspecting immense patient data to craft individualized treatment blueprints [27, 28]. Financial institutions leverage AI for risk assessment, fraud detection, and algorithmic trading as the transportation sector applies AI to autonomous vehicles and traffic management systems [29, 30].

The significance of AI in Industry 4.0 extends beyond technological progressions. AI is also critical in creating and examining colossal data sets, frequently called "big data." [31 - 33]. These data pools are fundamental for training AI models to perform complex tasks involving natural language, image recognition, and predictive analysis [34, 35]. AI's ability to extract meaningful insights from data enables organizations to make informed decisions, foresee trends, and react to market demands more strategically [36, 37].

Moreover, AI's impact on Industry 4.0 is characterized by its potential to spawn entirely new business paradigms and financial opportunities [38, 39]. The rise of AI-driven platforms and services is ushering in novel industries, reshaping job markets, and altering the competitive landscape. As AI continues evolving, its role in Industry 4.0 will likely expand further, driving additional innovation and transforming how sectors function globally [40].

Bibliometrics as a Research Method

Bibliometrics is a quantitative methodology for analyzing scholarly literature, yielding valuable insights into disciplinary frameworks. Examining citation patterns, authorship, keywords, and publication chronology, bibliometric evaluation aids in mapping intellectual terrain, recognizing landmark works, and uncovering nascent areas. It is especially practical for dynamically diversifying fields like AI in Industry 4.0's context. Len.org and similar databases delivering broad publication access empower researchers. By extracting citation tallies, coauthor networks, and keyword frequency, data can be examined, including citation analysis identifying influential papers, authors, and journals through impact and reach, co-citation analysis finding related research clusters through shared citations, keyword analysis highlighting topics and trends through frequency and co-occurrence, and co-authorship analysis revealing collaboration patterns and expertise distribution.

Bibliometrics enables comprehensive and objective investigation of large literature volumes, tracking evolution over time. Additionally, hidden connections may emerge invisible through traditional qualitative means, which is invaluable for understanding AI's complex, fast-evolving role in Industry 4.0. This chapter employs bibliometrics exploring AI research within Industry 4.0. Analyzing Len.org data, this study aims to uncover key tendencies, premier contributors, and emerging interests.

METHODOLOGY

Data Sources and Collection Methods

The dependent variable for this bibliometric exploration is the publication of a particular AI-related study in a peer-reviewed journal; therefore, it is a binary variable. The independent variables include many factors and aspects of artificial intelligence that can be explored and discussed in the academic literature. The initial database used in this study is Lens.org, which allows access to publications, patents, and associated bibliographic data. The keywords for this search include "Artificial Intelligence", "Industry 4.0", "Machine Learning", "Automation", "Smart Manufacturing", and other closely related terms and synonyms. The qualifier applied in this search is the requirement for the publication to be a peer-reviewed conference proceeding, journal article, or high-impact review.

The initial dataset is filtered to include only studies explicitly discussing AI innovations in the context of the Fourth Industrial Revolution. To refine the data further, the search is replicated in other sources, such as PubMed and Scopus, and the data collected there is compared to the core set in the Lens.org database. Other measures to ensure the relevance and accuracy of the collected data are coding both datasets, comparing the results, discussing the results with a group of experts, and revising the search terms and the sources. The final dataset will include the set of AI-related studies published in academic journals and represent the AI research trends for 2019-2024.

Bibliometric Analysis Techniques Used

The whole study is organized based on the bibliometric analysis which is used to provide a solid quantitative basis to examine the intellectual structure and dynamics of the AI research within Industry 4.0. To this end, it was essential to apply several key bibliometric techniques throughout the examination of the collected data, which allowed deriving valuable insights regarding different aspects of the research landscape within the chosen area. These methods or techniques included:

- **Citation Analysis:** This technique was used in the current context to assess the influence and impact of books, articles, authors, and other papers on the research in the area. The citation counts were employed to derive the list of the most cited works by other scholars who dealt with this topic, which implies that they are seminal works or initial studies in the chosen area of research.
- **Co-Citation Analysis:** This technique was also used to analyze the data collected by tracking how frequently publications are cited in other papers. Co-citation analysis reveals the so-called clusters of research within the examined field. This provides valuable data on the underlying structure and the mapping of such clusters. In this way, they are used to analyze the relationship between different studies.
- **Keyword Analysis:** This technique was used in the target context to concentrate on the effect of the keyword frequency and its relation to the number of times other words usually accompany the chosen word. In this way, the frequency of the co-occurrence of an examined word was analyzed to produce relevant insights into the AI research, including the periodic assessment of the dataset, which might allow us to conclude about some emerging trends or the dynamics in the attention to some keywords.
- **Co-Authorship** Analysis**: In the target context, the networks of co-authors were analyzed to provide insights regarding the patterns of how different authors or even entire institutions or countries collaborate.

Tools and Software Used for Analysis

To perform a full-scale bibliometric analysis, specialized software tools were used to process and visualize the obtained data. In this case, the leading software was VOS Viewer for multiple reasons. The software is highly capable and competent in creating and visualizing bibliometric networks, and it is traditionally well-regarded for being user-friendly, providing a straightforward and intuitive interface. In addition, VOS Viewer is equipped to comfortably process and analyze vast amounts of data at a time. It was utilized in the following ways:

- **Network Creation:** The software was used to generate networks of co-cited documents, co-occurring keywords, and co-authored publications, creating numerous visual representations of the internal relationships within multiple sources. This contributed to creating a clear, visual image of the research landscape under discussion and pinpointing the key clusters and hotspots of activity and development.
- **Clustering:** VOS Viewer is equipped with advanced clustering algorithms that group related publications, authors, and keywords based on their similarity. This allows for a concise image of the main research themes and emerging points of discussion within the topic of AI in Industry 4.0.
- **Density Visualization:** VOS Viewer was used to create dense maps of the data, thereby creating visual representations of highly cited articles and frequently used keywords. This created a nuanced image of the research hotspots and various topics' overall academic activity level.

Time Frame of the Study

This bibliometric analysis ranges from 2019 to 2024. It is advantageous for a few reasons: the period signifies rapid development and growth in AI research. Over the past five years, artificial intelligence has seen a notable expansion, and the introduction of AI in Industry 4.0. has become increasingly central. As such, the period helps capture cutting-edge research and the latest trends in AI studies, focusing on the most recent findings and the knowledge that is currently developing. Given that the end date of this period is 2024, the cut-off ensures that the study's findings are relevant and up-to-date. It covers some trends that have already existed and directions that have already been set for AI in Industry 4. 0. Overall, this time frame was selected to make it possible to study the current status of AI developed within the context of Industry 4.0., identifying its upwards trends in a satisfactory way for this type of research.

QUANTITATIVE ANALYSIS OF RESEARCH OUTPUT

Dataset Insights

It appears that the research landscape behind AI innovations in Industry 4.0 is quite robust and influential. I leveraged my dataset, finding that there were 4269 research works, with 2463 cited by other works. This indicates that over half of the works belonged to other researchers' bibliographies, underlining the field's significance. Moreover, the research appears quite interconnected; there are 36711 citing works and 79434 cited works, implying that on the one hand, the field is based on significant foundational and theoretical research, and on the other, it generates new impactful research. Finally, the number of total citations reaches 48037. Altogether, this work suggests that the research in this area appears highly impactful and dynamic, with a diverse range of works studied, cited, and used as the foundation for future research.

Scholarly Works Analysis

The data in Fig. (**1**) demonstrates a clear trend in scholarly output for different document types from 2019 to 2024. The number of journal articles shows the most significant growth; in 2019, there were only 151, which rose every year, and by 2023, there were already 659. The partial year showed 392 journal articles in 2024. The count of book chapters has also increased significantly, from 40 in 2019 to 284 in 2023. In 2024, there were already 179. The increase in conference proceedings articles is relatively constant, from 52 in 2019 to 191 in 2023, with 50 in 2024. The number of preprints also grows, though there are fewer of them in comparison to the other document types, from 4 in 2019 to 45 in 2023, with 27 in 2024. The output of books remains relatively stable, from 10 to 19 annually. In the partial data of 2024, there were 5 books. The data indicate that all document types' outputs have increased significantly from 2019 to 2023. However, only in the cases of journal articles and books is the growth particularly pronounced. The partial data for 2024 show that this trend will continue. However, the final numbers for this year of study are not yet available.

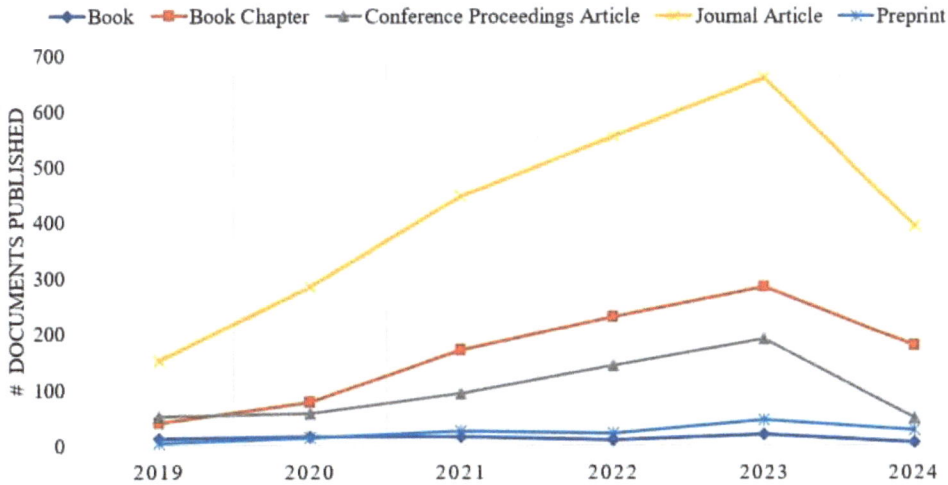

Fig. (1). Scholarly work over the time from 2019 to 2024 according to publication type.

The data in Fig. (**2**) depicts the dissemination of scholarly works across diverse publication outlets. Journal articles constituted the bulk of the output at approximately 58.26%, underscoring their preeminence in relaying research discoveries within academic circles. Book chapters accounted for the second largest share at 23.00%, highlighting their importance in contributing specialized knowledge within compiled volumes. Conference proceeding papers comprised about 13.75% of the total, emphasizing the value of conferences as platforms for debuting emerging scholarship. Preprints, with 3.19%, exhibited a growing tendency to share research before peer evaluation. In comparison, books tallied the smallest portion of 1.80%, signifying their role in furnishing exhaustive, comprehensive treatments of focused topics. This allocation stresses the panoply of publication formats in academic research, with periodical articles and book chapters representing the dominant forms.

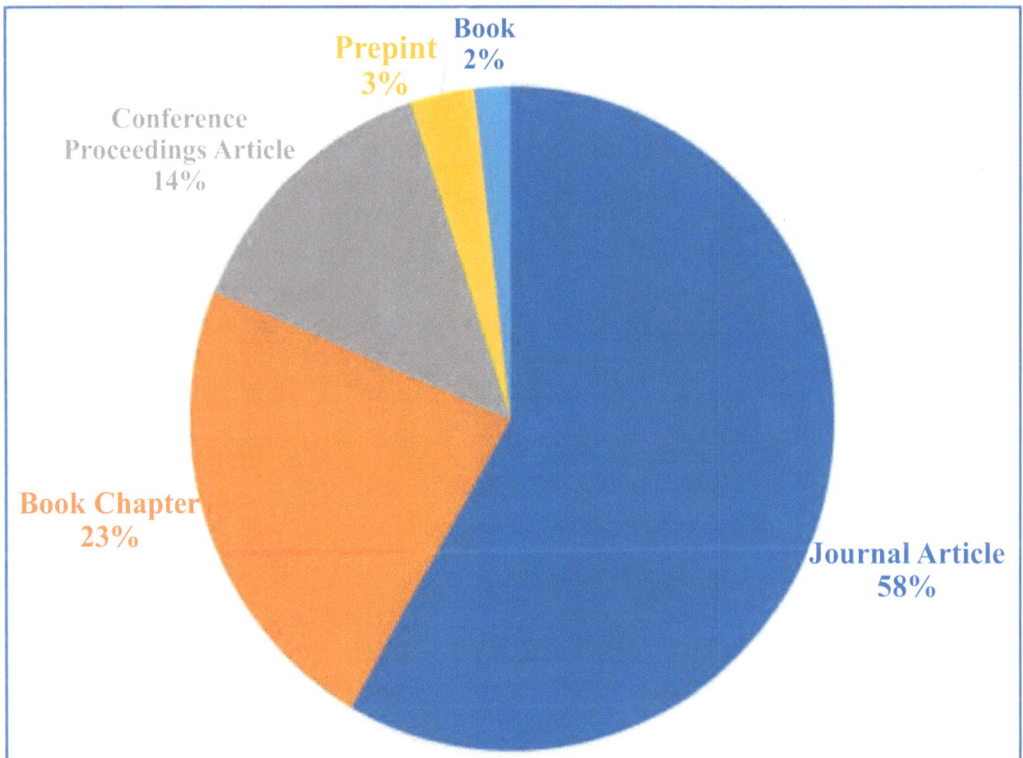

Fig. (2). Publication type distribution.

Data Analysis According to Institutions

Fig. (3) shows the top institutions internationally contributing research at the intersection of artificial intelligence innovations and Industry 4.0 initiatives between 2019 and 2024. Amity University, located in India, leads all others with twenty-one published documents delving into this dynamic area. Closely following in second is Deakin University in Australia with fifteen pertinent publications. In a narrow third-place tie are the Silesian University of Technology, based in Poland, and the University of Johannesburg in South Africa, each credited with fourteen impactful works. Next is Swinburne University of Technology from Australia, contributing thirteen papers. Meanwhile, Binus University in Indonesia and France's esteemed Centre national de la recherche scientifique each boast a dozen related documents. The last two of the top ten are the massive Chinese Academy of Sciences and the University of the Basque Country in Spain, which have added eleven publications each. Capping off the leading group of global institutions focused on advancing this interdisciplinary sphere is King Saud University from Saudi Arabia, credited with ten impactful works. This data evidences the widespread international focus on researching how AI is revolutionizing Industry 4.0, with top research facilities originating from diverse nations, including but not limited to India, Australia, Poland, South Africa, Indonesia, France, China, Spain, and Saudi Arabia. The close publication numbers among these institutions speak to the intensely competitive and progressively innovative nature of the research environment exploring AI's transformation of Industry 4.0, with multiple centers of excellence arising worldwide.

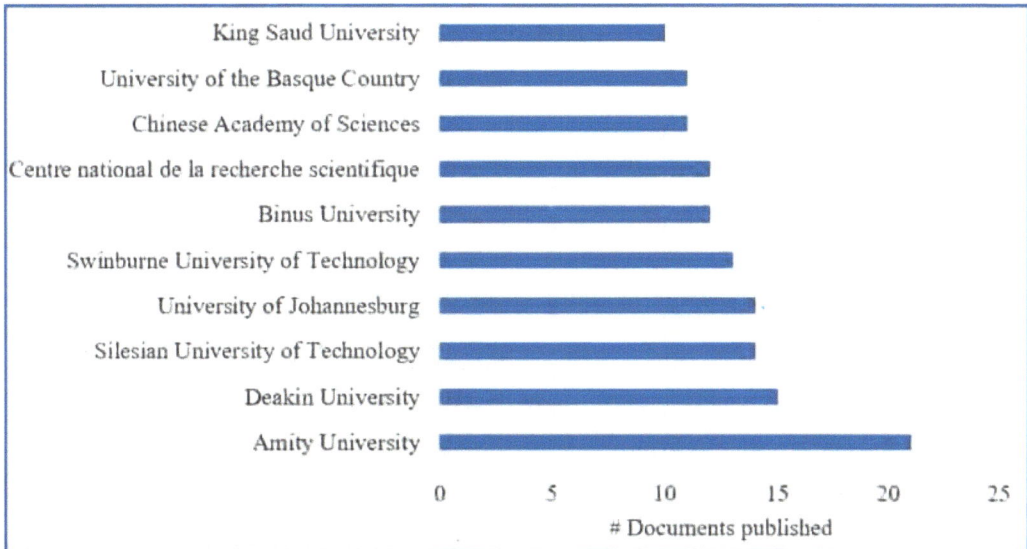

Fig. (3). Top research institute according to the number of documents published.

Fig. (**4**) exhibits the publication trends for the top 5 institutions in AI and Industry 4.0 research from 2019 to 2024. Amity University maintained a steady presence, peaking at eight publications in 2021 before declining slightly while still outputting consistently. In contrast, the Silesian University of Technology burst onto the scene, starting with zero publications from 2019 to 2021 before rapidly increasing output, notably releasing six papers in 2022 before a 10-publication peak in 2023. Similarly, Swinburne University of Technology spiked with 10 publications in 2021, though it maintained a powerful presence thereafter. Meanwhile, the University of Johannesburg demonstrated steady maturation, maximizing output with 10 publications in 2023. Lastly, the University of the Basque Country exhibited a stable pattern, publishing between 2 and 5 papers annually since 2020. Generally, these data indicate an ascending tendency in research output for these institutions, with most showcasing significant growth from 2021 onwards, signifying a deepening focus and prowess in AI and Industry 4.0 research.

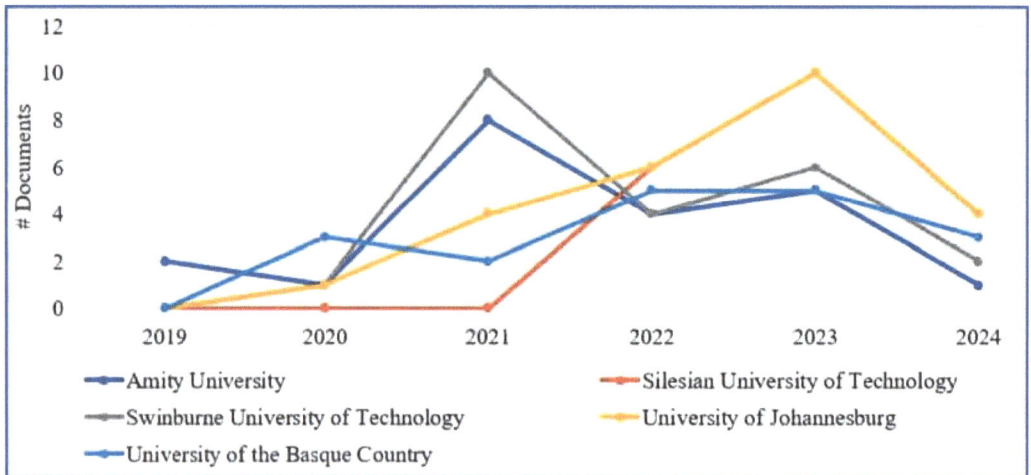

Fig. (4). Top 5 institutes over the time from 2019 to 2024.

Table **1** illuminates the diverse landscape of institutional contributions to AI Innovations in the Fourth Industrial Revolution research. Educational institutions led the way, with Amity University producing 17 documents, the University of Johannesburg authoring 14 texts, and Swinburne University of Technology producing 13 papers . Government institutions also played a sizable role, with the Centre national de la recherche scientifique and INRAE generating 12 documents each, closely followed by the Chinese Academy of Sciences and Russian Academy of Sciences with 11 documents . Consiglio Nazionale delle Ricerche represented nonprofit organizations, which developed 9 papers. Research facilities such as the Advanced Materials and Processes Research Institute and CSIR National Physical Laboratory of India contributed five documents each in differing styles. Interestingly, companies like Siemens also appeared on the list with four documents, indicating industry involvement in scholarship. This distribution highlights the collaborative and multifaceted nature of AI research in Industry 4.0, with robust contributions from academic, governmental, and research institutions, as well as some industry participation through various sentence structures.

Table 1. Different types of institutes.

Institution Type	Document Count	Institution Name
Company	4	Siemens
	3	Decision Sciences (United States)
	3	Ericsson
	3	IBM
	2	BMW
Education	17	Amity University
	14	University of Johannesburg
	13	Swinburne University of Technology
	12	Silesian University of Technology
	11	University of the Basque Country
Facility	5	Advanced Materials and Processes Research Institute
	5	CSIR National Physical Laboratory of India
	5	Centre national de la recherche scientifique
	5	Laboratoire Génie et Matériaux Textiles
	5	Norwegian University of Science and Technology
Government	12	Centre national de la recherche scientifique
	12	INRAE
	11	Chinese Academy of Sciences
	11	Russian Academy of Sciences
	5	Council for Scientific and Industrial Research
Nonprofit	9	Consiglio Nazionale delle Ricerche
	4	German Research Centre for Artificial Intelligence
	3	Institute for Systems and Computer Engineering of Porto
	3	Research Triangle Park
	3	University of Oxford

Data Analysis According to Institutions

Fig. (**5**) shows the most active authors according to the number of documents published. Anita Gehlot authored the most documents on AI Innovations in Industry 4.0's future, publishing 19 papers on the topic. Not far behind was the prolific duo of Abid Haleem and Rajesh Singh, each contributing 17 lengthy works exploring this burgeoning subject. Next was Abdo Hassoun, who added 15 complex publications to further our understanding. After a noticeable gap came a group of 7 authors putting forth varied analyses: Abderrahmane Aït-Kaddour, Bhekisipho Twala, Mohd Javaid, and Shaik Vaseem Akram. Then, 6 papers each from Alessandro Massaro, Amaresh Kumar, Christian Brecher, and Paul-Eric Dossou advanced the discussion. Wrapping up the list were 3 insightful contributions apiece from Ahmed Alkhayyat, Angelo Galiano, and Anjali S Nair. This metadata reveals a concentrated core intensely researching this field, with the top 4 far surpassing others. The diversity of nationalities implies international collaborations and universal interest in AI's Industry 4.0 implications. The leaders' high outputs demonstrate expertise and dedication to exploring this evolution.

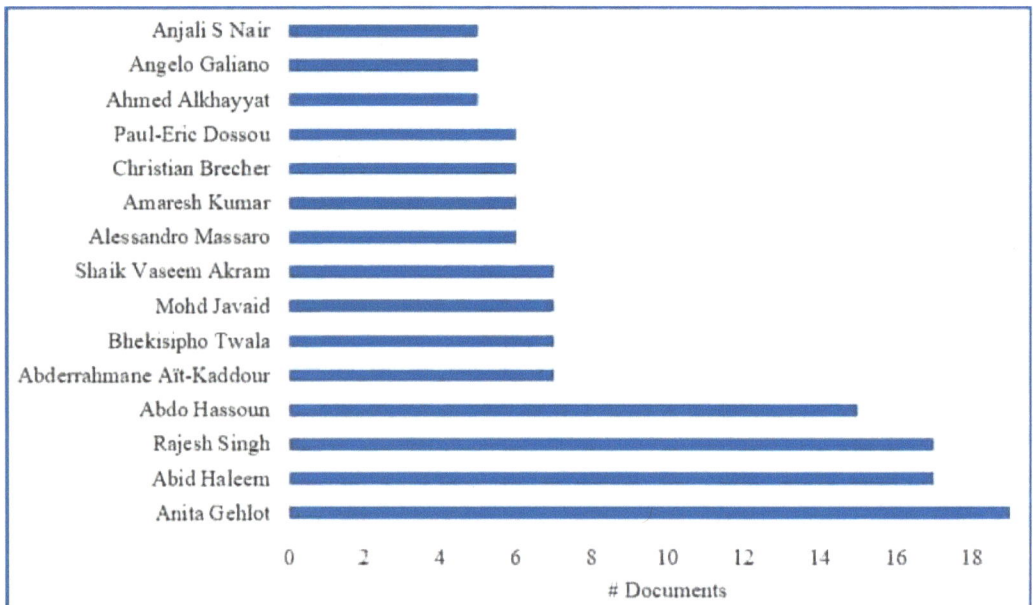

Fig. (5). Most active authors according to number of documents.

Fig. (**6**) highlights the top 15 scholars according to unique citations. Iqbal Sarker is the most influential researcher in AI innovations for Industry 4.0, garnering an impressive 3,135 singular citations. This considerably surpasses the subsequent group of authors, denoting Sarker's substantial effect on the field. A foursome of Aidan Fuller, Charles Day, Chris Barlow, and Zhong Fan each attract 1,105 unique references, implying probable collaboration or related study focuses. Abid Haleem and Mohd Javaid trail closely with 978 singular citations apiece. Ravi Pratap Singh (920 mentions) and Rajiv Suman (895 cites) complete the highest echelon of profoundly referenced experts. The list carries on with Fei Tao (815 cites), trailed by a trio of Andrew Nee, Lihui Wang, and Qinglin Qi - every with 753 citing works. Surajit Bag (641 references) and Cristiano da Costa (570 cites) finish the peak 15. This information unveils diverse researchers contributing significantly to the field, with citation matters proposing varying levels of impact and acknowledgment in the academic community. The span of citation counts from 570 to 3,135 indicates a field with established leaders and emerging influential researchers.

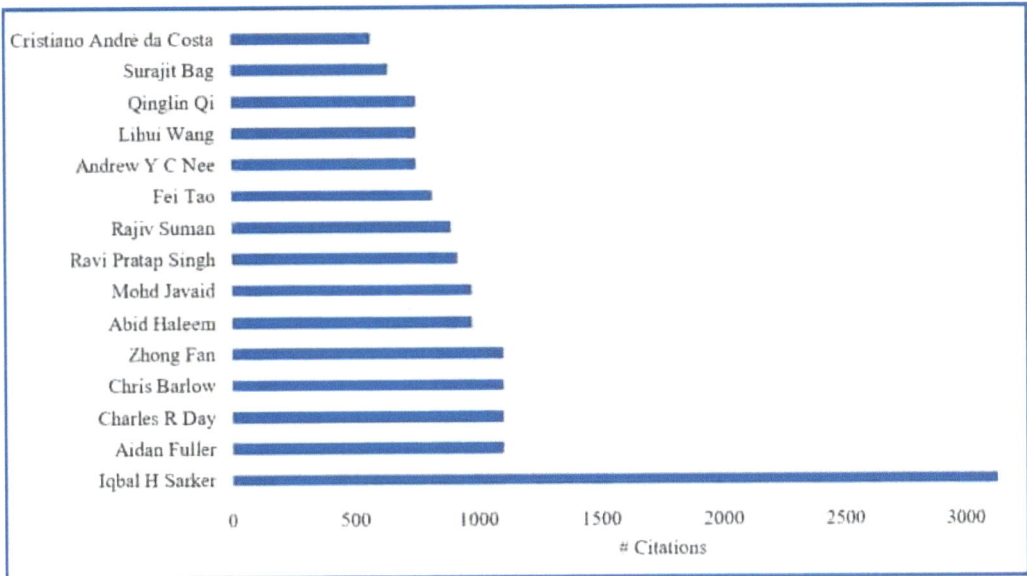

Fig. (6). Top 15 authors according to number of citations.

Fig. (7) depicts the fluctuating publication rates of the top 10 authors in AI Innovations in the Fourth Industrial Revolution from 2019 through 2024. A clear pattern emerges of growing scholarly output over time, with most researchers substantially ramping up their contributions from 2021 onward. Rajesh Singh is the most prolific, notably erupting with 10 documents in 2022 and a high of 13 publications in 2023. Anita Gehlot follows a comparable trajectory, peaking at 10 papers in 2022. Abdo Hassoun demonstrates a steady yield from 2022 to 2024, generating 6 pieces each in 2022 and 2023. Abid Haleem and Mohd Javaid exhibit an identical cadence, with both producing 7 works in 2021 and maintaining consistent productivity thereafter. Shaik Vaseem Akram sees a surge in 2022 with eight publications. Paul-Eric Dossou displays a more distributed scheme, contributing across all years, except 2024. Christian Brecher, Abderrahmane Aït-Kaddour, and Shweta Pandey illustrate climbing trends recently, with Pandey notably releasing 7 documents in 2023. The 2024 data remains incomplete but already signals continuing scholarly exertion. This breakdown unveils a dynamic research landscape with an intensifying focus on AI in Industry 4.0, particularly intensifying from 2021 onward.

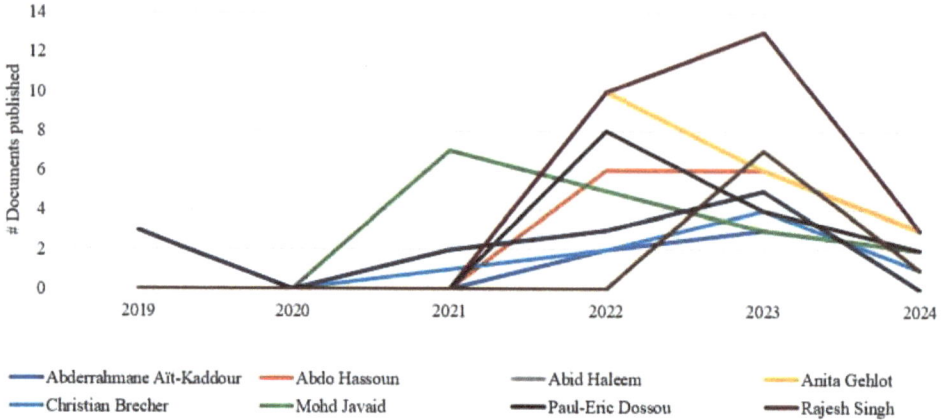

Fig. (7). Top 10 authors over the time from 2019 to 2024.

Data Analysis According to Funding Agencies

Table **2** shows the data about the Top Funding Recipients (Institutions by Funder). The landscape for financing innovations in artificial intelligence during the Fourth Industrial Revolution displays a diverse combination of sponsors and institutions. The Engineering and Physical Sciences Research Council is a substantial sponsor, supporting University College London with four scholarly papers. Another major benefactor is the European Commission, which financed multiple establishments such as the Faculty of Electrical and Computer Engineering and Faculty of Mechanical Engineering and Aeronautics at Rzeszów University of Technology, University of Bologna, University of Johannesburg, and University of Sindh - each with a pair of documents. The National Natural Science Foundation of China emerges as a prominent sponsor, backing Beihang University and the Chinese Academy of Sciences with four scholarly papers apiece, as well as institutions including the Beijing Institute of Technology, the National University of Singapore, and the Royal Institute of Technology with a duo of documents each. China's National Key Research and Development Program funds several establishments, like Beihang University, Loughborough University, the National University of Singapore, the Royal Institute of Technology, and the South China University of Technology, with two scholarly papers apiece. The European Regional Development Fund aids various institutions with a single document each, such as the Autonomous University of Queretaro, Clausthal University of Technology, and departments at universities in Romania, Italy, and Naples. This information exposes a global distribution of financing, with strong support from domestic funding bodies in China and Europe and international organizations, highlighting the worldwide importance and collaborative nature of research in AI and Industry 4.0.

Table 2. Top funding recipients (institutions by funder).

Funding	Document Count	Institution Name
Engineering and Physical Sciences Research Council	4	University College London
	3	University of Bristol
	2	Aberystwyth University
	2	University of Nottingham
	2	University of Oxford
European Commission	2	Faculty of Electrical and Computer Engineering, Rzeszów University of Technology, 35-959 Rzeszów, Poland.
	2	Faculty of Mechanical Engineering and Aeronautics, Rzeszów University of Technology, 35-959 Rzeszów, Poland.
	2	University of Bologna
	2	University of Johannesburg
	2	University of Sindh
European Regional Development Fund	1	Autonomous University of Queretaro
	1	Clausthal University of Technology
	1	Computer Science and Electrical Engineering Department, Lucian Blaga University of Sibiu, 550025 Sibiu, Romania
	1	Department of Computer Science, University of Salerno, 84084 Salerno, Italy
	1	Department of Management Studies and Quantitative Methods, Parthenope University, 80133 Napoli, Italy
National Key Research and Development Program of China	2	Beihang University
	2	Loughborough University
	2	National University of Singapore
	2	Royal Institute of Technology
	2	South China University of Technology
National Natural Science Foundation of China	4	Beihang University
	4	Chinese Academy of Sciences
	2	Beijing Institute of Technology
	2	National University of Singapore
	2	Royal Institute of Technology

Fig. (**8**) depicts a comparative analysis of the top ten funding agencies supporting AI innovation research in the Fourth Industrial Revolution. Emerging as the prime backer, the National Natural Science Foundation of China sponsored thirty-nine reports, underscoring China's robust commitment to interlinking AI and Industry 4.0 studies. The European Commission follows second by underwriting twenty-one papers, highlighting Europe's perceived importance of this domain. The Engineering and Physical Sciences Research Council, likely emanating from the UK, endorsed twelve documents. In addition, China's National Key Research and Development Program funded eleven reports, further amplifying China's investments in this arena. The European Regional Development Fund and the Natural Sciences and Engineering Research Council of Canada buttressed ten documents each, exhibiting significant North American and European participation. The Horizon 2020 Framework Programme and the Ministry of Science and Technology, Taiwan, each subsidized nine documents, indicating diverse international support. The U.S. National Science Foundation also supported nine reports, demonstrating America's interest in this sphere. Lastly, the Fundamental Research Funds for the Central Universities backed eight documents, presumably symbolizing extra Chinese backing. This allocation unveils a planetary curiosity in AI and Industry 4.0 studies, with particularly robust assistance from Chinese and European financing bodies.

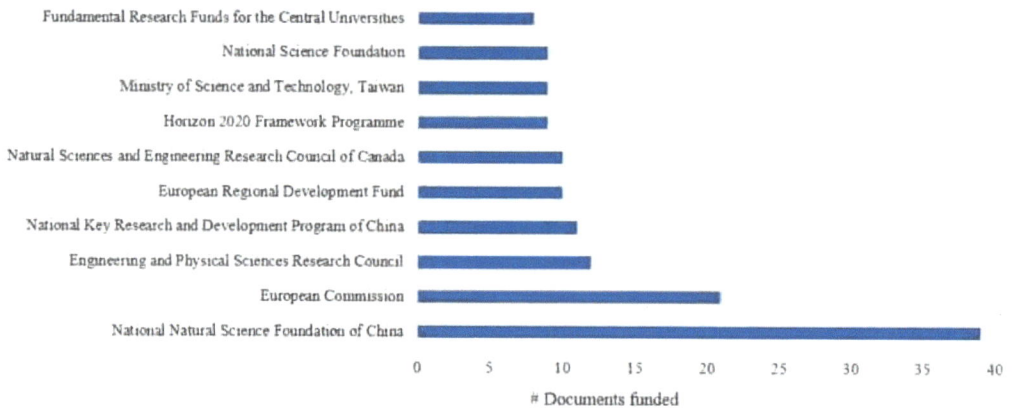

Fig. (8). Top 10 funding agency according to number of documents funded.

Fig. (**9**) analyses funding for AI innovation research from 2019 to 2024, revealing steady increases. The National Natural Science Foundation of China leads, consistently growing its supported documents from one in 2019 to eleven in 2024, peaking at nine in 2023. Meanwhile, the European Commission undergoes radical growth, starting with a sole document in 2020 before escalating to seven in 2023, indicating intensifying European participation. Conversely, the Engineering and Physical Sciences Research Council fluctuates oddly, with seven funded in 2021 but lesser amounts elsewhere. Similarly, both the European Regional Development Fund and Horizon 2020 Framework Programme accelerate from

2020 to 2023, reflecting Europe's burgeoning monetary commitments. Elsewhere, the Fundamental Research Funds for the Central Universities show a striking elevation from 2021 to 2023. The Ministry of Science and Technology, Taiwan, and China's National Key Research and Development Program have maintained constant backing over the years, with minor variances. Later, Canada's Natural Sciences and Engineering Research Council witnessed an amplification from 2021 onwards. Finally, the Fundação para a Ciência e a Tecnologia demonstrates an erratic sponsorship pattern throughout the years. Overall, the information unveils a general propensity to amplify finances for AI and Industry 4.0 inquiries from 2019 to 2024, with Chinese and European granting agencies playing major roles.

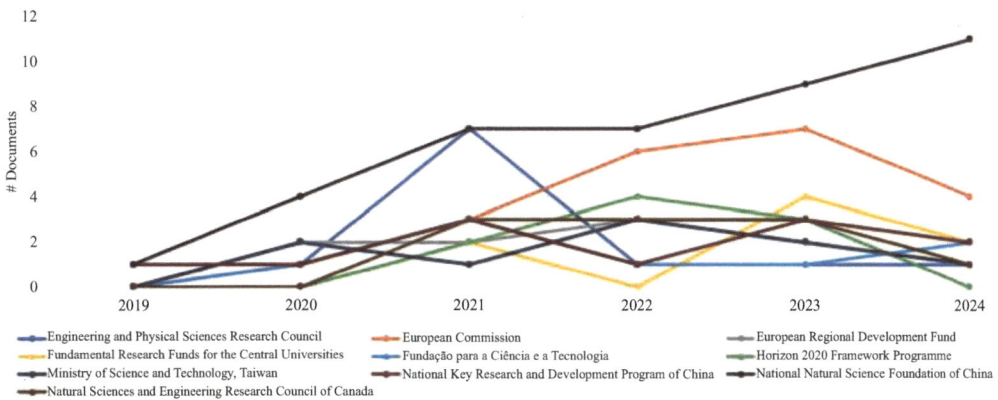

Fig. (9). Top 10 funding agencies over the time from 2019 to 2024.

Data Analysis According to Journals and Publishers

Fig. (**10**) shows the top journals. Procedia Computer Science emerges as the top journal publishing work on AI innovations for Industry 4.0, containing a sizable 56 documents focused on this area. Sensors are closely behind with 53 documents, indicating a strong emphasis on sensor-driven AI applications within manufacturing. SSRN Electronic Journal and Applied Sciences also make significant contributions, hosting 45 and 44 documents, respectively, exploring these interdisciplinary topics. Sustainability demonstrates the environmental concerns intersecting with this research theme through 41 documented studies, while IEEE Access highlights broad engineering implications with 37 publications. Delving deeper into specific engineering domains, Lecture Notes in Mechanical Engineering addresses relevance for mechanical processes through 32 documents, and Electronics publishes 25 papers on circuitry and system applications. Both IEEE Transactions on Industrial Informatics and IFAC contribute insightful industrial perspectives, each authoring 23 documents applying AI within operational settings. Energies and the importance of their related sectors, publishing 18 documents each investigating energy and production applications. The Journal of Cleaner Production signals the growing fusion of AI, Industry 4.0, and eco-friendly innovation through 16 documented studies. Journal of Physics: Conference Series and Advances in Business Information Systems and Analytics round out the list, presenting diverse avenues for disseminating this multidisciplinary research across 15 and 13 documents, respectively. This distribution reflects the cross-pollination of AI within Industry 4.0 across domains, including computer science, various engineering disciplines, sustainability concerns, and business functions.

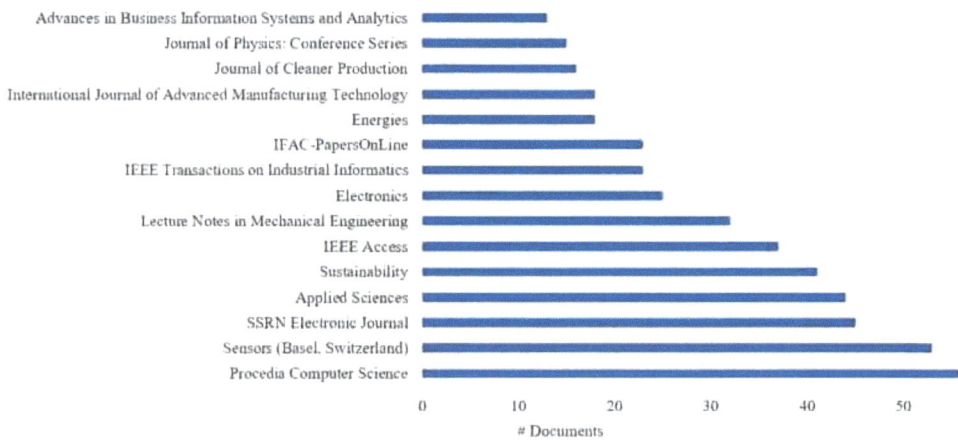

Fig. (10). Top journals.

Fig. (**11**) depicts a breakdown of the premier journals publishing work pertaining to AI advancements in Industry 4.0 from 2019 through 2024. Procedia Computer Science exhibits a marked upward trajectory, with contributions expanding from 5 in 2019 to a zenith of 18 in 2023 and 13 in 2024, signaling heightened interest in the domain. Comparably, Sensors (Basel, Switzerland) demonstrate an analogous pattern, increasing from 4 papers in 2019 to a maximum of 17 in 2023, with a minor decrease to 4 thus far in 2024. SSRN Electronic Journal presents fluctuations, peaking at 12 documents in 2023 but falling to 3 in 2024. Applied Sciences and Sustainability both showcase overall growth trends, with Applied Sciences hitting its apex at 12 submissions in 2022 and Sustainability achieving 16 in 2022. IEEE Access had its most substantial output in 2020, with 10 articles, but has shown a decline since. Lecture Notes in Mechanical Engineering presents variability, with a notable spike of 12 publications arising in 2023. The International Journal of Advanced Manufacturing Technology maintains a consistent production of 4-5 articles annually from 2020 onward. This metadata unveils a general propensity to increase publications in the domain of AI innovations for Industry 4.0 across most journals, alongside some irregularity and probable shifts in focus across the years.

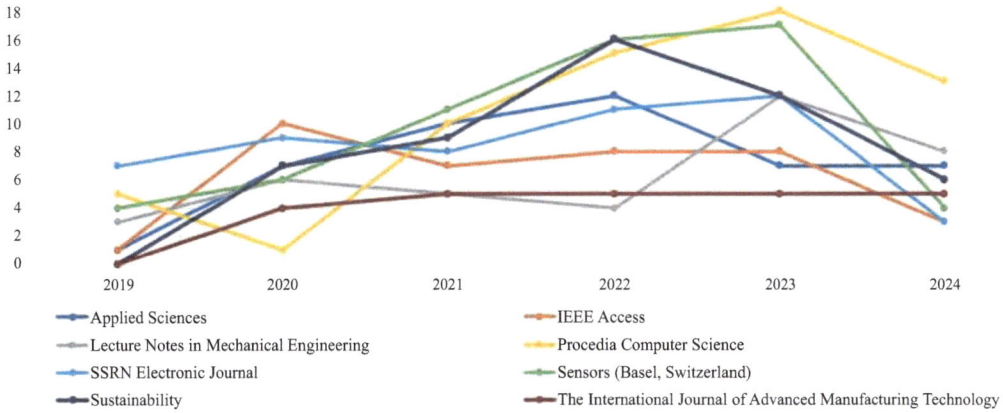

Fig. (11). Top 10 journals over the time from 2019 to 2024.

SN Computer Science dominates as the preeminent publication in its field, accumulating over three thousand citations according to the analysis shown in Fig. (**12**). Sustainability and IEEE Access come in close behind with over two and a half thousand citations, underlining their substantial impact. Ranking fourth is IEEE Transactions on Industrial Informatics, which has nearly two thousand citations, emphasizing its primacy regarding industrial applications of artificial intelligence. Technological Forecasting and Social Change demonstrates the interweaving of technology and the social realm, bridging these domains with over one thousand two hundred citations. Computers & Industrial Engineering accentuates artificial intelligence's industrial focus by amassing one thousand eighty citations. Engineering appeals to artificial intelligence's broad applicability across diverse engineering domains, with eight hundred and seven citations. Applied Sciences illustrates this versatility by garnering seven hundred eighty-seven citations. The International Journal of Advanced Manufacturing Technology, IEEE Communications Surveys & Tutorials, and Automation in Construction contributed significantly to their particular areas, notching over six hundred citations each. The Journal of Manufacturing Systems and Expert Systems with Applications complete the list with five hundred seventy-six and five hundred-eleven citations, respectively. This panoply of citations traversing an assortment of periodicals mirrors the multifaceted nature of research in Industry 4.0, intersecting computer science, engineering, sustainability, and industrial implementations with an accent on practical and industrial applications of artificial intelligence technologies.

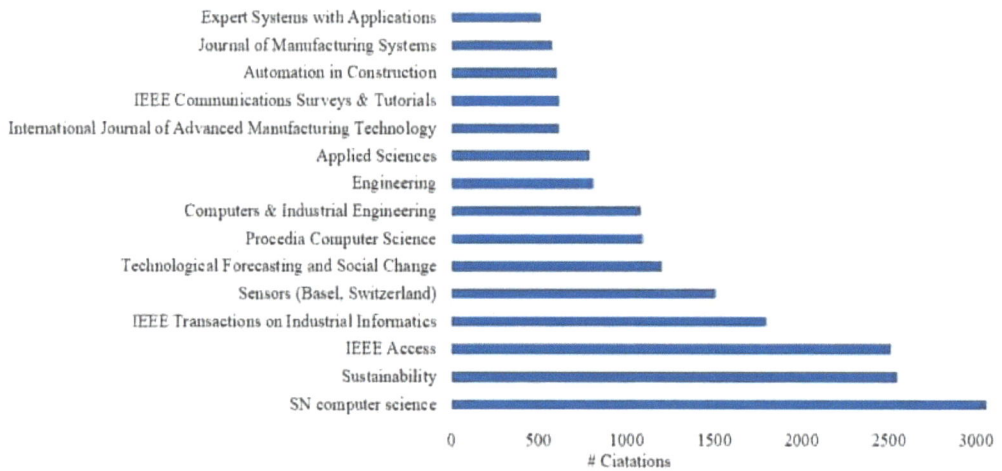

Fig. (12). Top journals according to the number of citations.

Elsevier BV remains the primary publisher with 458 documents, significantly ahead of their competitors, as shown in Fig. (**13**). IEEE conferences follow as the second most prolific publisher with 398 documents, underscoring the importance of conference proceedings in this rapidly transforming field. MDPI AG ranks third with 338 documents, exhibiting a powerful presence in open access publishing. Springer International Publishing and Springer Science and Business Media LLC contribute meaningfully with 249 and 160 documents, respectively, highlighting the Springer group's substantial involvement. IGI Global (138 documents) and the Institute of Electrical and Electronics Engineers (IEEE) (133 documents) also display considerable output. Springer Nature Singapore and Springer Nature Switzerland, with 106 and 102 documents in that order, further emphasize the global reach of Springer's publications on this topic. CRC Press rounds out the top ten with 92 documents. The list continues with Emerald Publishing Limited (70 documents), Wiley (59 documents), Elsevier (57 documents), Informa UK Limited (55 documents), and IOP Publishing (49 documents). This dispersion reveals a publishing landscape dominated by large, established academic publishers, with a blend of traditional and open access models, reflecting the diverse and dynamic nature of research in AI and Industry 4.0.

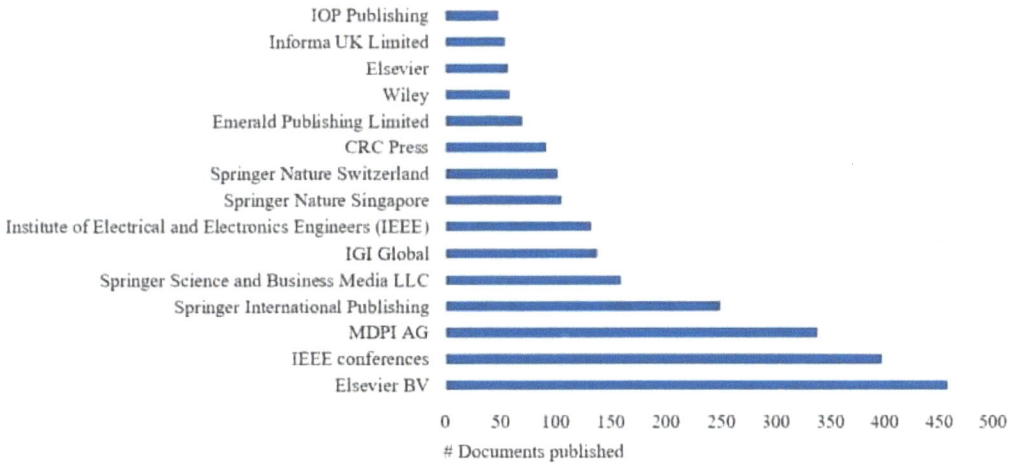

Fig. (13). Top publishers according to the number of documents published.

Elsevier BV consistently leads in publication volume, demonstrating significant increases from thirty-eight documents in 2019 to a high of one hundred twenty-four in 2022 and one hundred twenty-one in 2023, with sixty-eight already in 2024 as shown in Fig. (**14**). IEEE exhibits robust growth, expanding from forty-three documents in 2019 to one hundred twenty-four in 2023, though reflecting a decline to nineteen in 2024 thus far. MDPI AG shows swift increases, rising from nine documents in 2019 to seventy-six in 2023, with fifty-three in 2024, indicating a concentration of attention in this field. Springer International Publishing demonstrates variability, peaking at seventy-nine documents in twenty twenty-one but decreasing afterwards. Springer Nature Singapore and Springer Nature Switzerland both reflect considerable increases from 2021 onwards, with Springer Nature Switzerland notably noteworthy for its rapid amplification from three documents in 2022 to sixty-two in 2023. IGI Global and CRC Press portray more moderate but steady amplification over the period. The Institute of Electrical and Electronics Engineers (IEEE) presents fluctuations, with a notable peak of thirty-eight documents in 2023. Springer Science and Business Media LLC maintains a relatively consistent output throughout the period. Overall, the data uncovers a general trend of boosting publication volume in AI and Industry 4.0 research across most publishers from 2019 to 2023, with some unevenness and probable modifications in focus observed in 2024.

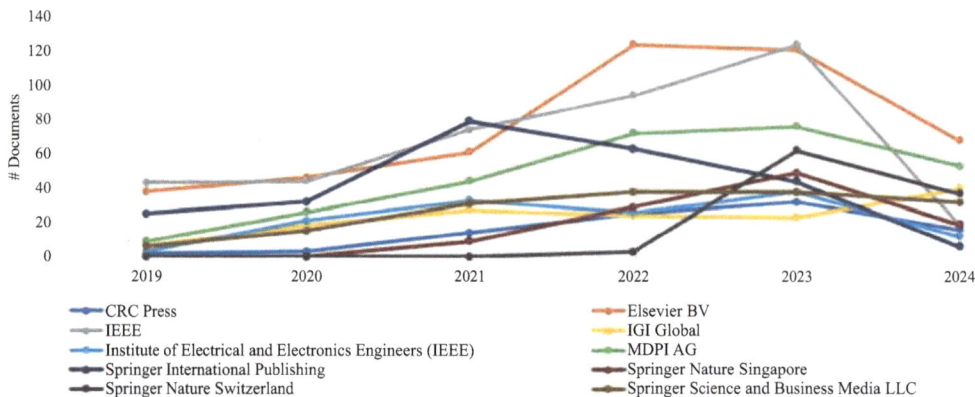

Fig. (14). Top 10 publishers over the time from 2019 to 2024.

Table **3** shows the top journals by publishers. The data uncovered a diverse landscape, with various publishers and journals contributing innovative AI technologies within Industry 4.0's new industrial age. Elsevier BV emerged at the forefront, with Procedia Computer Science as their most prolific journal by a wide margin, publishing sixty-two documents on its own, followed closely by SSRN Electronic Journal's fifty publications. IEEE demonstrated a strong presence through numerous conference proceedings, with multiple events each releasing between three to four documents. MDPI AG made significant contributions across diverse journals, most notably Sustainability, which had fifty documents and Applied Sciences, which had forty-four entries. Springer's involvement was apparent through several imprints, with Springer International Publishing focusing on book series and conference materials, where Lecture Notes in Mechanical Engineering topped out at fifteen documents. At the same time, Springer Science and Business Media LLC publishes in more traditional journal formats, foremost among them The International Journal of Advanced Manufacturing Technology and its twenty-three publications. This distribution underscores AI in Industry 4.0's interdisciplinary nature, crossing boundaries between computer science, sustainability, engineering, and manufacturing fields, with an assorted mix of journal articles, conference materials, and book series serving as principal publication venues.

Artificial intelligence and the Fourth Industrial Revolution intersect in manifold arenas of research. While engineering stands as the dominant domain, with its key functions highlighted in the boldest font, AI and Industry 4.0 likewise loom prominently as the bedrock technologies driving innovation, as shown in Fig. (**15**). Business, economics, and knowledge management materialize as significant spheres of cross-disciplinary study, underscoring the networked nature of progress in these fields. Terms like big data, machine learning, and data science denote the crucial roles of information gathering and analytics. Manufacturing systems, automated processes, and embedded technologies point to practical applications in industrial settings. Biology suggests possibilities of cross-domain research or bio-mimicked AI approaches. Of note, too, are computer security, cloud infrastructure, and the growing Internet of Things, indicating the digital architecture supporting advancements. Political science and law appear, reflecting societal implications as AI transforms Industry 4.0. This word cloud effectively portrays the multifaceted and interconnected character of scholarship addressing technological, economic, and societal dimensions of AI driving the Fourth Industrial Revolution across technical, managerial, and social domains.

Table 3. Journals by publisher.

Publisher	Document Count	Source Title
Elsevier BV	62	Procedia Computer Science
	50	SSRN Electronic Journal
	23	IFAC-PapersOnLine
	20	Procedia Manufacturing
	18	Procedia CIRP
IEEE	4	2022 IEEE 27th International Conference on Emerging Technologies and Factory Automation (ETFA)
	4	2023 3rd International Conference on Advance Computing and Innovative Technologies in Engineering (ICACITE)
	4	2023 IEEE 19th International Conference on Automation Science and Engineering (CASE)
	3	2019 IEEE 17th International Conference on Industrial Informatics (INDIN)
	3	2022 IEEE 28th International Conference on Engineering, Technology and Innovation (ICE/ITMC)
MDPI AG	50	Sustainability
	44	Applied Sciences
	25	Electronics
	18	Energies
	13	Processes

(Table 3) cont.....

Publisher	Document Count	Source Title
Springer International Publishing	15	Lecture Notes in Mechanical Engineering
	9	Advances in Intelligent Systems and Computing
	8	Lecture Notes in Networks and Systems
	8	Studies in Computational Intelligence
	6	Communications in Computer and Information Science
Springer Science and Business Media LLC	23	The International Journal of Advanced Manufacturing Technology
	8	International Journal on Interactive Design and Manufacturing (IJIDeM)
	8	Journal of Intelligent Manufacturing
	6	Artificial Intelligence Review
	5	Information Systems Frontiers

Fig. (15). Word cloud according to filed of study keywords.

The data shows in Fig. (**16**), the evolution of research focus in AI innovations for the Fourth Industrial Revolution from 2019 to 2024. Computer science consistently leads as the most prominent field, showing significant growth from 141 occurrences in 2019 to a peak of 1098 in 2023. Engineering follows a similar trend, rising from 40 in 2019 to 716 in 2023. Artificial intelligence, unsurprisingly, shows rapid growth, increasing from 53 in 2019 to 566 in 2023. Business also demonstrates strong growth, from 57 in 2019 to 586 in 2023. Industry 4.0 shows more modest growth compared to other fields, rising from 115 in 2019 to 371 in 2023. Fields like economics, embedded systems, and operating systems show dramatic increases from 2021 onwards, indicating emerging focus areas. Knowledge management and political science also show steady growth, highlighting the interdisciplinary nature of this research area. The data for 2024 is partial but suggests continued strong interest across all fields. Overall, this data reveals a rapidly expanding and diversifying research landscape in AI and Industry 4.0, with traditional tech fields leading but accompanied by significant growth in business and social science areas.

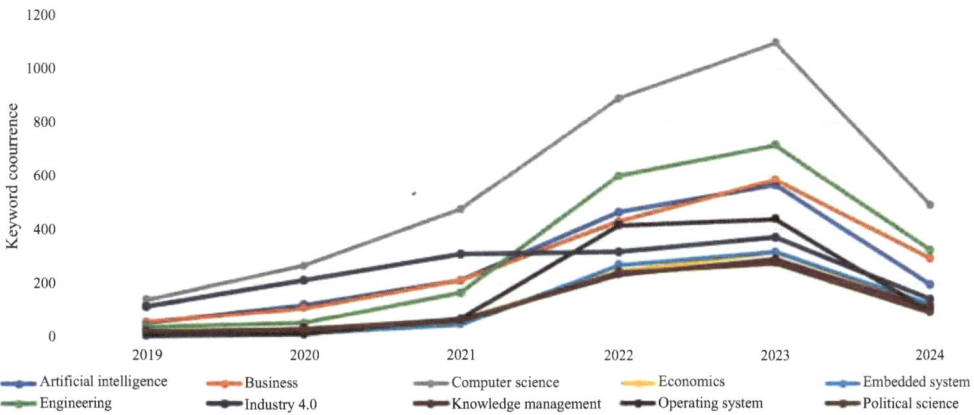

Fig. (16). Top 10 filed of studies over the time from 2019 to 2024 according to key word occurrence.

DISCUSSION

The bibliometric analysis explored here highlights the rapid expansion and branching out of AI investigation within the setting of the Fourth Industrial Revolution. The investigation demonstrates a tremendous surge in AI-related publications between 2019 and 2024, signifying a strong, escalating interest in comprehending how AI reshapes various commercial divisions. Publications like Procedia Computer Science and Sensors emerge as primary outlets, reflecting the multidisciplinary character of AI research that crosses domains from computer science to engineering and enterprise.

Geographically, the examination highlights significant contributions from institutions across diverse regions, such as Amity University in India, Deakin University in Australia, and the Silesian University of Technology in Poland. This worldwide distribution proposes a global interest and collaborative attempts to advance AI technologies within Industry 4.0 [41].

Emerging trends indicate an amplified concentration on mechanization, smart manufacturing, and utilizing AI for information examination and decision-making. Techniques like co-citation and co-authorship examinations uncover thick teamwork systems, specifically among experts like Anita Gehlot, Abid Haleem, and Rajesh Singh, whose remarkable yield underscores their impact in the field. Additionally, funding designs point to substantial backing from associations like the National Natural Science Foundation of China and the European Commission, stressing provincial strategic interests [42].

This investigation underscores the dynamic nature of AI research within Industry 4.0, demonstrating that while conventional technological fields dominate, there is an expanding interdisciplinary joining with business, financial aspects, and social sciences. Future examinations should continue investigating these crossroads to uncover novel applications and implications of AI in various industries, fostering further advancement, and addressing emerging challenges within the transformative landscape of Industry 4.0.

FUTURE RESEARCH DIRECTIONS

Adequate further research must focus on developing research on the role of AI in specific spheres within the context of Industry 4.0. For instance, while it is obvious that AI can be used in healthcare, transportation, or energy management, the extent of its impact and the ways in which it can optimize processes and support decision-making in these spheres are not discussed in the current academic literature [43]. Similarly, the implications of integrating AI in terms of socio-economic forces, such as workforce involvement or exclusion, operating developments, as well as ethical and regulatory issues, must be studied further. In addition, the future of the research must also focus on investigating the ways of creating AI technologies that can ensure the development of manufacturing systems and the adaptability of such systems to potential hazards such as pandemics or crises in supply chains that may occur anywhere in the world [44]. Finally, it is important to investigate the trends and technologies that are only emerging, such as quantum AI or edge technologies, that are likely to reconfigure the paradigms of research on innovation. The only way to achieve progress in these fields is to engage in collaborative research that combines insights from different academic disciplines and regions to develop a more complex understanding of the implications of AI for Industry 4.0.

CONCLUSION

The current chapter provided a detailed bibliometric examination of AI research prepared within the scope of the Fourth Industrial Revolution. A range of critical patterns, including the rapid rise of studies devoted to AI and the proliferation of the number of scholars and other stakeholders, contributed to this area of research. At the same time, the existing trends account for an accelerated emphasis on interdisciplinary research since AI-related studies appear in social sciences, as well as in economics, management, political science, and law. Moreover, some trends have identified that CS, engineering, and business remain the dominating research areas. However, this study also indicated that AI-related research has become more integrated into other areas of research, including economics, political science, and law. As the study shows, the role of AI in driving change within industrial processes, making better decisions, and becoming an AI component of a smart system is emphasized more regarding IR 4.0. At the same time, a range of limitations and further opportunities have been discovered in this type of research, including a limited number of studies addressing contextual factors and the social impact of AI, a lack of attention to the social implications of AI application within the fourth IR, sustainability, and emerging materials. Other limiting factors include the following: further potential of quantum AI, while other implications are edge computing and the socio-economic environment in which AI is developing. As such, this kind of analysis provides insights for further research by displaying its intellectual structure.

REFERENCES

[1]   A. Agarwal, A. Verma, and M. Khari, "Comparative assessment of machine learning methods for early prediction of diseases using health indicators", *Approaches to Human-Centered AI in Healthcare.,* pp. 160-186, 2024.
[http://dx.doi.org/10.4018/979-8-3693-2238-3.ch007]

[2]   S. Khan, M. Khari, and M. Azrour, "IoT in retail and e-commerce", *Electron. Commer. Res,* pp. 1-2, 2023.
[http://dx.doi.org/10.1007/s10660-023-09785-3]

[3]   T. Singh, A. Panwar, K.S. Kaswan, A. Jain, and U. Sugandh, "The datafication of everything: Challenges and opportunities in a hyperconnected world", *International Conference on Advancements in Smart Computing and Information Security,* pp. 254-268, 2024.
[http://dx.doi.org/10.1007/978-3-031-58604-0_18]

[4]   U. Sugandh, M. Khari, and S. Nigam, "How blockchain technology can transfigure the indian agriculture sector", *Handb. Green Comput. Blockchain Technol,* pp. 69-88, 2021.
[http://dx.doi.org/10.1201/9781003107507-6]

[5]   A. Panwar, and V. Bhatnagar, "Data lake architecture", *Int. J. Organ. Collective Intell.,* vol. 10, no. 1, pp. 63-75, 2020.
[http://dx.doi.org/10.4018/IJOCI.2020010104]

[6]   M. Khari, and A. Karar, "Analysis on intrusion detection by machine learning techniques : A review", *Int. J. Adv. Res. Comput. Sci. Softw. Eng.,* vol. 3, no. 4, pp. 545-548, 2013.

[7]   P. Singh, K. Chaudhary, G. Chaudhary, M. Khari, and B. Rawal, "A machine learning approach to detecting deepfake videos: An investigation of feature extraction techniques", *Journal of Cybersecurity and Information Management,* vol. 9, no. 2, pp. 42-50, 2022.
       [http://dx.doi.org/10.54216/JCIM.090204]

[8]   Saurabh, C. Sharma, S. Khan, S. Mahajan, H.S. Alsagri, A. Almjally, B.I. Alabduallah, and A.A. Ansari, "Lightweight security for IoT", *J. Intell. Fuzzy Syst.,* vol. 45, no. 4, pp. 5423-5439, 2023.
       [http://dx.doi.org/10.3233/JIFS-232388]

[9]   P. Singh, and M. Khari, "Necessity of time synchronization for IoT-based applications", *Internet of Things: Technological Advances and New Applications.,* pp. 285-297, 2023.
       [http://dx.doi.org/10.1201/9781003304609-15]

[10]   S.H. Reddy, H. Bathini, V.N. Ajmeera, R.S. Marella, T.V.V. Kumar, and M. Khari, "Startup unicorn success prediction using ensemble machine learning algorithm", *Lecture Notes in Computer Science (including subseries Lecture Notes in Artificial Intelligence and Lecture Notes in Bioinformatics).,* vol. 14532, pp. 330-338, 2024.
       [http://dx.doi.org/10.1007/978-3-031-53830-8_34]

[11]   M. Khari, R. Dalal, A. Sharma, and B. Mehta, "Person identification in UAV shot videos by using machine learning", *Multimodal Biometric Systems,* pp. 45-60, 2021.
       [http://dx.doi.org/10.1201/9781003138068-4]

[12]   P. Singh, M. Khari, and S. Vimal, "EESSMT: An energy efficient hybrid scheme for securing mobile ad hoc networks using IoT", *Wirel. Pers. Commun.,* vol. 126, no. 3, pp. 2149-2173, 2022.
       [http://dx.doi.org/10.1007/s11277-021-08764-x]

[13]   P. Gaba, A. Panwar, U. Sugandh, N. Pathak, and N. Sharma, "OptiCharge: A firefly algorithm-based approach for minimizing electric vehicle waiting time at charging stations", *Intell. Decis. Technol., no.,* pp. 1-14, 2024.
       [http://dx.doi.org/10.3233/IDT-230619]

[14]   U. Sugandh, S. Nigam, and M. Khari, "Ecosystem of technologies for smart agriculture to improve the efficiency and profitability of indian farmers", *Proceedings of the 17th INDIACom; 2023 10th International Conference on Computing for Sustainable Global Development, INDIACom,* pp. 1442-1449, 2023.

[15]   S. Vimal, M. Khari, N. Dey, R.G. Crespo, and Y. Harold Robinson, "Enhanced resource allocation in mobile edge computing using reinforcement learning based MOACO algorithm for IIOT", *Comput. Commun.,* vol. 151, pp. 355-364, 2020.
       [http://dx.doi.org/10.1016/j.comcom.2020.01.018]

[16]   S. Nigam, U. Sugandh, and M. Khari, "The integration of blockchain and IoT edge devices for smart agriculture: Challenges and use cases", *Advances in Computers.,* vol. 127, pp. 507-537, 2022.
       [http://dx.doi.org/10.1016/bs.adcom.2022.02.015]

[17]   G. Chaudhary, S. Srivastava, and M. Khari, "Generative edge intelligence for securing IoT-assisted smart grid against cyber-threats", *International Journal of Wireless and Ad Hoc Communication,* vol. 6, no. 1, pp. 38-49, 2023.
       [http://dx.doi.org/10.54216/IJWAC.060104]

[18]   S. Saif, P. Das, S. Biswas, M. Khari, and V. Shanmuganathan, "HIIDS: Hybrid intelligent intrusion detection system empowered with machine learning and metaheuristic algorithms for application in IoT based healthcare", *Microprocess. Microsyst,* p. 104622, 2022.
       [http://dx.doi.org/10.1016/j.micpro.2022.104622]

[19]   G. Chaudhary, M. Khari, and A. Mahmoud, "Intelligent video moving target detection based on multi-attribute single value medium neutrosophic method", *Journal of Intelligent Systems and Internet of*

Things, vol. 5, no. 1, pp. 49-59, 2021.
[http://dx.doi.org/10.54216/JISIoT.050105]

[20]   J. Khan, G.A. Khan, J.P. Li, M.F. AlAjmi, A.U. Haq, S. Khan, N. Ahmad, S. Parveen, M. Shahid, S. Ahmad, M. Raji, B. Ahamad, A.A. Alghamdi, and A. Ali, "Secure smart healthcare monitoring in industrial internet of things (IIoT) ecosystem with cosine function hybrid chaotic map encryption", *Sci. Program.,* vol. 2022, no. 1, pp. 1-22, 2022.
[http://dx.doi.org/10.1155/2022/8853448]

[21]   J.S. Dhatterwal, K.S. Kaswan, S. Saxena, and A. Panwar, "Big data for health data analytics and decision support", *Computational Convergence and Interoperability in Electronic Health Records (EHR).,* pp. 93-116, 2024.

[22]   U. Sugandh, S. Nigam, and M. Khari, "Blockchain technology in agriculture for indian farmers: a systematic literature review, challenges, and solutions", *IEEE Syst. Man. Cybern. Mag.,* vol. 8, no. 4, pp. 36-43, 2022.
[http://dx.doi.org/10.1109/MSMC.2022.3197914]

[23]   A.U. Haq, J.P. Li, B.L.Y. Agbley, A. Khan, I. Khan, M.I. Uddin, and S. Khan, "IIMFCBM: Intelligent integrated model for feature extraction and classification of brain tumors using MRI clinical imaging data in IoT-healthcare", *IEEE J. Biomed. Health Inform.,* vol. 26, no. 10, pp. 5004-5012, 2022.
[http://dx.doi.org/10.1109/JBHI.2022.3171663] [PMID: 35503847]

[24]   A.K. Dubey, A. Jain, A. Panwar, M. Kumar, H. Taneja, and P.S. Lamba, "UNet segmentation based effective skin lesion detection using deep learning", *2023 International Conference on Communication, Security and Artificial Intelligence, ICCSAI 2023,* pp. 470-474, 2023.
[http://dx.doi.org/10.1109/ICCSAI59793.2023.10421443]

[25]   U. Sugandh, S. Nigam, M. Khari, and S. Misra, "An approach for risk traceability using blockchain technology for tracking, tracing, and authenticating food products", *Information (Basel),* vol. 14, no. 11, p. 613, 2023.
[http://dx.doi.org/10.3390/info14110613]

[26]   S. Vimal, M. Khari, R.G. Crespo, L. Kalaivani, N. Dey, and M. Kaliappan, "Energy enhancement using Multiobjective Ant colony optimization with Double Q learning algorithm for IoT based cognitive radio networks", *Comput. Commun.,* vol. 154, pp. 481-490, 2020.
[http://dx.doi.org/10.1016/j.comcom.2020.03.004]

[27]   A.K. Dubey, A. Jain, A. Panwar, M. Kumar, H. Taneja, and P.S. Lamba, "Optimizing emotion recognition through weighted averaging in deep learning ensembles", *2023 International Conference on Communication, Security and Artificial Intelligence, ICCSAI 2023,* pp. 410-414, 2023.
[http://dx.doi.org/10.1109/ICCSAI59793.2023.10421386]

[28]   U. Sugandh, S. Nigam, S. Misra, and M. Khari, "A bibliometric analysis of the evolution of state-o--the-art blockchain technology (BCT) in the agrifood sector from 2014 to 2022", *Sensors (Basel),* vol. 23, no. 14, p. 6278, 2023.
[http://dx.doi.org/10.3390/s23146278] [PMID: 37514574]

[29]   S. Saif, P. Das, S. Biswas, S. Khan, M.A. Haq, and V. Kovtun, "A secure data transmission framework for IoT enabled healthcare", *Heliyon,* vol. 10, no. 16, p. e36269, 2024.
[http://dx.doi.org/10.1016/j.heliyon.2024.e36269] [PMID: 39224301]

[30]   M. Azrour, J. Mabrouki, A. Guezzaz, S. Ahmad, S. Khan, and S. Benkirane, "IoT, machine learning and data analytics for smart healthcare", *CRC Press,* 2024.
[http://dx.doi.org/10.1201/9781003430735]

[31]   K. Kumari, S.K. Pahuja, and S. Kumar, "Machine learning implementations in COVID-19", *Computational Modeling and Data Analysis in COVID-19 Research.,* Apple Academic Press, pp. 1-16, 2021.
[http://dx.doi.org/10.1201/9781003137481-1]

[32]   M.S. Rao, S. Modi, R. Singh, K.L. Prasanna, S. Khan, and C. Ushapriya, "Integration of cloud

computing, IoT, and big data for the development of a novel smart agriculture model", *3rd International Conference on Advance Computing and Innovative Technologies in Engineering, ICACITE,* pp. 2779-2783, 2023.
[http://dx.doi.org/10.1109/ICACITE57410.2023.10182502]

[33]   Z. Wang, "Digital Twin Technology," Industry 4.0 - Impact on Intelligent Logistics and Manufacturing. CRC Press, 2020.
[http://dx.doi.org/10.5772/intechopen.80974]

[34]   A. Haq, J.P. Li, S. Khan, M.A. Alshara, R.M. Alotaibi, and C. Mawuli, "DACBT: deep learning approach for classification of brain tumors using MRI data in IoT healthcare environment", *Sci. Rep.,* vol. 12, no. 1, p. 15331, 2022.
[http://dx.doi.org/10.1038/s41598-022-19465-1] [PMID: 36097024]

[35]   S. Sinha, A. Panwar, P. Gupta, and V. Bhatnagar, "Evolution of business intelligence system: from ad-hoc report to decision support system to data lake based BI 3.0", *Healthcare and Knowledge Management for Society 5.0: Trends, Issues, and Innovations.,* pp. 255-269, 2022.
[http://dx.doi.org/10.1201/9781003168638-18]

[36]   P. Chugh, M. Gupta, S. Indu, G. Chaudhary, M. Khari, and V. Shanmuganathan, "Advanced energy efficient pegasis based routing protocol for IoT applications", *Microprocess. Microsyst.,* vol. 103, p. 104727, 2023.
[http://dx.doi.org/10.1016/j.micpro.2022.104727]

[37]   K. Kumar, and M. Khari, "Energy gaps and bacteriochlorophyll molecular graph representation based on machine learning algorithm", *Biomedical Research Developments for Improved Healthcare.,* IGI Global, pp. 47-54, 2024.
[http://dx.doi.org/10.4018/979-8-3693-1922-2.ch003]

[38]   M. Khari, A.K. Garg, A.H. Gandomi, R. Gupta, R. Patan, and B. Balusamy, "Securing data in internet of things (IoT) using cryptography and steganography techniques", *IEEE Trans. Syst. Man Cybern. Syst.,* vol. 50, no. 1, pp. 73-80, 2020.
[http://dx.doi.org/10.1109/TSMC.2019.2903785]

[39]   R.O. Ogundokun, S. Misra, A.B. Adelodun, and M. Khari, "COVID-19 Detection system in a smart hospital setting using transfer learning and IoT-based model", *Internet of Things, vol. Part F1201.,* Springer International Publishing Cham, pp. 233-262, 2023.
[http://dx.doi.org/10.1007/978-3-031-28631-5_12]

[40]   A. Panwar, Shyla, and V. Bhatnagar, "Blockchain-based web 4.0: Decentralized web for decentralized cloud computing," in cloud IoT: Concepts, paradigms, and applications, 1st ed., Jitendra Kumar Verma, Deepak Kumar Saxena, Vicente González-Prida Díaz, Vira Shendryk, Ed. CRC Press, 2022, pp. 219–233.
[http://dx.doi.org/10.1201/9781003155577-19]

[41]   W. Jian, J.P. Li, A.U. Haq, S. Khan, R.M. Alotaibi, S.A. Alajlan, and M.B.B. Heyat, "Feature elimination and stacking framework for accurate heart disease detection in IoT healthcare systems using clinical data", *Front. Med. (Lausanne),* vol. 11, p. 1362397, 2024.
[http://dx.doi.org/10.3389/fmed.2024.1362397] [PMID: 38841592]

[42]   A. Panwar, and V. Bhatnagar, "Sentiment analysis of game review using machine learning in a hadoop ecosystem", *Handbook of Research on Engineering Innovations and Technology Management in Organizations.,* pp. 145-165, 2020.
[http://dx.doi.org/10.4018/978-1-7998-2772-6.ch008]

[43]   A. Panwar, and V. Bhatnagar, "Scrutinize the idea of hadoop-based data lake for big data storage", In: *Applications of Machine Learning. Algorithms for Intelligent Systems, First.,* S.P.P. Johri, J.K. Verma, Eds., Springer, 2020, pp. 365-391.
[http://dx.doi.org/10.1007/978-981-15-3357-0_24]

[44]   N. Pritam, M. Khari, L. Hoang Son, R. Kumar, S. Jha, I. Priyadarshini, M. Abdel-Basset, and H. Viet

Long, "Assessment of code smell for predicting class change proneness using machine learning", *IEEE Access,* vol. 7, pp. 37414-37425, 2019.
[http://dx.doi.org/10.1109/ACCESS.2019.2905133]

CHAPTER 9

Application of IoT-Based EEG Sensors in Industry 4.0

Sonu Kumar Jha[1,*], Somaraju Suvvari[1] and Mukesh Kumar[1]

[1] *Department of Computer Science & Engineering, National Institute of Technology Patna, Patna Bihar, India*

Abstract: Human-Machine Interaction (HMI) is definitely considered to play a pivotal role in advancing smart manufacturing systems in today's Industry 4.0 age. In this context, the chapter considers how IoT technologies are converging with EEG-based interfaces to refine HMI within Industry 4.0 frameworks. The introduction gives a thorough overview of the 4th industrial revolution (*i.e.*, Industry 4.0), focusing on its transformative influence on automation and data exchange within manufacturing processes. Real-time knowledge of cognitive states is essential to maximize human-machine collaboration, and EEG technology is presented as a key means for monitoring brain activity. The recognition of the relevance and impact HMI has in the context of smart manufacturing is demonstrated, evincing how it facilitates efficiency on factory floors, secures operations, makes them safer, and reinforces business decisions to be taken in real-time. The chapter also provides an explanation of how the Internet of Things can contribute to Industry 4.0 by connecting devices and exchanging data almost effortlessly. Incorporating EEG with IoT even allows formonitoring and analysis of human cognitive states in real-time, thus creating adaptive manufacturing environments where machines respond immediately based on updated human intent and condition. It also increases efficiency during operation hours by keeping workers in an optimal working condition. Machines look for factors that induce stress or fatigue and set them straight before they occur. Integrating EEG and IoT technologies represents a paradigm shift in HMI, offering manufacturers unprecedented insights into human cognition and behavior. By leveraging EEG data through IoT-enabled systems, manufacturers can optimize task allocation, personalize user interfaces, and even predict maintenance needs based on cognitive workload. This chapter argues that such advancements are critical for achieving higher productivity, quality, and safety standards in modern manufacturing. To sum up, this chapter elucidates EEG-based IoT-integrated interfaces for revolutionizing HMI from an Industry 4.0 perspective. These technologies improve operational confidence by facilitating real-time monitoring and adaptive responsiveness, making them ideal enablers for future smart manufacturing.

---

[*] **Corresponding author Sonu Kumar Jha:** Department of Computer Science & Engineering, National Institute of Technology Patna, Patna, Bihar, India; E-mail: sonukumarjha1990@gmail.com

Tanu Singh, Vinod Patidar, Arvind Panwar & Urvashi Sugandh (Eds.)

Keywords: Cyber-physical systems, Cognitive state monitoring, Data analytics, EEG sensors, Electroencephalogram, Human-machine interactions, Operational efficiency, Industry 4.0, Internet of Things, IoT sensors, Smart manufacturing.

INTRODUCTION

An Overview of Industry 4.0 and its Dependence on Human-Machine Interaction

Industry 4.0 is the fourth industrial revolution, primarily identified as a fusion of digital automation systems and physical processes necessary in biological environments. The role of EEG technology is shown in Fig. (**1**). This change has been possible thanks to technologies like artificial intelligence (AI), robotics, big data analytics, and the Internet of Things (IoT), thus giving birth to new-age smart factories and cyber-physical systems. At the heart of this revolution is Human-Machine Interaction (HMI), which emphasizes the incorporation of human operators with automated systems, ensuring a smooth transition. Good HMI is imperative in smart manufacturing. Human operators must be able to oversee, control, and cooperate with machines quickly, boosting productivity and safety.

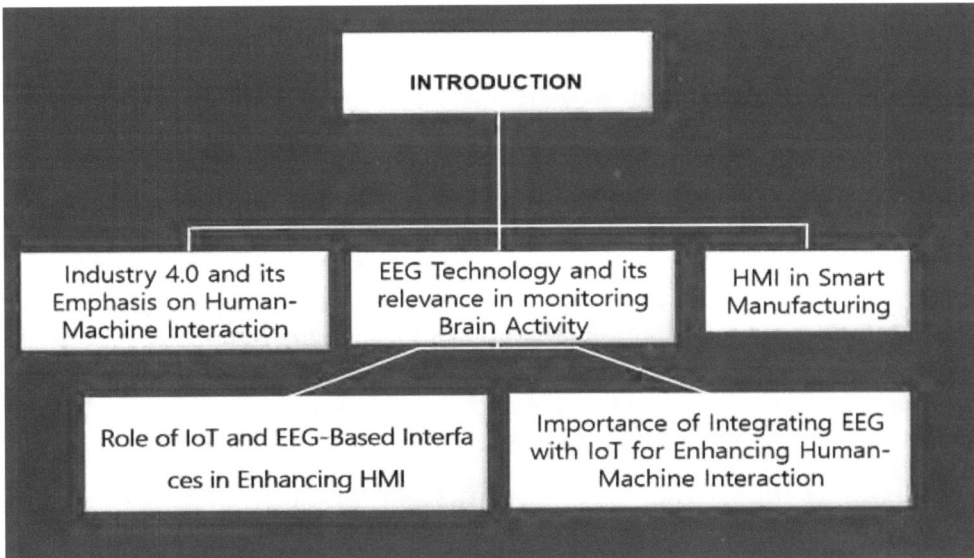

Fig. (**1**). Role of EEG technology.

Introduction to EEG Technology and its Relevance in Monitoring Brain Activity

EEG is a non-invasive way of tracking and recording electrical activity in the brain. By putting electrodes on the scalp, EEG measures electrical signals in the brain, thus informing about cognitive and emotional conditions. It is a technology that is used in a myriad of medical and psychological research, leading to advances ranging from the understanding of brain function to the diagnosis of neurological disorders and exploration into mental processes. From the perspective of Industry 4.0, EEG technology is a newer way to approach how HMIs perform within an industry by providing real-time data on the mental state and mental processes of workers/operators. It allows a more adaptive and responsive interaction with machines.

Importance of Human-Machine Interaction (HMI) in Smart Manufacturing

HMI is very important in smart manufacturing, and its efficiency and effectiveness have become more critical for various reasons. Human operators can operate complex automated systems in a natural manner, which reduces the risks of errors and improves operational safety. Secondly, it allows operators to make more informed decisions by making sure the right information is there and that they have control. It finally enables the amendment and improvement of manufacturing practices, facilitating changes in real-time due to human instruction and environmental variation. In this sense, industry 4.0 ambitions that strive to boost performance, quality, and customization levels are simply impossible without improved HMI capabilities.

Role of IoT and EEG-Based Interfaces in Enhancing HMI

The IoT bridges the gap in Industry 4.0 by interconnecting systems and devices to collect, process, and exchange real-time data. By integrating it with EEG-based interfaces, IoT can dramatically improve HMI by giving a live data stream of an operator's cognitive and emotional conditions. This real-time data can be used to alter the behavior of machines, human-machine interfaces, and systems, creating a more intuitive and responsive interaction environment. For instance, an EEG-based interface can detect fatigue in machine operators to change the pace of operation or notify the operator that they need a break, which would prevent incidents and promote greater efficiency overall.

Importance of Integrating EEG with IoT for Enhancing Human-Machine Interaction

When combined with IoT for the sake of HMI (Human-Machine Interface), EEG yields a few essential advantages. It allows the production of resilient systems that can react to the present mental states of the people operating them, leading to enhanced safety, performance, productivity, and user pleasure. Secondly, it enables the creation of customized HMI solutions that can match unique requirements and preferences of different operators. It can monitor and continuously analyse cognitive and emotional conditions, thus providing important information for further evolution of the HMI systems. This integration heralds the dawn of more gentle, responsive, and human-centric industrial ecologies.

In conclusion, the use of EEG technology, together with the Internet of Things, has a large potential for enhancing human-machine interfaces in the fourth industrial revolution. In the end, it can contribute to the success of factory certification programs through better, more flexible, and safer human-machine communication based on instant emotional feedback from the operators.

EEG TECHNOLOGY AND ITS RELEVANCE IN MONITORING BRAIN ACTIVITY

Electroencephalography (EEG) is a non-invasive neuroimaging technique that measures electrical activity within the brain. Developed within the early twentieth century, EEG has evolved to become one of the most critical tools in neuroscience, neurology, and cognitive science. The process involves placing electrodes on the scalp to discover tiny electrical indicators generated by neural activity. These signals are amplified and recorded as waveforms that offer insights into the brain's purposeful domain, starting from sleep styles and cognitive techniques to odd mind activity such as seizures. EEG is distinctly valued in brain monitoring because of its capacity to offer real-time data with high temporal resolution. Different imaging strategies, including useful Magnetic Resonance Imaging (MRI) or Positron Emission Tomography (PET), which provide excessive spatial resolution are confined by their delayed signal responses and excessive cost. Unlike these strategies, EEG offers a cost-effective and sensible method for non-stop tracking. This makes EEG mainly beneficial for programs that require real-time feedback, together with Brain-Computer Interfaces (BCIs), neurofeedback, and seizure detection.

The Mechanics of EEG Technology

The fundamental principle behind EEG is the detection of electrical potentials produced by the coordinated activity of neurons inside the brain. Neurons communicate through electric impulses, and when the networks of neurons fire synchronously, they generate electrical fields that may be detected on the scalp. EEG electrodes, typically crafted from conductive substances like silver or gold, capture those electric signals. The signals are then amplified and digitized for analysis. EEG indicators are classified into unique frequency bands: Delta (0.5-4 Hz), Theta (four-8 Hz), Alpha (8-12 Hz), Beta (12-30 Hz), and Gamma (30-60 Hz), as shown in Table **1**. Each of these bands is related to distinct cognitive states. For example, Delta waves are the most prominent during deep sleep, Alpha waves are related to relaxed wakefulness, and Beta waves are associated with energetic wondering and attention. Analyzing the amplitude and frequency of those waves allows researchers and clinicians to deduce the mind's state and locate abnormalities.

Table 1. EEG frequency band range representation [1].

EEG Frequency Band	Frequency Ranges
Theta	4-8 HZ
Alpha	8-12 HZ
Beta	12-30 HZ
Gamma	30-60 HZ
Delta	0.5-4 HZ

Relevance of EEG in Monitoring Brain Activity

EEG is essential for several clinical and research packages because of its capability to provide direct and instantaneous records about brain characteristics. In scientific settings, EEG is typically used to diagnose and reveal epilepsy. It can record epileptic spikes and seizures, permitting healthcare providers to pinpoint the affected areas in the brain to increase focused treatment plans. EEG is also used to diagnose other conditions, which include sleep disorders, brain tumours, head injuries, encephalitis, and cognitive impairments, imparting a complete view of brain fitness. Beyond scientific packages, EEG has won tremendous traction in research fields exploring cognitive neuroscience and psychology [2]. It is appreciably utilized in reading mind dynamics associated with interest, reminiscence, language processing, and sensory perception. Because EEG gives an instantaneous degree of neural interest, it has become an effective device for understanding how the mind processes data and how these processes are altered in different neurological and psychiatric disorders.

EEG in the Era of Industry 4.0 and IoT

The emergence of Industry 4.0 and the Internet of Things (IoT) has caused a revolution in EEG technology. The term "Industry 4.0" refers to the fourth industrial revolution, which is defined by data interchange, intelligent automation, and the integration of cyber and physical systems. One important part of this change is the Internet of Things (IoT), which basically just hooks up commonplace items and gadgets to the Internet so they can gather, share, and process data. EEG technology has enormous potential for creating cutting-edge applications in human-machine interaction, neuroscience, and healthcare when combined with IoT. IoT-connected wearable electroencephalography (EEG) devices can provide continuous, real-time monitoring of brain activity in non-clinical settings, including homes, offices, and even during everyday activities. This creates new possibilities for individualised treatment, where individuals might receive immediate feedback on their cognitive and emotional states, potentially preventing neurological illnesses from advancing. EEG systems, for instance, can be used by IoT-enabled Smart homes to monitor patients with epilepsy or other neurological diseases. If abnormal brain activity is observed, these systems can notify caretakers or medical experts [3]. Likewise, real-time monitoring of mental exhaustion, stress, and cognitive load in the workplace could be facilitated by EEG-based brain-computer interfaces, which could also improve worker safety and productivity. EEG Preprocessing is shown in Fig. (**2**).

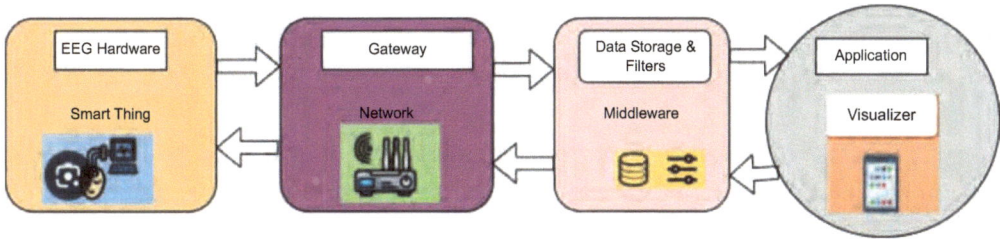

Fig. (2). EEG processing and application.

HMI IN SMART MANUFACTURING

Human-Machine Connection (HMI) Tech has developed significantly with the advent of the Fourth Industrial Revolution or Industry 4.0, focusing on the integration of cyber-physical systems, the Internet of Things (IoT), and smart manufacturing Methods. HMI is an important factor in forward industry environments as a medium between human operators and machines. It eases the efficient and effective control, watching, and management of complicated manufacturing systems, thereby enhancing productivity, safety, and flexibility in the production method.

Understanding Human-Machine Interface (HMI) in the Context of Smart Manufacturing

In the domain of smart manufacturing, HMI systems have revolutionized from simple control panels with buttons and switches to sophisticated connections that provide real-time Information visualization, remote control capabilities, and forecasting maintenance alerts. These connections are not but supine displays; they are reciprocal platforms that provide raw unbiased data and leave operators to make swift, knowledgeable decisions accordingly. Modern HMI systems [4] leverage advanced graphical connections, touchscreens, Augmented Reality (AR), and even voice recognition to improve operator encounter and operational productivity. The role of HMI in the forward industry is multi-dimensional. It involves not only the direct control and observation of machinery but also the aggregation and analysis of information from various IoT devices and sensors embedded in the production floor. These IoT devices collect large amounts of information relevant to operation, production, characteristics, and different name metrics. HMIs use this information to provide a comprehensive overview of the manufacturing method, allowing operators to identify and resolve problems, improve workflows, and minimize downtime promptly.

Integration of IoT with HMI for Enhanced Manufacturing Processes

Smart manufacturing now offers a new vision of connectivity and interaction, which will be highly applicable to the integration of IoT and HMI. Sensors and devices can continually monitor IoT-enabled machinery and ambient conditions, creating massive datasets sent to centralised systems for processing and analysis. These IoT networks enable real-time feedback and control when paired with HMI, opening the door to adaptive production methods, predictive maintenance, and energy management. HMI linked to Internet of Things devices can offer operators in a smart factory real-time machine health status updates, warning them of possible problems before they lead to equipment failure. This feature lowers maintenance expenses and unscheduled downtime dramatically. Furthermore, trend analysis using data from IoT devices by HMIs can reveal patterns in equipment utilisation and recommend the best maintenance schedules. HMIs with IoT integration also make remote control and monitoring possible. Remote monitoring and management of operations are crucial in a global manufacturing setting where factories may be spread across multiple geographic locations [5]. Through web-based dashboards or mobile apps, operators and engineers may access HMI interfaces and make real-time adjustments to the production process from anywhere in the world. This degree of adaptability guarantees a more responsive and nimble manufacturing process and improves decision-making.

Benefits of Advanced HMI Systems in Smart Manufacturing

The use of advanced HMI systems in smart manufacturing offers several significant benefits:

- **Greater Customization and Flexibility:** Modern HMI Systems can be customized to meet the particular needs, humidity levels, and other conditions of various production locations. These interfaces are designed to be user-friendly and adaptable to operators' skill levels, catering to both skilled labour and expert engineers.

- **Improved Operational Productivity:** With real-time information visualization and analytics, operators can make quicker and more informed decisions. Arsenic amp effect product is optimized to schedule blow decrease, resulting in extremely better general equipment strength (OEE).
- **Improved Guard and Compliance:** Advanced HMI systems are adequate for trip alarms or automatic shutdowns . This ensures that manufacturing methods comply with safety regulations and standards.
- **Reduced Downtime through Foretelling Maintenance:** By leveraging information analytics and calculator learning procedures, HMI systems can predict when a machine is likely to fail and schedule maintenance before a breakdown occurs. This proactive access significantly reduces downtime and extends the life of a machine.
- **Improved User Experience:** The integration of technologies such as Augmented Reality (AR) and Virtual Reality (VR) with HMI systems offers an immersive user experience. AR-based HMIs, for example, allow operators to visualise complicated data more intuitively by superimposing digital information onto physical objects.

Challenges and Future Directions

The use of HMI systems in intelligent manufacturing has several advantages, but there are drawbacks as well [6]. Integrating IoT-based sensors and devices with HMI systems to safeguard sensitive data and preserve system integrity can be difficult and expensive. Strong cybersecurity measures are therefore necessary. HMI design standardization is also necessary to guarantee interoperability across various platforms and devices. Future HMI in smart manufacturing will probably include more sophisticated interfaces driven by machine learning and Artificial Intelligence (AI). These intelligent HMIs will be capable of showing data and offering predictive insights and autonomous control, significantly eliminating the need for human intervention and opening the road for completely automated smart factories [7].

ROLE OF IOT AND EEG-BASED INTERFACES IN ENHANCING HUMAN-MACHINE INTERACTION (HMI)

The advent of the Internet of Things (IoT) and Electroencephalography (EEG)-based connections has revolutionized the field of Human-Machine Interaction (HMI) [8]. With the overlap of these technologies, we are witnessing a peak of perfection. This integration offers enormous potential across various sectors, including healthcare, automotive, smart homes, industrial mechanization, and gaming, where real-time information acquisition and operator-centered layout are decisive.

The Role of IoT in Enhancing HMI

The Internet of Things refers to the physical devices interconnected in a network that communicate and exchange data over the Internet. IoT facilitates the creation of intelligent environments where machines can sense, respond, and adapt to user needs dynamically with HMI [9]. The data gathered from several sensors that are integrated into gadgets and are capable of tracking and interpreting human movements, behaviours, and activities is the foundation of these innovative environments. IoT-enabled equipment, for instance, may recognise when people are in a smart home and appropriately change the entertainment, lighting, or temperature. IoT can enhance predictive maintenance in an industrial context by continuously monitoring equipment health and notifying operators of potential problems before they arise. Lowering downtime and preserving continuous operating flow not only increases operational efficiency and safety but also enhances user experience. The ability of IoT to interface with Machine Learning (ML) and Artificial Intelligence (AI) algorithms is another factor contributing to its strength in HMI [10]. Through these linkages, computers can gather information from user interactions and modify their replies over time to accommodate user preferences better. IoT-enabled voice assistants, like Google Home and Alexa from Amazon, for example, are constantly learning from the orders and actions of their users in order to deliver more precise and contextually relevant responses. As a result, users are far more satisfied with an ever-evolving, highly personalised interface that predicts and adjusts to their demands.

EEG-Based Interfaces: A New Dimension to HMI

Although the Internet of Things (IoT) connects and intelligently uses items, EEG-based interfaces provide a special, non-invasive method of tracking and interpreting human brain activity. Electrodes are applied to the scalp to detect electrical activity in the brain during electroencephalography, or EEG. By analysing the information obtained from these signals, it is possible to decipher user intentions, feelings, and mental states, which would exceed commands restricted to vocal or haptic input. EEG-based interfaces are handy in situations where traditional input devices, including touchscreens, mice, and keyboards, are impractical. Using brain waves alone, EEG-based solutions enable people with disabilities or motor impairments to engage with machines, removing barriers and promoting more inclusive human-machine interaction. Such systems have been successfully deployed in operating wheelchairs, prosthetic limbs, and communication equipment, allowing users to restore autonomy and independence.

Virtual Reality (VR) and gaming have also seen a lot of use for EEG-based interfaces [11]. Through the monitoring of a player's mental state, such as concentration, relaxation, or stress, games can dynamically modify their storylines, in-game locations, or difficulty levels to deliver a more personalised and engaging experience. By adjusting to each user's demands, this feature not only improves immersion but also fosters mental wellness and cognitive training.

Synergizing IoT and EEG for Enhanced HMI

IoT and EEG-based interfaces together have the most significant potential to improve HMI. When these technologies are combined, they form a potent synergy that can lead to more responsive feedback loops and deeper, context-aware interactions. Think about a smart-home setting, for example, where residents' mental states are continuously monitored by EEG headgear. With the help of IoT-enabled gadgets, the system may automatically dim the lights, play calming music, or change the temperature of the space if a user seems worried. When combined, IoT and EEG have the potential to greatly improve patient monitoring and care in the healthcare industry. While Internet of Things (IoT) sensors monitor physiological factors like body temperature, blood pressure, and heart rate, wearable EEG devices can continuously monitor a patient's mental and emotional states. Integrating those facts allows for greater holistic awareness of a patient's well-being, enabling personalized remedy plans, early detection of capability fitness problems, and extra effective management of chronic conditions. Similarly, EEG and IoT can work collectively in commercial automation to optimize human-system collaboration [12]. EEG sensors can monitor the mental workload and fatigue ranges of operators, whilst IoT gadgets offer real-time statistics about system performance and environmental conditions. By analysing these statistics, structures can dynamically modify machine behaviour, allocate responsibilities, or offer operators adaptive assistance, thereby improving safety and productivity. The 10-20 electrode placement system is an internationally recognised method for applying electrodes to the scalp to capture electroencephalography (EEG) [13]. Consistent and reproducible electrode insertion ensures dependable data collection, processing, and cross-study comparison [14]. An internationally accepted technique for placing electrodes on the scalp for electroencephalography (EEG) recording is the 10–20 electrode placement system. This device, invented by Herbert Jasper in 1958, has become a standard in clinical and research contexts for collecting brainwave activity. Consistent and repeatable electrode insertion guarantees dependable data collection, analysis, and cross-study comparison [15].

Regarding the relative distances between neighbouring electrodes, the term "10-20" (represented in Fig. (**3**)) describes them as percentages (10% or 20%) of the entire skull length from front to rear or left to right. Anatomical markers on the head, such as the nasion (the nasal bridge) and the inion (the bony bump at the rear of the skull), are used to determine where the electrodes should be placed. To preserve uniformity in the electrode placement while accounting for individual variations in head shape and size, this system's spacing has been designed [16].

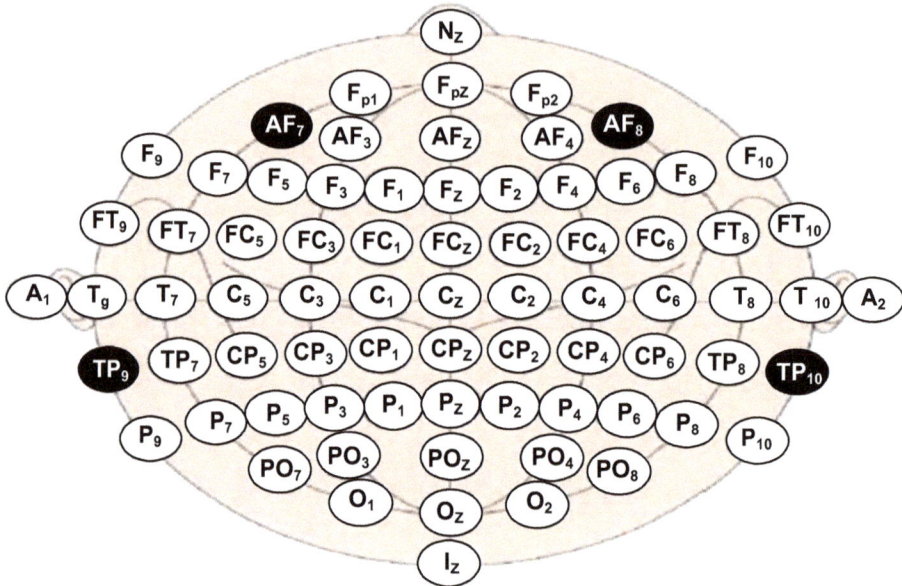

Fig. (3). 10-20 EEG electrode representation [3].

Electrode Placement and Naming Convention

The 10-20 system segregates the scalp into discrete zones that correlate to distinct regions of the cerebral cortex, each of which is linked to a distinct brain function. The letters on electrode labels correspond to the areas of the brain that they are closest to:

- **Fp**: Frontal pole
- **F**: Frontal
- **C**: Central
- **P**: Parietal
- **O**: Occipital
- **T**: Temporal

The labels for each electrode also have a letter (such as "z" for midline placements) or a number (even numbers for electrodes on the right hemisphere, odd numbers for electrodes on the left). For instance, "F3" designates an electrode located on the left side of the head's frontal region, whereas "Cz" designates an electrode situated at the head's centre midline. The frontal poles, temporal lobes, and occipital area are represented by the five crucial sites of the 10-20 system's principal electrodes, which are Fp1, Fp2, T3, T4, and Oz. To improve the granularity of the EEG data and allow for more accurate monitoring of brain activity, additional electrodes are placed between these.

Benefits of the 10-20 System: The 10-20 electrode placement approach is well known for striking a compromise between usefulness and comprehensiveness. Standardised electrode placements guarantee thorough scalp coverage and enable access to EEG signals linked to various brain areas. Because of the system's flexibility, additional electrodes can be added to create extended 10-10 or 10-5 systems, which provide higher spatial resolution for advanced research and diagnostic applications. Furthermore, the standardised nomenclature of the 10-20 system promotes collaboration and communication between physicians and researchers. The capacity to duplicate research and compare results using a standard framework is invaluable, especially given the growing significance of data sharing in neuroscience. This system's consistency lowers the electrode misplacement variability, which is crucial for analysing complicated signals like Event-Related Potentials (ERPs).

Application in EEG-based Human-Machine Interfaces (HMI)

The 10-20 electrode system plays a critical role in Human-Machine Interfaces (HMI) by precisely collecting brain impulses that operate external devices. To understand user intent, EEG-based HMIs frequently rely on real-time brainwave pattern analysis. Accurate electrode placement guarantees high-quality signal acquisition, which is essential for machine learning algorithms processing EEG data to identify particular commands or mental states. For example, motor imagery—brain activity linked to imagined movements—can be detected by electrodes positioned in accordance with the 10-20 system in Brain-Computer Interfaces (BCIs) used for neuroprosthetics or assistive devices. LVRT control is used for handling voltage dips, and EEG systems are used for emotion-adaptive applications like Brain-Computer Interfaces (BCI) [17]. By translating these signals into commands for robotic arms or communication aids, people with severe physical limitations can better engage with their surroundings. The integration of the Internet of Things (IoT) into EEG-based HMIs further enhances the significance of accurate electrode placement. IoT-enabled EEG devices can transfer real-time brain activity data to cloud-based platforms for processing and analysis, enabling continuous monitoring and feedback. This integration makes more individualised and adaptive HMI solutions possible, which can react quickly to shifts in a user's mental state. A quickly developing topic, integrating EEG technology into Human-Machine Interfaces (HMIs) uses EEG's real-time monitoring capabilities to enable direct brain-to-external device communication. Electroencephalography (EEG)-based Brain-Computer Interfaces (BCIs) translate brain impulses into commands that drive external devices like computers, cell phones, prosthetic limbs, and wheelchairs. This program is extremely life-changing for those with severe motor limitations since it opens up new channels for engagement and communication. EEG-based interfaces can potentially improve the responsiveness and interactivity of bright surroundings inside the Internet of Things. An IoT system that is integrated with EEG, for example, might monitor a user's cognitive state, such as stress, focus, or weariness, and modify lighting, temperature, or noise levels in the environment in accordance with that state. The user experience and comfort can be enhanced by more efficient and customised human-machine interactions brought about by this dynamic adaptability.

Challenges and Considerations

Electroencephalography (EEG) is a widely used technique that uses electrodes placed on the scalp to detect brain activity. One such electrode system is the 10-20 electrode system. This configuration, while widely used, has certain drawbacks compared to more sophisticated, high-density EEG devices. The lower spatial resolution resulting from the relatively sparse electrode distribution is one of the main downsides. More electrodes are used in high-density systems, which enables a more precise and in-depth depiction of brain activity. Nonetheless, the 10-20 system is still extensively used because it compromises performance and usefulness, particularly in situations where portability and usability are essential factors. The 10-20 wearable or portable EEG device system offers a functional trade-off between accuracy and usability. Despite being more accurate, high-density EEG systems can be heavy and unsuitable for non-clinical environments or applications that need mobility. The 10-20 system's design places a high value on wearability and simplicity of setup, making it perfect in scenarios where the user has limited time or must remain mobile. Because of this, it is instrumental in real-time applications such as brain-computer interfaces, where the necessity for the finest spatial resolution is not always as important as practicality. However, the quantity of electrodes is not the only factor that affects the 10–20 system's efficacy. In order to ensure the best possible signal quality, additional parameters are also essential. Electrode impedance, or the resistance to electrical signals between the electrodes and the scalp, is one such component. Low impedance is essential for accurate readings since high impedance can deteriorate the quality of the recorded signals. This can be controlled by properly prepping the skin before applying the electrodes and ensuring the electrodes establish good contact with the scalp.

Preparing the skin is another crucial element. Technicians frequently need to gently exfoliate the scalp to get rid of oils and dead skin cells that can interfere with the electrodes' capacity to detect electrical impulses. A conductive gel may be used to enhance signal transmission between the electrodes and the skin. An EEG recording might have higher quality and less noise if it is adequately prepared. Furthermore, the quality of the readings may be impacted by the kind of electrodes utilised. Various applications call for different kinds of electrodes. For instance, while some are optimised for quick setup and brief usage, others are made for long-term monitoring and provide more comfort to the user. The selection of the appropriate electrode is contingent upon the particular requirements of the EEG recording, such as the duration of the recording and the degree of mobility required of the subject during the session. Therefore, although the 10–20 electrode system might not provide as much spatial detail as high-density systems, it is still a valuable and dependable choice for a variety of EEG applications, especially those that call for portability and user-friendliness. The number of electrodes is not the only aspect that affects its efficiency; other factors include electrode impedance, skin preparation, and electrode selection. Users may maximise signal quality and guarantee correct results by carefully controlling these factors, making the 10-20 system a useful and adaptable tool in clinical and non-clinical EEG contexts.

IMPORTANCE OF INTEGRATING EEG WITH IOT FOR ENHANCING HUMAN-MACHINE INTERACTION

The convergence of multiple developing technologies has led to notable developments in the field of Human-Machine Interaction (HMI) in recent years. Electroencephalography (EEG) and the Internet of Things (IoT) are examples of such transformational technologies. Combined, these technologies present fresh opportunities to improve human-machine and human-environment interactions. By offering more user-friendly, responsive, and adaptable interaction mechanisms, integrating EEG-based interfaces with IoT systems can significantly enhance HMI and boost system performance. Enhancing Cognitive Awareness and Control: EEG is a non-invasive technique of recording electrical activity in the brain, providing treasured insights into a consumer's mental state, emotions, and intentions.

Analysing EEG indicators makes it feasible to recognize a person's awareness, pressure levels, fatigue, or even reason to move. When this real-time cognitive information is included in IoT environments, it could enhance the adaptability of machines and devices to the person's current situation. For instance, in smart-homes or offices, gadgets can adjust lighting, temperature, or ambient sounds primarily based on the occupant's mental state, developing a more comfortable and personalized environment. Furthermore, EEG-based interfaces allow customers to govern IoT-enabled gadgets even more intuitively *via* mind alerts. This kind of mind-machine interface (BMI) may be especially beneficial for people with mobility impairments. For instance, human beings with disabilities can manipulate IoT-connected devices along with smart wheelchairs, robotic hands, or household appliances solely through their mind, improving independence and the quality of life. This form of interaction is not the most efficient and reduces the cognitive load and effort required for users to carry out ordinary obligations.

Real-Time Data Processing and Decision Making

Real-time data collection, analysis, and decision-making are critical components of IoT ecosystems. A greater level of contextual comprehension and situational awareness is made possible by integrating EEG data into Internet of Things devices. EEG sensors, for instance, can be used in healthcare settings to continually monitor a patient's brain activity and identify indications of seizures, stress, or sleep disturbances. Then, the IoT framework can initiate emergency protocols, notify caretakers or healthcare providers, or modify treatment regimens as necessary. This smooth information flow and automated response can greatly enhance patient outcomes by facilitating prompt interventions. Moreover, incorporating EEG data into IoT systems facilitates more intelligent decision-making across multiple industries, including gaming, defence, and automotive. EEG sensors, for example, can track a driver's level of alertness in automotive applications. If the driver is detected to be distracted or tired, the IoT system can activate autonomous driving features or issue warnings. Similarly, EEG-based interfaces can offer a more immersive experience in virtual reality or gaming settings by customising the game environment or level of difficulty according to the player's emotional and cognitive states. This makes the experience more engaging and unique.

Adaptive Learning and Feedback Mechanisms

The integration of EEG and IoT in HMI offers several advantages, including implementing adaptive learning and feedback mechanisms. For example, EEG sensors can track a learner's emotional states, engagement, and attention in educational or training settings. In order to keep the student interested and to ensure that the content is presented at the right level of difficulty, the IoT system can use this data to modify the course material or give immediate feedback. This strategy is beneficial in neurorehabilitation, where patients can receive individualised training plans that adjust in real time based on their progress, increasing the efficacy and motivation of rehabilitation. In applications about mental health, the capacity to offer adaptive feedback is equally essential. Therapists and other mental health practitioners can create more effective treatment regimens for disorders like anxiety, depression, or ADHD by combining EEG and IoT. For instance, an IoT system might provide personalised therapeutic interventions, such as calming music, guided meditations, or cognitive behavioural therapy exercises, depending on real-time feedback. EEG data can also track a patient's emotional response to different stimuli.

Scalability and Interoperability of IoT-EEG Systems

Integrating EEG with IoT structures also brings forth challenges and possibilities in terms of scalability and interoperability. IoT frameworks are inherently designed to deal with huge volumes of data from heterogeneous sources, making them highly desirable for integrating EEG record streams alongside different sensory inputs. The real-time processing competencies of contemporary IoT architectures enable the seamless aggregation, analysis, and interpretation of EEG signals, facilitating sturdy decision-making tactics in dynamic environments. Moreover, the interoperability of IoT platforms allows EEG-based interfaces to be incorporated with an extensive range of devices and applications, from healthcare to entertainment and smart town infrastructures. This flexibility allows improving holistic HMI solutions that cater to various user needs and contexts. The scalability of IoT platforms ensures that those solutions may be deployed throughout numerous settings, from individual houses to large-scale public environments, thereby democratizing access to superior HMI technology. A Human-Machine Interface (HMI) system with EEG technology is seen below in Fig. (**4**) with an explanation:

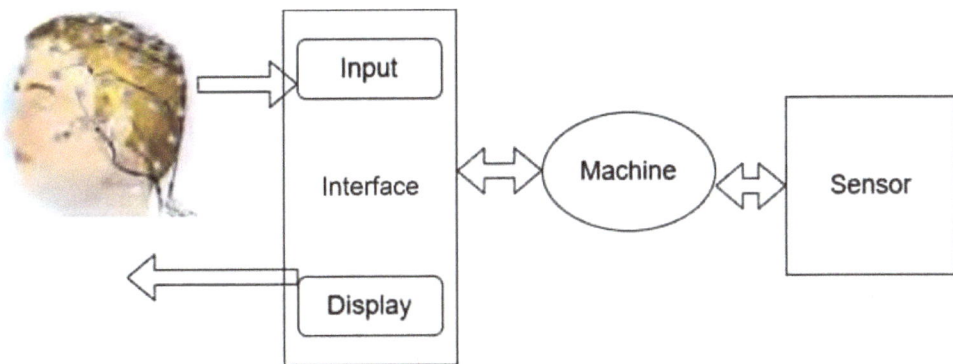

Fig. (4). EEG with sensors.

EEG sensor input: Brain signals are recorded by electrodes on the skull, enabling real-time cognitive state monitoring.

Interface: This talks to the machine and processes the data that is recorded. It can transmit information and obtain a response.

Machine and Sensors: The machine deciphers the processed signals, while the sensors offer operational feedback or more data.

Display: The user can interact in real-time with the computer by viewing information and cognitive states shown to them.

CONCLUSION

The integration of EEG and IoT technologies represents a massive jump within the evolution of Industry 4.0 with Human-Machine Interaction (HMI). As established in this chapter, this technology not only enhances the connectivity and flexibility of intelligent manufacturing systems but also fundamentally remodels the connection between people and machines. Real-time monitoring of cognitive states *via* EEG empowers machines to adapt and respond dynamically to human motives, situations, and overall performance. This capability creates an extra responsive and adaptive production environment in which an employee's well-being is prioritized by detecting stress, fatigue, or cognitive overload, ensuring safety and sustained efficiency. Furthermore, by means of leveraging IoT's ability to facilitate seamless data exchange across linked devices, and manufacturers can optimize production workflows, allocate responsibilities more effectively, and customize consumer interfaces based on real-time cognitive insights. These improvements offer producers remarkable control over their operations, fostering more precise decision-making and enhanced predictive maintenance to save them from gadget failures or human mistakes. The combination of EEG and IoT creates a particularly interactive and responsive machine that aligns each human's and device's abilities, using innovation in productivity, fine control, and protection. EEG-based IoT interfaces can transform HMI by providing new perspectives on human behaviour and thought processes. This integration makes Industry 4.0's smarter, safer, and more adaptable production processes possible. These technologies guarantee that smart factories may reach new heights of operational excellence by enabling real-time collaboration between humans and machines, making them essential to the advancement of modern production.

REFERENCES

[1]   S.K. Jha, S. Suvvari, and M. Kumar, "EEG-based emotion recognition: An in-depth analysis using deap and seed datasets", *11th International Conference on Computing for Sustainable Global Development (INDIACom)*, pp. 1816-1821, 2024.

[2]   N.S. Suhaimi, J. Mountstephens, and J. Teo, "EEG-based emotion recognition: A state-of-the-art review of current trends and opportunities", *Comput. Intell. Neurosci.,* vol. 2020, pp. 1-19, 2020.
[http://dx.doi.org/10.1155/2020/8875426] [PMID: 33014031]

[3]   S.K. Jha, S. Suvvari, and M. Kumar, "Emotion recognition from electroencephalogram (EEG) signals using a multiple column convolutional neural network model", *SN Computer Science,* vol. 5, no. 2, p. 213, 2024.
[http://dx.doi.org/10.1007/s42979-023-02543-0]

[4]   A. Topic, and M. Russo, "Emotion recognition based on EEG feature maps through deep learning network", *Engineering Science and Technology, an International Journal,* vol. 24, no. 6, pp. 1442-1454, 2021.
[http://dx.doi.org/10.1016/j.jestch.2021.03.012]

[5]   S. Koelstra, C. Muhl, M. Soleymani, Jong-Seok Lee, A. Yazdani, T. Ebrahimi, T. Pun, A. Nijholt, and I. Patras, "DEAP: A database for emotion analysis; using physiological signals", *IEEE Trans. Affect. Comput.,* vol. 3, no. 1, pp. 18-31, 2012.
[http://dx.doi.org/10.1109/T-AFFC.2011.15]

[6]   X. Du, C. Ma, G. Zhang, J. Li, Y-K. Lai, G. Zhao, X. Deng, Y-J. Liu, and H. Wang, "An efficient lstm network for emotion recognition from multichannel EEG signals", *IEEE Trans. Affect. Comput.,* vol. 13, no. 3, pp. 1528-1540, 2022.
[http://dx.doi.org/10.1109/TAFFC.2020.3013711]

[7]   S.K. Jha, S. Suvvari, and M. Kumar, "Maximizing emotion recognition accuracy with ensemble techniques on EEG signals", *Recent Advances in Computer Science and Communications,* vol. 17, no. 5, p. e170124225749, 2024.
[http://dx.doi.org/10.2174/0126662558279390240105064917]

[8]   S.B. Wankhade, and D.D. Doye, "Hybrid hunt-based deep convolutional neural network for emotion recognition using EEG signals", *Comput. Methods Biomech. Biomed. Engin.,* vol. 25, no. 12, pp. 1311-1331, 2022.
[http://dx.doi.org/10.1080/10255842.2021.2007889] [PMID: 35098819]

[9]   S. Liu, L. Zhao, X. Wang, Q. Xin, J. Zhao, D.S. Guttery, and Y.D. Zhang, "Deep spatio-temporal representation and ensemble classification for attention deficit/hyperactivity disorder", *IEEE Trans. Neural Syst. Rehabil. Eng.,* vol. 29, pp. 1-10, 2021.
[http://dx.doi.org/10.1109/TNSRE.2020.3019063] [PMID: 32833639]

[10]   F. Xu, D. Pan, H. Zheng, Y. Ouyang, Z. Jia, and H. Zeng, "EESCN: A novel spiking neural network method for EEG-based emotion recognition", *Comput. Methods Programs Biomed.,* vol. 243, p. 107927, 2024.
[http://dx.doi.org/10.1016/j.cmpb.2023.107927] [PMID: 38000320]

[11]   A. Mekler, "Calculation of EEG correlation dimension: Large massifs of experimental data", *Comput. Methods Programs Biomed.,* vol. 92, no. 1, pp. 154-160, 2008.
[http://dx.doi.org/10.1016/j.cmpb.2008.06.009] [PMID: 18667257]

[12]   T. Song, W. Zheng, P. Song, and Z. Cui, "EEG emotion recognition using dynamical graph convolutional neural networks", *IEEE Trans. Affect. Comput.,* vol. 11, no. 3, pp. 532-541, 2020.
[http://dx.doi.org/10.1109/TAFFC.2018.2817622]

[13]   S. Jirayucharoensak, S. Pan-Ngum, and P. Israsena, "EEG-based emotion recognition using deep learning network with principal component based covariate shift adaptation", *Scientific World Journal,* vol. 2014, pp. 1-10, 2014.
[http://dx.doi.org/10.1155/2014/627892] [PMID: 25258728]

[14]   A. Panwar, and V. Bhatnagar, "Data lake architecture", *Int. J. Organ. Collective Intell.,* vol. 10, no. 1, pp. 63-75, 2020.
[http://dx.doi.org/10.4018/IJOCI.2020010104]

[15]   S.K. Jha, S. Suvvari, and M. Kumar, "Exploring the impact of KNN and MLP classifiers on valence-arousal emotion recognition using EEG: An analysis of DEAP dataset and EEG band representations", In: *Advances in Computing and Data Sciences. ICACDS 2024. Communications in Computer and Information Science.,* M. Singh, Ed., vol. 2194. Springer: Cham, 2025. [http://dx.doi.org/10.1007/978-3-031-70906-7_1]

[16]   V.M. Joshi, and R.B. Ghongade, "EEG based emotion detection using fourth order spectral moment and deep learning", *Biomed. Signal Process. Control,* vol. 68, p. 102755, 2021. [http://dx.doi.org/10.1016/j.bspc.2021.102755]

[17]   D. Tyagi, A. Prakash, A. Pal, S.K.J. Jha, M. Rahul, and V. Yadav, "Control strategy for LVRT enhancement in photovoltaic fuel cell hybrid renewable energy system: Control strategy for lvrt enhancement in fuel cell hres", *J. Sci. Ind. Res. (India),* vol. 83, no. 2, pp. 204-213, 2024. [JSIR].

CHAPTER 10

Optimization Techniques for Predictive Maintenance in Industry 4.0

Arul Prakash A.[1,*], **S. Vignesh**[1], **Rahin Batcha R.**[1], **D. Saravanan**[1] and **Vijay Ramalingam**[1]

[1] *Department of Computer Science and Engineering, Sathyabama Institute of Science and Technology, Chennai, India*

Abstract: In Industry 4.0, "intelligent factories" collect and analyze data to keep tabs on the production process. Machine learning, data mining, and other statistical AI technologies can identify and forecast possible manufacturing procedure abnormalities, improving productivity and dependability. Nevertheless, the information retrieved from manufacturing information is sometimes presented in a complex structure due to the heterogeneous nature of the data. This puts up the semantic gap problem, which is shorthand for the reality that various production systems are incompatible. In addition, a unified knowledge model of physical assets and the ability to think in real time about analytical activities are essential for automating the decision-making process of Computerized Physical Systems (CPS), which are growing more data-intensive. Using symbolic AI in predictive maintenance could be a promising solution to these problems. Through numerous examinations, predictive upkeep offers a comprehensive review of the identification, localization, and identification of malfunctions in associated machinery. RAMI4.0 provides a structure to analyze the several initiatives that comprise Industry 4.0. The hierarchical structure, functional classification, and product life cycle are all encompassed. The Corporate Data Space, currently known as the International Data Space, is an online database that allows for the safe transfer and simple linking of data between corporate ecosystems using shared standards and governance frameworks. It guarantees data owners' online privacy while laying the groundwork for developing and using intelligent services and novel business procedures. In light of Industry 4.0, this article investigates potential ways to bolster maintenance prediction. Data exchange between businesses with varying security needs and the subsequent modularization of relevant functions are outcomes of implementing the RAMI 4.0 architecture, which facilitates predictive maintenance utilizing the FIWARE framework.

Keywords: AI, Computerized Physical System, Industry 4.0, Machine learning, Predictive Maintenance.

* **Corresponding author Arul Prakash A.:** Department of Computer Science and Engineering, Sathyabama Institute of Science and Technology, Chennai, India; E-mail: prakash875@gmail.com

Tanu Singh, Vinod Patidar, Arvind Panwar & Urvashi Sugandh (Eds.)

INTRODUCTION

Optimization techniques for predictive maintenance in Industry 4.0 focus on improving the efficiency and effectiveness of maintenance tasks using advanced technologies.

Machine Learning Algorithms: These algorithms analyze historical data to predict when equipment is likely to fail, allowing maintenance to be scheduled before issues arise.

IoT Sensors: Sensors collect real-time data on equipment performance, which is then analyzed to detect anomalies and predict failures.

Data Analytics: Advanced analytics processes large volumes of data to identify patterns and trends that indicate potential equipment issues.

Cloud Computing: Storing and processing data in the cloud provides scalability and accessibility, making it easier to manage and analyze data from multiple sources.

Digital Twins: Creating a digital replica of physical equipment allows for simulation and analysis, helping predict and prevent failure [1 - 3].

The introduction of cutting-edge technology like the Internet of Things (IoT), cloud computing, and big data analytics—the hallmarks of Industry 4.0—has revolutionized the way factories function. Industry 4.0's scheduled upkeep has quickly become an essential tactic for boosting equipment reliability, cutting maintenance expenses, and increasing operational effectiveness. Minimizing unplanned downtime and increasing the usable life for manufacturing assets are two goals of automated upkeep strategies. These techniques leverage data from sensors, machine learning methods, and analytics in real time to determine the ideal timing for maintenance interventions. The absence of sensors and connections in older machinery is a major obstacle to deploying predictive maintenance in brownfields or preexisting industrial settings. With the goal of integrating old systems with predictive maintenance capabilities, researchers have investigated ways to retrofit inexpensive sensors and establish an Industrial Internet of Things architecture.

AI and Deep Learning: These technologies enhance the accuracy of predictions by learning from vast amounts of data and improving over time.

Maintenance plays a crucial role in smart factories and in fulfilling operational priorities and plans. As noted, a significant chunk of a processing or manufacturing facility's operational expenses goes toward maintenance. The percentage of production expenses attributable to maintenance might range from fifteen percent to sixty percent, depending on the sector (Fig. **1**).

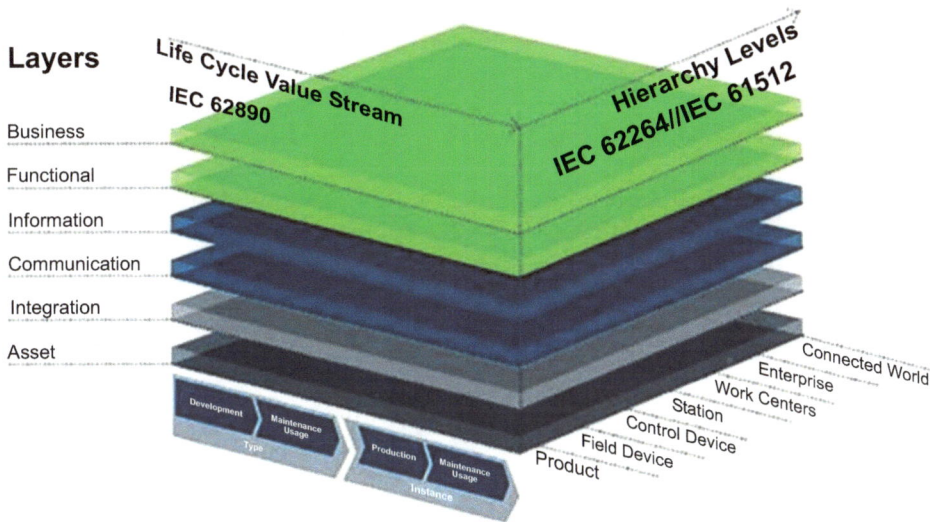

Fig. (1). Architecture layer of Industrial 4.0.

Equipment and machinery downtime may be decreased, efficiency can be increased, and production can be boosted with an effective maintenance method. It noted that to achieve environmental objectives within the framework of Industry 4.0, it is essential to choose the correct maintenance strategy due to the complexity and volatility of maintenance management and the difficulty in evaluating and cataloging the effectiveness of maintenance. The need for proper maintenance is stressed to prevent unanticipated plant and equipment failures. These failures incur various expenses for the business, such as labor, spare parts, rework, scrap, late order charges, and lost orders caused by unhappy consumers [4].

Small and Medium-sized Enterprises (SMEs) are the primary subject of this article. The hefty price tag of proprietary software and hardware solutions makes predictive maintenance a tough sell for Small and Medium-sized Enterprises (SMEs). Nonetheless, SMEs may build predictive maintenance apps using open-source tools far more affordably compared to proprietary remedies. It makes available a number of machine learning and statistical resources that are necessary for maintenance prediction. Assistance and additional helpful materials are readily available because of R's extensive ecosystem of developers and users who work together to improve the language of programming and its numerous packages.

Here are the sections that make up the paper: The third section discusses Internet of Things (IoT) equipment and sensors as a cornerstone of maintenance planning. Section four presents the predictive repair DSS prototype. This document provides an overview of the platform, its design and reason, the user interface using graphics, and the machine learning engine. It finishes with a case study of the platform in action [5].

STATE-OF-THE-ART OF PREDICTIVE MAINTENANCE

Many businesses are starting to employ predictive maintenance, even though it has existed since 1940. Infrastructure, emergency services, transportation networks, power plants, and communication systems are among the many businesses that have used predictive maintenance because of the crucial nature of their operation. Forecasts from Market Research Future Report indicate that predictive maintenance is becoming increasingly popular. The research study predicts that the overall preventative upkeep market will reach 23 billion dollars by 2025, expanding at a CAGR of 25.5% from 2019 to 2024. An action carried out on a system at predetermined intervals to minimize or eliminate cumulative degradation while maintaining satisfactory operation is defined. It isemphasized that predictive maintenance is often seen as a subclass of preventive maintenance [6 - 8]. Installed systems powered by predictive analytics technology enable predictive maintenance to monitor and detect system breakdowns and malfunctions. However, these safeguards kick in only when a catastrophic breakdown is imminent. This helps make the most of the money and resources available, ensures that systems and equipment are up and always running, improves quality and supply chain systems, and makes everyone happy.

Certain researchers see condition-based maintenance as a foundational step before predictive maintenance. However, there are others who, as said above, equate the two concepts [9]. Before the Internet of Things (IoT) concept, condition-based maintenance was a popular approach to industrial maintenance. The Internet of Things (IoT) is a component of predictive maintenance. According to the situation, there are three stages of condition-based upkeep, a program that uses data from condition monitoring to influence repair choices and suggestions.

The market includes traditional and sophisticated predictive maintenance procedures, which are further subdivided into two groups: methods using Big Data and the Internet of Things driven by machine learning.

Further evidence that the conventional methods subsegment dominated the market in 2018 comes from the Market Research Future Report [10]. Still, more development in the advanced techniques subsegment is anticipated. In this regard [10, 11], studies assert that most maintenance strategies depend on conventional, routine maintenance to ensure the uninterrupted operation of a system. However, you cannot discount the expense of maintenance-related components and oil replacements. As a result, predictive maintenance is becoming increasingly popular among businesses. In this approach, the system decides independently and schedules maintenance based on the needs [12]. Big data analytics and machine learning can help predict when assets will break and when to fix or replace parts before they fail, as pointed out by a study. Internet of Things (IoT) platforms may integrate data from many machines and production processes, considerably aiding predictive maintenance [13].

Equipment and machinery monitoring is the backbone of predictive maintenance strategies. Utilizing conventional and cutting-edge monitoring techniques allows for preemptive machine maintenance scheduling [14]. Instruments, including infrared thermography, vibration detectors, oil analyzers, electrical isolators, ultrasonic leak detectors, and temperature monitors, are all part of these monitoring approaches [15]. The business can run pre-programmed algorithms to anticipate when equipment will fail based on predictive maintenance calculations, monitoring and testing results with the right tools and instruments, and then start repairs only when a failure happens [16]. Furthermore, diagnostic and prognostic information is provided by predictive maintenance data, which shows what is wrong, where it is happening, why it is happening, if it is a malfunction or simply a failure, and when it will happen if it ever does [17].

Similarly, the primary goal of predictive maintenance is to reduce unnecessary maintenance and its costs by reviewing and assessing the needs and status of devices, systems, and machinery in real time to make maintenance decisions. Predictive maintenance, which ultimately leads to decision-making, revolves around condition monitoring. A control loop between the two parts of predictive maintenance, as shown in Fig. (**2**), is a graphic representation of the overall process.

Installed status sensors that communicate real-time operational and network state information are known as situation management and predictive maintenance technologies. State monitoring serves a twofold purpose, as explained by Ahmad and Kamaruddin [9], by allowing one to specify the status of devices within a system.

First, gathering information on the equipment's current state; second, learning more about what goes wrong and why regarding the impacts and patterns of equipment degradation. Numerous methods exist for mounting or retrofitting condition monitoring equipment and instruments to measure electrical currents, motion, temperature, pressure, oil, noise, and corrode levels.

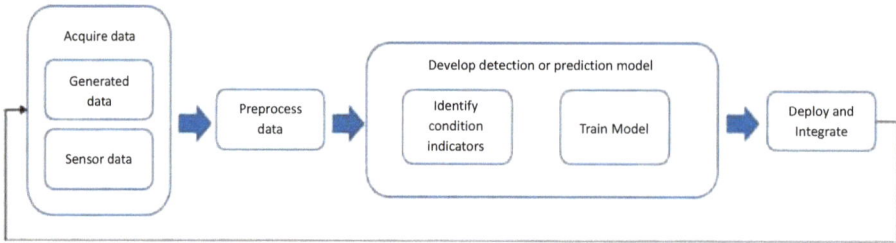

Fig. (2). Develop a detection or prediction model.

Condition monitoring data is the foundation of predictive maintenance since it can reveal several trends that point to impending machine or asset failure or degradation. The data gathered from condition monitoring also helps with maintenance planning, reducing the likelihood of failures and unexpected breakdowns. Reducing maintenance costs by discovering flaws early before they worsen, increasing protection and safety, efficiency, and dependability, and automating human inspection are ways condition monitoring benefits enterprises [18 - 20].

A Foundation for Predictive Maintenance: Internet of Things Devices and Sensors

World of Internet of Things Idea

The most basic explanation of the Internet of Things (IoT) is given by a study [21], which describes it as a mutually beneficial relationship between the physical and digital realms. The goal of the Internet of Things is to allow any device or person to connect to any other device or person at any location at any time through any network or service. Fig. (**3**) is a visual representation of the seamless connection between people and things or between things to address features like convergence, content, collections (repositories), computation, communication, and connectivity.

Numerous theoretical and practical publications on maintenance optimization attest to its growing popularity in academia and industry. Fig. (**1**) displays the change in the number of publications on maintenance optimization from 2000 to 2020. The information was culled from articles that were included in the Scopus database and had the words "maintenance optimization" along with one of the following: "scheduled," "opportunistic," "condition-based," "predictive," or "prescriptive" in the title, abstract, or keywords. Maintenance optimization is becoming increasingly focused, as seen by the rising ratio of articles mentioning the topic to all articles indexed by Scopus (rescaled in the image by dividing by 1000) (Fig. **3**).

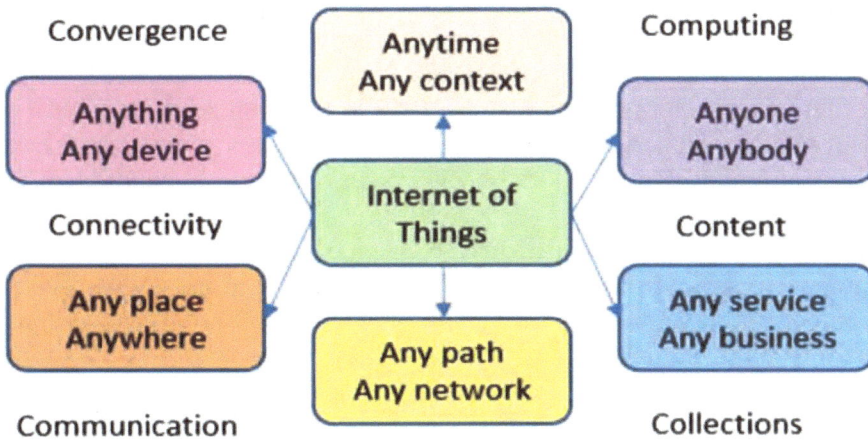

Fig. (3). Sample model of IoT 4C connections.

Precision Upkeep

It fixes an asset's malfunction and gets it working again. It consists solely of processes for fixing or replacing things. It works well for systems that are not mission-critical, meaning they can have their maintenance interventions done fast and cheaply and whose failures will not have significant effects [21].

Upkeep to Avoid Problems

Carrying out maintenance tasks prior to failure tries to keep the asset from losing its functioning.

Five distinct kinds of preventative maintenance plans are recognized:

1. **Set up a Maintenance Schedule:** By performing maintenance procedures at predetermined intervals, whether irregular or periodic, it hopes to keep the asset from becoming useless. The maintenance plan is usually constructed using asset statistical data, such as failure times and maintenance durations. Degradation mechanisms are complicated and marked by considerable uncertainty, making optimizing schedules challenging. Systems with a high potential for catastrophic failure, significant losses in production, or for which there are economic benefits to planning maintenance (*e.g.*, due to inconveniently unavailable spare parts) are good candidates for scheduled maintenance.

2. **Maintenance that Takes Advantage of Opportunities:** The goal is to

maintain more parts or subsystems of the asset simultaneously. To do this, it is possible to combine the maintenance of components with comparable failure rates and operating conditions or to take advantage of a scheduled shutdown or an unplanned breakdown to service many components at once. System types that share components or are subject to long-planned shutdowns (such as nuclear power plants) or those whose repair operations necessitate the rental of costly equipment (such as ships or cranes) are good candidates for this maintenance strategy.

3. **Upkeep Depends on Conditions:** Preventative maintenance, like planned maintenance, seeks to keep an asset from becoming useless; however, unlike scheduled maintenance, planning maintenance interventions is based on analyzing data obtained directly from the asset to determine its status. The availability of a monitoring system to gather data on physical quantities related to asset degradation is a prerequisite for applying condition-based maintenance. The next step is to use fault detection and diagnostic techniques to identify and diagnose aberrant circumstances, triggering the execution of specific maintenance activities. Suppose the benefits of avoiding failure-related unscheduled shutdowns outweigh the expenses of the monitoring system and the development of detection and diagnostic tools. In that case, condition-based maintenance is the way to go [22 - 24].

4. **Predictive Upkeep:** This method goes beyond condition-based maintenance by analyzing monitoring data for prognostics, which helps predict when something will break down and allows for proactive maintenance planning (Fig. **4**). Building the monitoring system and prognostic tools is necessary. The deterioration processes and failure mechanisms can be significantly impacted by operating, so it is essential to handle data characterized by multiple sources of uncertainty properly. Systems that may reap the benefits of condition-based maintenance and more can use predictive maintenance, for instance, when replacement components are not readily available and must be purchased.

APPROACHES FOR THE SELECTION OF OPTIMAL MAINTENANCE ACTIONS

Updated standards for optimization Industry 4.0 have some goals related to reducing energy consumption and ecological effects. However, its initial idea was to improve the industry's performance, efficiency, and safety by taking advantage of opportunities presented by advances in artificial intelligence, cyber-physical systems, the Internet of Things, and robotics. The focus of contemporary culture has shifted in recent years to address new issues of sustainability and resilience. Proposed as an expansion of Industry 4.0, Industry 5.0 considers the most pressing societal issues on a global scale and emphasizes the role of research and development to sustain industry for the benefit of humanity over the long term

[25]. As a result, optimizing for servicing will undoubtedly allow for incorporating new metrics alongside performance and safety-related ones. To do this, we need to define measurable quantities that can be used to assess how well a specific maintenance approach has been working in terms of the sustainability and resilience of the system. For example, a metric for measuring resilience has been established [26], and a new metric that considers safety, sustainability, reliability, and resilience simultaneously is based on return on investment [27]. Existing maintenance optimization methodologies are likely to see a flurry of activity as researchers work to define new ad hoc measures to incorporate new criteria of interest.

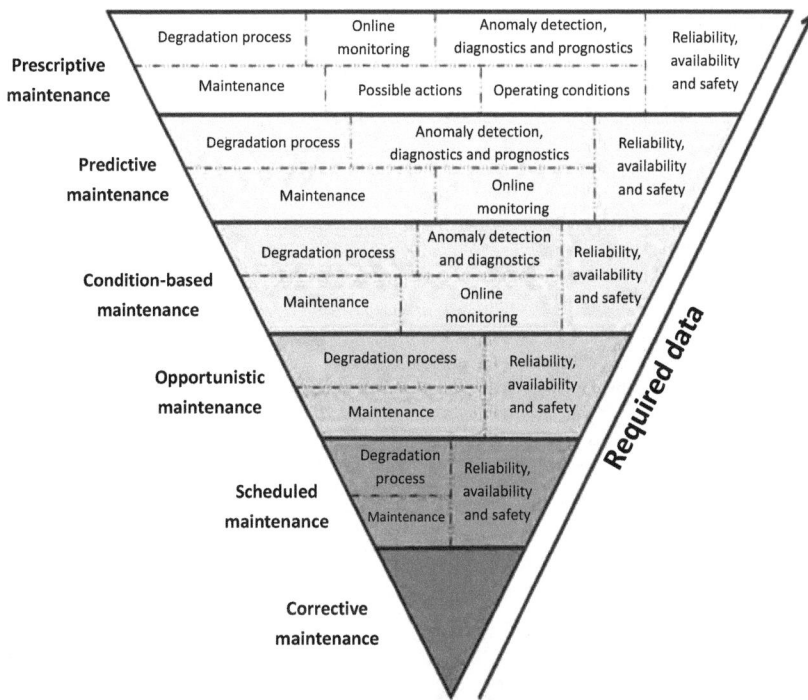

Fig. (4). Prescriptive maintenance for optimal maintenance action.

It is only sometimes the case that complex maintenance strategies and corrective maintenance are the way to go [28]. Instead, the best maintenance strategy should be chosen based on each component's specifics, considering factors like functionality, cost, criticality, environmental regulations, and business goals (Table **1**). As a result, it is best to use a maintenance plan that can change and adapt to the system's and environment's unique circumstances. This is why we anticipate the introduction of new approaches that call for maintenance engineers to document all potential operational and maintenance tasks rather than pre-deciding on a plan for each component under all circumstances. New methods will soon be suggested to maximize prescriptive maintenance, but in the meantime, MIP, D.P., and R.L. appear as potential solutions to this problem. Using MIP, MSAs, and R.L. in the industrial, energy, and aerospace sectors constitutes most Industry 4.0 applications. In contrast to the abundance of literature on general multi-unit systems, more needs to be written about actual case studies. This shows that there is still a need for more practical case studies and financial contributions from businesses to maintain theory and practice, which can only be addressed by more practical case studies and financial contributions from businesses. It was also noted that the created approaches are generalizable. Thus, they can be used by other industries with access to comparable KID sources.

Table 1. Literature review.

Paper Title	Methods Used	Practical Implications	Insights
ML-based failure detection approach for predictive maintenance in an industry 4.0-oriented web manufacturing control application.	ML-based approach for fault detection in predictive maintenance in Industry 4.0. Four supervised ML algorithms were compared for fault identification performance.	ML models used for fault identification in the predictive maintenance process. Web-based application developed for monitoring and sending alerts for anomalies.	ML algorithms, such as Grid Search along with Random Search, make fault identification better for predictive maintenance in Industry 4.0. This increases effectiveness and decreases downtime by anticipating faults before they happen.
A New Methodological Framework for Optimizing Predictive Maintenance Using Machine Learning Combined with Product Quality Parameters.	Framework tested in electromechanical components production line, reducing costs significantly.	ML combined with product quality parameters Product performance-based maintenance framework through ML.	In Industry 4.0, a new set of rules combines algorithmic learning with factors about the quality of the products to make predictive repairs that need better. This cuts charges and raises reliability by directing repair procedures better.
Enhancing Predictive Maintenance Hyperparameter Optimization and Adopted Strategies.	Investigates CNNs and LSTMs for predictive maintenance in manufacturing. Demonstrates optimized Parallel CNN-LSTM model enhancing prediction accuracy significantly.	Cost reduction in maintenance operations Improved efficiency in the manufacturing sector.	The CNN-LSTM simulation that was optimized got an RMSE of 14.98 on the test sample and an RMSE of 0.047 on the NASA charger sample.

(Table 1) cont.....

Paper Title	Methods Used	Practical Implications	Insights
Enhancing operational efficiency in industry 4.0: a predictive maintenance approach.	With scheduled upkeep for productivity, Industry 4.0 changes the way things are made.	• MATLAB-based code for predictive model development.	According to the study, proactive upkeep in Industry 4.0 uses strategies for optimization, such as Bayesian Inference and MATLAB-based models, to improve operational efficiency and keep work going without interruptions.

Lastly, as has been mentioned in other surveys on the optimization of maintenance, the absence of standards for evaluating maintenance techniques on clearly defined case studies should be mentioned. A benchmark for comparing the efficiency of various algorithms for optimizing power plant scheduled maintenance has been suggested in a study [29]. Despite its narrow focus on optimizing the maintenance schedule, it serves as a good foundation for assessing performance in this area.

RECENT ADVANCES IN BLOCKCHAIN TECHNOLOGY: PROSPECTS, APPLICATIONS, AND CONSTRAINTS IN THE MINERALS INDUSTRY

Security Protocols

Data security is the primary focus of this method. Every industry, including the mineral industry, relies on technology, and the security of that technology is paramount. Because of its delicate nature, blockchain attracts increased interest in implementing state-of-the-art security algorithms and mechanisms to protect all blockchain transactions. The necessity for authentication, non-repudiation, confidence, and integrity in information sharing is supported by cryptography [30]. This protects the integrity of the global network's data and information. Two types of encryptions are used to secure the data: symmetric and asymmetric. A key must erase or alter the stored data by its stringent tracking mechanism. With excellent resistance to tampering and protection using either a public key, a private key, or a mix of the two, the collection of documents, primarily financial records, is linked. This method significantly diminished the need for cash for transactions with individuals whose processes were delayed by banking institutions (Fig. **5**). Cryptocurrency, like Bitcoin, provides a safe and secure digital transaction ledger. The term "decentralization" describes how blockchain technology allows for the transfer of power and decision-making authority from a central authority to the network of events. This promotes understanding and builds confidence among those involved with this technology. This method also discourages users from exerting dominance or influence over one another to keep the blockchain network running smoothly. This method uses the nodes in the blockchain network to verify transactions that anybody can start at any time [31, 32].

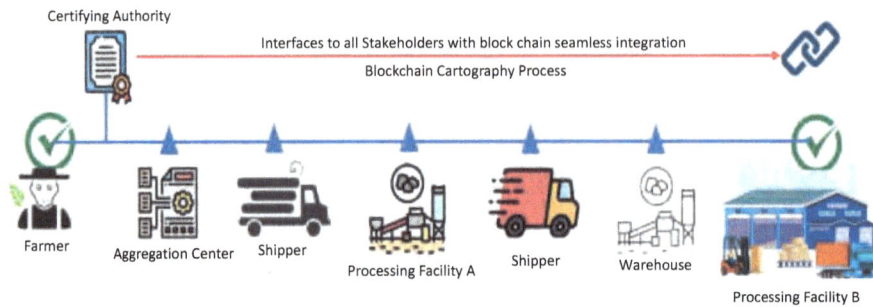

Fig. (5). Blockchain architecture process for transaction integration.

To keep the chain going, validated transactions are grouped into blocks, and when the limit of a block is reached, a new block is created. To add blocks to the chain, one must first obtain a unique identity called a Hash identity. Once recorded and transferred to the ledger, transactional values on the blockchain cannot be edited or amended, even by participants, thanks to its immutability. Like proof of state and other approaches, the nodes in a blockchain must reach an agreement in order for blocks to be admitted into the chain according to the concept of consensus. When mistakes happen during transactions, it is necessary to construct a new transaction to fix the mistake and make it accessible to the network. Order tracking, payments, and other types of transactions are recorded chronologically steadily. Before transactions may be created or accepted, the majority of members within the network must agree according to the stated norms for participant permission. Many people are getting on board with this technology because of this one big strategy, which would change the economy for the better in the future. Transactions are made safe and secure.

To sustainably monitor the performance and health state of a structure or piece of equipment while it is operating, planned upkeep makes use of instruments and condition monitoring methodologies. One thing that stands out in the literature about servicing 4.0 applications is how narrowly they target individual machines or pieces of machinery used in factories. One potentially game-changing notion is the development of a user-friendly, multi-purpose architecture that can combine several sensors and enable real-time *in situ* PdM on many types of machinery. Support for operational management and decision-making using collected data and PdM modeling is the core focus of this platform. At any point along the upkeep scheduling procedure, users and the maintenance team can alter and change proposed decisions based on their preset access levels to the platforms. Through user authentication safeguarded by a VPN (private virtual network), the platform grants remote access. As a result, alerts can be received using a cloud architecture that enables mobile and web communications. In addition to remote connectivity, this platform will deliver real-time in-person information tracking through a dashboard that computes KPIs and encourages API protocols for data individualization and alarm announcements. The data gets gathered by devices and systems. In addition to protecting data from intrusion and keeping it private, this allows for remote monitoring of plants from a browser on any device.

BLOCKCHAIN TECHNOLOGY AND PREDICTIVE MAINTENANCE SUPPLY CHAIN MANAGEMENT

Blockchain has many pros, including its ability to make the entire materials chain clear to the naked eye, verifiable, and traceable (Song *et al.*, 2019). As a result of the decentralized, secure, and unchangeable nature of blockchain technology itself, in supply chain processes like packaging and repackaging, transport, and final delivery, there are complexities very suitable for intelligent agents [33]. Many studies have shown the potential of blockchain technology in supply chain management. These cryptographers integrate blockchain with cryptographic solutions such as Elliptic Curve Cryptography (ECC) and the Generalized Menezes–Vanstone (or Fully Hashed) geometric hashing algorithm. In order to reinforce the security and privacy protection for decentralized supply chain systems [34], in the field of supply chain management, one important goal is to deliver materials and goods quickly. For this purpose, blockchain-based systems have been developed for tracking the origin and flow of materials. Renewable energy can be produced and consumed with blockchain. Wind farms and photovoltaic installations are connected to intelligent electric power systems.

Blockchain Technology in the Energy Sector

In the energy sector, there is a particularly interesting application for blockchain. Blockchain's decentralized and secure nature may well be able to meet the current challenges facing the energy industry: for example, how to integrate renewable energy sources into a system, management of an overloaded power grid and transmission network, or power architecture spanning multiple owners right down as far as homes in one or two apartment buildings connected in parallel. This is where directly used blockchain systems point out what could be done hitherto but could not be done in industrial process control and hence will find correspondence in every single such system based on electricity as it comes into existence. Furthermore, at present, the earliest instances have shown more efficient environmental protection achieved within industrial processes because, up until then, there was no way at all to ensure information about a single step carried over into another payment system eventually being held for public inspection.

CONCLUSION

We have provided a survey on optimizing servicing in this work. The readily accessible understanding, data, and knowledge within the context of Industry 4.0, the optimization criteria of interest, and the potential optimization outcomes have been the primary foci of the analysis. Academics and practitioners in the field of managing maintenance can use the example studies and guidelines provided in this review to help them choose the best upkeep optimization strategy to achieve their goals, considering the unique features of their respective industrial systems. The complexity of today's systems necessitates the creation of methods of optimization for management that can simultaneously optimize many goals while appropriately handling the substantial uncertainty impacting both the system's behaviors and its operating environment. When optimizing system-level maintenance, it is essential to consider the current and future health states of system components; new Artificial Intelligence (AI) and Machine Learning (ML) algorithms, as well as improvements in sensor technology, provide the opportunity to mine precious information on these states. Based on the optimization criteria research results, several industries are pushing to incorporate new sustainability and resilience measures into maintenance optimization. Prescription upkeep is also gaining popularity; it eliminates the need to choose an upkeep plan to apply to the system throughout its optimization time horizon, and it views operation and upkeep as complementary processes.

REFERENCE

[1]   R Meissner, H Meyer, and K Wicke, "Concept and economic evaluation of prescriptive maintenance strategies for an automated condition monitoring system", *Int. J. Progn. Health Manag.,* vol. 12, no. 3, pp. 1-17, 2021.
[http://dx.doi.org/10.36001/ijphm.2021.v12i3.2911]

[2]   S. Choubey, R. Benton, and T. Johnsten, "Prescriptive equipment maintenance: a framework. In: Proc. - 2019 IEEE Int. Conf. Big Data", *Big Data,* vol. 2019, pp. 4366-4374, 2019.
[http://dx.doi.org/10.1109/BigData47090.2019.9006213]

[3]   F. Tao, H. Zhang, A. Liu, and A.Y.C. Nee, "Digital twin in industry: state-of-the-art", *IEEE Trans. Industr. Inform.,* vol. 15, no. 4, pp. 2405-2415, 2019.
[http://dx.doi.org/10.1109/TII.2018.2873186]

[4]   M. Arvindhan, and D.R. Kumar, "Adaptive resource allocation in cloud data centers using actor-critical deep reinforcement learning for optimized load balancing", *Int. J. Recent Innov. Trends Comput. Commun.,* vol. 11, no. 5s, pp. 310-318, 2023.
[http://dx.doi.org/10.17762/ijritcc.v11i5s.6671]

[5]   J. Franzen, J. Stecken, R. Pfaff, and B. Kuhlenkötter, "Using the digital shadow for a prescriptive optimization of maintenance and operation", *Lecture Notes in Logistics,* vol. 1, pp. 265-276, 2019.
[http://dx.doi.org/10.1007/978-3-030-13535-5_19]

[6]   K. Worden, E.J. Cross, P. Gardner, R.J. Barthorpe, and D.J. Wagg, "On digital twins, mirrors and virtualizations", *Conference Proceedings of the Society for Experimental Mechanics Series,* vol. 3, pp. 285-95, 2020.
[http://dx.doi.org/10.1007/978-3-030-12075-7_34]

[7]   M. Mulders, and M. Haarman, "Predictive maintenance 4.0, predict the unpredictable", 2017.

[8]   K.L. Lueth, C. Patsioura, Z.D. Williams, and Z.Z. Kermani, "Industrial analytics 2016/2017: the current state of data analytics usage in industrial companies", 2016.

[9]   X Zhao, Z Lv, Z He, and W Wang, "Reliability and opportunistic maintenance for a series system with multi-stage accelerated damage in shock environments", *Comput. Ind. Eng.,* vol. 137, pp. 106029-106029, 2019.
[http://dx.doi.org/10.1016/j.cie.2019.106029]

[10]   P. Baraldi, M. Compare, and E. Zio, "Maintenance policy performance assessment in presence of imprecision based on Dempster–Shafer Theory of Evidence", *Inf. Sci.,* vol. 245, pp. 112-131, 2013.
[http://dx.doi.org/10.1016/j.ins.2012.11.003]

[11]   M. Marseguerra, E. Zio, and L. Podofillini, "Condition-based maintenance optimization by means of genetic algorithms and Monte Carlo simulation", *Reliab. Eng. Syst. Saf.,* vol. 77, no. 2, pp. 151-165, 2002.
[http://dx.doi.org/10.1016/S0951-8320(02)00043-1]

[12]   A.S. Yeardley, J.O. Ejeh, L. Allen, S.F. Brown, and J. Cordiner, "Integrating machine learning techniques into optimal maintenance scheduling", *Comput. Chem. Eng.,* vol. 166, pp. 107958-107958, 2022.
[http://dx.doi.org/10.1016/j.compchemeng.2022.107958]

[13]   M., Singh, H. "An Innovation development of cost wise task scheduling model for complex transmission in ultra dense cloud networks arvindhan". *2023 2nd Int. Conf. Innov. Technol. (INOCON),* 2023.

[14]   Y. Hu, X. Miao, J. Zhang, J. Liu, and E. Pan, "Reinforcement learning-driven maintenance strategy: a novel solution for long-term aircraft maintenance decision optimization", *Comput. Ind. Eng.,* vol. 153, 2021.
[http://dx.doi.org/10.1016/j.cie.2020.107056]

[15]   C.P. Andriotis, and K.G. Papakonstantinou, "Managing engineering systems with large state and action spaces through deep reinforcement learning", *Reliab. Eng. Syst. Saf.,* vol. 191, pp. 106483-106483, 2019.
[http://dx.doi.org/10.1016/j.ress.2019.04.036]

[16]   M. Arvindhan, "Effective motivational factors and comprehensive study of information security and policy challenges", In: *System Assurances* Elsevier, 2022, pp. 531-545.
[http://dx.doi.org/10.1016/B978-0-323-90240-3.00029-1]

[17]   J. Izquierdo, A. Erguido, P.X. Zubizarreta, and J. Uribetxebarria, "Framework for managing the operations and maintenance of wind farms", *J. Phys. Conf. Ser.,* vol. 1222, no. 1, p. 012046, 2019.
[http://dx.doi.org/10.1088/1742-6596/1222/1/012046]

[18]   Raj, A., Jadon, S., Kulshrestha, H., Arvindhan, M., Sinha, A. "Cloud infrastructure fault monitoring and prediction system using LSTM based predictive maintenance", *2022 10th Int. Conf. Reliab. Infocom Technol. Optim. (Trends Future Dir.) (ICRITO),* 2022.

[19]   L. Yang, R. Peng, G. Li, and C.G. Lee, "Operations management of wind farms integrating multiple impacts of wind conditions and resource constraints", *Energy Convers. Manag.,* vol. 205, pp. 112162-112162, 2020.
[http://dx.doi.org/10.1016/j.enconman.2019.112162]

[20]   X. Zhao, X. Huang, and J. Sun, "Reliability modeling and maintenance optimization for the two-unit system with preset self-repairing mechanism", *Proc. Inst. Mech. Eng. O. J. Risk Reliab.,* vol. 234, no. 2, pp. 221-234, 2020.
[http://dx.doi.org/10.1177/1748006X19890739]

[21]   M. Li, X. Jiang, J. Carroll, and R.R. Negenborn, "A multi-objective maintenance strategy optimization framework for offshore wind farms considering uncertainty", *Appl. Energy,* vol. 321, no. January, p.

119284, 2022.
[http://dx.doi.org/10.1016/j.apenergy.2022.119284]

[22]   J. Geng, M. Azarian, and M. Pecht, "Opportunistic maintenance for multi-component systems considering structural dependence and economic dependence", *J. Syst. Eng. Electron.,* vol. 26, no. 3, pp. 493-501, 2015.
[http://dx.doi.org/10.1109/JSEE.2015.00057]

[23]   R. Di Pasquale, and J. Marenco, "Optimization meets big data: a survey", *IEEE Congress on Evolutionary Computation (CEC),* 2017.

[24]   T. Yamagata, R. McConville, and R. Santos-Rodriguez, "Reinforcement learning with feedback from multiple humans with diverse skills", *NeurIPS 2021 Workshop on Safe and Robust Control of Uncertain Systems,* 2021

[25]   C. Ning, and F. You, "Optimization under uncertainty in the era of big data and deep learning: when machine learning meets mathematical programming", *Comput. Chem. Eng.,* vol. 125, pp. 434-448, 2019.
[http://dx.doi.org/10.1016/j.compchemeng.2019.03.034]

[26]   C. Wang, B. Wang, H. Liu, and H. Qu, "Anomaly detection for industrial control system based on autoencoder neural network", *Wirel. Commun. Mob. Comput.,* vol. 2020, pp. 1-10, 2020.
[http://dx.doi.org/10.1155/2020/8897926]

[27]   Z. Yang, P. Baraldi, and E. Zio, "A method for fault detection in multi-component systems based on sparse autoencoder-based deep neural networks", *Reliab. Eng. Syst. Saf.,* vol. 220, pp. 108278-108278, 2022.
[http://dx.doi.org/10.1016/j.ress.2021.108278]

[28]   A. Fuller, Z. Fan, C. Day, and C. Barlow, "Digital twin: enabling technologies, challenges and open research", *IEEE Access,* vol. 8, pp. 108952-108971, 2020.
[http://dx.doi.org/10.1109/ACCESS.2020.2998358]

[29]   A. Muthusamy, and R. K. Dhanaraj, "Dynamic Q-learning-based optimized load balancing technique in cloud", *Mobile Inf. Syst.,* vol. 2023, Hindawi Limited, pp. 1-16, 2023.
[http://dx.doi.org/10.1155/2023/7250267]

[30]   S. Carlos, A. Sánchez, S. Martorell, and I. Marton, "Onshore wind farms maintenance optimization using a stochastic model", *Math. Comput. Model.,* vol. 57, no. 7-8, pp. 1884-1890, 2013.
[http://dx.doi.org/10.1016/j.mcm.2011.12.025]

[31]   K. Atashgar, and H. Abdollahzadeh, "Reliability optimization of wind farms considering redundancy and opportunistic maintenance strategy", *Energy Convers. Manage.,* vol. 112, pp. 445-458, 2016.
[http://dx.doi.org/10.1016/j.enconman.2016.01.027]

[32]   L. Pinciroli, P. Baraldi, G. Ballabio, M. Compare, and E. Zio, "Optimization of the operation and maintenance of renewable energy systems by deep reinforcement learning", *Renew. Energy,* vol. 183, pp. 752-763, 2021.
[http://dx.doi.org/10.2139/ssrn.3875191]

[33]   Arvindhan, M., & Kumar, D. R.. "Adaptive Resource Allocation in Cloud Data Centers using actor-critical deep reinforcement learning for optimized load balancing". *International Journal on Recent and Innovation Trends in Computing and Communication*, 11(5s), 310-318, 2023.

[34]   G. Tripathi, M. A. Ahad, and G. Casalino, "A comprehensive review of blockchain technology: Underlying principles and historical background with future challenges," *Decision Analytics Journal,* vol. 9, no. 100344, p. 100344, 2023.

CHAPTER 11

Enhancing Predictive Maintenance through Optimization in the Era of Industry 4.0

Neha Sharma[1,*], Arvind Panwar[2], Rakesh Sharma[3], Urvashi Sugandh[4] and Manish Kumar[2]

[1] *Department of Information Technology, Bharati Vidyapeeth's College of Engineering, New Delhi, India*

[2] *School of Computing Science & Engineering, Galgotias University, Greater Noida, India*

[3] *McDermott International, Pune, Maharashtra, India*

[4] *School of Computer Science and Engineering, Bennett University, Greater Noida, India*

Abstract: The concept of Industry 4.0 is key to predictive maintenance, as it aids in balancing asset requirement utilization maximization, reducing downtime, and lowering maintenance expenditure. In this chapter, we look closely at the various methods of predictive maintenance strategies within Industry 4.0. It includes data analysis, machine learning, fault detection, anomaly prediction, sensor placement, and repair organization, as well as close reading with IoT and cyber-physical systems. In this way, companies can increase the performance of their assets, make them more reliable, and reduce insurance costs in Industry 4.0. This chapter dives deeply into how well optimized methods can be used in predictive maintenance. The lessons learned from such approaches by examining books, real examples, and useful experiences are also discussed, along with an understanding of effective results that come while you are studying data for your machine learning ways to get information based on lots of sensor data, which is what predictive maintenance essentially relies on as a bet against failure with early fault detection in place, yet avoiding downtime before problems start. Further, the chapter includes optimization techniques on the planning and scheduling of predictive maintenance. The integration of IoT and cyber-physical systems and the optimization of condition-based maintenance, as well as demonstrating their potential for autonomous decision-making and self-optimization, are also discussed. This chapter aims to provide a vision of using predictive maintenance, optimizing asset reliability, and driving operational efficiency in the era of Industry 4.0.

Keywords: Industry 4.0, IoT, Optimizing techniques, Predictive decision-making models, Predictive maintenance.

---

[*] **Corresponding author Neha Sharma:** Department of Information Technology, Bharati Vidyapeeth's College of Engineering, New Delhi, India; E-mail: neha.sh.2689@gmail.com

Tanu Singh, Vinod Patidar, Arvind Panwar & Urvashi Sugandh (Eds.)
All rights reserved-© 2025 Bentham Science Publishers

INTRODUCTION

Industry 4.0, also known as the Fourth Industrial Revolution, has brought digitalization and automation into manufacturing and industrial processes. At the crux of this revolution is the convergence and integration of cutting-edge technologies like Internet-of-Things (IoT), big-data analytics, Artificial Intelligence (AI), *etc.* with traditional industrial systems. Predictive maintenance has become a key application area that has been obtained using these technologies, with benefits dwarfing existing strategies for reactive and preventive maintenance [1, 2].

A Brief Introduction to Predictive Maintenance in Industry 4.0

Predictive maintenance is a proactive strategy with the goal of forecasting when an in-service asset will fall into a state of disrepair. Predictive maintenance systems can use machine learning to continuously monitor and analyze real-time data from sensors and other data sources in order to detect patterns, trends, and early warning signs of imminent failures. This allows minimizing unplanned downtime, reduces maintenance costs, and extends assets lifespan by scheduling necessary activities at the right time [3, 4].

Predictive maintenance scales with Industry 4.0. Predictive maintenance uses information from an array of sources that are produced by all the connected industrial systems—so it can assess precisely and be trusted [5, 6]. This data can be processed using advanced analytics techniques such as machine learning and deep learning to essentially go beyond the capability of human experts to identify complex patterns and relationships that are not straightforward.

The Significance of Optimization Techniques

As beneficial as predictive maintenance can be, it is also quite cumbersome to carry out and implement, especially in large industrial setups with myriad interconnected assets under multiple constraints. Optimization is a modeling tool that might help us to develop systems and decision-making in industrial maintenance. Fig. (**1**) shows IoT-enabled predictive maintenance.

These optimization techniques can be used to identify the best possible time and order in which maintenance activities should be done, considering asset criticality, resource availability, operational constraints, and more [7]. These same techniques can help optimize the managing of spare parts inventories to have the right parts available when needed and where they are needed at a minimum cost of carrying excess inventory [8].

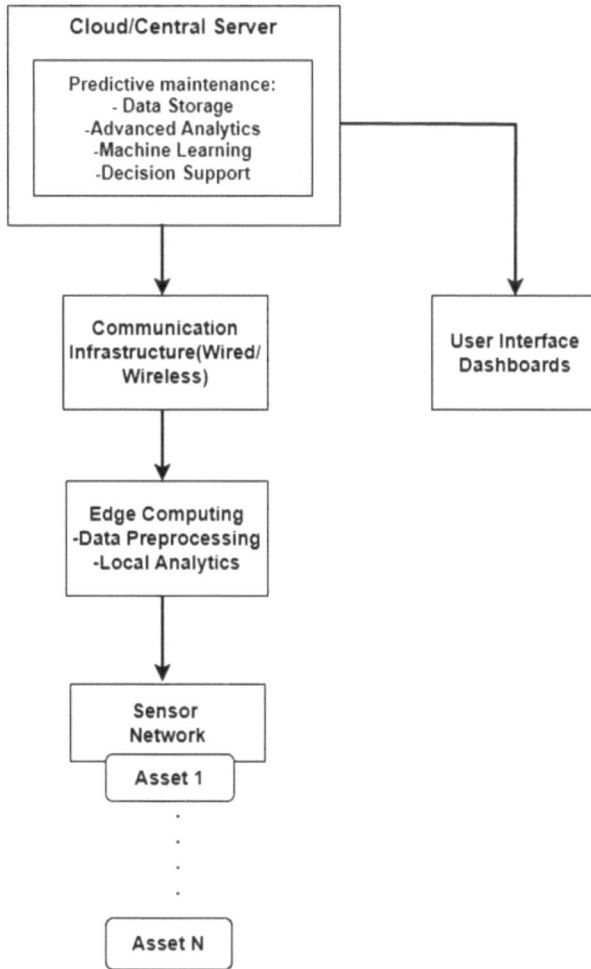

Fig. (1). IoT-enabled Predictive Maintenance.

Research Objectives and Scope

The main purpose is to investigate the performance of different predictive maintenance optimization approaches in an Industry 4.0 setting. In particular, the study tries to:

- Study the available approaches for fault diagnostics and predictive maintenance using mathematical programming, metaheuristics, machine learning-based solutions, *etc.*
- Study approaches for combining optimization methods with predictive maintenance models and frameworks in Industry 4.0 settings.

- Study the performance and effectiveness of the employed optimization techniques in real-world industrial challenges (*e.g.*, multi-component systems, resource constraints, and dynamic operational conditions). Evaluate the impacts of work on efficiency and system performance.
- Introduce data-driven predictive maintenance strategy in Industry 4.0 context as a unified framework or methodology with implementation and optimization suggestions based on a real case study.

This research primarily focuses on different sectors (industrial manufacturing, energy, transportation, and utilities) where the role of predictive maintenance technology is quite diverse to have smooth operations. The study of the research challenges and opportunities associated with the optimization of predictive maintenance in Industry 4.0 aims to contribute to the literature as well as offer some practical insights and recommendations on industrial practices for both practitioners and researchers.

DATA ANALYTICS AND MACHINE LEARNING

Role of Data Analytics in Predictive Maintenance

In the Industry 4.0 context, data analytics is one of the most important elements in predictive maintenance. Modern industrial systems create unprecedented volumes of data, such as sensor data, operational logs, and maintenance records — all of which help us understand the health and operations status of various components. However, analyzing this data in a way that can yield insights is easier said than done [9, 10]. It is with data analytics that one can pre-process these multiple sources of data and explore and analyze them, making way for predictive models and strategies for optimized maintenance developments. Fig. (**2**) depicts the data flow and integration in predictive maintenance.

Supervised, Unsupervised, and Semi-supervised Learning Techniques

Predictive maintenance solutions rely on ML techniques, which use historical data to identify patterns and make highly accurate predictions. There are many ways to do this, and broadly speaking, these methods can be classified as supervised, unsupervised, and semi-supervised learning techniques [11].

- **Supervised Learning:** Labeled data (instances of equipment failure or normal operation) is used to train models that can make predictions on future outcomes. Decision trees, random forests, support vector machines, and neural networks are the most commonly used supervised learning algorithms for predictive maintenance [12].

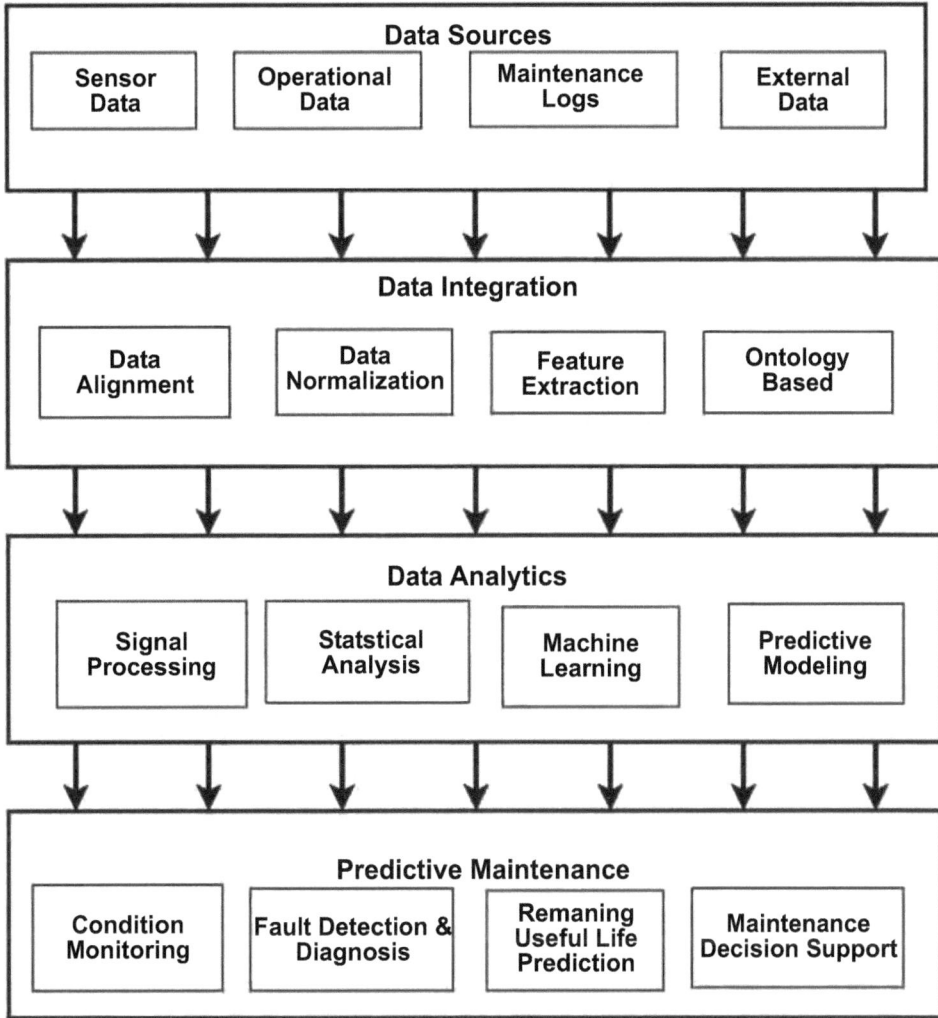

Fig. (2). Data Flow and Integration in Predictive Maintenance.

- **Unsupervised Learning:** If you have limited labeled data or no labeled data. These algorithms seek to reveal natural patterns, outliers, or clusters in the data, which can be invaluable for early detection of deterioration of equipment or potential failures. Some prominent examples are k-means clustering, hierarchical clustering, and dimensionality reduction techniques like Principal Component Analysis (PCA) [13, 14].
- **Semi-supervised Learning:** Labeled data is scarce in a lot of real-world

industrial cases, and many unlabeled data are available. Semi-supervised learning employs a small subset of labeled data with tremendous amounts of unlabeled data to boost the efficiency and accuracy of the model. They can be a helpful brainstorming tool in scenarios where operational conditions are changing or failure modes are rare [15, 16].

Feature Engineering and Selection

Quality and relevance of the input features are more important to the performance of machine learning models than model choice. Feature engineering is how we transform raw data into features, and feature selection techniques are usedto find a subset of informative features to fit our model [17, 18]. Feature engineering may be signal processing techniques, statistic feature extraction, or domain-specific transformations to capture features of the sensor data that are relevant to the problem at hand in predictive maintenance. Feature selection techniques, such as correlation analysis, recursive feature elimination, or embedded methods, help reduce dimensionality and improve model interpretability [19].

Model Training and Evaluation

After data pre-processing and feature selection are done, the data is used to train machine learning models. Cross-validation, ensemble methods, and hyper-parameter tuning are tools to improve model performance while, in most cases, avoiding overfitting. The performance measurements (precision, recall, F1-score, and AUROC) are then used to evaluate how well the model is able to predict failures or Remaining Useful Life (RUL) of assets [20].

FAULT DETECTION AND DIAGNOSIS

Challenges in Fault Detection and Diagnosis

Fault Detection and Diagnosis (FDD) are critical components of a predictive maintenance system. But there are multiple hurdles on the path to affordable and reliable FDD:

- **Industrial System Complexities:** The standard operating behaviors of machine operations have become so dependent on the coupled interactions between components and subsystems that it has become increasingly difficult to effectively compartmentalize abnormalities [21].
- **Noise and Uncertainty**: Sensor data and operational measurements are subject to noise, outliers, and uncertainties, which may not only distort a fault signature but can also result in false alarms or possible misses (False Positives/Negatives) from a fault detection system [22].

- **Dynamic Operating Conditions:** Industrial processes frequently operate in dynamically changing conditions, such as variations in load, environment-related influences, or operating modes that can alter the system's behavior and complicate the detection of normal *vs.* faulty operation [23].
- **Limited Fault Data:** In many industrial scenarios, data related to specific fault conditions may be scarce or unavailable, hindering the development and validation of fault diagnosis models.

Signal Processing Techniques

Signal processing techniques play a crucial role in feature and pattern extraction from raw sensor data for accurate fault detection and diagnosis. Predictive maintenance makes use of signal processing techniques such as the following:

- **Time-domain Analysis:** Techniques that involve statistical feature extraction, wavelet analysis, envelope analysis, *etc.*, are used to analyze time-series data and predict patterns corresponding to potential faults [24].
- **Frequency-domain Analysis:** Frequency analysis tools, such as Fourier, spectral, and order tracking methods, can be employed for frequency-based signal analysis that often provides information on system dynamics and incipient faults [25].
- **Time-Frequency Analysis:** Techniques like short-time Fourier transform (STFT) and wavelet transforms combine time with frequency information, enabling the analysis of non-stationary signals and transient events.

Model-based *vs.* Data-driven Fault Detection Methods

Four categories of fault detection methods exist on the basis of model-based approaches and data-driven solutions:

- **Model-Based Fault Detection:** This approach is based on mathematical models or simulations of the system behavior, which produce residuals as a function of the deviation between the actual and expected values. We use departures from expected behavior to detect adversarial and isolate failures. This includes methods for observer-based, parity space, and parameter estimation [26].
- **Data-driven Failure Detection:** These are the methods that use historical data and machine learning algorithms to detect patterns of normal *versus* fail conditions. Common techniques include Principal Component Analysis (PCA), Auto-Associative Kernel Regression (AAKR), and deep learning architectures such as autoencoders and convolutional neural networks [27].

Fault Diagnosis Algorithms

After a fault is detected, the fault diagnosis algorithms are conducted to detect the cause and type of the fault. The most common fault diagnosis techniques are as follows:

- **Rule-based and Expert Systems:** These types of fault diagnosis rely on expert knowledge in a domain to create predefined rules that are used to diagnose faults from observed symptoms and system behavior.
- **Pattern Recognition and Classification:** Based on the labeled fault data, machine learning algorithms such as decision trees, support vector machines, and neural networks are trained for classifying and diagnosing different fault conditions.
- **Model-based Diagnosis:** These techniques use analytical redundancy relations and residual analysis to isolate and diagnose faults by identifying discrepancies between observed and expected behavior.
- **Hybrid and Ensemble methods:** A combination of several fault detection techniques can provide a higher total precision and robustness, where, in this case, the advantages of different approaches can be exploited.

Integration with Control System

To achieve maximum predictive maintenance benefits, FDD systems should be integrated with industrial control systems and maintenance management platforms. This integration enables:

- **Real-time Monitoring and Feedback:** FDD systems give control systems visibility into the health and operation of assets in real time, enabling immediate corrective actions and optimized decision-making [28].
- **Closed-loop Control and Reconfiguration:** If a fault is detected, control systems can adjust operational parameters to minimize the progress of the fault, reconfigure system components to separate from the affected area, or activate failsafe procedures to reduce the risks of continuing operation [29].
- **Maintenance Planning and Scheduling**: Maintenance management systems can use the diagnosed fault information to allow predictive planning, scheduling, and execution of maintenance activities, reducing downtime and optimizing resource usage [30].

Use Cases and Real-World Examples

There are several examples of the application of fault detection and diagnosis techniques in different industrial domains; some include:

- **Rotating Machinery:** FDD methods have been used to monitor and diagnose faults of critical rotating machinery, including turbines, compressors, and motors, that help detect bearing failures, misalignment, or imbalance at an early stage.
- **Semiconductor Manufacturing:** FDD systems are widely used in the semiconductor industry to monitor and diagnose faults across complex manufacturing processes, increasing product quality and yield optimization.
- **Aerospace and Aviation**: FDD techniques come in handy to monitor and track the health of the aircraft systems, engines, avionics, *etc.*, for safety, which is critical from an aviation point of view.
- **Renewable Energy:** For the renewable energy industry, FDD is implemented for wind turbines and solar power plants to monitor conditions and diagnose failures to get the most from the energy production with minimum downtime [31].
- **Automotive sector:** Modern vehicles have FDD systems built for monitoring deliverables and failure diagnosis of various subsystems like engine, transmission, and ECU, hence ensuring scheduled maintenance and repairs [32].

The practical applications highlighted in this post explain the importance of such fault detection and diagnosis techniques throughout different industrial domains that would then optimize predictive maintenance strategies.

PROGNOSTICS AND REMAINING USEFUL LIFE (RUL) PREDICTION

Concepts of Prognostics and RUL Prediction

Prognostics is the process of forecasting the future health state and Remaining Useful Life (RUL) of an asset or system, given its current condition and operating history. Therefore, the accurate and reliable prediction of RUL is essential to help the maintenance planning in advance and it can direct related decision-based work [33]. The predictions enable the scheduling of maintenance activities and allow for planning for minimal equipment downtime while maximizing asset usage quotient. Degradation modeling in the context of prognostics and RUL prediction is critical. These methods try to model how an asset or system degrades through time, and then predict what this future health state may be [34]. Different types of degradation modeling approaches are:

- **Stochastic Process Models:** This is the approach that describes degradation as a stochastic process, taking randomness and uncertainties into consideration. For instance, some established diffusion models are the Brownian motion model, the gamma process, and Wiener process [35].
- **Physics-based Models:** These models employ laws of physics and science to explain in detail how an asset or a system degrades. Physics-based approaches

include Finite Element Analysis (FEA), fatigue crack growth models, and thermal-mechanical models [36].

- **Data-Driven Models:** When physical models are missing or impractical, the degradation patterns can be learned from historical data through machine learning and statistical techniques, known as data-driven models [37].

Time Series Analysis and Predictive Modeling

Prognostics and RUL prediction are heavily reliant on time-series analysis and predictive modeling techniques. The use of these methods is often based on historical data and information from condition monitoring to model future behavior, possible failures, or degradation processes and predict remaining useful life for assets or systems. Common techniques include:

- **ARIMA:** Autoregressive Integrated Moving Average ARIMA models are frequently employed for time-series forecasting and can be used to predict suitable wearing-out trends of the part in the upcoming future and estimate the RUL [38].
- **Recurrent Neural Networks (RNNs):** RNNs, especially Long Short-Term Memory (LSTM) networks, work well in sequential data and preserve the long-term dependencies that are essential for prognostics/RUL prediction tasks [39].
- **Non-parametric Bayesian Models:** Gaussian Processes (GPs) for regression and prediction tasks deliver uncertainty estimates and enable flexible degradation modeling.

Ensemble Learning Approaches

Ensemble learning methods are also popular for prognostics and RUL prediction as they combine multiple models to increase the overall predictive performance. Combining different models allows ensemble methods to be more accurate and robust as they make predictions by their diverse perspectives of the degradation process [40]. These are the popular ensemble techniques:

- **Bagging:** Bagging (Bootstrap Aggregating) builds many models and combines them in order to reduce overestimation and variance.
- **Boosting:** Different boosting algorithms such as AdaBoost or Gradient Boosting train weak models iteratively and ensemble them to achieve better accuracy.
- **Stacking:** Stacking relies on a meta-model trained to aggregate the predictions of different base models that capture their strengths.

Reliability and Uncertainty Quantification

Because prognostics and RUL prediction inherently have combined uncertainties from different sources, *e.g.*, measurements noise, model assumptions, future operating conditions, *etc.*, it is necessary to quantify and manage these uncertainties for reliable decision-making and risk assessment [41]. Uncertainty quantification techniques include:

- **Bayesian:** Bayesian methods, including Bayesian networks and Markov Chain Monte Carlo (MCMC) methods, provide a more consistent way to incorporate prior knowledge and measure uncertainties in the estimates of model parameters and predictions [42].
- **Conformal Prediction:** Conformal prediction provides confidence and uncertainty intervals on predictions for risk assessment and decision-making under uncertainty.
- **Sensitivity Analysis:** Sensitivity analyses, including variance-based sensitivity analysis and Sobol indices, provide a measure of how theycan affect model outputs and help prioritize areas for risk assessment and risk mitigation [43].

Case Studies in Industrial Use

The successful application of research in prognostics and RUL prediction across many industrial sectors has provided clear evidence for its practical value and impact:

- **Gaming and Sports:** Even in the gaming industry, companies can predict player trajectories more accurately using RUL logic for game obstacles and objects — making games more challenging.
- **Aerospace and Aviation:** Prediction of RUL is vital here to continuously monitor all aspects of aircraft engines, avionics, and structural parts, ensuring safety checks and operational readiness with minimum maintenance cost.
- **Energy:** In the energy field, prognostics and RUL prediction are for monitoring the health of wind turbines, solar panels, and power equipment, which allows for scheduling maintenance efficiently and maximizing energy production.
- **Manufacturing:** Using methods for predicting the RUL to critical production equipment, such as machine tools, robots and manufacturing lines, which decrease stopping time and improve product quality.
- **Transportation:** Transportation of vehicles, trains, and transportation infrastructure includes tracking the useful life (or RUL) that it predicts, which leads to traffic reliability and security to keep maintenance low.
- **Oil and Gas:** Regular scheduled maintenance using the RUL prediction helps oil and gas enterprises to monitor complex equipment like drilling rigs, pumps,

or compressors, which are typical in this industry. It allows efficient operations without putting overall integrity at risk of catastrophic failures due to aging-related damage, leading to unmanageable costs for repair or replacement [44].

This set of applications and case studies showcases the importance of prognostics and RUL estimation in predictive maintenance strategies, asset management, and operational efficiency across varied industrial sectors.

OPTIMAL SENSOR PLACEMENT

Importance of Sensor Placement Optimization

The sensor networks are instrumental in condition monitoring and data acquisition for predictive maintenance systems. On the other hand, the location of sensors is an important aspect and can influence the performance of these systems tremendously. The problem of optimal sensor placement aims to find the most informative locations and configurations for sensors by maximizing the information achieved while minimizing costs and practical constraints [45].

Sensor placement optimization can result in better fault detection and diagnostics, more accurate prognostics and Remaining Useful Life (RUL) predictions, and subsequently higher effectiveness of maintenance strategies. Alternatively, if sensors are placed in the wrong locations, they can deliver partial or even repetitive information and cause undetected defects and incorrect predictions that may ultimately result in highly expensive breakdowns and unexpected downtime [46].

Optimization Criteria and Objectives

One of the key steps in sensor placement optimization is that there exist multiple criteria and objectives, which can be summarized as:

- **Fault Mode Detection and Diagnosability:** Where possible, appreciate the need to place sensors so that faults in critical components or systems can be adequately detected and isolated.
- **Data Coverage and Informativeness:** Sensor locations must guarantee that the system's behavior can be fully observed with relevant information for correct understanding and prognostics.
- **Cost Minimization:** The overall cost in terms of acquiring, installing, and maintaining sensors should not exceed the minimum while we make sure to obtain data sufficiently enough in terms of quality and sense of coverage.
- **Practical Limitations:** The placement of sensors must be oriented by physical considerations (accessibility, environment, and system geometry) as well as

operational criteria regarding safety regulations or maintenance requirements [47].

Optimization Algorithms (*e.g.*, Genetic Algorithms, Particle Swarm Optimization)

Numerous optimization algorithms are used in solving the sensor placement problem; some of them are as follows:

- **Genetic Algorithms (GAs):** GA is a kind of metaheuristic algorithm that gets its roots in the principles of natural selection and heredity. They evolve a population of candidate solutions iteratively, using genetic operators such as selection, crossover, and mutation to locate optimal or near-optimal sensor configurations [48].
- **Particle Swarm Optimization (PSO):** A swarm intelligence-based optimization technique that imitates the living behavior of bird flocks or fish schools in looking for optimal solutions. Solution candidates move through search space while influenced by their personal best solutions and the global best solution [49].
- **Simulated Annealing (SA):** It is a probabilistic optimization algorithm, but the name and inspiration come from the annealing process of metallurgy. It will dive into the solution space and accept worse solutions (to some probability, thus escaping local optima).
- **Mixed-Integer Programming (MIP):** The sensor placement problem can be formulated as an optimization problem with integer and continuous variables, which can be modeled and solved using MIP formulations that benefit from efficient commercial solvers and branch-and-bound algorithms [50].

These heuristics are transformed into local optimization greedy algorithms that offer suboptimal results.

Trade-offs between Data Coverage and Cost

This is one of the important trade-offs in sensor placement optimization, which is the required data coverage and informativeness against associated costs. While more sensors can enhance the quality and coverage of data, they also increase the costs associated with acquisition, installation, and maintenance. Alternatively, reducing the number of sensors to decrease cost may result in insufficient data for effective condition monitoring and prognostics [51].

It results in a trade-off between cost and geographic coverage, which optimization algorithms and objective functions try to reconcile by, *e.g.*, adding constraints on the cost or formulating them as multi-objective optimization tasks that do not just account for re-data coverage, but also look at minimizing total costs.

Sensitivity Analysis and Robustness Evaluation

Some factors considered are sensitivity, the influence of noise on the algorithm solution, and robustness.

- **Measure Noise and Uncertainties:** Evaluate how sensor noise, calibration errors, and other uncertainties affect the performance of the optimized sensor configuration.
- **Operational Variability:** Changes in operational conditions like load patterns, environmental factors, or system configuration can impact the best sensor placement. This variability should be treated with solid solutions [52].
- **Facet Degradation and Failure Mode:** The optimal placement of sensors can change as components are impaired or fail with time. Sensitivity analysis can also be used to define regions where more sensors are needed for reliable monitoring [53].
- **Uncertainties in the Models:** Whenever conceptual/physics-based or data-driven models are being used to model the system/optimization problems, then one should try and assess whether solutions lie within certain bounds, which results in any perturbation/random realizations that might have been applied at such stages.

To assess the impact of these factors and steer the selection of robust sensor configurations, sensitivity analysis techniques are available (*e.g.*, Monte Carlo simulations, variance-based methods, or global sensitivity analysis).

Practical Considerations and Implementation Challenges

The insights and recommendations from sensor placement optimization are valuable. The deployment in industrial environments brings along some practical considerations and implementation challenges:

- **Physical Constraints**: Physical constraints such as inability to access certain areas, lack of space, and adverse environmental conditions lead to limitations on where sensors can be placed (*e.g.*, high temperature, in a vibration area, high corrosion rate, *etc.*) [54].
- **System Downtime and Installation Logistics:** For many applications, installation or changes (%) to sensor configurations require system downtime, which can be expensive and disruptive. This has to be done meticulously and synchronized with the schedules of operations.

- **Data Integration and Infrastructure:** The task of integrating data from the sensors placed at suitable strategic locations into older monitoring and maintenance systems may involve infrastructure changes, setting up data management codes, and integrating data with already installed software or hardware parts [55].
- **Verification and Validation:** After implementation, the optimized sensor setup needs to be verified and validated to satisfy needed performance goals/requirements.
- **Maintenance and Recalibration:** Systems will mature (or degrade) over time, so periodic re-evaluation and even reconfiguration of sensor locations may be necessary to realize optimal performance [56].

Solving these practical questions and issues inevitably involves a tight loop of researchers, engineers, and industrial practitioners (both potential users and providers), but even more careful consideration is needed to implement in real-world conditions.

PREDICTIVE MAINTENANCE PLANNING AND SCHEDULING

Role of Optimization in Maintenance Planning

Planning and scheduling are an integral part of realizing all the benefits of predictive maintenance. Maintenance is performed at the right time (not too early and not too late), asset availability is maximized, resource utilization is optimized, and operational disruptions are minimized, all by effective planning and scheduling. However, maintenance planning and scheduling in complex industrial settings might be difficult due to a variety of constraints like resource limitations, operational needs, dependencies among assets, *etc* [57].

To meet these challenges, optimization techniques offer convenient, ordered, and quantitative methods to identify optimal maintenance planning and scheduling. Optimization models explicitly include goals, constraints, and decision variables to determine cost-effective options while trade-offs among competing priorities are made and efficient resource allocation is realized [58].

Maintenance Optimization Objectives

The main objectives of maintenance optimization are the following:

- **Reducing Downtime:** Unexpected breakdowns may lead to huge loss of production and disruptions. The goal of optimization models is to minimize downtime by coordinating repairs with scheduled outages or off-peak demand, thus preventing unnecessary shutdowns [59].

- **Lowering Maintenance Costs:** These are fixed costs that are directly related to maintenance activity, which include labor, spare parts, and consumables. Optimization models have the ability to produce cost-effective maintenance plans by balancing preventive *vs* cure-paid maintenance, resource allocation, and over-maintenance.
- **Maximizing Asset Availability and Reliability**: Maintenance planning and scheduling in an optimal way will provide for high asset availability and reliability, which supports business productivity.
- **Extending Asset Life:** By prescribing maintenance activities just in time and of the right scope, models can help extend the useable lifetimes of assets as well asput off expensive replacements or upgrades.
- **Improved Safety and Compliance:** Maintenance optimization can take safety concerns as well as regulatory compliance constraints into account to make sure that any maintenance operations are carried out safely and in compliance with the regulations.

Optimization Techniques

There are several optimization techniques used for predictive maintenance planning and scheduling, which consist of:

- **Integer Programming (IP):** Binary decision variables are used in IP models to represent whether maintenance should be performed. Combined with linear or non-linear constraints, they can model a variety of maintenance scheduling problems. Optimization problems for these models can be solved using commercial solvers or custom algorithms [60].
- **Constraint Satisfaction Problems (CSPs):** This formulation models maintenance scheduling as a collection of constraints: resource availability, precedence relationships, and time windows. Feasible solutions are discovered using constraints propagation and search.
- **Genetic Algorithms (GAs):** GAs are metaheuristic optimization methods based on the theory of evolution and natural selection. This can be translated to scheduling problems by representing candidate schedules as individuals and then evolving them using selection, crossover, and mutation operations.
- **Ant Colony Optimization (ACO):** ACO is a swarm intelligence-based metaheuristics algorithm that mimics the behavior of ant colonies to find the optimal path. This can be used in maintenance scheduling to create and maintain pheromone trails for swarms, which can search optimal schedules.
- **Use of Simulation Models for Optimization:** Simulation models can be used in combination with optimization methods to test the performance of possible maintenance schedules over different operational scenarios and uncertainties. This method allows for more robust and natural optimization solutions.

Dynamic Scheduling and Rescheduling Strategies

An expert may know when to change the maintenance plan and schedule due to unexpected failures, resource limits, or changes in plant operation priorities. In case something goes wrong, there are dynamic scheduling and rescheduling strategies used.

- **Event-based Rescheduling:** Whenever there are unforeseen events or changes like component failures, resource unavailability, *etc.*, the maintenance schedules can be reassigned dynamically to compensate for these and minimize their effect.
- **Rolling Horizon Scheduling:** Instead, with rolling horizon scheduling, short-term schedules are rolled out periodically to replace existing ones as new information and forecasts roll in.
- **Real-time Scheduling**: Real-time scheduling allows for real-time monitoring of system conditions and updates to maintenance activities, which can quickly adapt to unplanned situations and changes in operating characteristics of systems.
- **Rescheduling Multi-objective Optimization:** When rescheduling is necessary, we can use multi-objective optimization models to balance objectives that might compete (*e.g.*, minimizing disruptions and resource utilization).

Case Studies Demonstrating Improved Efficiency and Cost Savings

The usefulness of optimized predictive maintenance planning and scheduling has been proven in many case studies and industrial settlements.

- **Manufacturing Sector:** A major automotive manufacturer integrated predictive maintenance into one of its largest plants, realizing a 25% reduction in unplanned downtime and an 18% decrease in maintenance costs, translating to tens of millions of dollars saved from improved productivity.
- **Power Generation:** A nuclear power plant implemented a scheduled optimization model for maintenance that brought industrial productivity to >100%, reducing the Mean Time Between Failure of this equipment by 10% and impasses with maintenance costs by 15%.
- **Semiconductor Manufacturing:** A fab operates more efficiently after applying predictive maintenance optimization techniques to gain a 20% reduction in unscheduled downtime and achieve a 12% increase in Overall Equipment Effectiveness (OEE).
- **Mining Industry:** An open pit mining operation deployed an on-demand type of maintenance scheduling system that could accommodate in-flight schedule

changes based on both the asset feature and operational need. This resulted in a 15% drop in maintenance costs and a 10% increase in equipment availability.

- **Aerospace Industry:** An airline company optimized its aircraft maintenance scheduling to reduce maintenance-related delays by 22% and cut overall maintenance labor cost by 12%.

CONDITION-BASED MAINTENANCE (CBM) OPTIMIZATION

Fundamentals of CBM and Condition Monitoring

Condition-Based Maintenance (CBM) is an ideal proactive strategy that assesses the actual operation of assets or systems in order to decide what the present maintenance necessity and their future life would be. More traditional CBM processes utilize different condition monitoring technologies such as vibration analysis, oil analysis, thermography, and acoustic emission testing to source real-time information from data produced by sensors and other sources [61].

This collected data is then analyzed for detecting anomalies from usual operating conditions, finding potential failures or degrading patterns and estimating the Remaining Useful Life (RUL) of the monitored assets. Through these methods, CBM can optimize maintenance activities and has the potential to help eliminate unnecessary maintenance and minimize downtime by making informed decisions on maintenance based on the actual condition of the assets, not just predetermined scheduling or run-to-fail methodologies [62].

Optimization of CBM Trigger Thresholds

One of the major issues in implementing a successful CBM program is identifying the trigger thresholds needed to initiate maintenance actions. These thresholds are generally derived from metrics that encapsulate a predefined condition indicator based on the detected health of assets from condition monitoring data. Setting thresholds too low can generate extra work and reduce the lifecycle of equipment, whereas setting them too high can result in breakdowns that could have easily been avoided [63].

The trigger levels for CBM can be determined by using optimization techniques, taking into account the criticality of those assets, maintenance costs, and also the underlying trade-off between preventive and corrective actions to avoid schedule congestion with limitations imposed due to operational constraints. Typically, these optimization methods are:

- **Cost-based Optimization:** Cost-based models for minimizing the total cost of maintenance actions (balance between proactive and reactive maintenance costs, with respect to the rate of asset degradation and associated probabilities/consequences)

- **Risk-based Optimization:**Here, methodologies like Failure Mode and Effects Analysis (FMEA) or Fault Tree Analysis (FTA) are employed to evaluate the causes of failures and associated risks, assess them in terms of their potential consequences, and subsequently optimize trigger thresholds.
- **Multi-objective Optimization:** The goal is to develop an optimization of the maintenance cost, asset availability, and risk into one solution; this is done by the use of genetic algorithms or particle swarm optimization.

Predictive Maintenance Decision-making Models

Apart from the optimization of CBM trigger thresholds, the decision rule models entail staging the value engineering analysis so as to indicate the optimal maintenance actions using CM data [64]. By combining factors, including asset criticality, remaining useful life estimates, resource availability, and operational constraints, these models inform the best decisions for maintenance. There are several contextual models for predictive maintenance that follow this fashion of decision-making, including:

- **Rule-based Decision Systems:**Use expert knowledge and predefined rules to suggest what action to take based on specific condition monitoring indicators or threshold violations.
- **Machine Learning-Based Models:** These models can help to leverage supervised or unsupervised machine learning techniques like decision trees, neural networks, and clustering algorithms to train over historical data, classify asset conditions, and predict maintenance actions.
- **Optimization-based Decision Models:** Mathematical optimization models that consider both maintenance costs, resource constraints, and operational requirements in determining the optimal maintenance strategy, including the timing of when to execute repairs. Details for optimimum timing and scope are expressed at a higher level than its components, the proper functioning of which eventually leads to growth/consequent expansion.
- **Hybrid Decision Models:** Combinations of rule-based systems, machine learning models, and optimization techniques to leverage the strengths of different approaches and improve decision-making accuracy and robustness.

Integration with Asset Management Systems

Integration with Enterprise Asset Management (EAM) is imperative to fully derive the benefits of CBM optimization [65]. The integration of these systems means the free flow exchange of data across all systems, centralized management of asset information, and coordinated maintenance planning and execution. The integration has been enforced in all key aspects, including

- **Data Integration:** All relevant data (condition monitoring, asset information, and maintenance records) must be inserted into a centralized Asset Management System to provide in-depth database analysis and decision support.
- **Maintenance Planning and Scheduling:** Set CBM trigger thresholds and recommended maintenance priorities on optimized levels to integrate with the maintenance planning and scheduling module for efficient resource allocation and minimize operational disruptions.
- **Inventory Management:** Integrating with inventory management systems to have the necessary spare parts and consumables in hand for maintenance activities (ultimately preventing delays and decreasing downtime).
- **Reporting and Analytics:** Complete reporting and analytics provide the ability to monitor performance, analyze trends, and enhance CBM optimization strategies on a continual basis.

Evaluation Criteria and Performance Metrics

To guide better performance metrics and evaluation criteria for CBM optimization strategies rather than make an isolated, case-based decision [66]. the following must be considered:

- **Cost of Maintenance:** Keeping a check on the overall maintenance expenses— labor, spares, and associated operating costs— to judge if predictive optimization would be cost-effective.
- **Availability and Reliability of Assets:** Tracking asset availability, Mean Time Between Failures (MTBF), and other reliability metrics to gauge the effect of optimized CBM on operational performance.
- **Reduced Downtime:** Tracking the impact of less unplanned downtime and comparing this to historical data or industry best practices can put a tangible figure on the benefits of improved CBM.
- **ROI:** The ROI of CBM optimization initiatives can be calculated by dividing the costs and benefits across the asset lifecycle.
- **Health & Safety and Regulatory Compliance:** Review the potential effects of CBM optimization on health and safety records, regulatory compliance, as well as environmental considerations.

Best Practices and Examples by Industry

CBM optimization has already been implemented effectively in different industry verticals; however, each industry comes with its own set of problems and opportunities.

- **Aerospace and Aviation:** In aviation, CBM optimization is implemented on vital components such as engines, avionics, and structural parts to maintain airworthiness. To maximize maintenance potential, we should integrate CBM with aircraft health management systems and use advanced condition monitoring techniques such as borescope inspections or oil debris monitoring.
- **Energy:** CBM optimization is used in the energy sector with wind turbines, power generation equipment, and oil and gas installations. So, remote monitoring will become increasingly important, as well as the ability to incorporate environmental factors like wind, dust, and heat into condition monitoring models with a greater level of intelligence and precision (especially when combined with CBM) integrated alongside an asset performance management system.
- **Manufacturing:** In the manufacturing industry, CBM methods are optimized for crucial ware production equipment, robots, and automated systems. These best practices call for taking advantage of advanced condition monitoring methods such as vibration analysis and thermography, combining CBM with Overall Equipment Effectiveness (OEE) metrics, and using machine learning to support predictive maintenance decision-making.
- **Transportation:** In the transportation sector, CBM is optimized for rolling stock, engines, and infrastructure assets. Examples of best practices are utilizing condition monitoring data from onboard diagnostics, combining CBM with fleet management, and using simulation and digital twin technologies for maintenance decision support.
- **Mining and Construction:** CBM optimization in mining and construction businesses focuses on heavy machinery, mobile equipment, and stationary assets. This utilization of ruggedized condition monitoring solutions, the incorporation of operational and environmental factors into CBM models, and the inclusion of CBM as part of equipment health and utilization monitoring systems are best practices.

This allows organizations to improve asset reliability, increase operational efficiency, and save costs while maintaining safety and environmental regulation compliance through the deployment of best practices specific to their industry and by refining continuous CBM optimization strategies.

CHALLENGES AND FUTURE DIRECTION

Key Challenges in Implementing Optimization Techniques for Predictive Maintenance

Even though optimization provides a lot of advantages in predictive maintenance, the implementation and deployment of these methods to industry raise many challenges:

- **Data Quality and Availability:** The quality and availability of data are crucial to help fit both the optimization model and in order for results produced by any given algorithm to be trusted. Incomplete, inconsistent, or noisy data can affect the capability of the model to predict accurately, which in turn may result in incorrect maintenance decisions. In particular, complex industrial environments with numerous legacy systems provide ongoing challenges when it comes to reliable data collection, integration, and preprocessing.
- **Accounting for Uncertainty and Dynamics:** Industrial processes are subject to multiple sources of uncertainty (*e.g.*, operational variability, environmental factors, unexpected events) and are inherently dynamic. Incorporating such optimization models, these uncertainties are extremely challenging problems to tackle that need advanced methods like stochastic optimization, robust optimization, or reinforcement learning [67].
- **Computational Complexity and Scalability:** With the size of industrial systems becoming ever-larger and more complex, it may not be feasible to run optimization algorithms with high computational requirements. A major challenge is the development of efficient and scalable optimization methods for large-scale optimization problems having a high number of decision variables and constraints.
- **Integration and Interoperability:** Predictive maintenance systems frequently involve multi-component solutions like sensors, control systems, asset management platforms, and optimization engines. Rapid integration and very high levels of interoperability between these heterogeneous systems are needed, with strict adherence to industry standards and protocols, which adds an extra level of complexity both technically and organisationally.
- **Cybersecurity and Data Privacy:** As predictive maintenance systems are grown in interconnection and operation based on data, ensuring cybersecurity against cyber threats. Privacy of confidential information looms as a quintessential point to ponder upon. Optimization solutions need to incorporate strong security and compliance with these regulations as fundamental to their design.

- **Model Validation and Maintenance:** The models need validation and more importantly, responsive capabilities to changing operational conditions, asset degradation patterns, as well as evolving maintenance practices. Developing procedures for model validation, refinement, and maintenance can be expensive from both a time and resource standpoint.

Emerging Trends and Future Research Directions

Despite the challenges, the field of optimization for predictive maintenance is rapidly evolving, with several emerging trends and future research directions:

- **Hybrid:** Hybrid and ensemble optimization techniques combining multiple optimization techniques such as mathematical programming, metaheuristics, and machine learning-based approaches can do this by exploiting the power of each of these to give a more robust and accurate solution. It is an active area of research to find such hybrid and ensemble optimization techniques that work effectively.
- **Optimization and Machine Learning/Deep Learning Integration:** The use of machine learning and deep learning within optimization algorithms is an exciting frontier. These methods might have the potential to change some of the traditional optimization approaches, as they can incorporate into a decision-making extension more optimally designed for data-driven optimizations, give us automatic feature extraction, and monitor equipment that adaptsitself according to changing environmental conditions.
- **Distributed and Parallel Optimization:** With industrial systems becoming increasingly distributed geographically, the development of distributed or parallel optimization algorithms will enable more coordinated and efficient decision-making across multiple sites or subsystems.
- **Multi-objective and Constraint-based Optimization:** Some predictive maintenance problems are multi-objective with numerous competing objectives and constraints. In the future, it is possible to investigate sophisticated multi-objective and constraint-based optimization techniques, which can provide more detailed and practical solutions.
- **Explainable and Interpretable Optimization:** Unlike traditional optimization, where the decision-making process is transparent, as optimization models become more complex and autonomous, there is a need for explainable and interpretable optimization techniques. These techniques can offer insight into how decisions are made, increasing transparency and confidence among stakeholders in the adoption of the system.
- **Collaborative and Federated Optimization:** Collaboration in industrial ecosystems with multiple stakeholders or organizations is in need of improvement.

Opportunities for Innovation and Collaboration

The remaining problems and the open areas for future research in optimization for predictive maintenance provide a vast arena of innovation and possible joint work:

- **Collaborative and Cross-Disciplinary Research:** Because the problems with these systems are complex, research teams of experts in operations research, computer science, data science, industrial engineering, and domain-specific knowledge (*e.g.*, manufacturing/energy/transportation) would work together to study specific topics.
- **Industry-Academia Partnerships**: Actively collaborating with industry partners ensures conceptual breakthroughs advance into practical applications and generate real-world problems and examples to inspire further research efforts.
- **Open Source Initiatives:** Open source initiatives and platforms to share optimization algorithms, models, and best practices can speed development and knowledge across distributed areas, further creating a cooperative ecosystem for predictive maintenance optimization.
- **Interdisciplinary Education and Workforce Development:** Effective implementation and use of optimization techniques for predictive maintenance require interdisciplinary education (that bridges optimization methodologies, data science, and industrial applications) and workforce development.
- **Standardization and Interoperability:** Collaborative efforts in the development of standards and interoperability frameworks allow the integration of optimization solutions in an unobtrusive way with industrial systems like OPC UA and enable cross-platform compatibility.
- **Innovation Challenges and Hackathons:** Innovation challenges, hackathons, and crowdsourcing can foster creativity and encourage collaboration with new ideas from outside the traditional organization to solve specific predictive maintenance optimization problems at scale.

Through cooperation, acquisition, and transfer of knowledge and transdisciplinary methods, the optimization community can make innovations to provide system solutions for nontrivial problems in predictive maintenance by capitalizing on contemporary themes so that industrial operations shall be more efficient, safer, and more sustainable.

CONCLUSION

In the time of Industry 4.0, a rationalized approach to predictive maintenance is essential for improved operational performance as well as asset longevity. This research proved that optimization techniques, data analytics, and integrated IoT with CPS architectures have the potential to revolutionize predictive maintenance practices. Predictive maintenance solutions will have to be more powerful, intelligent, and adaptive with the industrial systems that are several years along their evolution path. To meet these challenges, leverage emerging trends, and promote interdisciplinary collaborations, the optimization community has a unique opportunity to bring some breakthroughs that would pave the way for predictive maintenance in an era of efficient and robust industrial operations with sustainability. A literature survey has been conducted on different optimization tools, approaches, and applications to advance the state-of-the-art in predictive maintenance within complex industrial environments.

REFERENCES

[1]   A. Agarwal, A. Verma, and M. Khari, "Comparative assessment of machine learning methods for early prediction of diseases using health indicators", In: *in Approaches Hum.-Centered AI Healthc.* IGI Global, 2024, pp. 160-186.
      [http://dx.doi.org/10.4018/979-8-3693-2238-3.ch007]

[2]   S. Khan, M. Khari, and M. Azrour, "IoT in retail and e-commerce", In: *Electron. Commer. Res*, 2023, pp. 1-2.
      [http://dx.doi.org/10.1007/s10660-023-09785-3]

[3]   T. Singh, A. Panwar, K.S. Kaswan, A. Jain, and U. Sugandh, "The datafication of everything: Challenges and opportunities in a hyperconnected world", *Int. Conf. Adv. Smart Comput. Inf. Secur.,* pp. 254-268, 2024.
      [http://dx.doi.org/10.1007/978-3-031-58604-0_18]

[4]   U. Sugandh, M. Khari, and S. Nigam, "How blockchain technology can transfigure the indian agriculture sector", In: *Handb. Green Comput. Blockchain Technol*, 2021, pp. 69-88.
      [http://dx.doi.org/10.1201/9781003107507-6]

[5]   J.R. Ruiz Díaz Benítez, "Design of a reference architecture in intelligent warehouse supply logistics through the use of Industry 4.0 technologies. Case of retail Warehouses in the city of Pilar", *Revista Veritas de Difusão Científica,* vol. 4, no. 2, pp. 120-136, 2023.
      [http://dx.doi.org/10.61616/rvdc.v4i2.50]

[6]   A. Panwar, and V. Bhatnagar, "Data lake architecture", *Int. J. Organ. Collective Intell.,* vol. 10, no. 1, pp. 63-75, 2020.
      [http://dx.doi.org/10.4018/IJOCI.2020010104]

[7]   D. Gahlawat, U. Rani, S. Suhag, and S. Madavi, "Hybrid deep learning model for IT-OT integration in industry 4.0", *2023 2nd Int. Conf. Smart Technol. Smart Nation, SmartTechCon 2023,* vol. 11, pp. 1025-1030, 2023.
      [http://dx.doi.org/10.1109/SmartTechCon57526.2023.10391501]

[8]   M. Khari, and A. Karar, "Analysis on intrusion detection by machine learning techniques : A review", *Int. J. Adv. Res. Comput. Sci. Softw. Eng.,* vol. 3, no. 4, pp. 545-548, 2013.

[9]   A.M. Baimukhamedova, M.S. Aymurzinov, and G.S. Baimukhamedova, "Innovative management system for agro-industrial complex facilities within the framework of the "Industry -5.0" concept", *Problems of AgriMarket,* no. 4, pp. 37-45, 2023.
      [http://dx.doi.org/10.46666/2023-4.2708-9991.03]

[10] W. Sardjono and W. G. Perdana, "Adoption of artificial intelligence in response to industry 4.0 in the mining industry," *in Lecture Notes in Electrical Engineering,* vol. 1029 LNEE, Germany: Springer

Nature Switzerland, 2023, pp. 699-707.
[http://dx.doi.org/10.1007/978-3-031-29078-7_61]

[11] P. Singh, K. Chaudhary, G. Chaudhary, M. Khari, and B. Rawal, "A Machine learning approach to detecting deepfake videos: An investigation of feature extraction techniques", *J. Cybersecur. Inf. Manag.,* vol. 9, no. 2, pp. 42-50, 2022.
[http://dx.doi.org/10.54216/JCIM.090204]

[12] Saurabh, C. Sharma, S. Khan, S. Mahajan, H.S. Alsagri, A. Almjally, B.I. Alabduallah, and A.A. Ansari, "Lightweight Security for IoT", *J. Intell. Fuzzy Syst.,* vol. 45, no. 4, pp. 5423-5439, 2023.
[http://dx.doi.org/10.3233/JIFS-232388]

[13] A. Nagaraj, "Internet of Things (IoT) with AI", In: *in Role AI Enhancing IoT-Cloud Appl.* Bentham Science Publishers, 2023, pp. 21-72.
[http://dx.doi.org/10.2174/9789815165708123010006]

[14] S. Sharma, A. Malik, C. Sharma, I. Batra, M.S. Kaswan, and J.A. Garza-Reyes, "Adoption of industry 4.0 in different sectors: a structural review using natural language processing", *Int. J. Interact. Des. Manuf.,* no. Oct, 2023.
[http://dx.doi.org/10.1007/s12008-023-01550-y]

[15] R. Kamasak, D.P. Alkan, and B. Yalcinkaya, *Emerging trends of industry 4.0 in equality, diversity, and inclusion implementations.* Emerald Publishing Limited, 2023, pp. 129-148.
[http://dx.doi.org/10.1108/S2051-233320230000009008]

[16] F. Lamperti, K. Lavoratori, and D. Castellani, "The unequal implications of industry 4.0 adoption: evidence on productivity growth and convergence across Europe", *Econ. Innov. New Technol.,* no. Oct, pp. 1-25, 2023.
[http://dx.doi.org/10.1080/10438599.2023.2269089]

[17] P. Singh, and M. Khari, "Necessity of time synchronization for IoT-based applications", In: *in Internet Things: Technol. Adv. New Appl.* Apple Academic Press, 2023, pp. 285-297.
[http://dx.doi.org/10.1201/9781003304609-15]

[18] S.H. Reddy, H. Bathini, V.N. Ajmeera, R.S. Marella, T.V.V. Kumar, and M. Khari, "Startup unicorn success prediction using ensemble machine learning algorithm", In: *in Lect. Notes Comput. Sci. (incl. subser. Lect. Notes Artif. Intell. Lect. Notes Bioinform.).* vol. 14532. LNCS, 2024, pp. 330-338.
[http://dx.doi.org/10.1007/978-3-031-53830-8_34]

[19] Y. Lv, and Y. Shang, "Investigation of industry 4.0 technologies mediating effect on the supply chain performance and supply chain management practices", *Environ. Sci. Pollut. Res. Int.,* vol. 30, no. 48, pp. 106129-106144, 2023.
[http://dx.doi.org/10.1007/s11356-023-29550-1] [PMID: 37726630]

[20] M. Khari, R. Dalal, A. Sharma, and B. Mehta, "Person identification in uav shot videos by using machine learning", In: *in Multimodal Biometric Systems.* CRC Press, 2021, pp. 45-60.
[http://dx.doi.org/10.1201/9781003138068-4]

[21] K. Soni, N. Kumar, A.S. Nair, P. Chourey, N.J. Singh, and R. Agarwal, "Artificial intelligence: Implementation and obstacles in industry 4.0", In: *in Handbook of Metrology and Applications.* Springer Nature Singapore, 2023, pp. 1043-1065.
[http://dx.doi.org/10.1007/978-981-99-2074-7_54]

[22] R. Machhan, R. Trehan, P. Singh, and K.S. Sangwan, "Blockchain, artificial intelligence, and big data: Advanced technologies for Industry 4.0", In: *in Industry 4.0: Concepts, Processes and Systems.* CRC Press, 2023, pp. 141-160.
[http://dx.doi.org/10.1201/9781003246466-6]

[23] P. Singh, M. Khari, and S. Vimal, "EESSMT: An energy efficient hybrid scheme for securing mobile ad hoc networks using IoT", *Wirel. Pers. Commun.,* vol. 126, no. 3, pp. 2149-2173, 2022.
[http://dx.doi.org/10.1007/s11277-021-08764-x]

[24]   P. Gaba, A. Panwar, U. Sugandh, N. Pathak, and N. Sharma, "OptiCharge: A firefly algorithm-based approach for minimizing electric vehicle waiting time at charging stations", In: *Intell. Decis. Technol., no.* Preprint, 2024, pp. 1-14.
[http://dx.doi.org/10.3233/IDT-230619]

[25]   U. Sugandh, S. Nigam, and M. Khari, "Ecosystem of technologies for smart agriculture to improve the efficiency and profitability of Indian farmers", *Proc. 17th INDIACom; 2023 10th Int. Conf. Comput. Sustain. Glob. Dev., INDIACom 2023,* pp. 1442-1449, 2023.

[26]   A. Althabatah, M. Yaqot, B. Menezes, and L. Kerbache, "Transformative procurement trends: integrating industry 4.0 technologies for enhanced procurement processes", *Logistics,* vol. 7, no. 3, p. 63, 2023.
[http://dx.doi.org/10.3390/logistics7030063]

[27]   S. Vimal, M. Khari, N. Dey, R.G. Crespo, and Y. Harold Robinson, "Enhanced resource allocation in mobile edge computing using reinforcement learning based MOACO algorithm for IIOT", *Comput. Commun.,* vol. 151, pp. 355-364, 2020.
[http://dx.doi.org/10.1016/j.comcom.2020.01.018]

[28]   M. Shaikh, P. Shah, and R. Sekhar, "Communication protocols in industry 4.0", *2023 Int. Conf. Sustain. Emerg. Innov. Eng. Technol., ICSEIET 2023,* vol. 40, pp. 709-714, 2023.
[http://dx.doi.org/10.1109/ICSEIET58677.2023.10303397]

[29]   S. Nigam, U. Sugandh, and M. Khari, "The integration of blockchain and IoT edge devices for smart agriculture: Challenges and use cases", In: *in Advances in Computers.* vol. 127. Elsevier, 2022, pp. 507-537.
[http://dx.doi.org/10.1016/bs.adcom.2022.02.015]

[30]   S.S. Gupta, R. Goyal, and D. Gupta, "Artificial intelligence impacts on industry 4.0: A literature-based study", In: *Handb. Res. Data Sci. Cybersecur. Innov. Ind. 4.0 Technol.* IGI Global, 2023, pp. 30-44.
[http://dx.doi.org/10.4018/978-1-6684-8145-5.ch002]

[31]   G. Chaudhary, S. Srivastava, and M. Khari, "Generative edge intelligence for securing IoT-assisted smart grid against cyber-threats", *Int. J. Wirel. Ad Hoc Commun.,* vol. 6, no. 1, pp. 38-49, 2023.
[http://dx.doi.org/10.54216/IJWAC.060104]

[32]   S. Saif, P. Das, S. Biswas, M. Khari, and V. Shanmuganathan, "HIIDS: Hybrid intelligent intrusion detection system empowered with machine learning and metaheuristic algorithms for application in IoT based healthcare", In: *Microprocess. Microsyst,* 2022, p. 104622.
[http://dx.doi.org/10.1016/j.micpro.2022.104622]

[33]   M. Santhiya, J. Jeyalakshmi, and H. Venu, "Emerging networking technologies for industry 4.0", In: *in Priv. Preserv. Secur. Data Storage Cloud Comput..* IGI Global, 2023, pp. 322-340.
[http://dx.doi.org/10.4018/979-8-3693-0593-5.ch015]

[34]   G. Chaudhary, M. Khari, and A. Mahmoud, "Intelligent video moving target detection based on multi-attribute single value medium neutrosophic method", *Journal of Intelligent Systems and Internet of Things,* vol. 5, no. 1, pp. 49-59, 2021.
[http://dx.doi.org/10.54216/JISIoT.050105]

[35]   G. Dua, V. Arora, and R. Mulaveesala, "Artificial neural network based sub-surface defect detection in glass fiber reinforced polymers: Nondestructive evaluation 4.0", *Sens. Imaging,* vol. 24, no. 1, p. 38, 2023.
[http://dx.doi.org/10.1007/s11220-023-00445-2]

[36]   J. Khan, G.A. Khan, J.P. Li, M.F. AlAjmi, A.U. Haq, S. Khan, N. Ahmad, S. Parveen, M. Shahid, S. Ahmad, M. Raji, B. Ahamad, A.A. Alghamdi, and A. Ali, "Secure smart healthcare monitoring in industrial internet of things (IIoT) ecosystem with cosine function hybrid chaotic map encryption", *Sci. Program.,* vol. 2022, no. 1, pp. 1-22, 2022.
[http://dx.doi.org/10.1155/2022/8853448]

[37]   J.S. Dhatterwal, K.S. Kaswan, S. Saxena, and A. Panwar, "Big data for health data analytics and decision support", In: *in Comput. Converg. Interoperability Electron. Health Rec. (EHR)*. IGI Global, 2024, pp. 93-116.

[38]   U. Sugandh, S. Nigam, and M. Khari, "Blockchain technology in agriculture for indian farmers: A systematic literature review, challenges, and solutions", *IEEE Syst. Man. Cybern. Mag.,* vol. 8, no. 4, pp. 36-43, 2022.
[http://dx.doi.org/10.1109/MSMC.2022.3197914]

[39]   M.J. Labaran, and T. Masood, "Industry 4.0 driven green supply chain management in renewable energy sector: A critical systematic literature review", *Energies,* vol. 16, no. 19, p. 6977, 2023.
[http://dx.doi.org/10.3390/en16196977]

[40]   A.U. Haq, J.P. Li, B.L.Y. Agbley, A. Khan, I. Khan, M.I. Uddin, and S. Khan, "IIMFCBM: Intelligent integrated model for feature extraction and classification of brain tumors using mri clinical imaging data in IoT-healthcare", *IEEE J. Biomed. Health Inform.,* vol. 26, no. 10, pp. 5004-5012, 2022.
[http://dx.doi.org/10.1109/JBHI.2022.3171663] [PMID: 35503847]

[41]   A.K. Dubey, A. Jain, A. Panwar, M. Kumar, H. Taneja, and P.S. Lamba, "UNet segmentation based effective skin lesion detection using deep learning", *2023 International Conference on Communication, Security and Artificial Intelligence, ICCSAI 2023,* pp. 470-474, 2023.
[http://dx.doi.org/10.1109/ICCSAI59793.2023.10421443]

[42]   U. Sugandh, S. Nigam, M. Khari, and S. Misra, "An approach for risk traceability using blockchain technology for tracking, tracing, and authenticating food products", *Information (Basel),* vol. 14, no. 11, p. 613, 2023.
[http://dx.doi.org/10.3390/info14110613]

[43]   K. Ishfaq, M.D.A. Khan, M.A.A. Khan, M.A. Mahmood, and M.A. Maqsood, "A correlation among industry 4.0, additive manufacturing, and topology optimization: a state-of-the-art review", *Int. J. Adv. Manuf. Technol.,* vol. 129, no. 9-10, pp. 3771-3797, 2023.
[http://dx.doi.org/10.1007/s00170-023-12515-6]

[44]   S. Vimal, M. Khari, R.G. Crespo, L. Kalaivani, N. Dey, and M. Kaliappan, "Energy enhancement using Multiobjective Ant colony optimization with Double Q learning algorithm for IoT based cognitive radio networks", *Comput. Commun.,* vol. 154, pp. 481-490, 2020.
[http://dx.doi.org/10.1016/j.comcom.2020.03.004]

[45]   A.K. Dubey, A. Jain, A. Panwar, M. Kumar, H. Taneja, and P.S. Lamba, "Optimizing emotion recognition through weighted averaging in deep learning ensembles", *2023 International Conference on Communication, Security and Artificial Intelligence, ICCSAI 2023,* pp. 410-414, 2023.
[http://dx.doi.org/10.1109/ICCSAI59793.2023.10421386]

[46]   U. Sugandh, S. Nigam, S. Misra, and M. Khari, "A bibliometric analysis of the evolution of state-of-the-art blockchain technology (BCT) in the agrifood sector from 2014 to 2022", *Sensors (Basel),* vol. 23, no. 14, p. 6278, 2023.
[http://dx.doi.org/10.3390/s23146278] [PMID: 37514574]

[47]   I. Cvitić, A. Jevremovic, and P. Lameski, "Approaches and opportunities of using machine learning methods in telecommunications and industry 4.0", *Mob. Netw. Appl.,* no. Oct, 2023.
[http://dx.doi.org/10.1007/s11036-023-02241-4]

[48]   S. Saif, P. Das, S. Biswas, S. Khan, M.A. Haq, and V. Kovtun, "A secure data transmission framework for IoT enabled healthcare", *Heliyon,* vol. 10, no. 16, p. e36269, 2024.
[http://dx.doi.org/10.1016/j.heliyon.2024.e36269] [PMID: 39224301]

[49]   M. Azrour, J. Mabrouki, A. Guezzaz, S. Ahmad, S. Khan, and S. Benkirane, "Iot, machine learning and data analytics for smart healthcare", In: *IoT Mach. Learn. Data Anal. Smart Healthc.* CRC Press, 2024, pp. 1-94.
[http://dx.doi.org/10.1201/9781003430735]

[50]   K. Kumari, S.K. Pahuja, and S. Kumar, "Machine learning implementations in COVID-19", In: *in Computational Modeling and Data Analysis in COVID-19 Research.* Apple Academic Press, 2021, pp. 1-16.
[http://dx.doi.org/10.1201/9781003137481-1]

[51]   M.S. Rao, S. Modi, R. Singh, K.L. Prasanna, S. Khan, and C. Ushapriya, "Integration of cloud computing, IoT, and big data for the development of a novel smart agriculture model", *2023 3rd Int. Conf. Adv. Comput. Innov. Technol. Eng., ICACITE 2023,* 2023pp. 2779-2783
[http://dx.doi.org/10.1109/ICACITE57410.2023.10182502]

[52]   Z. Wang, "Digital Twin Technology", In: *Industry 4.0 - Impact Intell. Logist. Manuf.* CRC Press, 2020.
[http://dx.doi.org/10.5772/intechopen.80974]

[53]   A. Haq, J.P. Li, S. Khan, M.A. Alshara, R.M. Alotaibi, and C. Mawuli, "DACBT: deep learning approach for classification of brain tumors using MRI data in IoT healthcare environment", *Sci. Rep.,* vol. 12, no. 1, p. 15331, 2022.
[http://dx.doi.org/10.1038/s41598-022-19465-1] [PMID: 36097024]

[54]   S. Sinha, A. Panwar, P. Gupta, and V. Bhatnagar, "Evolution of business intelligence system: From ad-hoc report to decision support system to data lake based bI 3.0", In: *in Healthc. Knowl. Manag. Soc. 5.0: Trends Issues Innov.* CRC Press, 2022, pp. 255-269.
[http://dx.doi.org/10.1201/9781003168638-18]

[55]   A.G. Matani, "Industry 4.0 and 5.0 towards enhanced productivity and competitiveness", In: *in Industry 4.0: Concepts, Processes and Systems.* CRC Press, 2023, pp. 61-76.
[http://dx.doi.org/10.1201/9781003246466-3]

[56]   P. Chugh, M. Gupta, S. Indu, G. Chaudhary, M. Khari, and V. Shanmuganathan, "Advanced energy efficient pegasis based routing protocol for IoT applications", *Microprocess. Microsyst.,* vol. 103, p. 104727, 2023.
[http://dx.doi.org/10.1016/j.micpro.2022.104727]

[57]   K. Kumar, and M. Khari, "Energy gaps and bacteriochlorophyll molecular graph representation based on machine learning algorithm", In: *in Biomed. Res. Dev. Improv. Healthc.* IGI Global, 2024, pp. 47-54.
[http://dx.doi.org/10.4018/979-8-3693-1922-2.ch003]

[58]   M. Khari, A.K. Garg, A.H. Gandomi, R. Gupta, R. Patan, and B. Balusamy, "Securing data in internet of things (IoT) using cryptography and steganography techniques", *IEEE Trans. Syst. Man Cybern. Syst.,* vol. 50, no. 1, pp. 73-80, 2020.
[http://dx.doi.org/10.1109/TSMC.2019.2903785]

[59]   R.O. Ogundokun, S. Misra, A.B. Adelodun, and M. Khari, "COVID-19 detection system in a smart hospital setting using transfer learning and IoT-based model", In: *in Internet of Things, vol. Part F1201.* Springer International Publishing Cham, 2023, pp. 233-262.
[http://dx.doi.org/10.1007/978-3-031-28631-5_12]

[60]   A. Panwar, Shyla, and V. Bhatnagar, "Blockchain-based web 4.0: decentralized web for decentralized cloud computing", In: *Cloud IoT: Concepts, Paradigms, and Appl.* 1st ed., Jitendra Kumar Verma, Deepak Kumar Saxena, Vicente González-Prida Díaz, Vira Shendryk, Ed. CRC Press,, 2022, pp. 219-233.
[http://dx.doi.org/10.1201/9781003155577-19]

[61]   W. Jian, J.P. Li, A.U. Haq, S. Khan, R.M. Alotaibi, S.A. Alajlan, and M.B.B. Heyat, "Feature elimination and stacking framework for accurate heart disease detection in IoT healthcare systems using clinical data", *Front. Med. (Lausanne),* vol. 11, p. 1362397, 2024.
[http://dx.doi.org/10.3389/fmed.2024.1362397] [PMID: 38841592]

[62]   D. Siddharth, D. K. J. B. Saini, and S. Kumar, "Blockchain for the internet of things and industry 4.0 application", In: *Handb. Flex. Smart Sheet Form. Tech.* Industry 4.0 Approaches., 2023, pp. 167-181.

[http://dx.doi.org/10.1002/9781119986454.ch10]

[63]   A. Panwar, and V. Bhatnagar, "Sentiment analysis of game review using machine learning in a hadoop ecosystem", In: *in Handb. Res. Eng. Innov. Technol. Manag. Organ.* IGI Global, 2020, pp. 145-165.
[http://dx.doi.org/10.4018/978-1-7998-2772-6.ch008]

[64]   H. Mouhib, S. Amar, S. Elrhanimi, and L.E. Abbadi, "An extended review of the manufacturing transition under the era of industry 5.0", *in Colloquium in Information Science and Technology CIST,* no. Dec, pp. 709-714, 2023.
[http://dx.doi.org/10.1109/CiSt56084.2023.10410003]

[65]   A. Panwar, and V. Bhatnagar, "Scrutinize the idea of hadoop-based data lake for big data storage", In: *in Appl. Mach. Learn., Algorithms Intell. Syst., First.,* S.P.P. Johri, J.K. Verma, Eds., Springer, 2020, pp. 365-391.
[http://dx.doi.org/10.1007/978-981-15-3357-0_24]

[66]   G. Czeczot, I. Rojek, D. Mikołajewski, and B. Sangho, "AI in IIoT management of cybersecurity for industry 4.0 and industry 5.0 purposes", *Electronics (Basel),* vol. 12, no. 18, p. 3800, 2023.
[http://dx.doi.org/10.3390/electronics12183800]

[67]   N. Pritam, M. Khari, L. Hoang Son, R. Kumar, S. Jha, I. Priyadarshini, M. Abdel-Basset, and H. Viet Long, "Assessment of code smell for predicting class change proneness using machine learning", *IEEE Access,* vol. 7, pp. 37414-37425, 2019.
[http://dx.doi.org/10.1109/ACCESS.2019.2905133]

CHAPTER 12

Future Trends in Secure Healthcare Predictive Analysis: Homomorphic Encryption Perspectives

Prokash Gogoi[1,*] and **Joseph Arul Valan**[1]

[1] *National Institute of Technology Nagaland, Chumukedima, Dimapur, Nagaland, India*

Abstract: In the healthcare system, the application of predictive analysis is essential to the enhancement of patient benefits as well as the development of healthcare delivery systems. The digitization of health records presents an increasing threat of data leakage and breaches of patient privacy. This chapter discusses how homomorphic encryption can be applied as a solution to secure healthcare information. We discuss the state of the art of predictive analysis in healthcare organizations and realize that the issue of data security is still relevant and needs to be further investigated due to evolving healthcare regulations and rapid technological advancements. We then discuss an overview of different available encryption techniques. We particularly focus on homomorphic encryption that allows computations to be made on data without decryption while maintaining patient data privacy. After that, we discuss how predictive analysis techniques can be applied to encrypted healthcare data. Some of the issues arising when attempting to carry out predictive analysis on encrypted data are discussed, in addition to the advantages of and technical hurdles in homomorphic encryption. We examine trends and opportunities, focussing on how secure predictive analytics, as one of the potential solutions, can improve the trust and reliability of healthcare data and patients' care. Finally, we perform a case study on the use of predictive analysis techniques in encrypted heart disease data with the help of the Paillier Homomorphic encryption scheme to maintain data security.

Keywords: Case studies, Data security, Homomorphic encryption, Machine learning model, Privacy, Secure healthcare predictive analysis.

INTRODUCTION

In the context of healthcare, predictive analyses involve the application of data from the past mathematical models to estimate future outcomes. Hence, this methodology employs Electronic Health Records (EHRs), medical imaging, genetics, and patient demographic data to predict patients' future health events, treatment, and disease progression. Predictive models are useful to predict

---

* **Corresponding author Prokash Gogoi:** National Institute of Technology Nagaland, Chumukedima, Dimapur, Nagaland, India; E-mail: prokashgogoi25@gmail.com

Tanu Singh, Vinod Patidar, Arvind Panwar & Urvashi Sugandh (Eds.)
All rights reserved-© 2025 Bentham Science Publishers

diseases like diabetes, heart disease, and chronic kidney disease. Healthcare providers can use these outcomes to develop preventive actions, enhance treatment programs, and improve patient care [1].

In healthcare, predictive analysis has several uses that are vital in improving patient care and productivity. One of them is the use of analytical models to identify patients with risk factors associated with specific ailments, thus enabling early diagnosis and management of a disease. Personalized care is another important domain; with the help of predictive analytics, it is possible to come up with individual or even patient-specific care plans that would correspond to the specific patient data and his or her potential response to certain therapies, which would increase the effectiveness of the procedure as well as the outcome for the patient. In the context of resource utilization, the predictive analysis assists in estimating the number of patients in a given period. It thus ensures adequate utilization of the health facilities, personnel, and other resources in anticipation of the flow of patients. In the same regard, predictive analysis helps predict the success rate of a specific treatment type by providing estimates on the possibilities of treatment success, thus assisting clinicians in choosing the most suitable treatment interventions [1].

With the advancement in technology, patient data has turned out to be a sensitive issue, particularly with the enhancement of the use of technology in the healthcare sector. More so, in the context of healthcare, the data collected is highly confidential and personal since it consists of information relating to a patient's medical history, treatment, and genetics. This data, if accessed by unauthorized persons, can cause very serious violation of people's privacy, identity theft, and loss of confidence in healthcare systems [2].

Encryption is the technology that forms the basis of protection of data that is stored and transmitted through the internet. In this context, an algorithm and encryption keys are applied to transform the readable text, also known as plaintext, into an unreadable form known as ciphertext. In contrast to plaintext, for converting ciphertext back to plaintext, only authorized parties with decryption keys shall be eligible. This helps in determining that data, even if intercepted or viewed by unauthorized personnel, remains unreadable.

Homomorphic encryption is one of the most advanced encrypting methods by which computations are made on the encrypted data without needing decryption. This special feature makes it possible to input, store, analyze, and retrieve sensitive information without compromising its security. Due to this, the use of homomorphic encryption is capable of solving many of the privacy and security issues arising from the use of predictive analysis in healthcare by allowing computations to be run on the encrypted data, thus leading to efficient and secure use of patient data [3, 4].

CURRENT STATE OF PREDICTIVE ANALYSIS IN HEALTHCARE

Healthcare predictive analytics uses computational and machine learning approaches to diagnose patients, estimate their prognosis, predict future health issues, and provide the best treatment plans. Nowadays, various predictive models, methodologies, and tools are employed to facilitate decision-making and increase the effectiveness of healthcare [5].

Different techniques employed in prediction models in healthcare practice are used to balance between accuracy and interpretability. For example, in regression models, researchers can predict both continuous and binary outcomes. The different types of neural networks include CNNs and RNNs, which are used for undertaking functions such as image recognition and analyzing language. Boosting (for example AdaBoost, XGBoost) and Bagging are examples of the ensemble methods in which many models are employed. Methods used when improving predictive models in healthcare include selecting relevant features and generating new features from the raw data, which can be derived *via* methods such as PCA and mutual information. Cross-validation is used to evaluate the models' ability to generalize by selecting different subsets of data. Said differently, hyperparameter tuning aims at the ideal adjustment of model parameters, frequently utilizing grid search or random search techniques. Based on the concept of predictive models in healthcare, we have tools like libraries and frameworks like scikit-learn, TensorFlow, Keras, and PyTorch, among others, which are key to establishing models. Hadoop and Spark are some of the biggest data management systems that need to be used in the storage and analysis of the large amounts of healthcare data that are collected. Reporting tools like Tableau and Power BI help in understanding and passing the message of the outcome of the predictive models [6, 7].

Analytics in the forecast is especially valuable in the healthcare industry with its multiple areas of application based on the prediction of patient's health, treatment impact, and disease development. For instance, in healthcare services, predictive models apply in estimating patients' vulnerability to diseases such as diabetes, hypertension, and cardiovascular diseases to allow for early intervention and preventive measures particular to the patient. This personalization even reaches treatment efficacy, where the use of predictive analysis helps doctors predict and estimate the effects of different treatments on patients, thereby identifying the best therapy to use on a patient. Also, prescriptive tools track patients' compliance with the recommended treatments, estimate the level of compliance, and provide recommendations for increasing the likelihood of compliance and, therefore, the success of the treatments. In disease progression, predictive models enhance early thinking through imaging and patient data in diagnosing diseases such as cancer at early stages; thus, treatment can be commenced immediately. Moreover, these models monitor the disease processes in cases of Alzheimer's and Parkinson's diseases, *etc.*, so that healthcare professionals can predict disease progression and make corrections in further treatment plans concerning predominantly chronic diseases [6, 7].

ENCRYPTION IN HEALTHCARE DATA SECURITY

Ensuring that information or data in the healthcare industry is secure is a very important aspect to note because of the sensitive nature of the information. Electronic healthcare information relates to patients' health records, treatments, diagnosis tests, and other reported information about the patient and other personal identifiers, which, if disclosed, poses serious privacy breaches and risks to patients. The proper protection of the data is essential to retain patients' trust, satisfy legal or regulatory demands, and avoid data breaches and unauthorized use of sensitive information [8, 9].

Key reasons for prioritizing data security in healthcare include:

1. **Patient Privacy:** Privacy of data checks the access of unauthorized persons to maintain the confidentiality of the patient's health details.
2. **Preventing Data Breaches:** The theft of information can result in monetary losses, legal implications, and negative perceptions toward healthcare organizations.
3. **Ensuring Data Integrity:** Preventing data from being corrupted prevents false information from being used to make decisions concerning patient care.

Encryption is critical in safeguarding healthcare information since it transcribes the data into plain text called the Cipher text, which can only be opened by those in a position of authority who hold the keys. Various encryption techniques are there to secure healthcare data. There are four categories of encryption techniques: symmetric encryption involves the use of a single key to both map data into cipher text and map cipher text back into plain text, and it is efficient, but the key must be protected; asymmetric encryption provides flexibility whereby a public key is used to map data into cipher text and a private key is used to map cipher text back to plain text, and this is secure since the public and private keys must be protected; hybrid encryption uses a combination. It is pertinent to note that homomorphic encryption has vast applications in the field of healthcare data security since it allows for the computation and analysis of patient data in an encrypted form [10, 11].

Key features and benefits of homomorphic encryption:

1. **Privacy Preservation:** Data remains encrypted during the computation; hence patient's privacy is kept safe when performing these computations. This is because the data being processed in such an application may well be health-related, thereby demanding high levels of security.
2. **Secure Data Analysis:** The benefits of homomorphic encryption are that healthcare providers, researchers, and other stakeholders can process large amounts of data in a prediction analysis, machine learning, and other computations, and the data does not have to be decrypted for this to be done. This helps in making sure that data or information that must not be exposed is not exposed to the public domain during the analysis.
3. **Regulatory Compliance:** Since encrypted data is used during the computation process through HE, the storage of data is made secure, thus helping the healthcare organization adhere to the data protection regulations to minimize cases of hacks and unauthorized access to patient's data.
4. **Collaboration and Data Sharing:** Homomorphic encryption introduces the possibility of safely sharing and collaborating on information between physicians, researchers, and other entities. Processed data can be passed through networks and put through analytics without compromising on its content, hence stimulating creativity and analytical solutions.

Types of Homomorphic Encryption:

1. **Partially Homomorphic Encryption (PHE)**: This type allows the use of only a limited number of operations (such as addition or multiplication) on encrypted data.
2. **Somewhat Homomorphic Encryption (SHE)**: This enables only a certain amount of addition and multiplication operations. It is more efficient than fully homomorphic encryption, but it can only perform limited and simple computations.
3. **Fully Homomorphic Encryption (FHE)**: This type permits any computations on the encrypted data without restriction. On encrypted data, it is as flexible as with plain data and can perform any function on encrypted data that can be performed on plain data. Nevertheless, it involves a large amount of computation and is not efficient enough for practical purposes now.

Homomorphic encryption can be a promising solution for the future of healthcare data protection as it allows computation on encrypted data without revealing the patient's information. It enables the creation and use of diagnostic, therapeutic, and prognostic models based on encrypted information about patients while preserving their anonymity. As for clinical trials, homomorphic encryption can be used to share and analyze encrypted data collected from clinical trials, benefiting researchers while protecting patient information. It also enhances the safety of the telemedicine platforms since the patient data is encrypted during remote consultation and analysis so that information privacy is upheld. Also, as for the relation to the field of the study, homomorphic encryption allows for the analysis of genomic data, such as patients' personal information, which is integral to personalized medicine and is also sensitive to be left unencrypted. These applications demonstrate how homomorphic encryption can play a crucial role in the further development of healthcare by addressing the issues of data protection while at the same time enabling precise research and individual approaches to patients [12, 13].

PREDICTIVE ANALYSIS TECHNIQUES APPLIED TO ENCRYPTED HEALTHCARE DATA

Challenges and opportunities of applying the predictive analysis techniques based on the encrypted healthcare data are discussed in this section. First, there is the problem of computation on encrypted data, a challenge met by homomorphic encryption that permits secure and privacy-preserving predictive analysis. It starts with data pre-processing and then encrypting it such that the healthcare data is encrypted using homomorphic techniques that ensure the security and confidentiality of data during the analysis. Next, full-fledged machine learning models can be trained on encrypted data, allowing developers to apply the model to data without accessing the raw data, thus minimizing the risk of patient-data linkage and protecting patient privacy. The encrypted models can make predictions using the new encrypted data without compromising on security and confidentiality. Also, homomorphic encryption aids in the secure computation and sharing of encrypted datasets from different healthcare organizations or researchers to discover and develop as well as employ efficient and accurate prediction algorithms without revealing any sensitive information [14].

Fig. (1) shows how homomorphic encryption can be incorporated into secure predictive analysis for use in healthcare. In this process, the patient or doctor (acting as a client) encrypts medical data (medical records) using the public key generated from homomorphic encryption and sends the encrypted data to a third-party cloud service provider for predictive analysis service. The cloud service provider, which has a trained machine learning model, carries out the predictive analysis of the encrypted data. The results or the prediction outcomes are then sent back to the client. After that, the client can decrypt the results using the private key which was generated from homomorphic encryption.

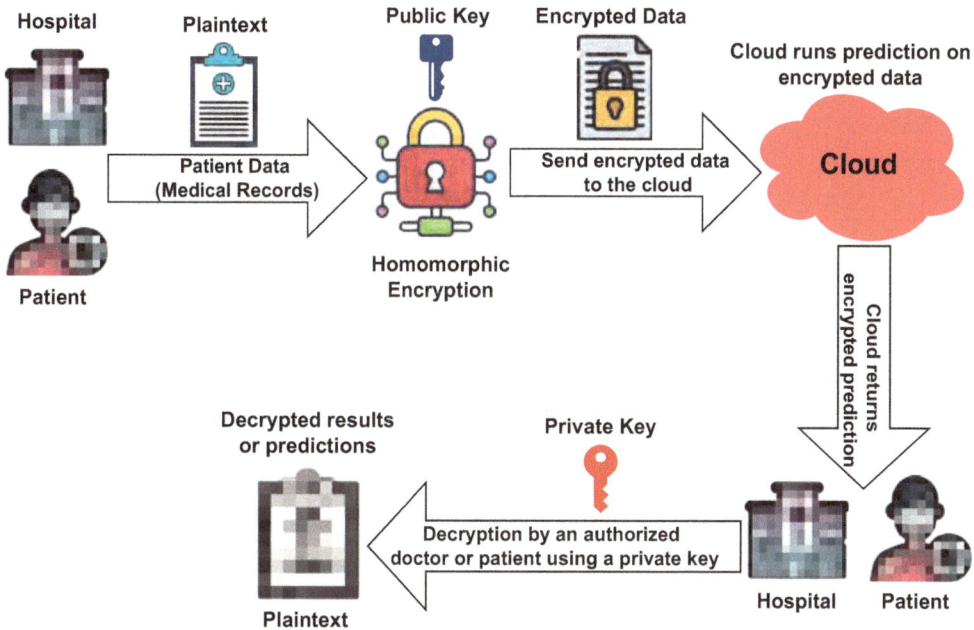

Fig. (1). Homomorphic encryption in secure predictive analysis for healthcare.

Over the past decades, different research works have been conducted using statistical analysis and modeling methods on encrypting healthcare information. For example, J. W. Bos *et al*. [14] employed homomorphic encryption to compute encrypted medical data without the need for decryption. Their research was centered on privately performing prediction analysis tasks through homomorphic encryption. A prediction service on Microsoft's Windows Azure runs on encrypted health data and provides the probability of cardiovascular disease in encrypted form. This cloud service demonstrated the cloud computing technology's possibilities in analyzing the submitted medical data while keeping it confidential. P. Gogoi *et al*. [15] highlighted the concern regarding privacy preservation in medical science, which is mandatory because of the sensitive nature of data associated with chronic kidney disease. They proposed a safe approach toward early identification of CKD, focusing on proper identification and data protection. The research was divided into two stages: utilizing meta-heuristic algorithms on feature selection and developing a privacy-preserving logistic regression model for encrypted data. The logistic regression model with the Paillier homomorphic cryptosystem and genetic algorithm achieved an accuracy rate of 98.75%. E. Sarkar *et al*. [16] discussed privacy-preserving cancer-type prediction based on homomorphic encryption on the vast numbers of genetic mutations available in the dataset. In this study, features were eliminated for computation, enforced by biological sense and statistical analysis. A new matrix multiplication algorithm for privacy-preserving logistic regression was presented. The final model added up enhancement in accuracy to the native 70.08% to 83%. It was optimized up to 61%, and at the same time, it increased the computational speed by 550 times. The method used in the process included compact encoding of the somatic mutations and features as well as reduction to predict the model. S. Behera *et al.* [17] described how data can be encrypted through a homomorphic process so that applied machine learning algorithms would not give leakage of sensitive data. The utilization made possible processing of data in an encrypted form while preserving privacy during prediction. They explained how to integrate linear regression with the Paillier homomorphic encryption technique and keep data anonymous during predictions. The output given by the model was encrypted and it was decrypted for analysis by using a private key of a homomorphic system. The validation of the results from the encrypted data was done by comparing the results to the ones that were obtained from plain text.

CHALLENGES AND OPPORTUNITIES IN PREDICTIVE ANALYSIS OF ENCRYPTED HEALTHCARE DATA

When using predictive analytics to analyze encrypted healthcare data, various challenges occur, including privacy limits and computational optimizations. A major complication that results from encryption is the issue of computational complexity involved. Algorithms such as homomorphic encryption optimize the time it takes to process information and require an enormous amount of computing power; current healthcare information technology cannot handle such solutions. Furthermore, several machine learning algorithms need to be modified significantly for encrypted data processing because of the introduced noise and limitations of the encryption techniques [18].

The other very significant implication is to ensure that different systems are integrated. Various encryption approaches may pose challenges when it comes to merging encrypted data from several sources hence restricted in safely sharing data between healthcare organizations without violating HIPAA and GDPR guidelines. Further, due to intrinsic complexity and lack of integrated end-to-end encryption and decryption, a good amount of care has to be taken in handling the keys so that privacy and security in the overall process of analyzing and providing predictable information are maintained.

However, homomorphic encryption presents remarkable advantages even with the above difficulties. It makes it possible to perform calculations on the data without revealing the information to unauthorized persons or patients' data; thus, the regulations on data privacy laws are followed. This capability enables secure multi-party computation among the researchers and physicians to enhance their research, taking advantage of the large amount of data available without necessarily compromising the individual patient data. Furthermore, in terms of analysis, it does not alter the raw data, hence addressing concerns about data leakage while still making patients stick to healthcare data management [19].

Security and flexibility costs are still seen as significant and exist in the form of performance overhead that generally outperforms traditional encryption techniques, thereby increasing the time taken to process and potentially overloading the resource. In addition, algorithmic constraints restrict the possibility of applying advanced predictive models on homomorphically encrypted data, thereby posing a problem for achieving high precision and accuracy in healthcare big data analysis.

As for the future work, there are a lot of prospects for research and development. Algorithmic efficiency in managing encrypted data and fine-tuning machine learning models, which may extend its applicability, are two major areas for improvement. Future developments in application-specific processing devices, including GPUs and quantum technologies, may make significant contributions towards rendering homomorphic encryption computations feasible, aspects currently associated with scalability challenges. The homomorphic encryption can be further extended and adapted by entailing standardization of the present encryption framework alongside the evaluation of new and more sophisticated privacy-preserving approaches, such as federated learning within the applications of the healthcare domain.

Since homomorphic encryption is an emerging field, real-life pilot projects and case studies will be crucial in proving the feasibility of the approach in the context of predictive healthcare analytics. Such initiatives can measure the effects of the outcomes in healthcare, data protection, and organizational effectiveness, and the findings can help healthcare information technology improve on defensive encryption approaches to bolster uptake in healthcare.

TRENDS AND FUTURE DIRECTIONS IN PREDICTIVE ANALYSIS ON ENCRYPTED HEALTHCARE DATA

Emerging trends and technologies driving predictive analysis in healthcare data analytics are in the process of evolution. One major trend is that artificial intelligence and machine learning are being gradually introduced into the design process. Methods such as deep learning, reinforcement learning, and ensemble methods are popular for improving predictive capacity and performance [20].

Another important trend is edge computing, which is the process of data computing in a location closer to the place where the data originates rather than waiting for cloud computing servers to provide the necessary data. This approach has low latency and allows for real-time predictive analytics, which is important for various use cases such as telemonitoring and emergency systems. Model training is going through a major shift through federated learning where devices or servers that participate in model training do not need to share raw data, and this maintains the privacy and security of the patients [21].

Blockchain technology provides a secure environment for the exchange of information while using distributed ledgers to guarantee data accuracy and consistency in the healthcare sector. Among predictive analysis techniques, there is a growing trend towards Explainable AI (XAI), which focuses on building transparent AI models. This is especially important in the health sector because health practitioners need to know why AI has made certain predictions so they can make informed decisions and have confidence in the AI applications being used [22].

As for future work, the study of predictive analysis on encrypted healthcare data will be directed to the enhancement of the homomorphic encryption algorithms. Future research will try to eliminate overhead and enhance performance, which can be done using algorithms for lightweight encryption and utilizing GPUs or Quantum Computing devices. The incorporation of homomorphic encrypted data with AI and machine learning algorithms will help in performing advanced encrypted analysis, leading to improving the factor of predictive healthcare analytics without compromising the security of data.

Privacy-preserving federated learning will help perform model training in a decentralized manner across different institutions to share the data, perform further analysis, and contribute to creating new knowledge without compromising the patient's information privacy. Prototypes will address the use in clinical trials, medical research, and remote patient monitoring, allowing for the safe processing of highly sensitive data, as well as further developments in tailoring medical interventions as well as the efficiency of treatments [23].

Healthcare data security and predictive analysis with the help of homomorphic encryption are going to be monumental improvements. This kind of computation enables prediction analysis to retain patient information anonymity from the computation stage as it is carried out on encrypted data, thereby effectively dealing with privacy issues and conforming to regulatory frameworks such as HIPAA AND GDPR. This makes data safe from breaches and also from unauthorized access, which, in turn, makes people have confidence in using artificial intelligence in clinical practice [24].

End-to-end secure encryption of the patient's data will enable the protection of predictive analysis of such information so that the interoperability between healthcare organizations, research organizations, and the pharmaceutical industries is enhanced for faster discovery of new medical knowledge and products. Following the development of homomorphic encryption possessing large-scale applicability for data analysis, population health management, epidemiological investigations, and a multitude of future clinical investigations will be based on homomorphic encryption solutions for healthcare's intricate issues [25].

CASE STUDIES AND EXAMPLES

From the real-life context, predictive analysis with homomorphic encryption has turned out to be fruitful in different healthcare applications. For example, in remote patient monitoring systems, private information about the patient is encrypted before transmission to the healthcare provider, especially one in a distant or poorly served region. This ensures privacy and security of the data while at the same time, the predictive models work on the data. It can give alerts on time for ailments such as heart disease or diabetes, thus facilitating early treatment. Another important area is pharmacogenomics or prescription drugs, which is the practice of developing unique therapies and treatments for each patient using his or her genetic profile and medical history. It helps to determine effective therapy when predictive models refer to patients' records, and homomorphic encryption enables safe data analysis with the help of such data. This method respects the patient's right to privacy, thus allowing healthcare practitioners to advance health recommendations that are closest to the patient's status without further compromising the patient's identity. Clinical Decision Support System (CDSS) keeps patients' data secured while making precise medical decisions concerning the patients' conditions since the data is first encrypted before being entered into the system for analysis. This helps in protecting the patient's identity, especially during diagnosis and planning on the best treatment options [26, 27].

Examples highlighting the application and impact of this technology:

- **Predictive Analysis for Early Detection of Chronic Diseases:** A hospital has implemented an analytical system that is used to determine patients who are prone to chronic diseases such as hypertension or diabetes. Personal information of patients, such as medical history, lab data, and personal characteristics, are employed in homomorphic encryption. This allows the encrypted data to be safely analyzed, hence determining the high-risk patients to enable their early intervention by the predictive model. As a result, alert messages are sent to the healthcare professionals and then, preventive and minimization measures of chronic diseases can be undertaken. In this process, the privacy of patients' information is maintained, confirming confidence in the health sector.

- **Secure Analysis of Genomic Data for Cancer Treatment:** A research institute applies homomorphic encryption to safely perform analysis on clusters of genomic data of cancer patients. The different treatment regimens are predicted using the biomarkers to identify the best therapy path based on specific genetic mutations. This is made to work in such a way that the genomic data is encrypted and this means that they are analyzed without first being decrypted in a way that ensures or protects the privacy of the patients. This kind of predictive analysis helps to discern the particular treatment, increases the chances of successful therapy, and decreases side effects at the same time. The proper management of any genetic data to protect the patients' information fosters confidence among the patients in research.

- **Enhancing Data Security in Collaborative Research:** Several healthcare organizations collaborate on a study to develop predictive models for rare diseases. A patient's data collected from several institutions is encrypted to be shared for analysis. This is advantageous since the data being worked on is encrypted, and thus, any privacy or data theft is limited throughout the process. It can also allow the researchers to securely integrate data from different sources and thereby improve the reliability and accuracy of the models that can be developed. Such a partnership model fosters the enhancement of the rare diseases' treatment more so without compromising the data protection.

Predictive Analysis of Encrypted Heart Disease Data

We performed a case study on the use of predictive analysis techniques in encrypted heart disease data with the help of a homomorphic encryption scheme to maintain data security. The objective was to increase the efficiency of the algorithms for heart disease prediction while preserving patients' privacy. From this case study, we were able to show how a trained model can run a predictive analysis on encrypted heart disease data. For this purpose, we used a heart disease dataset collected from the UCI Machine Learning Repository [28]. The dataset consisted of patient clinical data that are the medical indicators or attributes such as cholesterol, blood pressure, and heart rate. This dataset included 13 attributes and one target class. Since no values were missing within the dataset, no attempts were made to fill in for missing values as well. This heart disease dataset was divided into train and test data, where the train data was 80% and the test data was 20%. In feature selection, we employed the Mutual Information method on the training set; the Mutual Information scores of each feature were presented in a bar graph, as shown in Fig. (**2**). Values of Higher Mutual Information signify higher informativeness in helping to predict the target class [29]. In the analysis for this study, we used three sets of features containing 13, 9, and 7 features, as determined by higher Mutual Information scores.

The keys were created using the Paillier homomorphic encryption cryptosystem [30] and it generated both the public and the private key. Under the encryption process, we encrypted our test data with the public key. The training set was then trained using the Logistic Regression Machine Learning Model [31], and the trained model carried out the prediction analysis on the encrypted test data. The predicted outcomes or results from the analysis were obtained in encrypted form. After that, we decrypted the encrypted results with the Paillier private key to obtain the actual results.

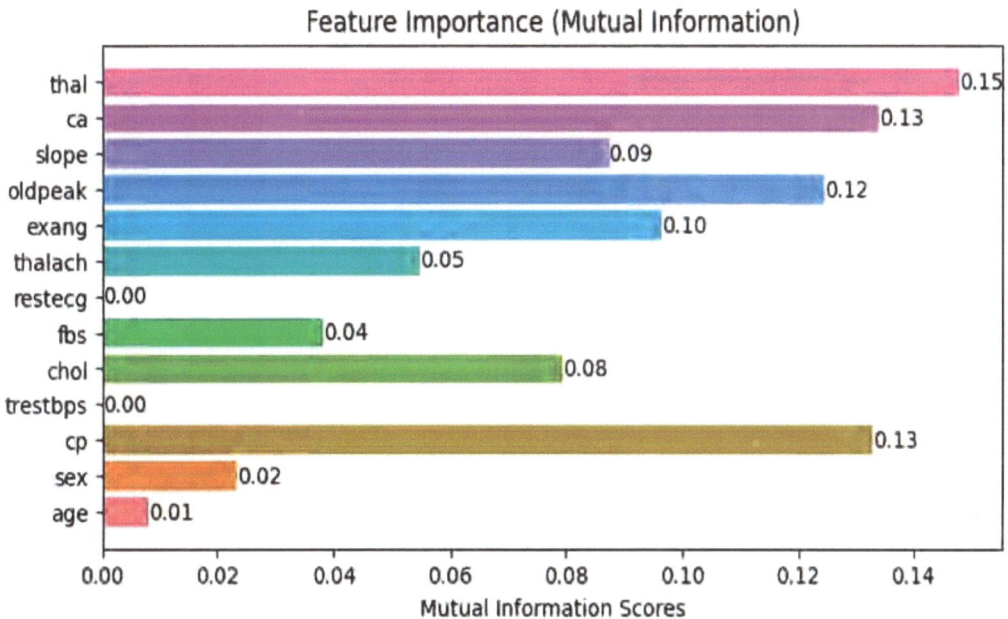

Feature Importance (Mutual Information)

Fig. (2). Mutual information scores of all features in the heart disease dataset.

In Fig. (**3**), we present the confusion matrices of the trained LR model on encrypted heart disease test data. The results or performance metrics of the trained LR models on encrypted test data with three different feature sets are shown in Table **1**. The LR model yielded better results with 9 features and attained an accuracy of 90.16%, which is the highest compared to other subsets of features.

Fig. (**4**) shows the ROC curves for all three subsets where the LR model employing 7 features yields the highest ROC-AUC of 93.91%.

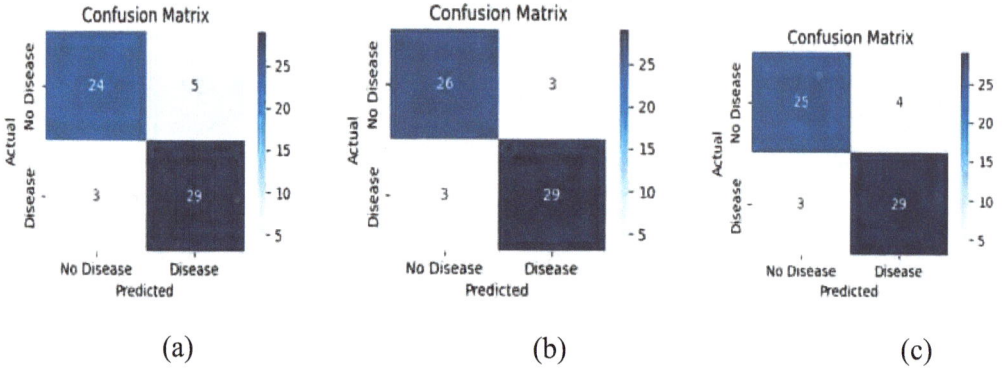

(a)   (b)   (c)

Fig. (3). Confusion matrices of the trained LR model on encrypted heart disease test data: (**a**) with all features (13), (**b**) with MI-selected features (9), (**c**) with MI-selected features (7).

Table 1. Performance metrics of the trained lr model on encrypted heart disease test data.

Model with Features	Accuracy	Precision	Recall	F1-score	ROC-AUC
LR with all Features (13)	86.89%	85.29%	90.62%	87.88%	91.49%
LR with MI (9)	90.16%	90.62%	90.62%	90.62%	91.92%
LR with MI (7)	88.52%	87.88%	90.62%	89.23%	93.91%

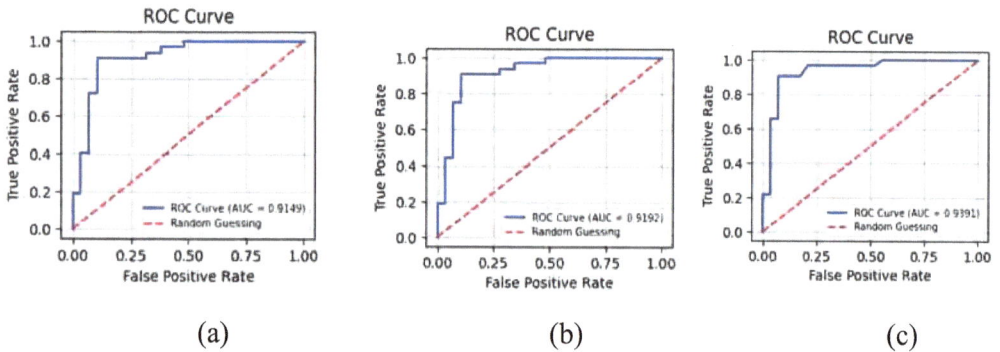

(a)   (b)   (c)

Fig. (4). ROC curves of the trained LR model on encrypted heart disease test data: (**a**) with all features (13), (**b**) with MI-selected features (9), (**c**) with MI-selected features (7).

Our experiments proved to be successful in the aspect of getting higher accuracy in determining the outcomes of heart diseases and, at the same time, ensuring that patients' privacy is protected in the course of predictive modeling. The analysis of encrypted data of heart disease and its application of predictive analysis in enhanced data analytics of healthcare concerning homomorphic encryption data compound the concept of protecting the patient's data privacy while advancing the analysis and analytics of the same. Our work is useful to the ongoing research and development of secure and accurate processing of encrypted health data to be used in the predictive modeling of healthcare systems. Other recommendations for future studies include looking at the issues related to the size scales and improving the models and their predictions with the help of bigger data sets as well as more complex cryptographic methods.

CONCLUDING REMARKS

In this chapter, we discussed the current state of predictive analysis in the healthcare sector more selectively, with a focus on the issues related to the protection of data. We explored different types of encryption approaches, with a strong focus on homomorphic encryption and its importance when it comes to the safe analysis of healthcare data. We provided detailed information about the advantages, disadvantages, and use cases of various types of predictive analysis methods and how they can be used in encrypted healthcare data. We also discussed some of the challenges and opportunities of applying the predictive analysis on the encrypted data, especially with the use of homomorphic encryption. This paper shows that homomorphic encryption solves the fundamental problem of data privacy and security while making it possible to perform computations on encrypted data for sophisticated predictive analysis. The case study conducted by us proves that a predictive model can be used on encrypted data, and the data can be secured as well. Further studies can be devoted to improving the speed and applicability of homomorphic encryption methods, which might be useful with greater amounts of data and higher orders of modeling. To some extent, by integrating homomorphic encryption in healthcare predictive analysis, a lot of benefits can be obtained as patients can obtain real-time personalized treatments with optimal outcomes. If the healthcare industry overcomes the difficulties and takes advantage of homomorphic encryption, then we can say that the predictions are accurate, data is more secure, and healthcare systems worldwide are more useful for the better treatment of patients.

REFERENCES

[1]   M. Badawy, N. Ramadan, and H.A. Hefny, "Healthcare predictive analytics using machine learning and deep learning techniques: a survey", *J. Electr. Syst. Inf. Technol.*, vol. 10, no. 1, p. 40, 2023. [http://dx.doi.org/10.1186/s43067-023-00108-y]

[2]   "Institute of Medicine (US), Committee on Health Research and the Privacy of Health Information", In: *Beyond the HIPAA Privacy Rule: Enhancing Privacy, Improving Health Through Research.* Nass SJ, Levit LA, Gostin LO, editors, Washington, DC: National Academies Press, 2009.

[3]   M. Ogburn, C. Turner, and P. Dahal, "Homomorphic encryption", *Procedia Comput. Sci.*, vol. 20, pp. 502-509, 2013.

[http://dx.doi.org/10.1016/j.procs.2013.09.310]

[4]   W. Yang, S. Wang, H. Cui, Z. Tang, and Y. Li, "A review of homomorphic encryption for privacy-preserving biometrics", *Sensors (Basel),* vol. 23, no. 7, p. 3566, 2023.
[http://dx.doi.org/10.3390/s23073566] [PMID: 37050626]

[5]   B. Van Calster, L. Wynants, D. Timmerman, E.W. Steyerberg, and G.S. Collins, "Predictive analytics in health care: how can we know it works?", *J. Am. Med. Inform. Assoc.,* vol. 26, no. 12, pp. 1651-1654, 2019.
[http://dx.doi.org/10.1093/jamia/ocz130] [PMID: 31373357]

[6]   Z. Zhang, "Predictive analytics in the era of big data: opportunities and challenges", *Ann. Transl. Med.,* vol. 8, no. 4, p. 68, 2020.
[http://dx.doi.org/10.21037/atm.2019.10.97] [PMID: 32175361]

[7]   D.S.E. Broekharst, R. Van de Wetering, W. Ooms, R.W. Helms, and N. Roijakkers, "Deploying predictive analytics to enhance patient agility and patient value in hospitals: A position paper and research proposal", *Healthc. Anal.,* vol. 3, p. 100141, 2023.
[http://dx.doi.org/10.1016/j.health.2023.100141]

[8]   P. Shojaei, E. Vlahu-Gjorgievska, and Y.-W. Chow, "Security and privacy of technologies in health information systems: A systematic literature review," *Computers,* vol. 13, no. 2, p. 41, 2024.
[http://dx.doi.org/10.3390/computers13020041]

[9]   A. Almalawi, A.I. Khan, F. Alsolami, Y.B. Abushark, and A.S. Alfakeeh, "Managing security of healthcare data for a modern healthcare system", *Sensors (Basel),* vol. 23, no. 7, p. 3612, 2023.
[http://dx.doi.org/10.3390/s23073612] [PMID: 37050672]

[10]   M. Mocydlarz-Adamcewicz, B. Bajsztok, S. Filip, J. Petera, M. Mestan, and J. Malicki, "Management of onsite and remote communication in oncology hospitals: Data protection in an era of rapid technological advances", *J. Pers. Med.,* vol. 13, no. 5, p. 761, 2023.
[http://dx.doi.org/10.3390/jpm13050761] [PMID: 37240931]

[11]   B. Basha, "Enhancing healthcare data security using quantum cryptography for efficient and robust encryption", *Journal of Electrical Systems,* vol. 20, no. 5s, pp. 1993-2000, 2024.
[http://dx.doi.org/10.52783/jes.2535]

[12]   N.N. Kucherov, M.A. Deryabin, and M.G. Babenko, "Homomorphic encryption methods review", *2020 IEEE Conf. Russ. Young Res. Electr. Electron. Eng. (EIConRus),* 2020pp. 370-373 St. Petersburg and Moscow, Russia
[http://dx.doi.org/10.1109/EIConRus49466.2020.9039110]

[13]   K. Vellore pichandi, V. Janarthanan, T. Annamalai, and M. Arumugam, "Enhancing healthcare in the digital era: A secure e-health system for heart disease prediction and cloud security", *Expert Syst. Appl.,* vol. 255, p. 124479, 2024.
[http://dx.doi.org/10.1016/j.eswa.2024.124479]

[14]   J.W. Bos, K. Lauter, and M. Naehrig, "Private predictive analysis on encrypted medical data", *J. Biomed. Inform.,* vol. 50, pp. 234-243, 2014.
[http://dx.doi.org/10.1016/j.jbi.2014.04.003] [PMID: 24835616]

[15]   P. Gogoi, and J.A. Valan, "Privacy-preserving predictive modeling for early detection of chronic kidney disease", *Netw. Model. Anal. Health Inform. Bioinform.,* vol. 13, no. 1, p. 16, 2024.
[http://dx.doi.org/10.1007/s13721-024-00452-7]

[16]   E. Sarkar, E. Chielle, and G. Gursoy, "Privacy-preserving cancer type prediction with homomorphic encryption", *Scientific Rep.,* vol. 13, no. 1661, 2023.
[http://dx.doi.org/10.1038/s41598-023-28481-8]

[17]   S. Behera, and J.R. Prathuri, "Application of Homomorphic Encryption in Machine Learning", *2020 2nd PhD Colloquium on Ethically Driven Innovation and Technology for Society (PhD EDITS),* pp. 1-2, 2020.

[http://dx.doi.org/10.1109/PhDEDITS51180.2020.9315305]

[18]   P. Goyal, and R. Malviya, "RETRACTED: Challenges and opportunities of big data analytics in healthcare", *Health Care Science,* vol. 2, no. 5, pp. 328-338, 2023.
[http://dx.doi.org/10.1002/hcs2.66] [PMID: 38938583]

[19]   A. Tolba, and Z. Al-Makhadmeh, "Predictive data analysis approach for securing medical data in smart grid healthcare systems", *Future Gener. Comput. Syst.,* vol. 117, pp. 87-96, 2021.
[http://dx.doi.org/10.1016/j.future.2020.11.008]

[20]   T. Davenport, and R. Kalakota, "The potential for artificial intelligence in healthcare", *Future Healthc. J.,* vol. 6, no. 2, pp. 94-98, 2019.
[http://dx.doi.org/10.7861/futurehosp.6-2-94] [PMID: 31363513]

[21]   J. Pérez, J. Díaz, J. Berrocal, R. López-Viana, and Á. González-Prieto, "Edge computing", *Computing,* vol. 104, no. 12, pp. 2711-2747, 2022.
[http://dx.doi.org/10.1007/s00607-022-01104-2]

[22]   H. Saeed, H. Malik, U. Bashir, A. Ahmad, S. Riaz, M. Ilyas, W.A. Bukhari, and M.I.A. Khan, "Blockchain technology in healthcare: A systematic review", *PLoS One,* vol. 17, no. 4, p. e0266462, 2022.
[http://dx.doi.org/10.1371/journal.pone.0266462] [PMID: 35404955]

[23]   S. Moon, and W. Hee Lee, "Privacy-preserving federated learning in healthcare", *2023 Int. Conf. Electron. Inf. Commun. (ICEIC),* pp. 1-4, 2023.Singapore

[24]   K. Munjal, and R. Bhatia, "A systematic review of homomorphic encryption and its contributions in healthcare industry", *Complex Intell. Syst.,* vol. 8, pp. 1-28, 2022.
[PMID: 35531323]

[25]   M.R. Abdmeziem, and D. Tandjaoui, "An end-to-end secure key management protocol for e-health applications", *Comput. Electr. Eng.,* vol. 44, pp. 184-197, 2015.
[http://dx.doi.org/10.1016/j.compeleceng.2015.03.030]

[26]   M. Paul, L. Maglaras, M. A. Ferrag, and I. Almomani, "Digitization of healthcare sector: A study on privacy and security concerns," *ICT Express*, vol. 9, no. 4, pp. 571–588, 2023.
[http://dx.doi.org/10.1016/j.icte.2023.02.007]

[27]   Y. Ma, J. Zhao, K. Li, Y. Cao, H. Chen, and Y. Zhang, "Research review on the application of homomorphic encryption in database privacy protection", *Int. J. Cogn. Inform. Nat. Intell.,* vol. 15, no. 4, pp. 1-22, 2021.
[http://dx.doi.org/10.4018/IJCINI.287600]

[28]   Machine Learning Repository, "Heart Disease Data Set", Available from: https://archive.ics.uci.edu/ml/datasets/Heart+Disease

[29]   J.R. Vergara, and P.A. Estévez, "A review of feature selection methods based on mutual information", *Neural Comput. Appl.,* vol. 24, no. 1, pp. 175-186, 2014.
[http://dx.doi.org/10.1007/s00521-013-1368-0]

[30]   P. Paillier, "Public-key cryptosystems based on composite degree residuosity classes", In: *Advances in Cryptology - EUROCRYPT '99.* Springer: Berlin, 1999, pp. 223-238.
[http://dx.doi.org/10.1007/3-540-48910-X_16]

[31]   C.Y.J. Peng, K.L. Lee, and G.M. Ingersoll, "An introduction to logistic regression analysis and reporting", *J. Educ. Res.,* vol. 96, no. 1, pp. 3-14, 2002.
[http://dx.doi.org/10.1080/00220670209598786]

CHAPTER 13

Future Trends and Emerging Technologies in Predictive Maintenance Research

Pranav Shrivastava[1,*], Prerna Agarwal[2], Saquib Hussain[2] and **Kareena Tuli[2]**

[1] *Department of Computer Sciences, Galgotias College of Engineering and Technology, Greater Noida, India*

[2] *School of Computer Science Engineering & Technology, Bennett University Greater Noida, India*

Abstract: Predictive Maintenance (PdM) refers to a forward-looking approach that uses data analytics to predict equipment failures and schedule maintenance at the most optimal time. This chapter explores the future trends and emerging technologies shaping PdM, focusing on its ability to enhance operational efficiency and reduce downtime. Key developments include the integration of Artificial Intelligence (AI) and Machine Learning (ML) to improve predictive accuracy, the use of IoT and sensor technologies for real-time monitoring, and the application of cloud and edge computing for decentralized data processing. Additionally, technologies such as Augmented Reality (AR) and Virtual Reality (VR) are transforming training and diagnostics, while blockchain ensures data security. The chapter also highlights quantum computing's potential to revolutionize predictive models. Despite these advancements, challenges like data privacy concerns, interoperability issues, workforce skill gaps, and high implementation costs are discussed, alongside recommendations for overcoming these obstacles to maximize PdM's benefits.

Keywords: Artificial intelligence, Augmented reality, Blockchain, Cloud computing, Edge computing, IoT, Machine learning, Predictive maintenance, Quantum computing, Real-time monitoring.

INTRODUCTION

Predictive Maintenance (PdM) is a proactive strategy that leverages data analytics to monitor machinery health, enabling timely maintenance actions, minimizing downtime, and optimizing repair costs. Its main goal is to pre-arrange the maintenance operations by selecting the right time in advance, guarantee that malfunction can be prevented, and reduce the cost of equipment repair. Among reactive maintenance (normally post FMEA), preventive maintenance, and

---
[*] **Corresponding author Pranav Shrivastava:** Department of Computer Sciences, Galgotias College of Engineering and Technology, Greater Noida, India; E-mail: pranav.paddy@gmail.com

PdM(Predictive Maintenance), predictivemaintenance is the one that processes data in real time using various mathematical methods to predict failures based on information about arrays of machines problems [1].

Maintenance Operations: Fig. (**1**) illustrates all the different categories of maintenance operations [2].

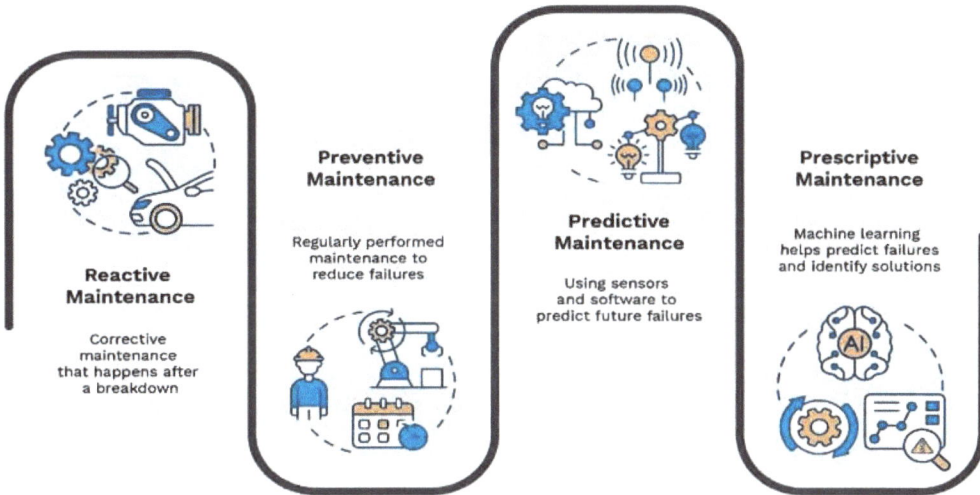

Fig. (1). Different types of maintenance activities [2].

Importance of Predictive Maintenance in Various Industries

Predictive Maintenance (PdM) is one of the powerful methodologies used across manufacturing, energy sector, transportation, and aerospace. This is further highlighted due to the fact it can add efficiency, minimize downtime, and extend the operational life of key assets. This might come in the form of unexpected downtime for manufacturing, which already leads to significant production decreases and even higher operational costs. PdM overcomes these issues by allowing maintenance to be done when it is required, which reduces unnecessary maintenance and prevents large failures [3]. The same goes for transportation vehicles where PdM keeps them running with maximal reliability and minimal sudden breakdowns. The efficiency of PdM in the aerospace industry leads to greater reliability and safety for full-size aircraft, faults occurrence on which may have catastrophic consequences [4]. Fig. (**2**) shows different benefits offered by PdM [2].

Fig. (2). Advantages offered by PdM [2].

Overview of Existing Predictive Maintenance Techniques

Throughout the years, many different Predictive Maintenance (PdM) strategies have been developed, where each presents its own advantages and use cases. They can broadly be grouped into statistical methods, machine learning methods, and model-based methods. A number of these statistical methods include regression analysis and time series analysis, which have been applied in the past for equipment failure predictions as they mine historical information. However, the introduction of PdM systems has changed the landscape by allowing the analysis of bigger and larger data sets for distinguishing patterns that other systems would not have been able to reveal. As a result, machine learning-based methods like decision trees, support vector machines, and deep learning model building have gained ground in the prediction of impending equipment failure, outpacing traditional predictive modeling techniques [5].

On the other hand, model-based frameworks concentrate their efforts on the creation of detailed mathematical models of equipment for simulating their behavior operating under various conditions. It also helps these models to predict the likeliness of component failure depending on operating conditions and degradation. PdM is a major strategy in almost all industries, bringing greater benefits, such as cost-effectiveness, safety, and dependability of the equipment. With continuous development, sophisticated condition-based monitoring using machine learning and data analytics is expected to add further value to PdM in the coming years. Fig. (3) depicts a survey conducted by marketsandmarkets.com, which estimates that the global PdM market is projected to increase from USD 10.6 billion in 2024 to USD 47.8 billion by 2029, at a CAGR of 35.1% during the forecast period [6].

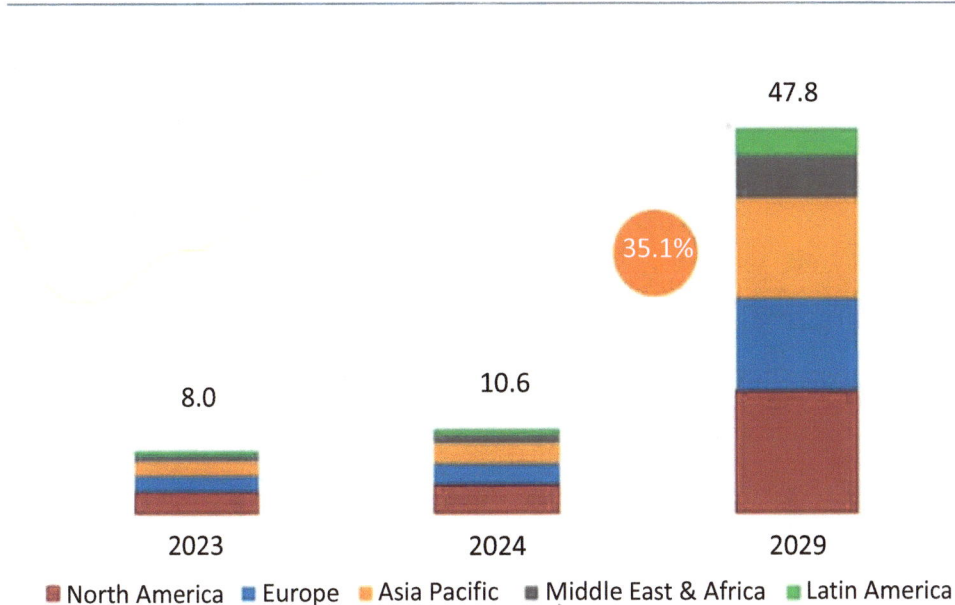

Fig. (3). PdM market global forecast for 2029 [6].

CURRENT STATE OF PREDICTIVE MAINTENANCE RESEARCH

Overview of Current Predictive Maintenance Technologies

Predictive maintenance has begun to take radical strides with the advent of state-of-the-art technologies, notably in areas like data analytics, machine learning, and the Internet of Things. Such innovative technologies have been able to capture, process, and analyze large volumes of data, which are essentially required to accurately predict equipment failures. The various kinds of predictive maintenance technologies at work today may be broadly grouped into a few basic categories. Primarily, sensor technologies are crucial in PdM, given their continuous temperature, vibration, and pressure metrics that allow for critical insights into equipment operational integrity. This is further enhanced by the integration of IoT devices that allow the acquisition of data in real time and foster communication between machinery and analytical platforms [1]. Fig. (**4**) shows top seven PdM trends and innovations for the year 2023, retrieved from StartUsInsights [2].

The utilization of data analytics accompanied by machine learning algorithms has emerged as a cornerstone of Predictive Maintenance (PdM).

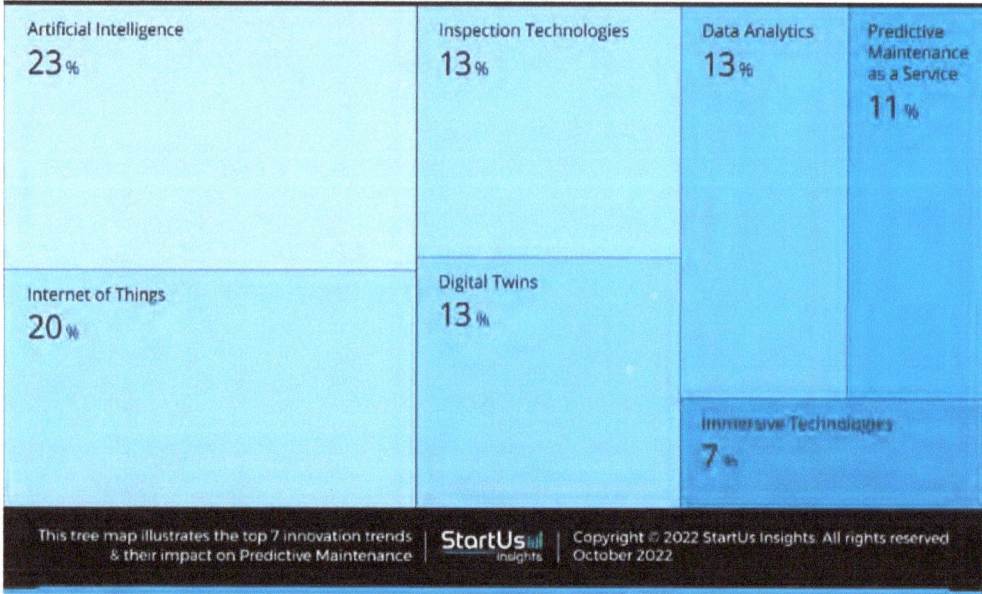

Fig. (4). The top seven PdM trends and innovations in 2023.

These computational frameworks analyze historical datasets and real-time information representative of patterns and trends of impending malfunction occurrences in equipment. Methods such as regression analysis, SVM, neural networks, and deep learning architectures have been widely applied for building predictive models that are usually associated with very high accuracy regarding the forecast of failures [3]. Cloud computing has substantially increased both the scalability and the accessibility of the PdM systems. With cloud-based platforms, companies can store and analyze massive volumes of data, run elaborate predictive algorithms, and gain insights from anywhere in the world with ease. Such development makes PdM more practical for companies of different sizes and reduces the need for heavy on-premise infrastructure [3]. Finally, there is something known as the digital twin-a virtual model of a physical asset-whose incorporation into a PdM system has been increasingly realized. Digital twins now allow the simulation of real operation scenarios in real time for equipment. Predictive algorithms can, therefore, run simulations on various conditions and predict which failures may occur [5].

Analysis of Strengths and Weakness of Existing Techniques

One of the major strengths of PdM includes its reduced downtime and maintenance costs. Companies are able to reduce the risk of unexpected breakdowns and minimize disruptions to operations since failures can be scheduled at the best time. This leads to increased equipment lifespan and improved operational efficiency [3]. Another advantage of PdM is its flexibility. The PdM systems can be customized on the type of equipment or the nature of the industry in which they are applied. Companies will then implement a solution that answers to their needs. By using machine learning and data analytics, PdM systems have the capacity to improve over time, learning new data and adjusting predictive models accordingly [7].

At the same time, current PdM technologies have some limitations. Among the major challenges, there is a demand for high-quality and complete data. Most of the PdM systems depend on valid and full data in order to perform well. Sometimes, some companies may not have sufficient data infrastructure or enough historical data. All this may result in limited accuracy of the predictive models [8]. Thirdly, PdM is also quite expensive to deploy. The deployment of PdM systems requires investing in sensors, data storage, and analytics platforms and integrating these with existing maintenance processes. Small companies, in particular, may find such costs hard to justify in those cases where the return on investment cannot be clearly foreseen in advance [9]. Finally, machine learning algorithms, though powerful, are not perfect. Predictive models have a tendency to sometimes produce false positives or false negatives, leading to erroneous maintenance or missing failures. These small errors decrease the overall effectiveness of the PdM system and may require constant vigilance and tweaking [5].

Case Studies Highlighting Successful Implementations of Predictive Maintenance

Predictive maintenance has been utilized for several years in numerous industries, which have gained immense benefits in terms of efficiency and cost-cutting. General Electric uses PdM consistently in its line of jet engines. With the utilization of advanced analytics along with Internet of Things sensors, General Electric can constantly monitor the health of engines and predict when maintenance will be needed. This program has allowed for a 30% reduction in unexpected downtime and a 20% decrease in maintenance costs [10]. In a related fashion, the French National Railway Company, SNCF, has utilized PdM to monitor its trains and also the supporting infrastructure. By deeply analyzing sensor data from rolling stock and railways, SNCF is able to predict potential breakdowns and proactively perform the necessary maintenance. This cuts down the delay times of the trains by 25% and dramatically lowers the costs involved [11].

For instance, in the manufacturing sector, Siemens has implemented PdM on its production floors to monitor critical equipment health. Siemens was able to reduce maintenance costs by 15% and increase equipment availability by 10% by leveraging digital twin technology combined with machine learning algorithms [12]. These examples represent a few important benefits of PdM across different verticals and depict how this technology can enhance operational efficiency, economize, and thereby extend the lives of critical assets. Keeping in view further improvements in the technologies used by PdM, more and more sectors are expected to use this methodology, whereby their contribution toward developing newer maintenance paradigms will also increase.

FUTURE TRENDS IN PREDICTIVE MAINTENANCE RESEARCH

Integration of Artificial Intelligence (AI) and Machine Learning (ML)

In the future, predictive maintenance will be increasingly linked to the continued integration of artificial intelligence and machine learning. These sophisticated technologies are now changing PdM by providing high-level analytical tools that help improve the accuracy and speed of predictions concerning the need for maintenance. AI and ML allow for handling big datasets, explaining intricate patterns, and giving much more accurate predictions of equipment failures that would enable even more effective strategies for maintenance.

Use of AI/ML Algorithms for Predictive Maintenance Analytics

AI and ML algorithms epitomize the leading edge of PdM analytics. These algorithms enable investigations into large datasets to extract hidden patterns and relationships that may be invisible using conventional methods and, as such, develop predictive models continuously fed by new data, which in turn keeps refining their accuracy over time [13]. Supervised learning algorithms like decision trees, random forests, and SVM find their applications in classification and regression tasks for PdM, which use historical maintenance data to predict the likelihood of future equipment failures [14].

The following case studies highlight the extensive ability and usage of supervised learning algorithms in PdM:

I. **Decision Trees:** In a case study on a power plant, decision trees were used to predict turbine failures based on sensor data, such as vibration intensity and temperature thresholds. The algorithm split the data into decision nodes and identified critical operational ranges linked to failures. Although the method was simple, it proved highly interpretable for maintenance teams [15].

II. **Random Forest:** The random forests algorithm was used on a wind turbine dataset for motor failure prediction. The aggregation of predictions by multiple decision trees helped to avoid overfitting and increase the accuracy of the algorithm. For example, features like wind speed, torque, and historical failure logs were used. The model could recall 92% of critical failures, rarely missing any of them [16].

III. **Support Vector Machines (SVM):** SVMs were used to classify the state of aircraft engines (healthy *vs.* faulty) using high-dimensional acoustic emission data. The algorithm separated faulty signals with 90% accuracy using an optimal hyperplane. Scalability to larger datasets was computationally challenging [17].

At the same time, unsupervised learning techniques, such as clustering and anomaly detection, are helpful in identifying abnormal patterns that might represent the early stages of a failure [4]. Some examples of the usage of unsupervised learning algorithms are:

I. **K-Means Clustering**: In a building management system, clustering was used to group HVAC units based on their energy usage patterns. Units falling outside of their cluster were highlighted as possible points of failure and allowed for proactive maintenance before breakdowns occurred [18].

II. **Anomaly Detection**: Autoencoders, a form of unsupervised neural network, were used to identify early-stage failure patterns in industrial motors. The method detected subtle deviations from normal behavior by reconstructing sensor input and analyzing reconstruction errors, thus predicting failures with high precision [19].

Deep learning, an advanced subcategory of ML, has also shown great promise for PdM applications. It conventionally included CNNs and RNNs that are immensely capable of processing elaborated forms of data, such as time-series sensor information, hence driving very effective forecasts of failure. These models are further capable of probing into multi-layers of data with the capture of intricate relationships among several variables [5]. Some example case studies are:

I. **Convolutional Neural Networks (CNNs)**: CNNs have been used to classify images of conveyor belts to determine wear and tear. The approach involved convolutional and pooling layers that extracted surface cracks, achieving 95% accuracy in classification. These methods had high requirements in terms of labeled data for training but provided actionable insights [20].

II. **Recurrent Neural Networks (RNNs)**: RNNs were used for predictive maintenance in railway systems, analyzing time-series data from accelerometers installed in trains. The network captured temporal dependencies, like the way the anomalies of vibrations propagate with time, and produced accurate failure forecasts up to two weeks in advance [21].

The following Table **1** presents a structured and systematic comparative analysis of key Artificial Intelligence (AI) and Machine Learning (ML) algorithms commonly applied in Predictive Maintenance (PdM) systems across various industrial domains. The choice of algorithm is crucial, as each comes with its own strengths, limitations, and suitability for specific data types and use cases. The table outlines six widely used algorithms—ranging from traditional classifiers like Decision Trees to advanced deep learning models like CNNs and RNNs—along with their practical strengths, computational or methodological constraints, real-world applications, and relevant performance evaluation metrics.

Table 1. Structured representation of a systematic comparative analysis of various AI/ML algorithms used in PdM.

Algorithm	Strengths	Limitations	Use Case	Performance Metrics
Decision Trees	Simple, interpretable, good for small datasets	Overfits easily, struggles with noisy data	Predicting replacement needs for critical parts	Accuracy, Precision
Random Forest	Handles noisy and large datasets effectively	Computationally expensive for large-scale data	Fault prediction in wind turbines	Recall, Feature Importance
SVM	Effective for high-dimensional and smaller datasets	Poor scalability to large datasets	Classifying healthy *vs.* faulty machinery	Classification Accuracy, ROC-AUC
K-Means clustering	Fast and intuitive for clustering tasks	Sensitive to initial centroids, requires tuning	Grouping similar operational patterns in machines	Silhouette Score
CNN	Ideal for image-based data processing	Requires large labeled datasets, high compute	Identifying physical damage in industrial equipment	Precision, Recall
RNN	Handles sequential/time-series data	Suffers from vanishing gradient problem	Forecasting anomalies in railway maintenance	RMSE, MAE

Advantages and Challenges of AI/ML Integration

The integration of AI/ML into PdM has a lot of key benefits. Of major importance is the fact that maintenance forecasting will be automated, hence reducing human surveillance and minimizing the incidences of human error. AI/ML models can process vast volumes of data in relatively less time and make information available in real time to support proactive maintenance routine strategy formulation [5]. Moreover, AI/ML-based PdM systems are very adaptive. As they receive new data, they continuously revise their models and, therefore, provide a higher predictive accuracy with time. This adaptability proves very useful in

dynamic contexts where the status of equipment changes much more frequently [3].

The integration of AI/ML methods into PdM also creates some challenges. Among them is the necessity for substantial volumes of good-quality data for the successful training of predictive models. Many organizations may face problems with a shortage of historical data, or there may be some issues in data collection and processing from heterogeneous sources7. Another important challenge is that AI/ML algorithms often are so complicated that their development, implementation, and maintenance require deeply specialized knowledge. This may automatically force an organization to invest in training activities or to hire skilled professionals who can manage such advanced systems. The "black-box" feature of some AI/ML models- most having deep learning inheritance- make understanding the rationale for certain predictions impossible, therefore easily undermining trust and hindering the wider adoption of such models, as discussed in a study [12].

Internet of Things (IoT) and Sensor Technology

The IoT, along with the evolution of sensor technology, forms the very base for predictive maintenance to bloom, setting in this way the critical foundation for acquiring and analyzing real-time data.

Role of IoT in Enabling Real-Time Data Collection

IoT technology is always at the core of implementing PdM; thus, it will be able to establish a bridge between physical assets and digital platforms by helping in the timely acquisition of data and monitoring. IoT instruments, encompassing sensors, actuators, and edge computing nodes, can be deployed across a diverse array of machinery to collect data pertaining to variables such as temperature, vibration, pressure, and humidity [11]. This information is relayed to centralized or cloud-based analytical systems, where it undergoes processing and evaluation to identify potential anomalies. The instantaneous capabilities inherent in IoT-driven PdM empower organizations to discern and rectify equipment malfunctions prior to their escalation into expensive breakdowns, thus reducing downtime while enhancing operational efficacy [22]. Besides, IoT allows the creation of digital twins, virtual versions of physical assets that model their actual performance in real time. Digital twins allow for a comprehensive point of view about equipment conditions, enabling predictive algorithms to simulate many situations and predict possible failures for various circumstances [22].

Sensor Advancements Enhancing Predictive Maintenance Capabilities

Advances in sensor technology significantly improved the functionality related to PdM systems. The sensors developed today are more accurate and reliable and can measure a greater range of parameters compared to their forerunners. Further, the miniaturization trend enabled widespread implementation of sensors in various environments [12]. A key improvement is that of wireless sensors, which eliminate the need for complicated wiring and allow for more flexible installations. Sensors can now be easily deployed in hard-to-reach or remote locations to ensure comprehensive monitoring of critical assets [23]. Another important development is multisensory systems, which integrate input from multiple sensors to provide a more integrated view of equipment health. Such systems enhance the preciseness of predictive models and reduce the likelihood of false positives and negatives by monitoring multiple parameters all at the same time [24].

Predictive Analytics and Big Data

The large volume of information emanating from IoT devices and other sources has given birth to big data analytics in the domain of predictive maintenance. In this domain, the integration of predictive analytics with big data opens new perspectives for the development of an anticipatory maintenance strategy and informed decision-making.

Leveraging Big Data for Predictive Maintenance Insights

Big data comprises massive volumes of structured and unstructured data emanating from several sources, including sensors, IoT devices, maintenance logs, and operational systems. In predictive maintenance, big data is the required component in analyzing equipment health and performance. Big data enables organizations to develop more accurate and holistic predictive models by taking into account several factors contributing to equipment failure. For instance, a combination of several sensor data with the history of prior maintenance and environmental conditions may provide complex patterns and relationships that cannot be noticed in individual source data only [25]. Furthermore, analytics of big data permits the detection of long-term trends as well as anomalies that may lead to complications. The gradual growth in the level of vibration, along with the fluctuation in temperature, can indicate the generation of mechanical problems that need intervention [26].

Predictive Analytics Techniques for Proactive Maintenance Planning

Predictive analytics encompasses various techniques of analysis of data to predict future outcomes. Predictive maintenance deals with using these techniques to predict equipment failures for optimized scheduling of maintenance and reduced operational risks. The most common technique that is followed regarding PdM is time series analysis; this technique looks for patterns in historical data, which is collected on a regular basis to make an estimate regarding future values. Models such as ARIMA and exponential smoothing can be widely used to predict when equipment fails based on experience from relevant indicators of past performance [27].

Another important method is survival analysis, in which the probability is estimated that equipment will continue to operate without failure throughout a specified period of time. This is an especially crucial methodology when it comes to the RUL prediction of critical assets, enabling an organization to effectively prioritize effort in the upkeep of such assets on a failure likelihood basis. The scope of predictive analytics can also be expanded to prescriptive maintenance, enabling failures to be foreseen and giving specific advice on maintenance interventions. By embedding predictive models with decision-making algorithms, organizations can reach an optimum maintenance strategy that minimizes their chances of downtime and improves the dependability of equipment [28].

Blockchain Technology in Predictive Maintenance

Blockchain technology, well-recognized due to its use in cryptocurrency and similar secure transaction purposes, is finding great interest because of its potential role in enhancing data integrity and security in predictive maintenance systems.

Potential Applications of Blockchain for Data Integrity and Security

Blockchain is a kind of decentralized, immutable ledger that records transactions in a network of computers in such a way that it is highly secure and transparent. In the PdM context, this deployment of blockchain protects the integrity and authenticity of data acquired through sensors and other relevant sources EN. One of the strongest value propositions of blockchain technology is its ability to create a tamper-resistant record of information. Each entry in it is time-stamped and interconnected with its previous one, which makes the modification of historical data almost impossible not to notice. The latter is highly relevant for PdM, where having available valid and reliable data supports the decision-making process on maintenance activities.

Also, the blockchain can enhance the security of PdM systems through a secure and decentralized infrastructure of data dissemination. For instance, when there are several actors that can be involved in the operational chain of PdM- different manufacturers, maintenance service providers, and equipment operators- the possibility exists to exchange data with the assurance that all parties will have identical, tamper-proof information [29].

Integration of Blockchain with Predictive Maintenance Systems

Coupling blockchain technology with PdM systems may offer a wide range of benefits, such as increased transparency in data, improvement in traceability, and strengthening of trust among a variety of stakeholders. With the introduction of blockchain technology, the ability to maintain records can be transparently audited for all activities related to maintenance, ensuring that every action is accurately recorded and traceable with ease [30]. For instance, blockchain can be used as a tool to maintain an overall record of the maintenance history of equipment, including sensor data, maintenance documents, and inspection data. This then gets shared securely with relevant parties for complete knowledge of the status of the equipment and at what timeline the performed maintenance has been carried out on it [31].

Besides, smart contracts are self-executing agreements where the stipulations are directly encoded, and as a result, they can be deployed in a PdM setting to automate such a maintenance operation. Intelligent contracts can automatically set off an independent maintenance procedure when the conditions reach the threshold level as designed in the sensor data, hence reducing the need for manual intervention [32].

Conclusively, the combination of AI/ML, IoT, big data analytics, and blockchain technologies will make the pace at which predictive maintenance advances quicker than before. As these technologies evolve further, they will drive even more accurate, efficient, and secure PdM systems to further improve asset management and optimize operational performance across a wide range of industries.

EMERGING TECHNOLOGIES IN PREDICTIVE MAINTENANCE RESEARCH

Augmented Reality (AR) and Virtual Reality (VR)

AR and VR change many different industries; a maintenance methodology is no exception. These innovative technologies allow deeply immersive and interactive experiences, significantly enhancing PdM procedures.

AR/VR Applications in Maintenance Training and Diagnostics

AR and VR have started finding wide applications in the fields of training in maintenance and diagnostics by efficiently filling the gap between theoretical knowledge and practical application. In AR, virtual information can be superimposed on a real environment; this means that, among other things, maintenance personnel will be able to view, for example, detailed information such as the condition of equipment on the equipment itself [1]. In a scenario like this, AR might assist technicians in finding step-by-step maintenance procedures superimposed directly on the equipment being serviced, therefore diminishing the possibility of human error and improving operational efficiency.

On the other hand, VR offers realistic training environments wherein maintenance personnel can apply practices in the safety of their virtual environment. The medium is a particularly valuable tool for training on complex or hazardous machinery, where realistic training would be prohibitively expensive or potentially hazardous to undertake. The potential of virtual reality to simulate any scenario opens up the possibilities for the trainees to take care of any potential difficulties without risk or real-world consequences [33]. The integration of AR and VR in training curricula enables organizations to enhance competencies within their maintenance teams, helping them become so much more proficient and timely in maintenance interventions.

Enhancing Predictive Maintenance through AR/VR Visualization

Going beyond mere training, Augmented Reality (AR) and Virtual Reality (VR) also significantly extend the effectiveness of predictive maintenance with modern visualization tools. With AR, it is possible to project real-time sensor data onto the actual apparatus, thus allowing technicians to quickly assess whether machinery is working within operational parameters. This real-time visualization enables the early identification of potential issues, thus allowing for the accomplishment of proactive maintenance with interventions. For example, AR-enabled glasses offer instant on-site access to past equipment history, diagnostic data, and predictive analytics, thereby offering informed decision-making and reducing problem diagnosis time for maintenance staff [13].

This is while VR can simulate equipment functionality under a wide range of operating conditions, allowing engineers to predict with reasonable accuracy when it is likely to fail and thus optimize maintenance. AR/VR integrated with analytics on predictive maintenance enables organizations to visualize complex information in an intuitive and accessible way, further enhancing productivity and the effectiveness of their maintenance tasks.

Edge Computing

Edge computing is progressively establishing itself as an essential technological paradigm in the realm of predictive maintenance, particularly within contexts that necessitate instantaneous data processing and informed decision-making.

Utilizing Edge Computing for Real-Time Predictive Maintenance

In contrast, edge computing is the processing of information closer to its source, usually at the device itself or close by, rather than *via* a centralized cloud infrastructure. This reduces latency and makes it possible to process real-time data, which is very important for predictive maintenance. With predictive maintenance, the edge devices can aggregate the sensor data in real time and analyze it in such a way that it provides anomaly identification and failure forecasts with high immediacy. This high-speed analysis further enables quick decisions and timely maintenance activities, which, in turn, reduces the chances of unplanned shutdowns. Another important advantage involves edge computing, which drastically decreases the amount of data to be transported to the cloud. This reduces bandwidth usage and related costs. This attribute makes edge computing quite useful in industries where real-time processing is key, for example, manufacturing, oil and gas, and transportation, among others.

Advantages of Edge Computing in Remote or Harsh Environments

The main advantage of edge computing is its effectiveness in remote or harsh environments where connectivity to centralized cloud infrastructures is either limited or intermittent. In such conditions, operating independently of continuous connectivity, edge devices perform data processing locally to sustain predictive maintenance functionalities. For instance, edge computing has ensured that vital maintenance data is analyzed on-site, with poor Internet connectivity in place- for example, offshore oil platforms or remote mining operations- facilitating timely interventions. This function not only increases equipment reliability but also enhances safety in such harsh environments [9].

Besides, edge computing can easily integrate with IoT networks in smart manufacturing facilities where real-time data processing is crucial for maintaining continuous production flows. An organization should be assured, with the power of edge computing, that predictive maintenance frameworks are robust, resilient, and run efficiently across a variety of operational contexts.

Quantum Computing

Quantum computing represents another advanced niche area, enabling new predictive maintenance models by solving complex optimization problems and enhancing the capability of prediction algorithms.

Potential Impact of Quantum Computing on Predictive Maintenance Algorithms

Quantum computing is a form of computation that uses the basic tenets of quantum mechanics to perform tasks much faster than would otherwise be achievable and thus enables the processing of huge volumes of data and the solution of complex problems beyond the reach of any classical computational system. Quantum computing can prove to be revolutionary when it comes to formulating predictive algorithms for predictive maintenance, as it would enable one to build more complex models that analyze a wider range of variables and their interactions.

For example, quantum computing can refine predictive models by running large numbers of failure modes and situational scenarios concurrently. This would provide higher accuracy predictions and better scheduling maintenance events to minimize equipment downtimes and thereby extend operating lifetime. Additionally, quantum machine learning, the study of quantum systems regarding machine learning, is one branch that would take predictive maintenance further by giving speed and thoroughness to the data being processed. It would enable the development of more advanced predictive models, which would reflect more adequate uncertainties and fluctuations in equipment performance [11].

Challenges and Opportunities of Quantum Computing in Maintenance Optimization

While quantum computing offers substantial prospects for predictive maintenance, it concurrently encounters various obstacles. The technology remains in its formative phases, with functional quantum computers being constrained in both accessibility and performance. Moreover, the formulation of quantum algorithms requires specialized knowledge and expertise that may not be readily available within numerous organizations [12]. The integration of quantum computing with current predictive maintenance frameworks would also necessitate considerable infrastructural modifications and innovative methodologies for data storage and processing. As a result, the extensive adoption of quantum computing in predictive maintenance is anticipated to be a long-term endeavor rather than an immediate actuality [23].

In spite of these obstacles, the potential advantages are considerable. As advancements in quantum computing technology materialize, it may result in transformative developments in predictive maintenance, enabling organizations to enhance their maintenance strategies with unparalleled accuracy. Early adopters of quantum computing in predictive maintenance can attain a significant competitive advantage by realizing elevated levels of operational efficiency and dependability. In conclusion, the amalgamation of emerging technologies such as augmented reality/virtual reality, edge computing, and quantum computing into predictive maintenance is poised to facilitate substantial progress in the domain. These technologies will support the formulation of more precise, efficient, and robust maintenance strategies, ultimately bolstering operational performance across a variety of industries.

CHALLENGES AND CONSIDERATIONS

As PdM continues to advance and integrate novel technological innovations, there are a lot of challenges and considerations that need to be taken into view to ensure proper implementation and optimize its benefit. The challenges encompass several sectors: data confidentiality, complexities of integration, workforce education, and economic viability.

Data Privacy and Security Concerns

Data security and privacy are considered the biggest concerns in predictive maintenance, wherein both the volume and sensitivity increase manifold with IoT, artificial intelligence, and cloud technologies. The Predictive Maintenance System works on continuous gathering, transmission, and analysis of data received from various sources, including sensors attached to critical infrastructure. This can also include very sensitive information about the operational status, performance metrics, and possible vulnerabilities of equipment, which naturally will make them a very exciting target for cyber-attacks.

A salient risk is related to unauthorized possibilities of sensitive data disclosure. In case of a breach within the PdM system, malicious actors will have access to confidential operational information that can be used either for espionage purposes or to disrupt continuity. For instance, a PdM system compromise within power generation facilities may lead to blackouts or equipment damage, which are catastrophic in nature [34].

Also, the usage of cloud-based systems for storing and processing data enables a whole set of new risks related to data breaches. Even though cloud service providers take every precaution with tightly developed security protocols, the shared architecture of the cloud environment means that data can be exposed if security vulnerabilities are used [33]. These risks force organizations to implement holistic data protection strategies involving encryption, mechanisms for access control, and periodic security audits. Blockchain technology will further help in data integrity and security by creating immutable records of maintenance data [29].

Integration Complexities and Interoperability Issues

Effective implementation of a PdM system requires professional integration with existing operational technologies and enterprise systems. It is usually quite complex and often creates critical challenges, especially in industries that have been built around legacy systems that were never designed with today's PdM technologies in mind. Among the critical challenges is that interoperability among various systems and devices will be a key problem. In most industrial settings, equipment by different manufacturers uses proprietary communication protocols, data formats, and interfaces, impeding seamless data exchange [12]. The lack of standardization would inhibit the implementation of the PdM solution, where considerable customization and configuration are expected to ensure compatibility.

The integration of PdM with enterprise resource planning and computerized maintenance management systems can be quite a challenge since these systems have their own ways of data architecture and workflows not aligned with PdM applications. Because of this, an organization might be forced to use resources on middleware or custom integrations that resolve the disjunction between these systems, increasing both the complexity and costs concerned with the implementation process.

To transcend these limitations, industry stakeholders must focus on building standardized protocols and frameworks that would allow interoperability. Industrial Internet Consortium-IIC, along with the International Society of Automation-ISA, are working on standards that will increase integration and interoperability within a wide range of systems and devices [9].

Skill Gap and Workforce Training Needs

Advanced PdM systems require professionals with data analytics, machine learning, IoT technologies, and cybersecurity competencies. For this reason, the core issue for most organizations is the significant skill gap that already exists within the maintenance staff, who might currently lack some key competencies to manage such complex systems effectively. The transition to PdM indicates a paradigm shift from conventional methodologies that are generally reactive or preventive to one that is proactive and data-driven. This itself demands the development of new skills in areas such as understanding data, prediction models, and the use of advanced diagnostic tools. AI and ML adoption also requires algorithm development and management skills related to machine learning models [22].

Overcoming this skill gap needs a more integrated approach to workforce development and engagement with educational institutions - reaching optimal levels of education, training, and upskilling. Organizations may have to invest in lifelong learning opportunities for their staff to ensure familiarity with current technologies and best practices in predictive maintenance. In addition, the innovative culture and adaptability of the workforce play a very significant role in determining their success in the adoption and implementation of PdM solutions. It would be very easy to transition and accept PdM systems if motivation among the employees was present to welcome new technologies and methodologies.

Cost-Effectiveness and Return on Investment Considerations

While PdM has great potential in reducing equipment downtime, improving reliability, and optimizing the cost of maintenance, it also involves a huge upfront capital investment in technology and infrastructure along with the development of human resources. It is very tricky to do cost-effectiveness or ROI analysis while implementing a PdM solution by any organization [5].

The implementation of PdM systems requires several costs: buying and installing sensors, upgrading already working equipment with IoT connectivity, implementing data analytics platforms, and integrating PdM with other enterprise systems. Moreover, ongoing costs deal with the system's maintenance, updating, and personnel training and reskilling [3].

Calculating the ROI of PdM is likely to be complicated because the benefits come gradually and can be difficult to measure. This includes preventing critical equipment failures or reducing unplanned downtime. The value of these will be saved immensely, but the outcome may not be directly seen. Returns from investment for PdM will also differ based on industries, complexity of the equipment, and usage in particular applications.

With that said, full cost-benefit analyses to determine whether the investments in PdM are economically viable should be implemented by organizations, including direct and indirect benefits. For that, this analysis should cover reduced maintenance costs, extended equipment lifespan, improved operational efficiency, and increased safety measures, among others [24].

Another advantage will be that implementation of PdM can be made in a gradual approach. In this regard, starting with a pilot project will provide the organizations with an opportunity to test the viability and effectiveness of the technology before full-scale deployment. This kind of graduated approach would reduce some of the risks and allow better decision-making on investments in PdM [31].

In a nutshell, predictive maintenance does indeed come with a lot of benefits, but its successful implementation requires considerations of data privacy and security issues, integration challenges, workforce training requirements, and, finally, cost-effectiveness. Organizations can completely exploit the benefits of PdM if such challenges are proactively addressed by them to achieve continuous operational improvements.

CONCLUSION

This study demonstrated that predictive maintenance has achieved considerable development owing to several critical technologies and, therefore, has dramatically revolutionized the methods of equipment maintenance management for industries. A few distinguished trends and novelties are highlighted in this discussion. First, the integration of AI and ML in enhancing the accuracy of prediction models has proved paramount in making effective and more accurate predictions of equipment failures [14]. IoT and advanced sensor technologies allow the aggregation of data continuously and, in turn, provide input to predictive analytics platforms for real-time monitoring. Other technologies such as AR, VR, Edge computing, and Quantum computing will further take PdM to the next level through enhanced diagnostic insight, reducing latency in processing data and enabling more sophisticated predictive algorithms. The introduction of blockchain technology is another huge step that brings maximum security and integrity to bulks of data created by PdM systems. However, there are also obstacles, including data privacy, issues related to integration, shortage in the workforce personnel with relevant skills, and, last but not least, the cost-effectiveness of the PdM solutions. The above-mentioned obstacles must be addressed if the full realization of the benefits of predictive maintenance is to be achieved.

Implications for the Future of Predictive Maintenance Research

Indeed, the embedding of advanced technologies into PdM frameworks is a significant evolution in maintenance methodologies for many industries. As AI and ML algorithms continue to evolve, they are expected to boost the accuracy and reliability of PdM systems, contributing toward reduced levels of downtime and maintenance costs and extending the lifetime of equipment operations. Continuous improvements in IoT and sensor technologies will continue to simplify better data acquisition, thereby improving predictability. The concept of edge computing is also about enhancing the efficiency of PdM systems in remote and challenging fields and extending their usage in different industries. Although it is still in its infancy, quantum computing solves complex optimization problems that are well beyond the capabilities of today's computers and may take PdM systems to the next level [35]. Meanwhile, blockchain is going to play an increasingly important role in data integrity and security since the growth of PdM data will expand. But for all these technologies to work successfully, many hurdles are to be crossed before they can become a reality, such as requirement of skilled people, problems in integration that might be at hand, and the higher implementation costs.

Recommendations for Further Research and Industry Adoption

With many of these areas still requiring research and development in the area, the vast possibilities of predictive maintenance are fully realized. This requires a next-generation development of AI and ML algorithms to deal with the volume and complexity of data streaming from PdM systems; however, transparency and interpretability will need to be injected into these models if confidence in these systems is going to engender trust for their adoption in industrial applications [14]. The second has to do with interoperability, which involves standardization of communication protocols and uniformity in data formats. Such standardization will be developed through the cooperation of industry stakeholders, technology innovators, and standards organizations. Further, training of the workforce must be conducted to overcome the shortage of skills. This has to cover not only technical competencies related to PdM system operations but also cultural competencies focusing on continuous learning and innovation.

Economic aspects are also equally compelling in this area. The organizations should take a step-by-step strategy toward PdM implementation, initiating the adoption of pilot projects that can prove cost-effectiveness and return on investment. This process can be initiated through incentives for the adoption of the PdM technologies by the governmental and industrial sectors in areas of industries where failure to provide maintenance could have led to some severe economic or safety consequences. In other words, predictive maintenance brings quite considerable improvements in the practice of industrial maintenance. However, attaining maximum benefits requires conquering a number of technical, organizational, and economic challenges. Maximization of advantages can be realized by continuous research, collaboration, and strategic investments, thus translating into more efficient, reliable, and economically feasible industrial operations.

REFERENCES

[1]   L. Leemis, and S. Park, *Discrete-event Simulation: A First Course.* Pearson: Williamsburg, 2006.

[2]   StartUs Insights, "Top predictive maintenance trends & innovations you should follow in 2023", Available from: https://www.startus-insights.com/innovators-guide/predictive-maintenance-tr-nds-innovation/ [Accessed 16 September 2024].

[3]   J. Lee, H.A. Kao, and S. Yang, "Service innovation and smart analytics for industry 4.0 and big data environment", *Procedia CIRP,* vol. 16, pp. 3-8, 2014.
[http://dx.doi.org/10.1016/j.procir.2014.02.001]

[4]   A.G. Parlos, "Advanced fault diagnostics and self-recovery in large-scale industrial processes", *IEEE Int. Conf. Syst. Man Cybern.,* 2009 San Antonio, TX, USA

[5]   B. Yan, and Z-X. Zhang, "A novel machine learning framework for predictive maintenance using deep learning and big data", *IEEE Trans. Ind. Electron.,* vol. 65, no. 3, pp. 2401-2410, 2018.

[6]   MarketsandMarkets, "Operational predictive maintenance market by component, deployment type, organization size, end user, and region - global forecast to 2026", Available from: https://www.marketsandmarkets.com/Market-Reports/operational-predicti-e-maintenance-market-8656856.html [Accessed 16 September 2024].

[7]   P. Dray, "Predictive maintenance brings big savings to rail networks", *Railway Technol.,* 2017.

[8]   P. Nyhuis, H. Fischer, and M. Busse, "Digitalization in manufacturing: A framework for the digital transformation of production", *Procedia Manuf.,* vol. 43, pp. 163-170, 2020.

[9]   P. Okoh, P. Roy, and A.K. Parlikad, "Risk-based maintenance modelling of complex systems for operational resilience", *Reliab. Eng. Syst. Saf.,* vol. 182, pp. 158-168, 2019.

[10]   R. Evans, "Digital twins and predictive maintenance at GE Aviation", 2019. Available from: https://www.iotforall.com/digital-twins-predictive-maintenance-ge-aviation [Accessed 16 September 2024].

[11]   M. Grieves, *Digital twin: Manufacturing excellence through virtual factory replication.* Florida Institute of Technology: Melbourne, FL, USA, 2014.

[12]   R. Ahmad, and S. Kamaruddin, "An overview of time-based and condition-based maintenance in industrial application", *Comput. Ind. Eng.,* vol. 63, no. 1, pp. 135-149, 2012.
[http://dx.doi.org/10.1016/j.cie.2012.02.002]

[13]   H. Boyes, B. Hallaq, J. Cunningham, and T. Watson, "The industrial internet of things (IIoT): An analysis framework", *Comput. Ind.,* vol. 101, pp. 1-12, 2018.
[http://dx.doi.org/10.1016/j.compind.2018.04.015]

[14]   S. Zhang, Y. Li, and W. Zhu, "A survey of machine learning methods for big data processing", *Knowl. Base. Syst.,* vol. 102, pp. 100-118, 2016.

[15]   A. Imad, N. Vasileios, M. Charilaos, T. Konstatinos, C. Eleni, N. Dervilis, K. Warden, and E. Maguire, "Fault diagnosis of wind turbine structures using decision tree learning algorithms with big data", *Proc. 28th Eur. Saf. Reliab. Conf. (ESREL 2018)*, 2018 Zurich

[16]   A. Zaher, S. McArthur, D. Infield, and Y. Patel, "Online wind turbine fault detection through automated SCADA data analysis", In: *Wind Energy.* Wiley, 2009, pp. 574-593.

[17]   D. Lucking-Reiley, D. Bryan, N. Prasad, and D. Reeves, "Pennies from eBay: The determinants of price in online auctions", *J. Ind. Econ.*, vol. 55, no. 2, pp. 223-233, 2007. [http://dx.doi.org/10.1111/j.1467-6451.2007.00309.x]

[18]   K.M. Alam, M. Saini, and A. El Saddik, "Toward social internet of vehicles: Concept, architecture, and applications", *IEEE Access,* vol. 3, pp. 343-357, 2015. [http://dx.doi.org/10.1109/ACCESS.2015.2416657]

[19]   Y. Zhao, and L.J. Bassham, "Comparison of multiple linear regression and artificial neural networks for predicting the performance of air-to-air heat exchangers", *Energy Build.*, vol. 43, no. 10, pp. 3181-3187, 2011.

[20]   S. Sagiroglu, and D. Sinanc, "Big data: A review", *2013 international conference on collaboration technologies and systems (CTS)*, 2013 San Diego, CA, USA [http://dx.doi.org/10.1109/CTS.2013.6567202]

[21]   N. Elgendy, and A. Elragal, "Big data analytics: A literature review paper", *2014 IEEE/IFIP Conf. Data Min. Workshops (ICDMW)*, 2014 Shenzhen, China [http://dx.doi.org/10.1007/978-3-319-08976-8_16]

[22]   H.M.H. Nguyen, S. Das, and B.B. Gupta, "Blockchain-based secure data sharing in industrial IoT with deep reinforcement learning", *IEEE Trans. Industr. Inform.*, vol. 16, no. 9, pp. 6245-6254, 2020.

[23]   D. Yaga, P. Mell, N. Roby, and K. Scarfone, *Blockchain technology overview.* IEEE Computer Society: Gaithersburg, MD, USA, 2018. [http://dx.doi.org/10.6028/NIST.IR.8202]

[24]   S. Nakamoto, "Bitcoin: A peer-to-peer electronic cash system", 2008. Available from: https://bitcoin.org/bitcoin.pdf [Accessed 16 September 2024].

[25]   M. Crosby, P. Pattanayak, S. Verma, and V. Kalyanaraman, "Blockchain technology: Beyond bitcoin", *Applied Innovation,* vol. 2, pp. 71-81, 2016.

[26]   F. Tao, Q. Qi, L. Wang, and A.Y.C. Nee, "Digital twins and cyber–physical systems toward smart manufacturing and Industry 4.0: Correlation and comparison", *Engineering (Beijing),* vol. 5, no. 4, pp. 653-661, 2019. [http://dx.doi.org/10.1016/j.eng.2019.01.014]

[27]   A.K. Sood, *Augmented reality: A game-changer for predictive maintenance.* IEEE Computer Society: Los Alamitos, CA, USA, 2018.

[28]   P.W. Shor, "Algorithms for quantum computation: Discrete logarithms and factoring", *35th Annu. Symp. Found. Comput. Sci.,* 1994 Santa Fe, NM, USA [http://dx.doi.org/10.1109/SFCS.1994.365700]

[29]   D. Riste, M.B. Shadbolt, and A.G. Fowler, *Toward fault-tolerant quantum computing with superconducting qubits*, 2017.

[30]   A. Gandomi, and M. Haider, "Beyond the hype: Big data concepts, methods, and analytics", *Int. J. Inf. Manage.*, vol. 35, no. 2, pp. 137-144, 2015. [http://dx.doi.org/10.1016/j.ijinfomgt.2014.10.007]

[31]   A. Verma, V. Roy, and R. Kumar, "Big data analytics: Challenges and applications for text, audio, and video data", In: *Big Data Analytics.* Springer: Singapore, 2018, pp. 69-89.

[32]   J.W. Taylor, and P.E. McSharry, "Short-term load forecasting methods: An evaluation based on

European data", *IEEE Trans. Power Syst.,* vol. 22, no. 4, pp. 2213-2219, 2007.
[http://dx.doi.org/10.1109/TPWRS.2007.907583]

[33]   C.B. Zio, *Data-driven methods for predictive maintenance and fault diagnosis.* CRC Press: Boca Raton, FL, USA, 2014.

[34]   X. Xu, C. Pautasso, L. Zhu, and I. Weber, "A decentralized architecture for enforcing end-to-end IoT security and privacy in edge-based IoT platforms", *Proc. IEEE,* vol. 107, no. 4, pp. 850-864, 2019.

[35]   N. Szabo, "Smart contracts: building blocks for digital markets", *Extropy, J. Transhumanist Thought,* vol. 16, 1996.

SUBJECT INDEX

www.ingramcontent.com/pod-product-compliance
Lightning Source LLC
Chambersburg PA
CBHW050809220326
41598CB00006B/156